WHO WERE THE PHOENICIANS ?

NISSM. R. GANOR

WHO WERE THE PHOENICIANS ?

NISSIM R. GANOR

KIP – Kotarim International Publishing LTD

WHO WERE THE PHOENICIANS? NISSIM R. GANOR

KIP - Kotarim International Publishing ltd
www.kotarim.com

Design: Daphna Ganor
Rachel Shamir

ISBN: 978-965-91415-2-4

Printed in Israel

This book is dedicated to my friend, partner and spouse Magda, whose unlimited devotion and support made this research possible. To my late parents Avraham D. and Simcha Mizrachi *Alehem Hashalom*. And last, to my sons – Elon ,Ido and their families.

ACKNOWLEDGMENTS

I would like to express my gratitude to the management and employees of the 'Eretz Israel' Museum library for all their assistance. Many thanks to the management of the Rockefeller Museum and specifically to Mrs. Cassuto.

I would also like to extend my thanks to Mr. Regulant who helped me at different stages of my research. Thanks to Mr. Norbert Segal for the photographs he provided. Special thanks are due to Mr. Heineman, formerly the manager of the 'Eretz Israel' museum library, and to Mrs. Rebecca Twaig who both edited the English translation at different stages. To my granddaughter Daphna Ganor for her work and dedication on the graphics editing of this book and to my grandson Ori Ganor for his help with editing work.

Many thanks to Meir Ben Dov for his support and for the introduction written for this book.

Many thanks to Mr. Yosef Elkony and Mr. Aviel, for their help in publishing this book. Thanks to its publisher Mr. Moshe Alon.

Special thanks are due to the late Professor Yehuda Fried, who inspired me to write this book. Finally I would like to thank all the many friends and supporters who could not be mentioned here.

Dr. Nissim R. Ganor
Summer 2009

CONTENTS

HEBREW NAME	PHOENICIAN SCRIPT OF 9th CENT. B.C. BAAL LEBANON KARATEPE		OLD GREEK SCRIPT OF 8th CEN. B.C.	HEBREW CURSIVE OF c. 600 B.C.	GREEK NAME
ALEPH	⟨	⟨	⟨	⟨	ALPHA
BETH	ᑫ	ᑫ	ᗷ	ᑫ	BETA
GIMEL		∧	Γ	˥	GAMMA
DALETH	Δ	◁	Δ	◁	DELTA
HE		ⅎ	ⅎ	⅊	EPSILON
WAW		Y	F	⅄	
ZAYIN	I	I	I	⅂	ZETA
HETH	⊟	⊟	⊟	⊟	ETA
TETH			⊗	⊘	THETA
YODH	⅂	⅃	⟨	⅁	IOTA
KAPH	⅄	⅄	K	⅁	KAPPA
LAMEDH	⅃	⅃	∧	⅃	LAMDA
MEM	ᙢ	⅄	ᙢ	⅄	MU
NUN	⅃	⅃	N	⅄	NU
SAMEKH	⅀		⅀	⅀	XI
AYIN	O	O	O	◑	OMICRON
PE		⅃	Γ	⅃	PI
SADE		ⱳ	ᙢ	ⱳ	
QOPH	φ	Φ	Φ	φ	
RESH	◁	◁	ᗡ	◖	RHO
SHIN	W	W	⧹	W	SIGMA
TAW	†	✗	T	✗	TAU

EGYPT MAP AND THE EXODUS PATH

LIST OF ABREVIATIONS

A. Periodicals

AAA. Annals of Archaeology and Anthropology.
AASOR. Annual of the American Schools of Oriental Research.
AJA. American Journal of Archaeology.
AJSLL. American Journal of Semitic Languages and Literature.
AR. Archaeology.
AS. Anatolian Studies.
ASOR. American Schools of Oriental Research.
BA. The Biblical Archaeologist.
BAR. Biblical Archaelogy Review.
BASOR. Bulletin of the American Schools of Oriental Research.
BIE. Bulletin de L'Institut d'Egypte.
BSA. Annual of the British School of Athens.
BSAE. British School of Archaeology in Egypt.
IES. Israel Exploration Society.
JAOS. Journal of the American Oriental Society.
JBL. Journal of Biblical Literature.
JEA. Journal of Egyptian Archaeology.
JNES. Journal of Near Eastern Studies.
JPOS. Journal of the Palestine Oriental Society.
OA. Opuscula Archaeologica; Acta instituti Romani Regni Sueciae.
PEF/P/Q. Palestine Exploration Fund; Paper, Quarterly Statement.
QDAP. Quarterly of the Department of Antiquities in Palestine.
PSBA. Proceeding of the Society of Biblical Archaeology.
RAr. Revue Archaéologique.
RB. Revue Biblique.
RES. Revue des Etudes Sémitique.
RHR. Revue de l'Histoire des Religions.
RS. Revue Sémitique.
SY. Syria, Revue d'Art oriental et d'Archaéologie.
VT. Vetus Testamentum.
ZAW. Zeitschrift für die alttestamentliche Wiesenschaft.
ZDPV. Zeitschrift des Deutschen Palästina –Vereins.

B . Books

ANET. Ancient Near Eastern Texts Relating to the Old Testament. Pritchard. J. B. (princeton 1954).

ANE. The Ancient Near East. A New Anthology of Texts and Pictures. Pritchard J. B. Princeton paper printing 1973.

Ant. Josephus Flavius–Antiquities.

CAH. Cambridge Ancient History.

CIS. Corpus Inscriptionum Semiticarum.

Con. Ap. Josephus Flavius –Contra Apionem.

Diod. Sic. Diodorus Siculus.

EB. Encyclopaedia Britanica.

EI. Enciclopedia Italiana Di Scienza, Lettere ed Arti, Treves–Trecani 1932.

ERE. Encyclopaedia of Religion and Ethics. New York, Scribners'.

EWA. Encyclopedia of World Art, N. Y. 1966.

Fr. His. Gr. Fragmenta Historicorun Grecorum.

Lods–Israel. A. Lods, Israël des origines au milieu du VIIIe siècle. edit. L'Évolution de L'humanité, Paris, 1949.

RECORDS. Breasted, Ancient Records of Egypt, Historical Documents, Chicago 1906 II.

STU. PH. Studia Phoenicia, I–II, Leuven, 1983; III, 1985; IV, Namur, 1986. V, Leuven 1987.

TEAT.; EAT.; Tel el Amarna Tablets; el Amarna Tablets. Knudtzon; Knudtzon, J. A. Die El Amarna Taffeln, Leipzig 1915. Mercer, S. A. The Tell El Amarna Tablets, Macmillan 1939.

C. Books of the Old Testament

Gen. Genesis.

Ex. Exodus.

Le. Leviticus.

Nu. Numbers.

Deut. Deuteronomy.

Jos. Joshua.

Ju. Judges.
1Sam. 1 Samuel.
2Sam. 2 Samuel.
1Kn. 1. Kings.
2Kn. 2 Kings.
1Chr. 1 Chronicles.
2Chr. 2 Chronicles
Ez. Ezra.
Ne. Nehemiah.
Ps. Psalms.
Pr. Proverbs.
Je. Jeremiah.
Is. Isaiah.
Ezk. Ezekiel.
Ho. Hosea.
Mi. Micha.
Ze. Zephaniah.
Sol. Song of Solomon.

Words

A.V. Authorized Version.
Heb. Hebrew.
L. line.
O.T. Old Testament.
Tab. Tablet.
Trans. Translation.

INTRODUCTION

There is little doubt that the invention of the phonetic alphabet was a pivotal event in the development of human culture, paralleled in importance by only a handful of events such as the beginning of tool-making and the invention of Gutenberg's printing press. The ability to record ideas through different combinations of twenty-two letters advanced mankind in all cultural domains. Earlier forms of writing (such as the ancient Egyptian, Chinese or Mesopotamian cuneiform scripts) required knowledge and memorization of thousands of symbols and were, therefore, the estate of a meager few. The powerful yet simple idea of the phonetic alphabet paved the way for lasting human communication of unlimited content and scope, and in doing so facilitated the cumulative progress of science, technology, culture and religion as we know them.

The development of the phonetic alphabet is commonly attributed to a mysterious ancient civilization, known as 'Phoenician'. The Phoenicians were a nation based in the Mediterranean coastal regions of modern day Lebanon, Syria and Israel. The Phoenicians are known for being a fierce clan of sailors and merchants who settled the shores of the southern and eastern Mediterranean, and whose famous later descendant Hannibal of Carthage almost conquered Rome. However, when studied carefully, it is clear that the coherence of this common description abounds with logical flaws. First, the earliest phonetic alphabet symbols were discovered in the area of Serabit El-Khadem in the Sinai Peninsula, and were dated to the 18th-19th centuries B.C., long before any documented mention of the Phoenicians. Their language is Semitic and is commonly considered 'proto-Phoenician', namely, a precursor to the later language known as Phoenician. Moreover, no mention of the term 'Phoenician' is found prior to Homer, several hundred years after their time (not even in the Phoenician writings themselves). From where and when then did this influential culture 'emerge'? Who were the Phoenicians?

Many researchers have addressed this mystery, and a multitude of ideas and conjectures have been made in hundreds and thousands of articles and books. As in many research fields, a genuine breakthrough was hard to achieve.

Preconceptions, inferences and dogmatic opinions are entrenched in the academic teaching of history, archeology and biblical science and are inevitably accepted by professionals through academic study without realizing it. Therefore, in history as in all fields of science, it is not uncommon to find major breakthroughs and fresh unbiased views made by people who were not formally educated within the specific discipline. A good example of this is the German researcher Wellhausen, whose 19th century research on Arab tribes indirectly led him to a new understanding of the origins of the Bible – an understanding that is now key to all modern-day biblical research.

In my view, the same applies to the current study, originally published in Hebrew three decades ago. Dr. Ganor, a pediatrician and a self-taught history scholar, began his research on the Phoenician language and people by pure coincidence. Studying the field with outstanding intellectual curiosity, he saw what could only be seen through the eyes of a skeptic outsider unbound by preconceptions. Dr. Ganor's approach is novel and revolutionary, and his perspective is drawn from a completely different angle and outlook to that to which we are accustomed in historical research.

Over the course of more than thirty years, Dr. Ganor analyzed hundreds of books and articles, and studied every piece of information on the subject. It is evident that he has researched the subject comprehensively, as attested by the rich bibliography. Finding many fundamental contradictions and logical flaws in the conventional scholarly views, he embarked on extensive, step-by-step detective-like work, reshuffling the basic elements composed of uninterpreted hard evidence and gradually formulating his own unique interpretation. He then fitted many pieces of the puzzle into new places, arriving at surprising and far-reaching conclusions in unexpectedly diverse aspects in the history of the near east, from the dating of the Children of Israel's exodus from Egypt to the evolution of monotheism.

Dr. Ganor's conclusions, the significance of his challenges to common dogmas and his propositions regarding many fundamental yet unresolved problems cannot be overruled by any serious scholar of the history of the near-east, the Bible, and the land and people of Israel. For that alone, this work deserves a proper place in the library of anyone studying these subjects. One can also not remain indifferent when reading this book, which despite being an in-depth scholarly study is far from being a dull read. Rather, it reads like an exciting adventure in intellectual discovery.

I strongly recommend the publication of this new translation and hope it will reach the audience and gain the recognition it so deserves. I also hope that this study will inspire and induce other researchers to inquire further into the history and genealogy of the nations and peoples of the Mediterranean basin.

Meir Ben-Dov, Historian & Archeologist

PREFACE

I never dreamed that I would one day write a book on the Phoenicians, but pure coincidence turned things otherwise and brought it about that in course of time I ended with this book.

At the age of twenty five my voice was yet unaltered and high pitched as in my boyhood. One day by sheer chance I met someone who told me he had had the same experience, and explained to me that my voice is the result of misphonation and misuse of vocalization and vocal cords. He instructed me how to use correctly my vocal chords and vocalize properly. I followed his instructions and performed the exercises he set me while a radio was turned on full volume in the background with me trying to overtop the radio sound. The result was overwhelming, and within two days my voice changed utterly from high pitched to low pitched. At the time I was a medical student and curiosity drove me to inquire into this phenomenon from the anatomical point of view. This, I came to realise, would involve a better understanding of the vowels and the basis of phonetical writing. In my quest for more information on the subject I came across a book on phonation, which mentioned, among other things, that the Phoenicians are considered the inventors of the first system of phonetic writing in the world. My first reaction was to go to the university library and look up the entry "Phoenicia" in both the Encyclopedia Britannica and Larousse Encyclopedia. There I learned that the Bible is regarded as a primary source for knowledge on the Phoenicians, and so I naturally referred to the Bible. I was amazed to discover that certain passages in the biblical writings were clearly misunderstood and misinterpreted, and this inevitably led to an erroneous approach. The more I delved into the study of the history of the region the more I was astonished to perceive what sort of "scientific basis" constitutes the accepted reconstruction of Israelite and regional history.

The study of the history of a nation is the study of a succession of events. In this study of the past, the historian is assisted by whatever he can lay his hands upon; archaeology, epigraphic texts, linguistic terms, philology and the like. An error in the interpretation of terms or findings will inevitably cause misunderstandings in the comprehension of historical events. This may have a repercussion on the understanding of other developments connected with these events. Reasons for mistakes may be either subjective errors resulting from the erroneous approach of scholars; or objective ones due to ideas and theories based on concepts, and beliefs which were in accordance with data available at a specific period. Accumulation of new data in the wake of new findings, lead to new ideas, but concepts and theories formed earlier may still remain unchanged. For example; when epigraphic findings were rare, the invention of phonetic writing was ascribed to the 10th century B. C. Accordingly, most of the biblical narratives such as the Exodus, conquest of Canaan, tribal settlement, etc. were assigned to an orally transmitted tradition which was only later written down. This together with certain interpretations (Biblical, . archaeological and alike) led to the assumption that the biblical narratives have no historical value and cannot be regarded as a reliable or trustworthy source (Graf, Wellhausen; Alt and others), even though the Bible assures us that Moses himself recorded the comings and goings of the Israelites in the desert. In time, new epigraphic findings brought the date of phonetic writing back to about 1500 B. C. There is therefore no longer any reason to deny the possibility of written records or documents dating from the time of the Exodus and conquest of Canaan, as indicated in the Bible. However although our attitude toward the history of phonetic writing has fundamentally changed, this has not effected any change in our viewing of the biblical narratives as oral transmission.[1]

Permutation and alteration in the meaning of terms and words taking place in the course of time, may also lead to erroneus understanding. For example, the Hebrew word "Iy" (אי) today means an island. Biblical verses such as "Iy Caphtor" (the original homeland of the Philistines according to the Bible), were accordingly understood and translated as the 'island of Caphtor' . This rendering of the term brought in its wake a mass of conceptions relating to the Philistines who presumably "came" from the island of Crete, etc. We will see that the word "Iy" in the Bible meant "land" and not "island", thereby undermining the very basis for the view that the Philistines came from Crete. Yet the "Philistine theory" is so firmly rooted in our times apparently corroborated by archaeological findings that its origin is already forgotten. If we now try to show that it is basically erroneous we shall probably be confronted by the various archaeological findings, although the problem is really one of interpretation given to these findings.

InTel Ed–Dweir ostraka were found written in ancient Hebrew. The mound was identified as ancient Lachish. and the ostraka, known as the 'Lachish letters', were ascribed to the period of the destruction of the first Temple (578 B. C.). There are grounds for dating the ostraka to the period of king Rehoboam c. 917 B. C.[2] We therefore have to "move" backward

---

1   However Dussaud points out that Israelite history must be reexamined in light of the fact that writing was known already in the region in the patriarchal period. (La notion d'ame chez les Israelites et Phéniciens, SY., 16, 1935, p. 277.)
2   Ganor. N. R. The Lachish Letters. P. E. Q. . 1967. p. 74.

the date of many of the findings discovered in that mound Different points of departure inevitably bring about radical changes of attitude to certain problems in the present, past or future. If we assume that the Exodus occurred in the period of Raamses II (the prevailing theory), then the Israelites must have invaded Canaan in c. 1200 B. C. Then the inevitable conclusion is that when they reached the cities of Jericho, Bet–El, Ai and other cities they must have found them already destroyed bieng that their destruction is assigned archaeologically to an earlier period. The outcome is: theories of two exoduses or alternatively negation of biblical historicity. findings like the Ras Shamra (Ugarit) tablets (assigned to the 14 th century B. C. and with a context very similar to that of the biblical narratives) inevitably constitute "proof" that the Israelites "borrowed" their culture from the "Phoenicians" as is widely believed. But if we accept that the Exodus took place about 1400 B. C. (following biblical evidence), then the assertion of "borrowing" or two exoduses etc. has no basis whatsoever.

One of the main sources for studying the history of our region was and still is the Old Testament. Every scholar, directly or indirectly, returns to the Old Testament as a main source. The Jews recognising the Old Testament as a holy book accepted it literally and in the past did not question its veracity. Their attitude towards it was of elucidation and exegesis rather than criticism, Compared with them the first gentile investigators, most of whom were members of various churches, were motivated by the understanding of Christianity, and their wish to see it enhanced. Naturally this attitudes, as we will see later, had implications for the history of the entire region. For myself also, the Bible serves as the basic ground, yet my approach is not either to negate or to affirm. My point of departure is that the Bible is a book which was written by Jews for the nation of Judah, and it has a main trend which is to assert that the Jewish God is the almighty power and all–ruling providence in the universe. These two points must be borne in mind in evaluating biblical statements. Nevertheless, the very fact that the O. T. includes stories such as the concubine of Gibeah (Ju. 19); David and Bat–sheba (2Sam. 11); Amnon and Tamar (2Sam. 13), etc. shows clearly that this is not a book which depicts events and their protagonists in merely a praiseworthy and glorifying light. It presents objective happenings but in a manner which betrays the subjectivity and tendencies of its editor.

In the 18th century (Astruc Jean 1684–1766), there began what has been regarded as scientific biblical criticism and research. Although ostensibly this was objective scientific investigation in actual fact it continued like any other investigation to be founded on former investigations. This approach challenged biblical historicity and veracity and led to a dismembering of the Bible (O. T.). Eventually it was "proved" that the biblical text was merely an assemblage of aetiological legendary narratives (Alt, Noth etc.): We are told, for example, that the conquest of the cities Ai and Jericho as reported in the Bible, never happened or at most the biblical editors "confused" the conquest of Ai with that of Beit–El (Albright and others). We are further told that the Exodus, which is the climax and major turning point in the history of the nation of Israel and which forms a strong basis for the Jewish religion never existed (Nibuhre, Finkelstein etc.) or alternatively that there were two Exoduses, (Rowe, Albright and others), etc. Whenever the "scientific archaeological facts" did not correspond with the biblical narrative, it was always the Bible that was at fault It was either unreliable traditions transmitted from one person to another, or copyist mistakes, aetiological tales, etc. I have not come across many cases where archaeologists confessed that perhaps they were the ones at fault in the understanding and interpretation of archaeological findings. As we will see these ideas were corollary and conesequential to dating the Exodus wrongly to c. 1200 B. C.

When writing this book I tried to preserve as objective a stern as possible and suppress entirely the subjective personal point of view. I have tried to base myself and tried to obtain an objective picture. as much as possible on primary sources only, and not on the views and theories a succession of different scholars, which generally contradict each other. It is only after arriving at conclusions from the primary sources, that I turn to the discussion of those theories and archaeological findings relating to them. By adopting this approach, I believe the reader will encounter views and conclusions already advanced by others but which I arrived at by my own methods. However, our ultimate conclusions differ.

The sources from which I took material to write this book, were partly read by me in the original and partly in translation. In cases where I was aided by translation, I was not satisfied with only one source but examined and compared various sources. I should note here that translations of historical sources, are always a reflection of the translator's understanding of the source; and it is according to this understanding that historical knowledge is formed and not according to the source itself. As regards this book, it is not the sources themselves that are important but the way they were understood and explained; these are reflected by and can be studied from the different translations. However it should be noted that because of the intricacies of historical events and developments certain problems raised and discussed were of necessity left unresolved until later chapters. The main outlines of this book were published earlier in Hebrew in two booklets and a book entitled "Who were the Phoenicians"? The first of these was published in 1952 in Geneva, the second at the beginning of 1962 in Israel, and the book in 1974, but their arguments are discussed here in greater detail. In this book I set out to controvert the by now universally accepted view that the Phoenicians were an ancient Canaanite people, whose homeland is the region of today's Lebanon. The thesis advanced is that "Phoenicians" was the name applied by the ancient Greeks to the people of Israel, but because of a long series of misinterpreted and misunderstood facts, linguistic religious and archaeological, this truth was not recognized up till now. As a result certain key historical events recounted in the Bible, such as the Exodus, the conquest of the land of Canaan etc., were wrongly understood, leading inevitably to a distorted reconstruction of the history of this region. Another important factor contributing to this distorted view is the religious secession within Israel that climaxed at the time of Ezra the Scribe. This secession eventually led to the formation of a new nation – the Judeans – who seceded from the majority of the Israelite nation. Following this, the name 'Phoenicians', which previously had referred to the whole of the Israelite nation, was now applied only to the Israelite majority remnant, and in time became restricted to the people living on the Levantine coast.

The conclusions advanced in this book differ from those generally accepted today. Nevertheless I arrived at them only after deep and careful thought, and my decision to publish them in book form is because I am persuaded of their veracity and their appropriateness. Though I am sure this book, like any book, is not exempt from technical defects, I hope nonetheless the reader will be persuaded of the truth of the arguments put forward here.

A NOTE TO THE ENGLISH EDITION

While translating this book into English I was faced, for the most part, with the problem of how to present the English reader with questions based on the interpretation and pronunciation of Hebrew words and quotations which lie at the very source of the erroneous understanding and interpretation of biblical history as discussed here. Translation into English of these words and passages was patently impossible for the very reason that such translation would deprive them of their main essence and would not express the actual connotation in the original tongue. Added to this difficulty was that of Bible translations which in many instances neither overlap with, nor are identical to the Hebrew source. Such inaccuracies frequently constitute the very basis for the distortion of certain events concerning the history of the region. To the reader trained in the Hebrew language, these numerous inaccuracies can be easily pointed out. But it is almost impossible to do so for the English reader, because to quote from an erroneous English translation of the Bible in order to expose inaccuracies in that same English translation is obviously self–defeating. In any case, it would perpetuate misunderstanding and misinterpretation of the citations and so frustrate their purpose. In order to overcome such difficulties and to provide the English reader not conversant with the Hebrew language with the means of understanding the words and passages cited in the text, and of following the arguments laid out in this book, I have cited, in several instances, the words and quotations in the original Hebrew, transcribed and explained in English, so that the English reader might be able to get a more exact sense of the citations. Another problem was that of the spelling and pronunciation of certain names which differ in Hebrew and in English such as Raamses–Rameses, Yehuda–Judah, Yehoshua–Joshua, etc. I have referred to these names in their original Hebrew pronunciation, except for certain names already familiar in their English form such as Joshua, Judah, etc. I referred to these occasionally in their Hebrew form side by side with the English one when a specific reason called for it, e. g. Joshua (Yehoshua) etc. I trust that the English reader will thus surmount the unavoidable difficulties and be able get at the heart of the matter discussed here.

WHO WERE THE PHOENICIANS?

It is universally accepted today that the Phoenicians were a nation which had settled on the Mediterranean coast, along a narrow strip of land bordered by Aradus to the north, Mount Lebanon to the east, and Mount Carmel to the south. The city of Jaffa is sometimes mentioned as the southern border, and the Eleutherus river (Nehar el–Kebir) as the northern one. Pliny[1] mentions Jaffa as "Jaffa the Phoenician" though he designates the city of Dor as the border between Phoenicia and Judea. Raymond Weill, relying on various sources, infers that the term Phoenicia implied at first a vast section of the Aegeo–Asiatic world, and that only in the course of centuries it became restricted to the above–mentioned narrow coastal strip. For Weill this puzzling fact remains inexplicable[2]. According to Herodotus (II, 84) "these Phoenicians dwelt in old time, as they themselves say, by the Red Sea"[3] This quotation from Herodotus was taken by many scholars to mean they came from the region surrounding the Persian Gulf[4] while others thought they were from the Erythrean region[5]. Strabo (I, II, 35; XVI, 27) refers with astonishment to the claim of the inhabitants of the Persian Gulf that two cities in their region are named Tyros and Aradus, whereas Pliny[6] states that the name is not Tyros but Tylos.

With respect to political and geographical relations, Phoenicia held a foremost position in the history of the ancient world. The Phoenicians were known as brave and courageous merchants and seafarers. They were the first to venture great distances from shore and to navigate the open seas aided by the north star as guide. In their travels they gained the Atlantic Ocean, and were the first to reach the British Isles. Herodotus states (IV, 42) that Phoenician seafarers were the first to circumnavigate the African continent. Through their constant travelling, the Phoenicians expanded their commercial

---

1   (v –14, 17).
2   Weill, Phoenicia and Western Asia etc., pp. 15–17. see also; Rawlinson, Phoenicia, pp. 1–2.
3   Trans. A. D. Godley, Loeb Classical Library (London. 1946); see also I, 1.
4   Harden, The Phoenicians, ch. i, n. 1.
     Whitaker, Motya – a Phoenician Colony in Sicily, p. 5.
     Barnette, Phoenicia, E. B. (1968), p. 886.
     Perrot – Chipiez, History of Art in Phoenicia etc., pp. 11; 25.
5   e. g.: Moscati, the World of the Phoenicians, p. 4.
     Montgomery – Harris, the Ras Shamra Mythological Texts, p. 5.
6   Natural History, VI, 32.

ties with many countries and served as link between east and west. Another consequence of their travels was the founding of many settlements, especially in the Mediterranean Basin. The army of one of these – Carthage – nearly vanquished Rome.

The Phoenicians had an enormous influence on the ancient world, particularly upon the Greeks, in architecture, religion, language, and other spheres. Pliny[7] ascribes to the Phoenicians the invention of the glass industry. Whether this statement is accurate or not, there is no doubt that they raised the art of glass–making to a high degree of perfection. He also ascribes to them the invention of astronomy, navigation and military strategy. From the Phoenicians the Greeks received their system of weights and measures[8]. However, the most important invention attributed to them[9] is that of phonetic writing which was and still is, the main basis and cause for the development and advancement of the human race.

The term "Phoenicians" appears in later centuries – first and foremost in early Greek literature. Homer, the ancient Greek poet (c. 1000 B.C.) is the earliest source mentioning "Phoenicians (Phoinikes – Phoiniké) from Tyre and Sidon" and telling of "Sidon which is in Phoenicia". Nevertheless, in epigraphic inscriptions from that part of the world where Phoenicia is supposed to have existed, no such name appears. The Bible refers to the inhabitants of this area as Tyrians and Sidonians, whereas in the Amarna letters we read of Sidon or Canaan, although the latter is used to denote a general term for the whole area. In Egyptian inscriptions, the names "Kharu" or "Retenu" are employed to designate the region of Phoenicia and Israel[10] It should be noted that in certain Egyptian texts from the 3rd millenium B. C., the name "Pnhu" appears which Seth finds similar to the Greek "Phoinikes", and he identifies it with the Phoenicians.

It should be emphasised that in ancient Greek literature, including Homer, despite the use of the term Phoenicians, the term Sidonians is more generally employed. The interpretation of "Phoenicia" as identical with Canaan appears only in later periods (Stephen of Byzantium, Sanchoniathon) to be followed accordingly by the Church Fathers who identified Canaan with Phoenicia. Hecateus[11] tells us that "Phoenicia was formerly called Chna" (Canaan), However Philo Byblius[12] mentions in his Mythology "Chna who was afterwards called Phoinix". This informs us that the name Canaan was changed to Phoenicia. Yet today it is customary to see the terms Phoenicians, Sidonians, and Canaanites as a single identity, and therefore interchangeable;

7   Pliny, Natural History, v – xiii.
8   Whitaker, ibid. p. 13.
9   Pliny, ibid. V – XIII, Herodotus, V – 58
10   For example: Dunand, Byblia Grammata, p. 21.
11   Fr. Hist. Grec. I – 17.
12   Fr. Hist. Grec. III – 569

which has produced the tendency to designate as "Phoenicians" the inhabitants of the region even in periods prior to the appearance of this name in history[13]. To cite Albright[14], "The word 'Canaanite' is historically, geographically, and culturally synonymous with 'Phoenicia'".

Who, therefore, were these people which settled in the region of Tyre and Sidon?

The Bible classifies the inhabitants of the world into three ethnic groups: Shem, Ham and Japhet,[15] a division which is still in use with the modification that instead of the Japhet group we speak of the Indo–European group. Since the Bible associates the Sidonians with Canaan the son of Ham, they are still linked nowadays with the Canaanite race. However, the linguistic and cultural characteristics of the nation that inhabited the region of Sidon, as revealed by archaeological findings, are those of a Semitic people. This evidence induced scholars to accept the biblical division only in part: namely, that the Phoenicians were Canaanites by race, yet were not of Hamitic, but rather of Semitic origin This paradoxical explanation is the general belief today. In support, the analogy is made with today's Afro–American descendants, with their English language culture. Interestingly, Autran claims their origin to have been entirely different, calling them Aegeo–Asiatics[16]. Perrot,[17] while trying to classify the Phoenicians, states: "...relying upon the genealogical table in the tenth chapter of Genesis some have supposed them to belong to the stem of Cush so they would be cousins of the Egyptians, like the Canaanites who according to the same genealogy were also sons of Ham. But, on the other hand, since the Phoenician inscriptions have been deciphered it has been recognised that the Phoenician and Hebrew languages resembled each other very narrowly – so narrowly – that they might almost be called two dialects of one tongue. If this be so, ought we not rather to connect the Phoenicians with the great Semitic race of which the Hebrews are the most illustrious representation. We cannot say how close the relationship may have been, but in any case the Phoenicians must have been much more nearly connected with the Hebrews than with the Egyptians and other nations whom we know as Cushites and Hamites".

The principal object of this book is to try, in the light of sources known

---

13   For example: Perrot – Chipiez, ibid. p. 30.
      Moscati, ibid. pp. 31; 34. ; p. 24 . in article "Who Were The Phoenicians"in The Phoenicians Edit.
      Bompiani 1988.
      Renan, Histoire du peuple d'Israel, Tome I. p. 10
      Mazar, The Philistines and The Rise of Israel And Tyre p. 3.
14   Albright, The Bible and The Ancient Near East, p. 328. see also: Muhly, Homer and The Phoenicians, Berytus, 19, 1970, p. 27.
15   Gen. 10.
16   Autran, "Pheniciens".
17   Perrot – Chipiez, ibid. p. 12.

to us, to trace the course of events in the area of Sidon, (known to be in Phoenicia), from the remotest periods in time, and by so doing to provide an answer to the question: Who were the people that dwelt in that region? In other words, who were the people whom the Greeks called "Phoenicians"?

The sources from which historical investigators derived their knowledge of Phoenician history can roughly be divided into two: epigraphic and archaeological. In the main we will discuss the epigraphic sources, and then go to examine how far the archaeological findings are in conformity with the conclusions deriving from these sources.

Until the discovery of the Tell el–Amarna and Ras Shamra tablets our main source for the knowledge about the Phoenicians were the Latin and Greek literatures. But these are not to be considered a primary source, since they originated in later periods: Homer, c. 1000 B. C.; Herodotus between c. 480–425 B. C.; Strabo, 50 B. C.; Josephus and Diodorus Siculus in the first decade A. C. etc.

The most ancient epigraphic sources in our possession today are the Ras–Shamra tablets, el–Amarna tablets, and the Bible. Of these, only the last two refer to political events, therefore we shall try to extract information from these two sources about the region of Sidon.

THE CONQUEST OF CANAAN ACCORDING TO THE BIBLE AND THE T.E.A.T.

The Tell el – Amarna tablets provide us with the description of wars and the invasion by certain tribes of the land of Canaan; Furthermore we learn that the region of Sidon was conquered at that period by Aziru[1]. In some tablets the name appears as Aziru son of Abd Ashera (Abdi Ashirta)[2]. The name "Aziru" and "Abd Ashera" (Abdi Ashirta) are generally identified as proper names, therefore Aziru is supposed to be the son of a certain man called Abd Ashera (Abdi Ashirta). They are also identified as Amorites[3]. Mercer[4] believes Aziru to be an Amorite prince. son of a man called Abdashera who was hated by his contemporaries and was an enemy of the king of Egypt. Conder believes Aziru to be a proper name of an Amorite person who betrayed the king of Egypt, and the letters of this Aziru to the king of Egypt he assembles in a special chapter entitled "The Amorite Treachery"[5]. According to Barton[6] "The kings of the Amorites during this period were Ebed Ashera and Aziru". Elsewhere in his book (p. 442), Barton conjectures that "if the Asirta, Abd Asratu, etc. 'ebed' were dropped out of the phrase 'sons of Ebed Ashera' there

---

1   tablet 118, lines 23, 30.
2   Conder transcribes the name as Abd Ashera, whereas Mercer and Knudtzon render it Abdi Asirta, Alod Asrata, etc.
3   Conder, TEAT
    Albright, The Amarna Letters From Palestine, CAH, ch. 20, vol. II, pp. 5, 6
    Jack, The Date of The Exodus In The Light of External Evidence, p. 177.
    Lods, Israel, P. 152.
    D'horme, Les Pays Biblique Au Temps d'el – Amarna, RB. 1909, pp. 59; 70.
    – Les Nouvelles Tablettes d'el–Amarna, RB 1924, p. 7.
    – La Question Des Habiri, RHR. 1938, p. 170.
    – Les Habiru et Les Hebreux, JPOS. 1924, p. 164.
    Contenau, La Civilisation Phénicienne, p. 49.
    Campbell, The Amarna Letters and Amarna Period, BA. 1960, p. 8.
    Kapelrud, Interpreters Dictionary Of The Bible – Phoenicia.
    Berard, Les Phéniciens et L'Odysée, p. 208.
    Slouschz, Sefer hayam, p. 68 (Heb.); Motzaei haivrim, p. 42. (Heb.).
    Aharoni, Eretz Israel bitkufat hamikra, p. 150. (Heb.).
    Bondi, The Origins In The East, p. 34 – article in "The Phoenicians", Bompiani 1988.
    Swiggers p. Byblos dans Les Lettres d'el Amarna; Stu. Ph. 1985. pp. 54–55
4   Mercer, TEAT
5   Conder, TEAT
6   Barton, Archeology And The Bible, p. 153

would remain 'sons of Ashera' or 'sons of Asher'", referring to the conquest of the tribe of Asher.

The biblical narrative of Israel's settlement in Canaan refers initially to the conquest of the east side of the Jordan River under the leadership of Moses The first conquests are of the lands of Sihon the Amorite king and of Og king of Bashan. This conquest is recorded in the Bible as follows: "And we took the land at that time out of the hand of the two kings of the Amorites that were beyond the valley of the Arnon unto mount Hermon" (Deut. 3: 8). Their land is settled by the tribes of Reuben, Gad and half of Menashe (Nu. 32). Then the Israelites cross to the west side of the Jordan. Before crossing the Jordan we find the Israelites camping"...in the plains of Moab by Jordan near Jericho...from Beth–Jeshimot even unto Abel–shittim (Nu. 33: 48–49)."And Israel abode in Shittim..." (Nu. 25: 1). Here Moses died and was buried "in the valley in the land of Moab" (Deut. 34: 6). From Shittim Joshua sent the spies to Jericho (Jos. 2: 1), and from Shittim the Israelites crossed the Jordan to conquer the west side of Canaan (Jos. 3: 1).

Some verses allow us to infer that the encampment of the Israelites in Shittim lasted from two to three months. Aharon, the high priest, died on Mount Hor "in the fortieth year after the children of Israel were come out of the land of Egypt, in the first day of the fifth month" (Nu. 33: 38). and in "the fortieth year in the eleventh month on the first day of the month that Moses spake unto the children of Israel. in Moab" (Deut. 1: 3–6). In the plains of Moab the children of Israel mourned Moses for thirty days (Deut. 34: 8). On the tenth day of the first month the people of Israel came up out of Jordan and encamped in Gilgal (Jos. 4: 19). Therefore at least two and a half months must have elapsed from the time Moses spoke unto Israel in Moab (Shittim) until they crossed the Jordan. And about eight and a half months from the time of Aharon's death. During their journey from Mount Hor to Shittim the Israelites encamped eight times (Nu. 33: 39–49). Thus we shall not be at fault if we add about one month to the said period of two months. This means the children of Israel stayed in Shittim for only two or three months. After crossing the Jordan, the Israelites "encamped in Gilgal in the east border of Jericho". (Jos. 4: 19). From Gilgal they went out to attack Jericho, Ai, and Beth– El. It was to Joshua in Gilgal that the Gibeonites came (Jos. 9: 6), and from Gilgal Joshua went up to fight Adoni–zedek, king of Jerusalem. Hoham king of Hebron, Piram king of Jarmuth and Japhia king of Lachish, and Debir king of Eglon (Jos. 10: 9). The text informs us that at the end of the battle "Joshua returned, and all Israel with him, unto the camp to Gilgal" (Jos. 10: 15).

This battle is followed by the conquest, one after the other of the cities Makkeda, Libnah, Lachish, Eglon, Hebron and Debir (Jos. 10: 28–40). These cities were destroyed and the Bible points out "so Joshua smote all the country of the hills, and of the south, and of the vale, and of the springs, and all their kings: he left none remaining. And Joshua smote them from Kadesh–barnea even unto Gaza, and all the country of Goshen, even unto Gibeon. And all these kings and their land did Joshua TAKE AT ONE TIME...And Joshua returned, and all Israel with him unto the camp to Gilgal" (Jos. 10: 40–43) (emphasis–N. G.). Thus, after the battles Joshua and the sons of Israel return to Gilgal. The Israelites do not settle in the conquered places, but return to Gilgal which most probably served as assembling center as well as a religious and political one. Some verses allow us to estimate approximately. the number of years that Gilgal served as a center for the Israelites.

In Jos. 4: 19 we read: "And the people came up out of Jordan on the tenth day of the first month. and encamped in Gilgal, in the east border of Jericho". Thus they reached Gilgal on the forty first year after leaving Egypt, in the first month of the year. In Jos. 14: 6 – 10 we read: "Then the children of Judah came unto Joshua in Gilgal: and Caleb the son of Jephuneh the Kenezite said unto him...forty years old was I when Moses the servant of the Lord sent me from Kadesh–barnea to espy out the land: ...And now, behold, the Lord had kept me alive as said, these forty and five years...". As we know, the spies were sent from the desert of Paran (Nu. 13) where the Israelites had arrived on the second year after the Exodus (Nu. 10: 11–12). Hence, about six years must have elapsed from the crossing of the Jordan until Caleb addresses Joshua in Gilgal (45–40 + 1 and two months). Evidently this is about the number of years that Gilgal served as center till this was transferred to Shiloh. For we read thereafter: "And the whole congregation of the children of Israel assembled at Shiloh" (Jos. 18: 1). From now on all the activities of Joshua and the Israelites are linked with Shiloh. In Shiloh Joshua apportions the country by lot to seven tribes (Jos. 18; 19: 51; 21: 2;). it is from Shiloh that the children of Reuben, Gad and the half tribe of Menasseh departed to return to the Gilead (Jos. 22: 9), and it is to Shiloh that the "whole congregation of the children of Israel" gathers to go up to war against the tribes of Gad, Reuben and the half of Menasseh (Jos. 22: 12). From the biblical text we learn that after Shiloh, and still within Joshua's lifetime, Shechem became a place of holiness to God, and a national center for the Israelites: "And Joshua gathered all the tribes of Israel to Shechem..." (Jos. 24: 1)."So Joshua made a covenant with the people that day, and set them a statute and an ordinance at Shechem. And Joshua wrote these words in the book of the law of God, and took a great stone, and set it up there under an oak, that was by the sanctuary of the Lord" (Jos. 24: 25–27).

To sum up: From the biblical account it is clear that the Israelites while penetrating deeper into the country and advancing in their conquest of the land, established different centers: Shitim, Gilgal, Shiloh and Shechem. These centers form reference points for the conquest; moreover the entire process will be more comprehensible if reviewed in the order of these points.

At Shitim, the Israelites, after the death of Moses and Aharon, organised for a military assault upon the west side of the Jordan. Who are their leaders? According to the biblical narrative "Moses commanded Eleazar the priest, and Joshua the son of Nun, and the chief fathers of the tribes of the Children of Israel" (Nu. 32: 28). Elsewhere there is more detail: "And the Lord spake unto Moses, saying, These are the names of the men which shall divide the land unto you: Elazar the priest and Joshua son of Nun. And ye shall take one prince of every tribe, to divide[7] the land by inheritance. and the names of the men are these: ...". We learn therefore that we deal here not with just a single leader, as would appear at first sight, but with a leadership comprised of twelve men holding the function of chiefs (princes) and leaders of their tribes, who are, at the same time, subject to a higher dual authority consisting of Eleazar the priest and Joshua son of Nun, neither of whom exercises power alone; the first being a religious leader, and the second a military leader[8]. With this leadership the Israelites cross the Jordan and centre upon Gilgal, from whence they go out to conquer the towns of Jericho and Ai (Jos. 6: 8). After the conquest of these towns, follows a description of a campaign against the confederation of Adoni–Zedec, king of Jerusalem, Hoham king of Hebron, Piram king of Jarmuth, Japhia king of Lachish, and Debir king of Eglon. Joshua defeats them and finally seizes them as they hide in a cave (Jos. 10: 16–28). Then follows the conquest of Makkedah "And that day Joshua took Makkedah...he utterly destroyed them, and all the souls that were therein; he let none remain: and he did to the king of Makkedah AS HE DID UNTO THE KING OF JERICHO" (Jos. 10: 28) (my emphasis – N. G.). From Makkedah he goes on to Libnah and conquers it: "...and he smote it with the edge of the sword, and all the souls that were therein; he let none remain in it; but did unto the king thereof AS HE DID UNTO THE KING OF JERICHO" (Jos. 10: 30, emphasis – N. G.). From Libnah he goes to Lachish, but here the biblical account varies: "And the Lord delivered Lachish into the hand of Israel, which took it on the second day, and smote it with the edge of the sword, and all the souls that were therein, according to all that he had done to Libnah" (Jos. 10: 32). Here the addition of "as he did unto the king of Jericho" is lacking. The account refers only to "all the souls" "all that he had done to Libnah". This same variation is also found in the account of the conquest of Eglon, which follows that of Lachish; "and they took it on that day, and smote it with the edge of the sword, and all the souls that were therein he utterly destroyed that day, according to all that he

---

7   Hebrew – yinhalu, meaning to inherit, to conquer.
8   A dual leadership as of two judges can be found at a later period in Carthage

had done to Lachish" (Jos. 10: 35). From Eglon Joshua goes up unto Hebron: "And they took it and smote it with the edge of the sword, and the king thereof, and all the cities thereof, and all the souls that were therein; he left none remaining, according to all that he had done to Eglon; but destroyed it utterly, and all the souls that were therein" (Jos. 10: 36–38). From Hebron he returns to Debir: "And he took it, and the king thereof, and all the cities thereof, and they smote them with the edge of the sword, and utterly destroyed all the souls that were therein; he left none remaining: as he had done to Hebron so he did to Debir, and to the king thereof; as he had done also to Libnah, and to her king" (Jos. 10: 39). Why this variation? Is it of any significance? . On the face of it the addition "...And he did to the king...as he did unto the king of Jericho" seems to imply the kings' death, but why does the text reserve this expression only for certain kings while not using it with others, although their death is mentioned? Does any difference exist between what was done to the king of Jericho and what was done to the other kings?

To clear up this problem, let us see what happened to the king of Jericho. The biblical narrative of the conquest of Jericho (Jos. 6) has no detailed description of what happened to the king, but this can be clarified from verses elsewhere. We are told that Joshua was ordered: "And thou shalt do to Ai and her king as thou didst unto Jericho and her king" (Jos. 8: 2). This order was carried out duly as we learn from the verse: "...When Adoni–Zedec king of Jerusalem had heard how Joshua had taken Ai, and had utterly destroyed it, as he had done to Jericho and her king so he had done to Ai and her king" (Jos. 10: 1). Therefore it is evident that the king of Ai suffered the same fate as the king of Jericho; concerning what was done to the king of Ai, the description is detailed: "So Joshua burnt Ai...And the king of Ai he hanged on a tree until the eventide: and at the going down of the sun Joshua commanded, and they took his body down from the tree, and cast it at the entrance of the gate of the city, and raised thereon a great heap of stones, unto this day" (Jos. 8: 28–29). Thus we see that the king of Ai, after he was hanged, was buried under a heap of stones "AT THE ENTRANCE OF THE GATE OF THE CITY", and likewise this must have been the fate of the king of Jericho. On the other hand, the kings of Lachish, Hebron, Eglon, etc. were also hanged, but buried either in a cave in Makkedah (Jos. 10: 16–28) or elsewhere. The only difference subsequent to their death, compared to that of the kings of Jericho and Ai, was the latter's burial at the entrance of the gate of the city. The phrase "and he did to the king...as he did unto the king of Jericho" was probably inserted to indicate the burial of the king at the gate of his city. Accordingly this was done to the kings of Jericho, Ai, Makkedah and Libnah, though not to the kings of Lachish, Eglon and Hebron. However, the fate of the towns and their inhabitants was the same. Most probably the Israelite conquerors used to bury the kings of the conquered cities at the gates of their destroyed and burnt cities. Perhaps this had symbolic significance. It is notworthy that in the Amarna letters, in a letter by Abdi–Hiba (Tablet 288)[9], the writer mentions that "Turbazu has been killed in the gate of Zilu" (lines 41–42), and that "Iaptih–Ada is slain in the city gate of Zilu" (lines 45 – 46). As will be discussed later, there is the possibility that the Bible and the Amarna letters depict the same sequence of events.

After the conquest of the cities mentioned above, we read: "So Joshua smote all the land, the hill – country, and the South, and the lowland, and the slopes, and all their kings: he left none remaining, but he utterly destroyed all that breathed. as Jehovah, the god of Israel, commanded. And Joshua smote them from Kadesh–barnea even unto Gaza, and all the country of Goshen even unto Gibeon.

And all these kings and their land did Joshua take at onetime, because Jehovah, the God of Israel, fought for Israel. And Joshua RETURNED and all Israel with him, UNTO THE CAMP TO GILGAL" (Jos. 10: 40–43).

It would appear from the foregoing that Joshua conquered the entire country in one action. But further consideration makes us realise that the blow administered by Joshua to "all the land, the hill country, and the south, and the lowland..." etc. refers only to the southern part of the country, and not to the whole of Canaan. This had taken place while the centre was still in GILGAL, for it was to Gilgal that Joshua and all the Israelites with him returned after the battle. The account is, therefore, of a single, continuous battle in which Joshua conquered a part of the southern region. Immediately after, the biblical account speaks of another battle against an alliance of kings headed by Jabin king of Hazor: "And it came to pass, when Jabin king of Hazor heard thereof, that he sent to Jobab king of Madon, and to the king of Shimron, and to the king of Achsaph, and to the kings that were on the north, in the hill–country, and in the Arabah south of Chinneroth, and in the lowland, and in the heights of Dor on the west, to the Canaanite on the east and on the west, and the Amorite, and the Hittite, and the Perizzite, and the Jebusite In the hill–country, and the Hivite under Hermon in the land of Mizpah." (Jos. 11: 1– 5). In this battle Joshua conquers the city of Hazor (Jos. 11: 10)."And all the cities of those kings, and all the kings of them did Joshua take." (Jos. 11: 12). The narrative continues: "So Joshua took all that land, the hill – country, and all the South, and all the land of Goshen, and the lowland, and the Arabah, and the hill – country of Israel, and the lowland of the same; from mount Halak[10], that goeth up to Seir, even unto Baal–gad in the valley of Lebanon under mount Hermon" (Jos. 11: 16–17)."So Joshua took, THE WHOLE LAND, according to all that Jehovah

---

9   The numbers of the tablets are according to Mercer, TEAT. and Knudtzon, TEAT. When different numbers are employed, this is noted.

10   in Hebrew ḥalak (חלק) means smooth, slippery, Har = mountain, since the biblical text has ההר החלק ha–har he–halak, i. e. a noun preceded by a definite article, (ha –he= ה) it must be translated: the "slippery" mountain, and not mount Halak.

spake unto Moses; and Joshua gave it for an inheritance unto Israel according to their divisions by their tribes. And the land had rest from war."[11] (Jos. 11: 23 –emphasis–N. G.). From this passage summing up Joshua's activities, and from the account of the conquest so far, it might be assumed that the Israelites had conquered the entire western part of Canaan in a single whirlwind campaign, after which "the land had rest from war". The expression "all the land" does not imply a reference to the whole country of Canaan, but only to the land (cities) which were at war with the Israelites. On the other hand, in the Bible the word war (Hebrew – milḥama(מלחמה) is often taken to signify battle: "When Joab saw that the battle (Heb. – milḥama) was against him..." (2Sam. 10: 9); "Set ye Uriah in the forefront of the hottest battle..." (Heb. – milḥama) (2 Sam. 11: 15); "David asked of him how Joab did, and how the people fared, and how the war (Heb. – מלחמה milḥama) prospered."(2Sam. 11: 7); "...and they set the battle (Heb. – – מלחמה milḥama) in array against them in the vale of Siddim" (Gen. 14: 8), and elsewhere (1Sam. 17: 2 ; Ju. 20: 20, 22, 34, 39). Therefore, the quoted passage from Joshua 11: 23 should be seen as summing up a battle (or battles) and not an entire war: Accordingly "and the land had rest from war" (Heb. – milama) realy means – and the land was void of battles. And indeed the first sentence of chapter 12, continues to summarize the battles: "Now these are the kings of the land, whom the children of Israel smote, and possessed their land beyond the Jordan toward the sunrising, from the valley of the Arnon unto mount Hermon, and all the Arabah eastward" (Jos. 12: 1). From verse 7 onward there follows an account of the conquest on the west side of the Jordan: "And these are the kings of the land whom Joshua and the children of Israel smote beyond the Jordan westward, from Baal–gad in the valley of Lebanon even unto mount Halak, that goeth up to Seir and Joshua gave it unto the tribes of Israel for a possession according to their divisions; in the hill –country, and in the lowland, and in Arabah, and in the slopes, and in the wilderness, and in the South; the Hittite, Amorite, and the Canaanite, the Perizzite, the Hivite, and the Jebusite: ". This account is followed by a detailed list of the kings who were killed and their cities taken (Jos. 12: 9ff); it includes only thirty one kings along with their cities, i. e. not the whole land of Canaan. Immediately after this accounting we read in chapter 13: "Now Joshua was old and well stricken in years; and Jehovah said unto him, Thou art old and well stricken in years, and there remaineth yet very much land to be possessed" (Jos. 13: 1); " Now therefore divide this land for an inheritance unto the nine tribes, and the half – tribe of Manasseh, With him the Reubenites and the Gadites received their inheritance, which Moses gave them beyond the Jordan eastward." (Jos. 13: 7–8).

Thus, not all the country was conquered by Joshua, but only thirty –

---

11 The Hebrew text reads milḥama (מלחמה).

one cities, after which the land rested from battle. This conquest took place under Joshua's leadership when the center was in Gilgal. When Joshua was old and stricken in years, with the conquest already in an advanced phase, only the tribes of Reuben, Gad and half tribe of Menasseh had received their inheritance on the east side of the Jordan, whereas nine tribes and half of Menasseh had not yet received their inheritance, that is all the west part was not yet divided, although thirty – one cities had already been conquered. By the time the center was transferred to Shiloh, there still remained seven tribes which had not yet received their inheritance: "And the whole congregation of the children of Israel assembled themselves together at Shiloh, and set up the tent of meeting there: and the land was subdued before them. And there remained among the children of Israel seven tribes, which had not yet divided their Inheritance" (Jos. 18: 1–2). From the above verses we learn that the conquests of Joshua so far described refer to a period when the center was in the Gilgal, and that this same center still existed when Joshua was "old and well stricken in years". Moreover, only two tribes and a half received their inheritance at Gilgal at the end of this period, while the remaining seven tribes got their inheritance at Shiloh.

Returning to chapter 14 we read: "And these are the countries which the children of Israel inherited in the land of Canaan, which Eleazar the priest, and Joshua the son of Nun, and the head of the fathers of the tribes of the children of Israel, distributed for inheritance to them. By lot was their inheritance...Then the children of Judah came unto Joshua in Gilgal: and Caleb the son of Jephunneh the Kenezite said unto him...Now therefore give me this mountain...for thou heardst in that day how the Anakim were there, and that the cities were great and fenced: if so be the Lord will be with me, then I shall be able to drive them out[12] ...And Joshua blessed him, and gave unto Caleb the son of Jephunneh Hebron for an inheritance" (Jos. 14: 1–14). Caleb asks Joshua for Hebron to be given him, but this is before Hebron was even conquered, since his request is "if so be the Lord will be with me, then I shall be able to drive them out" From these verses it is quite evident that Joshua IN GILGAL agrees that Hebron be given as an inheritance to Caleb, though it still remains for Caleb to conquer it. We must remember that the consent of Joshua was needed for allotting the inheritances to the tribes, as indicated by the first verse of this chapter: "And these are the countries which the children of Israel inherited..." etc. In this same sense we should interpret the verse "then the children of Judah came unto Joshua in Gilgal: and Caleb...said unto him..." to mean that when the children of Judah came to Gilgal to receive their lot, Caleb son of Jephunneh, who was a Kenezite, asked personally for the city of Hebron, which was in the territory allotted

---

12 The Hebrew text reads "veorashtim"- והורשתים future tense of the verb leorish להוריש – the meaning of leorish will be discussed later.

to Judah, to be given to him, this is in accord with: "And unto Caleb the son of Jephunneh he gave a part among the children of Judah, according to the commandment of the Lord to Joshua, even the city of Arba the father of Anak, which city is Hebron" (Jos. 15: 13).

This episode in Gilgal is followed by the account of the inheritance assigned to the tribes of Judah, Ephraim and half the tribe of Menasseh (Jos. chaps. 15; 16; 17). Immediately after this we read: "And the whole congregation of the children of Israel assembled together in Shiloh..." (Jos. 18: 1). It is evident, therefore, that according to the biblical narrative the division of the inheritance started in Gilgal at the end of the "Gilgal period" when Joshua was "old and well stricken in years" with two and a half tribes receiving their inheritance in Gilgal. After this, the center was transferred from Gilgal to Shiloh where the division of the inheritance was continued among the seven remaining tribes which had not received their inheritances in Gilgal. The verse: "And the whole congregation of the children of Israel assembled themselves together at Shiloh, ...and there remained among the children of Israel seven tribes, which had not yet received their inheritance" points up and draws the reader's attention to the continuity of the partitioning activity which had begun in Gilgal and which ended in Shiloh. The text also emphasizes that at Shiloh "they made an end of dividing the country" (Jos. 19: 51).

From chapter 18, Joshua, we learn how the partition was carried out. Joshua adresses the sons of Israel: "How long will you be remiss in going to possess the land, which the Lord God of your fathers given you? Assign from among you three men for each tribe: and I will send them, and they shall rise, and go through the land, and mark it out according to their inheritance; and they shall come back to me. And they shall divide it into seven parts: ...You shall therefore mark out the land in seven parts, and bring the description to me here, that I may cast lots for you here before the Lord our God... And the men went and passed through the land, and wrote it down by cities into seven parts in a book, and came back to Yeoshua to the camp at Shilo. And Yeoshua cast lots for them in Shilo before the Lord: and there Yeoshua divided the land to the children of Yisra'el according to their divisions" (Jos. 18: 3–11)[13]. Thus we are informed that the country was partitioned into seven sections and each tribe was apportioned its part by lot. It must be remembered that this took place when the areas assigned had not yet been conquered. This is confirmed by the fact that Hebron was conquered by Caleb after the city had been allotted to him, and by Joshua's statement: "Behold I have allotted unto you the nations that remain, to be an inheritance for your tribes, from Jordan, with all the nations that I have cut off, even unto the great sea toward the going down of the sun. And the Lord your God, he shall thrust them out from before you, and drive them from out of your sight" (Jos. 23: 4–5).

---

13   Translation – Koren Bible, Jerusalem 1969.

Concerning the conquest of the cities which had fallen to the lot of each tribe, we read in Judges 1: 1–3: "And it came to pass after the death of Joshua, that the children of Israel asked of the Lord saying, Who shall go up for us first against the Canaanite to fight against them, and Jehovah said, Judah shall go up: behold, I have delivered the land into his hands. And Judah said unto Simeon his brother, come up with me into my lot, that we may fight against the Canaanites; and I likewise will go with thee unto thy lot...". We learn therefore that each tribe had to fight individually to conquer the cities that had fallen to its lot. However, there also existed the possibility of mutual assistance, as for instance, the tribe of Judah calling on the Simeonites for help. Accordingly the book of Judges (Chapter 1) records the conquests of each tribe separately: "And the house of Joseph, they also went up against Beth–el:", "And the children of Judah fought against Jerusalem" and so on. Whenever the text refers to the destruction (Heb. lehorish)[14] of the Canaanite cities it lists the battles of each individual tribe."Asher drove not out the inhabitants of Acco"..., "And Manasseh did not drive out the inhabitants..." etc.

The two (differing) biblical accounts, 1) The individual tribal campaigns; contrasting with 2) the combined, all–out one time campaign under the leadership of Joshua, led many scholars to consider them as two different and contradictory accounts of the same campaign[15], They believe that the account of a combined, all–out campaign is a later idealisation by the editor of the book of Joshua, while the reality was that of a conquest carried out by means of slow and steady infiltration. According to Burne[16], the differing accounts represent a combination of several traditions to form a single unified account. Alt and Noth totally reject the account of the conquest, and see it as an aetiological story, i. e. a story created at a later period to explain an existing custom or name (of place etc.). Noth discredits the conquest narrative as given in the book of Joshua and regards it as having no historical value whatever; the same tendency is evident among many scholars today. There are various reasons for these opinions: On the one hand, a number of verses in the book of Joshua report that Joshua "took the whole land", "and the Land had rest from war", these verses

---

14   Translated: drive out.
15   Wright, Biblical Archaeology Today, BA. 1947, p. 13; The Literary and Historical Problem of Joshua 10 And Judges 1, JNES, 1946, pp. 105 – 114.
       Biblical Archaeology, pp. 69–70.
       Lods, Israel, pp. 12; 380.
       Burney, Israel Settlement In Canaan, 1921, pp. 15–17.
       Rowley, From Joseph to Joshua, pp. 100–103.
       Bright, A History of Israel, pp. 117–118.
       Meek, Hebrew Origins, pp. 23; 45.
       Liver, Iyunim besefer Yehoshua, pp. 46–47 (Hebrew).
       Aharoni, Iyunim besefer Yehoshua, p. 8 (Hebrew).
16   Burney, ibid. pp. 16–27.

are generally understood to mean that the whole land of Canaan was conquered by Joshua in a single campaign[17]; yet we have already noted that this is clearly a misinterpretation. On the other hand, the partition of the land by lot has been understood to have taken place after the conquest of the allotted cities[18]. Since the text states that the Israelites "lo horishu – לא הורישו" (translated in A. V.: "did not drive out") the inhabitants from many cities, this was understood to imply that they failed to conquer these cities. Therefore it was assumed that the list of the allotted cities is a purely arbitrary list introduced by later editors.

It was deduced from certain verses that some of the cities were conquered in separate battles by different leaders. In Joshua 10: 36–39 we read "And Joshua went up from Eglon, and all Israel with him unto Hebron and they fought against it; and they took it... And Joshua returned and all Israel with him, to Debir, and fought against it, and he took it..."etc., while elsewhere (Jos. 15: 13–17; Ju. 1: 10–13) it is related that Hebron was conquered by Caleb the son of Jephunneh, and Debir by Athniel the Kenezite. Verses as the above, together with differing descriptions of campaigns, have led scholars to regard the conquest narrative of the book of Joshua as containing a mass of discrepancies and contradictions. Further substantiation of this is provided by the apparent similarity of phrasing of various segments of the text taken as evidence that the books of Joshua and Judges were composed at the end of the 7th century and at the beginning of the Second Temple period. Another similar factor is the date of the conquest which is linked to the date of the Exodus (generally taken as being c. 1200 B. C. the Raamses – Merneptah period). This topic has not yet been treated here but will appear in a chapter on the Exodus.

The account of the conquest as single combined campaign, under the leadership of Joshua, relates (evidently) to a campaign when GILGAL was yet the center of the Israelites, that is to the first period of the conquest. By contrast the conquest by each single (individual) tribe took place subsequent to the death of Joshua after the center had been transferred to SHILOH. What we have here are different accounts of two separate campaigns. The reasons for believing that we have different accounts of the same conquest were outlined above; we must assume that they result from a misunderstanding the biblical text. Turning to Joshua 21: 10–14 we read: "...which the children of Aaron, being of the families of the Kohathites who were of the children of Levy, had: for theirs was the first lot. And they gave them the city of Arba the father of Anak, which city is Hebron in the hill country of Judah, with the suburbs thereof round about it. But the fields of the city, and the villages thereof gave they to Caleb the son of Jephunneh for his possession. Thus they gave to the children of Aaron the priest Hebron with her suburbs to be a city of refuge

---

17   For example see: Bright, ibid, p. 117; Liver, ibid. pp. 46–49.
18   For example see: Bright, ibid. p. 117.

for the slayer...". The Hebrew text reads: ויהי לבני אהרן ממשפחות הקהתי מבני
"לוי...וַלבני אהרן הכהן נתנו את – עיר מקלט הרצח את־חברון ואת מגרשיה"

It will be seen that the Hebrew verse includes the letter waw (ו) that is a conjunctive (=and), which literally translated reads: "AND TO the sons of Aaron the priest they gave the city of refuge Hebron and its suburbs". This means that additionally to the children of Aaron of the families of the Kohathites–the Levites. – the children of Aaron the priests also received their lot. Verse 19 enumerates all the cities given to "children of Aaron THE PRIESTS". Quite evidently, these cities were given to the children of Aaron THE PRIESTS, (note: plural Heb. הכהנים – Hakohanim – priests), who did not include the Levites. One should remember that the families of the Levites were merely attached to the families of Aaron the priest. Numbers 3: 9–12, informs us of the prevailing sacerdotal hierarchy

1. Aaron and his sons were "consecrated to minister in the priest's office"
2. The Levites performed the service of the tabernacle and accordingly "keep all the instruments of the tabernacle of the congregation, and the charge of the children of Israel to do the service of the tabernacle"(Nu. 5: 5–9).

It should be understood, therefore, that Hebron was partitioned into three sections:

1. to certain families of the Kohathites sons of Aaron, who were nevertheless Levites, attached to the family of Aaron
2. to Caleb the son of Jephuneh.
3. to the PRIESTS (not Levites), the actual sons of Aaron.

From the statement that"...the fields of the city, and the villages thereof gave they to Caleb..." etc., it is to be understood that the name Hebron does not apply to just one city, but to a whole region which was divided into three parts. The fact is that Caleb asks Joshua: "...now therefore give me this mountain...for thou heardest in the day how the Anakim were[19] there and that the cities were great and fenced...And Joshua blessed him and gave unto Caleb the son of Jephunneh Hebron for inheritance" (Jos. 14: 12–14). Hence "this mountain" in which there are great and fenced cities is called Hebron. The name Hebron thus indicates not just one city but an entire region that includes a number of cities. In fact, we are told that the Israelites took Hebron "and all the cities thereof" (Jos. 10: 37) and that David and his men "dwelt in the CITIES of Hebron:" (2Sam 2: 3; emphasis N. G.).

It is obvious that the biblical text refers to the conquest of different areas in a region called Hebron, and that there is no contradiction whatsoever in the biblical narrative. In the same manner we have to understand the conquest of Debir "and all the cities thereof" (Jos. 10: 39) and the conquest

---

19   The original Hebrew text reads "are".

of Jerusalem, Josephus remarks that: "...the lower town they mastered in time and slew all the inhabitants but the upper town proved too difficult to carry through..." (Ant. V–124), whereas regarding Hebron he writes: "...This town they gave to the Levites as a choice boon, along with a tract of two thousand cubits; but of the rest of the land they made, in accordance with the behests of Moses, a present to Caleb" (Ant. V, 126)[20].

According to the above data, we understand the conquest of the land of Canaan to have been as follows: When the center was in Gilgal, the Israelites, under the leadership of Joshua, managed to conquer part of the country (i. e. thirty–one cities and their suburbs) in an all – conquering single campaign comprised of several battles. After these, the land was quiet for some years. At the end of this period, when Joshua was already aged, the land was partitioned among the tribes by lot. The partition also included cities not yet conquered. It began in Gilgal where two and a half tribes received their lot, after which the center was transferred to Shiloh where the partition was resumed by allotting land to the seven remaining tribes. With the death of Joshua the fighting recommences. The center is now in Shiloh, and now each tribe, under the leadership of its chief (prince) fights alone or with the aid of another tribe to conquer the cities allotted to it.

The book of Joshua (chaps. 15–18) ennumerates the cities allocated to each tribe, whereas Judges 1 briefly describes the separate campaigns for their conquest. Thus it emerges that there is no conflict whatever between chapter 1, Judges, and the account of the battles in the book of Joshua since we are concerned here with different battles fought at different periods.

If each tribe was expected to fight by itself to conquer the cities allotted to it, then, the tribe to which the region of Sidon was allotted would have to engage by itself in the conquest of that region. In Joshua 19: 24–32 we read: "And the fifth lot came out for the tribe of the children of Asher according to their families. And their border was Helkath, and Hali, and Beten, and ACHSHAPH, and Allamelech, and Amad, and Mishal, and it reached to CARMEL westward, and to Shihor – libnath; and it turned toward the sunrising to Beth–dagon, and reached to Zebulun, and to the valley of Iphtah – el northward to Beth – emek, and Neiel; and it went out to Cabul on the left hand, and Ebron, and Rehov, and Hammon, and Kanah, even unto great SIDON; and the border turned Ramah and to the fortified city of TYRE; and the border turned to Hosah; and the goings out thereof were at the sea by the region of Achzib; Ummah also, and Aphek, and Rehob: twenty and two

---

20   Loeb translation – One may note that S. Yeivin (Mekhkarim betoldot Israel veartzo, 1960, pp. 135, 145). believes there is no contradiction between the books of Joshua and Judges but that the same events are narrated from different points of view. in these two books.

cities with their villages. This is the inheritance of the tribe of the children of Asher according to their families..."

From the above it emerges that the region of Sidon was awarded to the tribe of Asher; yet we read in Judges (1: 31–32) that "Asher...drove not out[21] the inhabitants of Acco, nor the inhabitants of Sidon, nor of Ahlab, nor of Achzib, nor of Helba, nor of Aphik, nor of Rehob; BUT THE ASHERITES dwelt among the Canaanites the inhabitants of the land, for they did not drive them out". This verse has been taken to indicate that the tribe of Asher was not successful in conquering the mentioned Canaanite cities, since they did not drive out their inhabitants, but settled among the Canaanite population. Various Bible translations give it this sense.[22]. Thus Renan; "Asher did not conquer the cities awarded to him" and cites this particular verse in proof of his assertion[23]. In many scholarly books[24] this verse still serves as proof text that the tribe of Asher did not conquer the region of Tyre (Zor) and Sidon. Moreover, similar verses concerned with other tribes were likewise seen to indicate that these particular tribes, also failed to conquer the cities allotted to them. Albright[25] notes: "Excavations at Gezer, Taanach, Megiddo, and Beth – Shan were not calculated to throw any direct light on this question since all of these towns remained in Canaanite hands during the periods of the Judges, according to explicit Hebrew tradition".

Before attempting to clarify the meaning of the verse in Judges, let us first examine the interpretation of the verb "lehorish" – להוריש. This verb is usually taken to derive from "lareshet" – (לרשת Hebrew for " inherit")"Hence Judges 1: 31–32, whose Hebrew text includes the word – (להוריש lehorish),

---

21   The Hebrew reads "lo horish –"לא הוריש".
22   The Vulgate translates: "Asher quoque non delevit..." ('destroy, annhilate').
23   Renan, Histoire Du Peuple D'Israel, Tome I, p. 253.
24   Barrois, Manuel D'Archeologie Biblique. 1953, II, p. 94.
      Meek, ibid., pp. 22–23.
      Autran, ibid., p. 63.
      Wright, Epic Of Conquest, BA. 1940 (3), p. 27.
      – The Literary And Historical Problem Of Joshua 10 And Judges 1, JNES. 1946, p. 109
      Phytian – Adams, Mirage In The Wilderness, PEQ. 1935, p. 75.
      Wiener, The Conquest Narratives, JPOS. 1929, p. 1.
      Kaufman, The Biblical Account Of The Conquest Of Palestine, pp. 58; 91.
      Petrie, Palestine And Israel, pp. 39 – 40.;
      Lods Israel, p. 381.
      Garstang, Joshua – Judges, p. 241.;
      Sayce, The Early History Of The Hebrews, p. 246 – 248.
      Slouschz, Hébreo – Phéniciens et Judéo – Berbères, p. 76.
      Burney, ibid., pp. 18; 22. ;
      Braver, Haaretz, p. 320. (Hebrew)
      Aharoni, Eretz Israel In Biblical Period, P. 18: Eretz Israel In the Late Canaanite Period: The Settlement of Israelite Tribes In Upper Galilee, p. 69 (Hebrew)
25   Albright, Archaeology and The Date of The Hebrew Conquest of Palestine, BASOR, 1935, (58), p. 10.

was understood to indicate that Asher did not – "lehorish"– the inhabitants of Acco...Sidon etc., that is, he did not inherit their land; and it was therefore translated "Asher did not drive out..."

In Judges 1: 33 we read that "Naphtali drove not out (the Hebrew reads "lo horish" – לא הוריש) the inhabitants of Beth–Shemesh, nor the inhabitants of Beth–anath; but he dwelt among the Canaanites, the inhabitants of the land; nevertheless the inhabitants of Beth–Shemesh and Beth–anath became subjects to task work". It is evident therefore, that the tribe of Naphtali subjugated the Canaanite inhabitants as well as the inhabitants of Beth–Shemesh and Beth–anath, for the latter "became subject to task work"; this means that Naphtali conquered their cities. However the verse reads that he "drove not out" (Hebrew: lo horish– לא הוריש) their inhabitants. Joshua 13: 8–13 tells of the conquest of the entire eastern part beyond the Jordan and we are told, inter alia, that the Reubenites and the Gadites conquered the cities of the Geshurites and of the Maacathites, but though the text clearly speaks about the conquest of their land, we read there: "nevertheless the children of Israel drove not out (Hebrew: lo horish – לא הוריש) the Geshurites, nor the Maacathites; but Geshur and Maacath dwell in the midst of Israel unto this day".

In Judges 1: 31 we read that Asher drove not out (Hebrew: lo horish לא הוריש–) the inhabitants of the city of Rehob, but from Joshua 21: 31; and 1 Chronicles 6: 59 we learn that this city was handed over to the Levites, that is, it was conquered, nevertheless we learn that Asher did not drive out (Hebrew: lo horish – לא הוריש) their inhabitants. Therefore, the above verses plainly indicate that "lehorish" cannot be translated "drive out". The same verb "lehorish" but in its future plural form "torishemo –,–תורישמו" is found in Exodus 15: 9, where we read" torishemo yadi"= my hand will lehorish them. However, though elsewhere this verb is translated "drive out", here it is rendered "destroy": "The enemy said, I will pursue, I will overtake, I will divide the spoil: my lust shall be satisfied upon them: I will draw my sword, my hand shall DESTROY them". Why was the translator not consistent here and render lehorish –"drive out" as he did elsewhere?

Nothing can better demonstrate the absurdity of translating lehorish as "drive out" than rendering the lehorish of the quoted verse in this sense. For if the Israelites were running away because they wanted to leave Egypt, why then should the Egyptians run after them in order to drive them out? . Ibn Ezra explains – torishemo – "destroy them, as see also lo horisho". So also Onkelos. (Aramaic translation). In Deut. 28: 42, we encounter the word "yeyaresh" (3rd person future of "lehorish"). translated "possess". Onkelos, Rasag, (Seadiah ben Joseph) and Ibn Ezra construe – "to destroy". In Numbers 33: 50–55 we read: "And the Lord spake unto Moses. Speak unto the children of Israel, and say unto them, when ye are passed over Jordan into the land of Canaan; then ye shall drive out (Hebrew: veorashtem–...והורשתם second person plural, imperative form of "lehorish") all the inhabitants of the land from before you, and destroy all their pictures, ...And ye shall dispossess (Hebrew: veorashtem) the inhabitants of the land, and dwell therein: ...But if ye will not drive out (Hebrew: torishu ותורישו– second person plural, future form of lehorish) the inhabitants of the land from before you: then it shall come to pass, that those which ye let remain of them shall be pricks in your eyes, and thorns in your sides...". This is translated in the Vulgate:

"Quando transieritis Iordanem intrantes terram Chanaan, DISPERDITE... cunctos habitatores terrae illius..." that is, the Hebrew verb lehorish is translated by the Latin disperdite meaning "to ruin, squander, annihilate". Onkelus (Aramaic), translates: vetetrahun; and Rabbi Saadia Gaon (Rasag) translates (to Arabic) fatakardahom; both versions mean: "to annihilate". Rashi however construes– to drive out. Ibn Ezra explains "torishemo– to destroy, like in the verse –if you will not torishu ". The command to Moses to lehorish all the inhabitants of the land from before them, is cited in other words (varia lectio) in Joshua 9: 24ff, where we read of Joshua reprimanding the Gibeonites for their trickery saying: "Wherefore have you beguiled us, saying we are very far from you; when you dwell among us?", and the Gibeonites answer Joshua: "because it was certainly told thy servants, how that the Lord thy God commanded his servant Moses to give you all the land and to DESTROY[26] all the inhabitants of the land from before you". This instruction which is a mere repetition of the above cited command to Moses (Nu. 33: 50–55), confirms beyond all doubt that "lehorish' from before you" means to destroy. (annihilate).

The same command to Moses is found in yet another version in Joshua 11: 14–15 where we read: "And all the spoil of these cities and the cattle, the children of Israel took for a prey unto themselves; but every man THEY SMOTE WITH THE EDGE OF THE SWORD, until they had DESTROYED them, neither left they any to breath. As the Lord commanded Moses his servant, so did Moses command Joshua, and so did Joshua; he left nothing undone of all that the lord commanded Moses". The same relation recurs in Joshua 11: 20 "...that he might DESTROY them, as the Lord commanded Moses".

Josephus (Ant. IV, 305) writes: "When they had utterly vanquished the land of Canaan and destroyed its whole population"; and elsewhere (Ant. V, 49): "...the Gibeonites. . yet resolved not to implore mercy of Joshua; for they did not think to obtain any tolerable terms from a belligerant whose aim was the extermination of the whole race of the Canaanites".

It is evident therefore, that the verb lehorish means 'to destroy, to

---

26   The Hebrew reads "lehashmid = להשמיד to annihilate, instead of "lehorish" as in the verses in Nu. 33: 50–55.

annihilate', and not "drive out". This is corroborated by several verses in the Bible that refer to the Israelite settlement in Canaan, e. g.: "The Horites also dwelt in Seir afore time, but the children of Esau succeeded them; and they DESTROYED them from before them, and dwelt in their stead; AS ISRAEL DID UNTO THE LAND OF HIS POSSESSION, which Jehovah gave unto them" (Deut. 2: 12). "They did not destroy the peoples, as Jehovah commanded them" (Ps. 106: 34); "Yet destroyed I the Amorite before them" (Amos. 2: 9); "As for all the people that were left of the Hittites, and the Amorites, and the Perizzites, and the Hivites, and the Jebusites...whom the children of Israel were not able utterly to destroy" (1Kn. 9: 20–21); "But of the cities of these people, which the Lord thy God doth give thee for an inheritance, thou shalt save alive nothing that breatheth; But thou shalt utterly destroy them; namely the Hittites, and the Amorites, the Canaanites and the Perizzites, the Hivites, and the Jebusites; as the Lord thy God hath commanded thee" (Deut. 20: 16–17). In these verses the words "destroy, consume" translate the Hebrew "lehorish".

To sum up: lehorish is not to be translated or understood as "inherit" (Hebrew – yarosh ירש) or "drive out", but rather, as seen above, as "destroy, annihilate".[27] Deut. 2: 12; "The Horites also dwelt in Seir afortime, but the children of Esau succeeded them; and they destroyed them...and dwelt in their stead...:" etc. clearly shows that annihilation of populations was customary of old days, the Amonites destroy the Rephaim, the children of Esau destroy the Horites, and Caphtorites the Avites, etc. (Deut. 2: 16–25).

As will be seen below the Hebrew verbs "yarosh"– (ירש to inherit), and "lehorish" להוריש (to destroy, to annihilate) are both likely to be related to the same noun –"rosh" – ראש (= head). The former "yarosh" means to become the head, that is, the head (master) of a property, house etc., i. e. to inherit; whilst the latter lehorish signifies 'to behead', 'to decapitate', to annihilate, a common practice in antiquity.[28] Given that lehorish means to "annihilate", 'exterminate' we must interpret the biblical statement that the tribe of Asher did not lehorish the inhabitants of Acco, nor the inhabitants

27 S. L. Gordon in his Hebrew Bible commentary, glosses lehorish –'to destroy, 'though he cites no reason for this. On the other hand Ibn Genah (– Abu'lwalid Merwan – Hebrew grammarian) in his book "The Roots" (Hebrew – Berlin 1896, p. 206 gives lehorish as to destroy ("because it is incorrect to explain the sentence 'to inherit them from before you,' as deriving from the verb to inherit since it does not fit in either with 'from before you' nor with 'from before them'").
   With regard to lehorish and torishemo meaning to "destroy" because both derive from rosh (= head). I have dealt with, as far back as 1952 and 1962 in two booklets also entitled "Who were the Phoenicians".
28 David cuts off Goliath's head (1Sam. 17: 57); The Philistines cut off Saul's head and send it throughout their land. (1Sam. 31: 9); See also: 2Kn. 10: 7; 2Sam. 20: 22.

of Sidon, ...etc. as meaning that Asher did not exterminate them. This does not, however, imply that he did not subjugate them, or that he did not take over their land. On the contrary, the conclusion of the verse[29]: "...but the Asherites dwelt among the Canaanites...for they did not 'lehorish' them" evidently means that the sons of Asher subdued the Canaanites. It is quite unreasonable to assume that the Canaanites allowed Asher – their enemy, to settle amongst them[30]. The verse makes the point "that he did not 'lehorish' the inhabitants..." that is, he did not exterminate them and evidently this is to clarify why the Canaanite element continued to exist in the territory of the tribe of Asher. Further corroboration is supplied by: "And the children of Israel dwelt among the Canaanites, the Hittites, and the Amorites, and the Perizzites, and the Hivites, and the Jebusites" (Ju. 3: 5), which summarizes the wars of the Israelites in Canaan, notwithstanding the fact that the preceding chapters repeatedly emphasize their victory over these nations. Most probably certain cities capitulated on condition that their inhabitants not be destroyed, and it is to these cities that the text alludes when it says that the Israelites did not lehorish them, that is did not destroy them.

Biblical evidence clearly shows that the tribe of Asher conquered the region of Tyre and Sidon, yet owing to erroneous translation and misinterpretation of the word lehorish this was entirely disregarded.

On the other hand, the el–Amarna tablets report that this region was conquered by Aziru.

Who, therefore, had first conquered this area, Aziru or Asher? Or, perhaps, was this one and the same conquest?

To answer this, let us try to establish the dates of these two conquests.

The el–Amarna tablets in which Aziru's conquest is mentioned were sent to Amenophis III and Amenophis IV. According to Petrie the period of the reign of Amenophis (Amenhotep) III, is c. 1413–1372 B. C.,[31] while Breasted has c. 1411–1375 B. C.[32]. According to Garstang[33] c. 1375 B. C. is the last year of Amenophis (Amenhotep) III, whereas the wars mentioned in the Tablets refer to the years c. 1380–1365. B. C. . In the preface to his book Mercer dates most of the EAT. to between c. 1411–1358 B. C.[34] According to Breasted,[35] we can safely assume that of thirty six years of Amenhotep III's reign, thirty four passed eventless, and moreover he claims that the wars mentioned in the el–Amarna tablets took place in

29   Ju. 1: 27– 36
30   For unmentioned reasons the statement that "he settled amongst the Canaanites" is regarded by Burney as proof that the Canaanites were not subjugated and that Asher merely settled amongst them. see: Burney, Israel Settlement In Canaan, p. 22.
31   Petrie, Revision of History, Ancient Egypt, March 1931.
32   Breasted, Histoire de L'egypte, 1926, Tome II, p. 363.
33   Garstang, Joshua – Judges, p. 253.
34   Mercer. TEAT, Toronto, 1939.
35   Breasted, ibid. p. 363.

either the last year or the last two years of his life, that is., the wars began between c. 1377–1375 B. C. (according to the chronology of Breasted,) or between 1379–1377 B. C. (according to Petrie's chronology). Hence. this is also the approximate date of Aziru's conquest of the region of Sidon.

Next let us examine when according to the Bible it was that the tribe of Asher fought its wars of conquest. The Bible states that the Exodus took place four hundred and eighty years before the erection of the Jerusalem Temple, in the fourth year of Solomon's reign[36]. Since the reign of Solomon is considered to have begun in c. 970 B. C.[37], this means that the Exodus took place in 970 – 4+480 =c. 1446 B. C.[38]. If we then add the number of years elapsed from the time of the Exodus till the beginning of the wars conducted by the tribe of Asher in Canaan, we shall arrive at the approximate date of its conquest of Sidon

According to the Bible, the Israelites wandered for forty years in the desert until they reached settled land. However, it must be borne in mind that the war of the tribe of Asher which led to the capture of Sidon followed immediately Joshua's death[39], that is more than forty years after the Exodus. The Bible does not specify exactly the number of years, but these can be deduced approximately from certain verses: We read in Joshua 24: 29 that Joshua died at the age of one hundred and ten. Further we read that when Caleb the son of Jephunneh asked Joshua to annex the city of Hebron to his lot, he told him: "Forty years old was I when Moses the servant of Jehovah sent me from Kadesh–barnea to spy out the land; ...And now, behold Jehovah hath kept me alive, as he spake, these forty and five years from the time that Jehovah spake this word unto Moses. And Now, lo, I am this day fourscore and five years old".[40]. Also we are told that Joshua was send to spy out the land together with Caleb; and. moreover, we know that both were leaders (princes) of their tribes[41], and that both survived all the rest of the spies. From this may be concluded that both were approximately of the same age. As we know that Joshua died at the age of one hundred and ten, and the spies were sent to spy out the land from the desert of Paran when Caleb was forty years old, it will be seen that a period of seventy years had elapsed

---

36   1Kn. 6: 1 ; 2Chr. 33: 2

37   See CAH. (Solomon). Some scholars differ by a few years in their dating ; Oesterly and Robinson (A History of Israel) – 976 B. C. Wardle – 974 B. C. (EB. 1929, article– Solomon).

38   A number of different theories on dating the Exodus in later periods (Raamses II – Merneptah period), are current, but as stated in my introduction, I deliberately refrain from basing myself on theories but depend on epigraphic texts only. This question will be discussed more fully below; in the meantime we refer solely to epigraphic sources.

39   Ju. Chap. 1.

40   Jos. 14: 7–11.

41   Nu. chap. 13

between these two events. The Israelites reached the desert of Paran in the second month of the second year after leaving Egypt[42]; hence, according to our computation, seventy – one years must have passed from the time of the Exodus until the death of Joshua, which means that about thirty – one years elapsed from the time of Israel's entry into Canaan until Joshua's death, at which point the war of the tribe of Asher against Sidon began. This inference finds support in two paragraphs in Josephus[43], one of which says of Joshua that "he died having lived one hundred and ten years; of which he passed forty in the company of Moses receiving profitable instructions, and after his master's death had been commander in chief for five and twenty years", and the other (Ant. V, 115) that "after Joshua dismissed the multitude to their several provinces Joshua himself abode at Sikima. Twenty years later in extreme old age, having sent for the chief notables of the cities...and so, after this address to the assembled company he died...". Shalit[44], in a note to this paragraph, writes: "Therefore according to Josephus it emerges that Joshua and Caleb were of the same age, for Joshua lived one hundred and ten years, twenty of which since the end of the conquest of the land. In other words, when the conquest was over he was 85 years old, like Caleb".

In addition, we may deduce from the account in Josephus that about seventy – one years passed from the Exodus until Joshua's death. Thus the wars of the tribes following immediately after Joshua's death must have started in c. 1374–5 B. C. (i. e. from the date of the Exodus c. 1446 plus 71 years and two months. Therefore the conquest of the region of Sidon by the tribe of Asher also occurred about this date, which is contemporaneous with that of the conquest of Sidon by Aziru (see above.)

According to both sources – the Bible and the TEAT – neither of the two conquests of Sidon preceded the other, but both Asher and Aziru evidently conquered the same region at the same time. Seemingly, there appears to be a conflict between the two sources. The tablets mention Aziru son of Abd–Ashera (Abdi–Ashirta) as conqueror of Sidon, whereas the Bible reports that the tribe of Asher conquered the same region at this very same period of time. How is one to resolve this issue? .

The Amorite letter Z or the S is known sometimes to represent the Hebrew letter SH (Shin). Conder, referring to the name Akizzi in the EAT. notes that "as the Amorite Z or S seems sometimes to represent the Hebrew SH, this name might be compared with the Philistine Achish"[45]. The same applies also to Aziru, in which the Z can be seen to represent the Hebrew SH, yielding the pronunciation "Ashiru". Be it noted that the name Aziru appears in the

---

42   Nu. 13: 26 ; 10: 11–12.
43   Ant. V, 117
44   Ant. book V–117, note 110 (Heb. translation, Shalit,).
45   TEAT Note 2, p. 11.

EAT. also as Azira and Aziri.

Many names in the TEAT. reappear in the Bible in slightly modified form Thus in the tablets we have Abimilki, Kinaani, Kinaana, Kinaanu, Lakisi, Lakisa, Gazri, Shakmi, Shakmu, Beit –Shani, Beit–Shana, Seiru, Seiri, Askaluna, Adumu, etc., whereas in the Bible these are without their suffix – Abimelech, Knaan (Canaan) Lakish, Gezer, Shechem, Beit – Shan, Seir, Ashkelon, Edom, etc. Accordingly the suffix of these names is perhaps only indicative of the genitive form. and thus the name Aziru in the TEAT. would be transcribed in the Bible Ashir or Asher, which is remarkably similar to the name of the tribe of Asher. This resemblance coupled with the fact that the TEAT ascribe the conquest of the region of Sidon to Aziru–Ashir, while the Biblical evidence points to the tribe of Asher as conqueror of the same area, in the very same period, leads to the inference that Aziru and Asher are in fact the same entity. However this inference raises certain difficulties.

Aziru is commonly thought to signify:

1. A personal name.
2. An Amorite.
3. The son of a person named Abd–Ashera (Abd–Ashirta)[46].

However, Asher in the Bible signifies:

1. The name of a tribe.
2. An Israelite.
3. An offshoot of Asher the son of Israel (Jacob).

How can these discrepancies be explained?:

To examine each point in turn:

1. Aziru is considered to be a personal name, because in many TEAT it appears in singular form[47]. We find repeated references to "Aziru the son of Abdi Ashirta (Abd Ashera)"."this man Aziru" etc, . and this has led scholars to regard Aziru as the personal name of a single person, the son of a man named Abd Ashera. But is there, in such phrases, any confirmation that Aziru is indeed a personal name?

In many tablets one reads about the "Gaz people",[48], and there is no dissent whatever that the referance here is to a group of people and that the term "Gaz "does not represent a personal name. However, though Gaz usually denotes "Gaz" people in the plural, it sometimes appears in singular form, as "the mighty Gaz man", "this Gaz man"[49]. In a letter to the king of

---

46 Mercer and Knudtzon write Abdi–asirta, Conder spells it Abd–Ashera. Lods (ISRAEL p. 152) writes: "in the period of Tell el–Amarna one of the most notable princes of the Syrian region was called Abd – Asirta or Abd–Asratu, that is, the servant of Ashera":

47 For example: Conder, TEAT tablet B. 61 last line. BM 19, line 8. Mercer 107 line 26.

48 For example see: tablets 74; 77; 82; 83; 108.

49 Tab. 71, line 21.

Egypt, Rib–Adi writes: "Why dost thou sit and hold back, so that HE takes thy cities the Gaz– MAN the dogi".[50] Again there is the verse "neither did Asher drive out..., which in the Hebrew appears in the singular: "Asher lo horish – "אשר לא הוריש" though there can be no doubt that it refers to the people of the tribe of Asher. It is a common biblical linquistic usage for the singular to serve in place of the plural: "And Moses sent messengers from Kadesh unto the king of Edom, thus saith thy brother Israel ".[51]. Here Israel "saith" is singular in the Hebrew original ("amar– ,"אמר" and likewise "Israel thy brother"; "...and Israel abode[52] in Kadesh"[53]. In Samuel one reads: "And the men of Israel, when they saw the man ,fled from him, and were sore afraid. And the men[54] of Israel said..."[55]. As already stated, the singular serving in place of the plural, is common biblical usage especially when in reference to a nation, a tribe or a single group of people, and still obtains today. Hence, in the el – Amarna tablets Aziru in the singular form should not be read as definite proof to denote a single person since, quite possibly, it may in fact refer to a single unit or tribe.

2. It is generally accepted that Aziru is an Amorite. This view is based chiefly on verses that tell of Aziru dwelling in Amurri, e. g.: "Aziru the son of Abd Ashera who comes from Amurri land..."; "Azira in the land of Amurri"; etc In a letter by Rib–Adi king of Gubla to the king of Egypt he asks the latter for help against Abd–Ashera, and informs him: "Knowest thou not that the land of Amurri day and night strives for archers"[56]. The fact that in many tablets Aziru is named the son of Abd–Ashera (Abdi Ashirta), and that Aziru and Abd–Ashera are both found in the land of Amurri, has led scholars to infer that Aziru is the son of a man called Abd–Ashera (Abd–Ashirta) and that Aziru, like his father Abd–Ashera, was an Amorite.

Assuming that the tablets indeed indicate an Amorite by the name of Aziru, what confirmation is supplied by the tablets themselves for such an assumption? In a tablet sent by Rib–Adi to the king of Egypt[57] he assures the king that "if one regent would make common cause with me, then I would drive Abdi–Asirta out of Amurri". As pointed out, Abd–Ashera is considered by scholars the father of Aziru, and both are thought to be Amorites. If this is indeed the case, why then does Rib–Adi need to assert: ' to drive him' "out of Amurri"?

After all, it is self–evident that if Abd – Ashera is an Amorite and lives in the land of the Amorites, that is, lives in his own land, one would expect

---

50   Tab. 91, lines 3–5 ; see also Tab. 112, line 46.
51   Nu. 20: 14.
52   In Hebrew, the singular is employed.
53   Ju. 11: 17
54   The Hebrew reads: "Ish Yisrael"=man of Israel, in the singular.
55   1Sam. 17: 24
56   Tab. 82, lines 47–50
57   Tab. 85, L. 68–69.

Rib–Adi to state: straightforwardly "to drive Abd–Ashirta out from his land" or "subjugate him".

In another tablet[58], Rib–Adi writes to the king of Egypt: "and let the king my lord know that Amurri long (day and night) for the departure of the archers, in the day when the archers come Amurri will join themselves unreservedly to the king, my lord" (i. e. to fight against Abd – Ashera and Aziru – N. G.) In yet another tablet[59]: "behold on the day that thou comest all the country will rally to the king". A similar message is found in tablet 73[60]: "dost thou not know of the land of Amurri that it is an abode of mighty men? Therefore, behold now are they not friendly with Abdi Asirta. But what does he do to them. And so they wait day and night for the departure of the archers and (say) 'we would join with them' and all regents strive to do this to Abdi Asirta". On the other hand, in tablet 13 BM.[61] Rib – Adi informs the king about Aziru who makes war against him,[62]: "All who are in the land of the Amorites have gathered " (i. e. to fight against Rib–Adi–N. G). If Aziru is an Amorite this means that all the Amorites unite with Aziru against Rib–Adi, while in the preceding verse, all the Amorites, WITHOUT EXCEPTION, will unite to fight against Aziru. There is a flagrant contradiction here. Looking at another tablet of Rib–Adi to the king of Egypt.[63] we find that Rib–Adi informs the king: "Behold Aziru, a son of Abdi – Asirta is with his brother in Dumassqa". In many tablets sent by Akizi from Qatna, Akizi informs the Egyptian king: "The people of Qatna, my servants that Aziru takes and puts them out of the land of my lord".[64] Consequently, the conquest of Damascus was considered a Hittite one; In fact Conder[65] even assembles and publishes all the tablets that refer to the conquest of Damascus and that were sent by Akizi from Qatna, under the title "The Hittite Invasion of Damascus."

If Aziru is indeed an Amorite, it follows that his "brother" who fights with him in Damascus was also an Amorite. How are we to explain that in the letters from Akizi he (the brother) figures as a Hittite, or at least served a Hittite king?

In letter 103[66], sent by Rib–Adi, we read: "the sons of Abdi–Asirta have entered Amurra, to them the whole land belongs". What is obvious from

---

58   Tab. 70, L. 23–30.
59   Tab. 129, L. 62 – 64.
60   Tab. 73, L. 14–25.
61   No. . of tablet according to Conder., according to Mercer and Knudtzon . No. 114
62   Line 21.
63   Tablet 107, L. 26.
64   The city of Damascus was considered to be Akizi's. . Tab. 55, L. 44 – 45.
65   TEAT
66   L. 9–12. Knudtzon translates here "sind eingedrungen in Amurra", that is, invaded Amurra.

his letter is that the "sons of Abd–Asirta" are not Amorites but have merely conquered the land of the Amorites. Moreover other letters supply further information about the conquest of the Amorite land . Thus in tablet 55[67] we read: "For six days has Azira in the land of Amurru remained and he will indeed take them if however in this year the troops of my lord do not go forth and do not take (them) they will subject themselves to Azira". In letter 142 (L. 24), Rib-Adi refers to "The enemies of the king who are in the land of Amurri". In tablet 156[68] Aziru writes to the Egyptian king: "and may he allow me to enter Amurru". A closer look establishes that the el–Amarna Tablets consistantly refer to Aziru and Abd–Ashera (Abdi-Ashirta)" who is in the land of Amurri", or "coming from the land of the Amurri" etc., and then always attach the word "land" to their names. Hence we never read of "Aziru the Amorite" or "Abd–Ashera the Amorite". One may conclude therefore that Aziru and Abd–Ashera are in the land of the Amurri though no other significance attaches to this fact.

We can definitely establish that Aziru was indeed in the land of the Amorites, but there is no evidence whatever in the tablets to indicate that he was an Amorite. On the contrary, this is contradicted by other verses which can be clarified only by assuming that the name Aziru serves to denote the name of the tribe of Asher.

The tribe of Asher together with the other tribes settled in the cities they had conquered; we know from our earlier discussion (see above) that the first cities conquered by the Israelites were the Amorite cities. It is clear therefore, why Aziru, i. e. the tribe of Asher, is always characterized as "coming from the land of the Amorite" and not as "Aziru the Amorite". We are also now in a position to understand why it is said that "all who are in the land of the Amorites have gathered themselves": since this refers to Aziru, that is, to the people of the tribe of Asher who are in the Amorite land (and possibly also to a part or the remainder of the Israelite tribes). Further we can now understand why "The Amorite long for the archers" and "in the day when the archers come Amurri will join thenselves unreservedly to the king", to fight Aziru. This evidently refers to the native Amorite population who had come under the subjugation of the tribe of Asher and of the rest of the remaining Israelites. Moreover, it is made plain now why in the letters sent by Akizi from Qatna, Aziru is seen as a Hittite, for he finds himself there with his "brother" (i. e. most probably another tribe which abode in an area of Hittite land) to whose aid Aziru had come. Finally we may also get some idea of letters nos. 103; 55, and 156, which tell of the sons of Abdi–asirta (Ashera) and Aziru who conquer the land of the Amorites.

3. It is generally agreed that Aziru was the son of a man named Abdi–

---

67   L. 23–27.
68   L . 13.

Asirta (Ashera), whereas, according to the biblical account, Asher was the son of Israel, that is Jacob. One reads in many tablets "Aziru son of Abdi–Asirta", though sometimes the name Abdi–asirta (Ashera) occurs by itself without linkage to Aziru. Occasionally, we have the sons (plural) of Abdi – Asirta[69]; from which scholars concluded that Abdi–Asirta (Ashera) was a single person, with a son named Aziru, but with other sons besides.[70] Assuming that this Aziru is here correctly identified, what evidence is there. in TEAT to make this identification accord with our assumption. In one of the tablets[71] by Rib – Adi there is the following passage: "No allies marched to Abd Ashera. But behold this Aziru has chosen all the men of blood". Obviously the subject initially is Abd Ashera but it later changes to Aziru. Abd Ashera and Aziru are in fact interchangeable. Passages such as the foregoing in which the writer begins with Abd Ashera (Abdi–Asirta) as the subject and ends with Aziru or Sa Gaz, or the other way round, are frequent in the TEAT[72].

The suspicion that Aziru and Abd Ashera do not constitute two separate identities is increased with reading Tablet 75, sent by Rib–Adi[73] king of Gubla which states that Abd–Ashera killed "Aduna king of Irqata", while in tablets 140 (L. 10) and 139 we read: "Behold Aziru has killed Aduna king of Irqata". How are we to explain the fact that both Aziru and Abd–Ashera, who are supposed to be two different persons, killed the same man? Mercer already referred to this contradiction: "according to 140/10 Aziru killed Aduna, king of Irqata, but here this act seems to be ascribed to Abdi–asirta"[74]. Does this mean that here also Abd–Ashera (Abdi–Asirta) and Aziru are identical? .

In another tablet[75] Rib–Adi begs the king of Egypt to send an army against Abd – Ashera, and writes among other things: "And to slay Abd–Ashera the king shall set him against them"; "THEM" in the plural refers to Abd–Ashera. In tablet 104[76] we read that "Pubahila, a son of Abdi Asirta has entered Ullaza to THEM belong Ardata...all cities belong to THEM" (emphasis –N. G.); here again the plural form is used for a supposedly single individual, but this time in reference to the supposed son of Abd–Ashera. How are we to explain the use of plural pronouns in reference to names of what are considered single persons? Taking all these facts together, it will no longer be possible for us to accept the supposition that Abd–Ashera is the name of a single person and the father of Aziru, as this leads to unresolved contradictions.

---

69 For example tab. 61 no. according to Conder. Tablets 108; 123; 132; 137; 138 according to Mercer and Knudtzon.
70 See Mercer tab. 60 note to line 2.; note to line 26 tab. 107. See also Lods, Israel, p. 152.
71 Tab. 18 BM l. 22–23 according to Conder: Tab. 132 –Mercer and Knudtzon.
72 For example tablets 79; 81; ; 88; 104; 116.
73 Tab. 75. L . 25
74 See note to line 25 tablet 75, p. 278. Mercer, TEAT
75 Conder, TEAT, tab. 44BM L. 16–17.
76 Lines 7–14.

Perhaps the facts can be explained otherwise: In many tablets one finds composite names of which "Abdi" comprises the first part of the name, e. g. Abdi–Adi (Ada)[77], Abdi–Uras[78], Abdi Rišha[79], Abdi–Hiba (or Hiva)[80]. In regard to the last name, Mercer notes that: "Abdi Hiba consists of two parts: abdi – which is the Semitic for servant and Hiba which is the same as the word hepa, the name of the Hittite goddess".[81]

The name Abd–Ashera (Ašratu, Asirta) may be seen as a personal name; however, if the abd serves an adjectival function, as with the name Abdi–Hiba, then compound names such as "Aziru son of Abdi–Asirta" (or asratu) signify "Aziru son and servant to Ashera", this means that "son and servant to Ashera" refers to Aziru, thus reversing the meaning entirely[82].

There are many examples in the biblical writings when the Hebrew "ben" (son), when joined to another word, has an adjectival function, thus ben – beliaal, ben–boshet, etc; the meaning here is therefore not of the son of a man named Beliaal or Boshet. In Hebrew beliaal means 'rascal' ', worthless', and "son of Beliaal" means a wicked person (yet, curiously enough, some Bible translations read "son of Beliaal")[83].

The foregoing view allows us to explain how in one tablet Aziru is reported to have killed Aduna king of Irqata, while in another Abdi–Asirta, i. e. Abd–Ashera, is said to have killed Aduna. We may now understand the text when it says "the sons of Abd–Ashera" that is servants of Ashera, i. e. a cognomen of Aziru, and not the sons of a man of this name. "Sons" (in the plural) of Abd–Ashera applies when speaking of the tribal people in general, whilst "son" (in the singular) of Abd–Ashera applies when dealing with a particular member of the tribe, or with the tribe as one unit. Sometimes it appears without the addition of "son", thus "Abd–Ashera" servant of Ashera, which is identical in meaning to 'son of Abd–Ashera', and also refers to Aziru.

Following our assumption that Asher and Aziru are identical, we are led to conclude that Asher was servant to Ashera. Yet, this appears to be a contradiction, for Asher is a son of Israel and the Israelites are worshippers of Jehovah.

---

77   Tablet 120 . Lines 32–36.

78   Tab. 170.

79   Tab. 176a.

80   Tab. 285, L. 4.

81   See Mercer TEAT p. 285 note to line 2. ; See also Albright, Palestine In The Early Historical Period, p. 127.

82   Lods, Israel, (p. 152) states in respect of the Amarna Tablets that "one of the princes in the region was Abdi Asratu that is a servant to Ashera"

83   1. Sam. 25: 17 "for he is such a son of Belial"; (A. V.); 1Sam 2: 12, "Now the sons of Eli were sons of Belial" (A. V.) (they were either the sons of Eli or the sons of Belial). i. e. they could not be the sons of both. Gideon Bible (N. Y. Nelson) translates Belial as"worthless". L. Segond in his French translation writes "mechant" (wicked).

How is this contradiction to be resolved?

Compared phonetically, the names "Asher" and "Ashera" are remarkably similar. It is easily possible therefore that Asher may have been derived from "Ashera", and scholars in the past have tried to link these two names[84]. According to the biblical account, the sons of the tribe of Asher were, like all the other Israelites, descendants of Jacob, who is of course a forefather of the Israelite nation, and who was also named Israel because he "hast striven (– שׂרית – sarita, past tense of the Hebrew verb saro –to strive) with God and with men, and hast prevailed" (Gen. 32: 28). The story of Jacob wrestling with the angel of God is not in keeping with the general tenor of the biblical narrative. The Bible tells us about the worship of one god, the God who selects Jacob and regards him as his chosen son[85]; yet the text here speaks of the angel of God wrestling with Jacob. Why does the angel wrestle with Jacob, God's chosen? The biblical explanation for this is far from satisfactory, the impression gained is that this story is a disguise for something other. Renan[86], claims that the biblical explanation of the name Israel (ישראל) is completely imaginary. He thinks the real explanation is that since the Hebrew letters Shin (שׁ) and Sin (שׂ) were identical in antiquity, the name probably read "Yeshar – El", that is, it articulates Jacob's servitude toward El=God.

In I Chronicles[87] occurs the name Asarel (אשראל) elsewhere[88] we find a variant of this name – Asriel .(אשריאל) Both names are phonetically closely similar to the name Israel. We know that in Arabic the name Israel is written with and sounded as A (– א– Aleph) instead of I (י –Yod). Hence, the name Asarel may well have been an archaic form of the name Israel; possibly the name Yesarela 1 (ישראלה Chr. 25: 14) should be seen as an intermediate form of Asarel and Israel.

It is evident that in the names "Asarel" and "Asriel" the element "el" is a recurring form to which another element is joined. Substitution of the two different elements gives us the names "Asera –El" and "Aseri–El". Given that the Hebrew letters "Shin" and "Sin" are interchangable, one reads "Ashera–El" and "Asheri–El", that is: " Ashera is the god "(Ashera el); and "my Ashera is the god" (Asheri el). Most probably the name Israel originally was Asarel (Ashera–El), a derivation of Ashera, which eventually was changed to Israel; Moreover, for reasons yet to be stated, the story of Jacob's wrestling with the

---

84   Burney attempts to link most of the Israelite tribal names to the names of deities, as for instance: Asher to Ashera, Gad to the "Phoenician" deity Gad. Dan to Dan etc. Burney, Israel Settlement In Canaan, pp. 54–55. See also: Patai, The Goddess Ashera, JNES, 1965, pp. 1–2; Petrie, Palestine And Israel, p. 38.

85   See: Is. 41: 8 ; 45: 4.

86   Renan, Histoire du Peuple D'Israel, tome I, p. 106. About the identity of the letters Sin and Shin see Gesenius Hebrew grammar p. 33§ 6 i.

87   1 Chr. 4: 16.

88   Nu. 26: 31; Jos. 26: 2; 1Chr. 7: 14.

angel was introduced to disguise the real meaning of the name Israel We may now also understand why one of the Israelite tribes was called Asher; which is most probably derived from the name Ashera.

From the above, it appears that the sons of Israel worshipped the Ashera, and that the name Israel derives therefrom. However, what is the Ashera, and what does the worship of the Ashera betoken?

In Deut. 16: 21, the sons of Israel are commanded: "Thou shalt not plant thee an Ashera of any kind of tree beside the altar of Jehovah thy God which thou shalt make thee", the Hebrew literally translated reads "Thou shalt not plant thee an Ashera any tree beside the altar of Jehovah..."[89]. It is clear therefore that the Ashera is a tree, and that the cult of the Ashera must be that of tree–worship. This is confirmed by the story of Gideon who cuts down the Ashera that is by the altar of Baal and with the wood thereof offers a burnt offering (Ju. 6: 25–27). Robertson Smith[90] likewise cites this verse from Deuteronomy, and states that the Ashera "must have been either a living tree, or a tree like post" (p. 188), that is an object of worship. He argues against certain Assyriologists who claim that the Ashera was a goddess. (ibid. 189). In Genesis (21: 33) we read of Abraham: "And Abraham planted a Tamarisk tree in Beer–Sheba, and called there on the name of Jehovah". The fact that these two acts are linked together in the biblical text, shows that they are closely interrelated: Abraham plants a tree and at the same time calls on the name of God. This plainly illustrates the worship of the Ashera, as shown above. In Genesis 35: 2–4 we read: "Then Jacob said unto his household and to all that were with him. Put away the foreign gods that are among you, and purify yourselves, ...and Jacob hid them under the oak[91] which was by Shechem". Jacob buries the idols under the terebinth tree, which clearly shows that Jacob's household worshipped idols, and we may suspect that the terebinth was Jacob's personal deity. This act of jacob can be seen as having symbolic significance: that is, he buries the foreign gods under his personal deity. Likewise we are told of Deborah, Rebekah' s nurse, that she "died and she was buried below Beth–el under the oak".[92] (Gen. 35: 8). This burial under the oak tree leads us assume that for Jacob the oak was sacred. In Joshua 24: 25–26 we read: "So Joshua made a covenant with the people that day, and set them a statute and an ordinance at Shechem. And Joshua wrote these words in the book of the law of God: and he took a great stone, and set it up there UNDER THE OAK[93] THAT WAS BY THE SANCTUARY

---

89   "לא תטע לך אשרה כל־עץ אצל מזבח יהוה אלהיך" (Lo tita lekha ashera kol etz etzel mizbakh yehova eloheka)

90   R. Smith, The Religion of The Semites, p. 188, (pp. 185–196). See also: Oesterly and Robinson, Hebrew Religion, p. 59.

91   In the Hebrew original "ela – = אלה" terebinth tree.

92   In the Hebrew original "alon – אלון" = oak tree.

93   In the Hebrew original "ela –= אלה" terebinth tree.

OF JEHOVAH". Also, we read in Judges 9: 6: "And all the men of Shechem assembled themselves together, and all the house of Millo, and went and made Abimelech king, by the oak of the pillar that was in Shechem". These verses inform us of the fact that in Beth–el there stood an oak tree near the house of God, or as the text puts it THE oak (with the definite article). In Shechem there was THE terebinth tree (with the definite article), whilst in Beer–Sheba there was a tamarisk. it is interesting to note that according to the biblcal account, Abraham and Isaac lived in Beer–Sheba, whilst Jacob lived in Shechem and Beth–el. It is known that these three places constituted important centers in the life of the Israelite nation, and the trees in these centers are qualified in the Bible by the definite article, as well known and well recognized objects. Accordingly it may be inferred that the Tamarisk was Abraham's and Isaac's deity, while the Terebinth and Oak were Jacob's deities. It is noteworthy that the narrative of Jacob's descent into Egypt states that he "came to Beer–Sheba and offered sacrifices UNTO THE GOD OF HIS FATHER ISAAC". Why does the text here refer to and emphasize, "unto the God of his father"? At any rate, if the God of Isaac is the same god as for Jacob, it would be logical for the read: "and offered sacrifices to God" or "his God". But seeing, as stated, the oak and the terebinth, (i. e. Jacob's deities), were located in Shechem and Beth–el, whilst the tamarisk (i. e. the deity of Abraham and Isaac) was located in Beer–Sheba; it may well be understood that on his way to Egypt Jacob passed through text to Beer–Sheba where the tamarisk tree of his father and grandfather was planted, and there he would pray to this deity which is not his own but that of his father[94] Likewise it may be understood that the verse, "seek ye me, and ye shall live; but seek not BETH–EL, nor enter into GILGAL and pass not to BEER– SHEBA"[95], clarifies that Beer–Sheba, Beth–El and Gilgal were places of pilgrimage involving pagan–worship.

Jacob calls his god "El Shaddai[96] – אל שדי" and presumably Shaddai was the name of the Israelite deity till the time of Moses, as stated in Exodus[97]: "And God spake unto Moses and said unto him, I am Jehovah; and I APPEARED UNTO ABRAHAM, UNTO ISAAC, AND UNTO JACOB AS GOD ALMIGHTY (the Hebrew here is EL SHADDAI – (אל שדי) BUT BY MY

---

94 Gen. 46: 1. Various jewish commentators such as Rashi(Solomon ben Isaac), Ramban (Nahmanides). Sforno, and Rashbam (R. Shmuel ben Meir), noticed the problematic nature of this sentence and tried to clarify it in different ways. Nahmanides even stresses that it is suitable to write: "to the god of his forefathers"

95 Amos, 5: 4–5.

96 See: Gen. 43: 14 ; 48: 3 . The name "El Shaddai" occurs in the Hebrew text but is transcribed in the Vulgate "Deo Omnipotente" In the Septuagint "Pantochrator", and in English "God Almighty".

97 Ex. 6: 2–3.

NAME JEHOVAH I WAS NOT KNOWN TO THEM". Offord[98] equates this name to the Assyrian or Sumerian name Shaddu which he believes to mean mountain, and therefore ventures that El Shaddai perhaps means: "God of the mountains". Maclaurin interprets it along similar lines[99]. Most biblical exegetes believe that the name is a derivation of the Hebrew verb – שָׁדַד shadod = to plunder, to rob; and therefore El Shaddai = Omnipotent, which produces the translation for instance "God Almighty", as in the Vulgate. Robert[100] suggests that the name is derived from the Hebrew "shad" = שַׁד breast, and accordingly El Shaddai = "God of Fertility".

The name "Shaddai" will be better understood if we recall that in ancient Hebrew the letters "Shin" (SH – שׁ) and "Sin" (S – שׂ) are interchangable, so that "Shaddai" might equally read "Saddai". In the biblical text one often meets the word "saddai" in place of "Sadeh" (Hebrew; field); "And he did eat the increase of the field"[101]; "Let the field exult and all that is therein. Then shall all the trees of the wood sing for joy[102]; ...and the beasts of the field"[103] etc[104].

We may now conclude that El Shaddai mean God of the field (or fields), and moreover since we already know that Abraham and Isaac worshipped the tamarisk whereas Jacob adored the terebinth and the oak, all trees of the field, the connection between the name "Shaddai–Saddai" and the trees – the oak, terebinth and tamarisk – becomes quite clear. The name "El"(God) most probably derives from elah (terebinth) and alon (oak), but over time the original deity concept became enlarged and more abstract[105]. Incidentally it may be noted that for the people called Phoenicians, "Alonim" (plural of alon = oak) signified the plural of "El" (God)[106].

From the information given in the TEAT, we may now conclude:

1.   Aziru conquered the region of Sidon in c. 1375 B. C.
2.   The name Aziru should not be regarded as the personal name of any individual, but possibly serves as the name of an entire group or of a tribe.
3.   Aziru appears to be present in the land of the Amorites but there is no evidence whatever to indicate that he was an Amorite, Moreover, if we were to accept the Amorite theory this would lead to serious contradictions.

---

98   Offord, Babylonian And Hebrew Theophoric Names, PEQ. 1916.
99   Maclaurin, VT. 1962, (12), p. 444.
100 Robert, La Revelation Du Nom Divin Jehovah, RB. 1894, p. 162.
101 Deut. 32: 13; the Hebrew text here reads "saddai – שדי ".
102 Ps. 96: 12. In the Hebrew text, field reads "saddai".
103 Ps. 8: 7. In the Hebrew text the word field reads "saddai"
104 Ps. 104: 11; Jer. 4: 17. In the Hebrew text, field reads"saddai"
105 On" Ela" and "El", see also: Zimerman, El and Adonai, VT. 1962, p. 190.
106 See: Contenau, La Civilisation Phénicienne, p. 89; Cook, Phoenicia, EB. 1929; CIS. no. 3, I. 9, 22.

4. The belief that Abdi–Asirta (Abd–Ashera) is a personal name has no basis whatever. There is evidence for seeing it as signifying a 'servant of Ashera' ; moreover, the text implies that Aziru was a worshipper of the Ashera, but not that he was the son of a man of this name.

As against this, we may conclude from the Bible:

1. It was the tribe of Asher which conquered the region of Sidon in this same period (c. 1375 B. C.).

2. The tribe of Asher together with the rest of the Israelites settled in the Amorite land, since the Amorite cities were the first to be conquered by them.

3. The tribe of Asher, like all the other Israelite tribes, worshipped the Ashera which evidently represented a tree–cult; the name Asher is derived from the name of this deity.

It has been shown that the name Aziru, in Hebrew transcription, produces Ashir – Asher. As the identity between the two names, is absolute, and political events, as reported in TEAT and Bible, closely interconnect and overlap, our notion that Asher and Aziru are identical entities goes beyond mere conjecture .

Additional points to the above:

1. According to the biblical account the war of the tribe of Asher began after Joshua's death, and as noted above, about thirty – one years elapsed from the time of entry of the Israelites into the land of Canaan until the death of Joshua. However, in the el–Amarna Tablets the exact period of the wars is not mentioned, though in a letter from the people of Tunip to the king of Egypt[107] one reads (line 13): "and now for TWENTY YEARS we have been sending to the king...". Further in the same letter (lines 40–44) we read: "Tunip thy city weeps, and her tears are running and there is no help for us. We have been sending to the king for TWENTY YEARS but not one word has come to us from our lord". Hence the period when Tunip was at war lasted at least twenty years, which correlates with the chronology of the Israelite wars, as shown earlier.

2. The accounts of the wars in the TEAT and the Bible. are remarkably similar, In each case, the earliest conquests are of the Amorite cities, and proceeds from there. Both accounts depict the invasion as utterly devastating and destructive in its effect on the cities of the land[108]. Campbell, Haynes, Conder, Headlam and others[109] previously pointed

---

107 Tab. 59 (41 BM – Conder).
108 For instance; Tab. 185, lines 16–37.
109 Haynes, The Date of The Exodus, PEF. 1806, pp. 251–252.
     Conder, The Hebrew of The Tel el Amarna Letters, PEP. 1891–2 p. 251.
     Headlam, PEQ. 1931, p. 128.
     Meek, The Israelite Conquest of Ephraim, BASOR, 61, pp. 17–19.

to certain parallels in the two accounts.

3. We saw that in the biblical Hebrew "lehorish" denotes to "annihilate", "exterminate", and therefore, if it is written that Asher did not "lehorish" the inhabitants of Sidon, we can take it that he did not exterminate them. However, he did conquer the city, which of course led to the capitulation of the enemy but not necessarily to his annihilation. At the same time, the TEAT tells us of a treaty of capitulation between the city of Sidon and Abd–Ashera (whom we have identified as the sons of the tribe of Asher).[110]

4. Many names of cities, whose destruction is mentioned in the TEAT also occur in the Bible in the list of cities destroyed by the Israelites during their invasion of Canaan e. g. Ashkelon, Hazor, Gezer, Megiddo, Beit–Shan, etc. Hence, if we reject the theory that Aziru's and Asher's conquests are in fact the same conquests, this obliges us to admit that these cities were destroyed twice over within a very short period of time[111] (within the space of 200 years, at most)[112]. Barton, quoting Paton, makes just this inference[113]. He states "that there were two conquests, one in the el–Amarna period and the other about 1200 B. C." However there is no archaeological evidence, for this inference; on the contrary, archaeological findings Campbell, The Amarna Letters and The Amarna Period, BA. 1960 (3), p. 11. utterly disagree with it. To quote Prof. Yadin on the subject: "There is decisive evidence that the above mentioned Canaanite cities were destroyed in the same archaeological period. They were destroyed, burned, and not rebuilt by their settlers. This fact is not disputed. In what consists the difference of opinions between archaeologists? It is in the ultimate determination between the different dates"[114]

5. Certain names in the TEAT resemble names appearing in the Bible. Tablet 104 mentions "Pubahila son of Abdi–Asirta". Possibly this is a corruption of the name Pedahel who was the contemporary prince of the tribe of Naphtali[115]. As noted above, each prince stood at the head of his tribe in the war of the conquest of the land. Another name "Iliap"[116] phonetically echoes the Hebrew name "Eliab"; which is the name of the contemporary prince of the tribe of Zebulun; that is in full Eliab son of

---

Yeivin, Kibush Haaretz, Maarakhot 24–25, Feb. Mai. 1945 (Heb).

110 Tab. 83, Lines 24–27.

111 Headlam dealt with this in the Sixtieth Annual General Meeting, PEQ. 1931, p. 128.

112 If we accept that the Exodus occurred c. 1200 B. C.

113 Barton, The Habiri Of The El–Amarna Tablets And The Hebrew Conquest Of Palestine, JBL, 1929 (48), p. 144.

114 Iyunim Besefer Yehoshua, p. 76 (Hebrew).

115 Nu. 44: 28.

116 Tablet 168, L. 12.

Helon[117]. (The letters P and B are interchangeable in Semitic languages, as in Parzel=Barzel=iron, etc.)[118]

6. In Tablet 256 occur the three names Benenima, Tadua, and Jasuia. Hallock believes, and is followed in this by some scholars, that the name Benenima should perhaps be equated with Benjamin while Jasuia is possibly equivalent to the Hebrew name Joshua but as he states[119] "this, too, is far from certain." We are told in the Bible that Jacob called his son Benjamin, yet his mother "called his name Ben–Oni" (Gen. 35: 18). The Oni of the name Ben–Oni indicates the possessive pronoun in Hebrew, that is, "my Ben–Onim"[120]. which means that in its original form the name was Ben–Onim, If written " Benonim" we discover a remarkable resemblance between 'Benonim 'and 'Benenima.'

    The name Tadua is probably related to the Hebrew word toda = praise, thanks; from which the name Yehuda (Judah) is said to derive.[121]

    The resemblance between the names Jasuia and Yehoshua (Joshua) is quite obvious.

7. In Tablet 288[122] sent by Abdi–Hiba from Jerusalem to the king of Egypt, the writer points out that "Turbazu has been killed in the gate of Zilu..." and so also with "Iaptih–Addi". There is biblical support for the view that the Israelites used to hang the kings of cities at their town gates; these quotations from Abdi–Hiba might well reflect this.[123]

8. It is noteworthy that in the TEAT there are names such as Rib–Addi, of which the suffix is Addi–Addu (i. e. the deity Addad), whereas subsequent to the period of the conquest these names are linked to the prefix "Baal". Contenau already pointed this out earlier.[124]

In the Tablets there is talk of local kings,[125] whereas after the period of conquest we read about judges (in Sidon).

---

117 Nu. 7: 24.
118 see Gesenius: Hebrew – Chaldee Lexicon to the Old Testament, p. 689.
119 See Mercer, TEAT, Excursus VII, The Habiri and The Sa Gaz In the Tell el–Amarna Tablets, by F. H. Hallock p. 843, L. 13–17, and notes
120 Onim (אונים–) In Hebrew – strength, grief, sorrow.
121 Gen. 29: 35.
122 Tab. 288, L. 41–46.
123 Albright identifies Zilu with Sile, east of Kantara. (Albright, The Town Of Selle (Zaru) In The Amarna Tablets, JEA 1924, pp. 6–8), which seems a curious identification given that Abdi–Ḫiba sends his letter from Jerusalem, and the Sile that Albright mentions is on the border of Egypt very far from Jerusalem. What connection could Abdi–Ḫiba of Jerusalem possibly have with the region of Kantara, and for what reason would he send to the king of Egypt a message informing him about events in this city, considering that Kantara is close to the border of Egypt and at a considerable distance from Jerusalem? . Far more logical to accept Conder's identification with the city of Shilo, situated as it was not far from Jerusalem, which explains why it is mentioned in the letters of Abdi–Ḫiba.
124 Contenau, La Civilisation Phénicienne, p. 97.
125 For example: Tablets 46; 66; 88; 147.

In Deut. 3; 9. we read"Which Hermon the Sidonians call Sirion and the Amorites call it Shnir". We realise therefore that according the Bible Sidonians are not Amorites.

Having established, on the basis of the above evidence, that Sidon was conquered by the tribe of Asher and that this conquest is the same as the conquest of Aziru in the el–Amarna period, (c. 1375 B. C.), the inevitable question arises: When did the Exodus take place? .

THE EXODUS

The Exodus occupies a place of utmost importance in the study and understanding of the history of ancient Israel and the ancient Near East. Subsequent historical events, such as the conquest of the land of Canaan and related events, drastically change their meaning according to the date fixed for the Exodus. Two interrelated problems have to be considered: one–when did the Exodus take place, and the other, from where did it start out, that is the location of the land of Goshen, in which the Israelites are reported to have dwelled.

The date of the Exodus varies depending on what location is accepted for the land of Goshen, and the opposite also applies. If, for instance, Goshen is located in the Nile Delta, then the Exodus could not have taken place before c. 1200 B. C. (i. e. the period of Raamses II), for it is commonly assumed on the basis of archaeological evidence that there was no extensive building activity in the area of the Nile Delta before Raamses II, whereas the Israelites are reported in the Bible to have built the two cities Pithom and Raamses. This circumstance has been cited by several scholars to prove that the oppression of the Israelites took place during the period of Raamses II[1]. Rowley[2] writes: "We may note that the fifteenth–century date for the Exodus would make Thotmes III the Pharaoh of the Oppression. No known building operation of this Pharaoh took place in the Nile Delta region and he is not known to have had a royal residence in the district" He cites Mallon[3] in support of his contention: Wright who considers Goshen was located in the Delta region, states[4]: "Lack of evidence for Egyptian building in the Egyptian

---

*   For the identification of place names see attached map.
1   e. g. Rowley, The Date of The Exodus, PEQ, 1941, p. 154.
      Wright, Biblical Archaeology Today, BA, 1, 1947, p. 14.
      Wright, Two Misunderstood Items In Exodus Conquest. etc., BASOR, 86, 1942, pp. 32–35.
      Loewenstamm, S. E., The Tradition of The Exodus In Its Development, Magness Press,
      Jerusalem, 1965, p. 6. (Heb.)
      Eisfeldt, O. The Exodus And Wanderings, CAH. 1975, Vol. II. part II. Chap. XXVI, p. 321,
2   Rowley, From Joseph To Joshua, pp. 23–24.
3   Mallon, Supplement Au Dictionnaire De La Bible II, 1934, col. 1340, see Rowley ibid. p. 24, n. 1.
4   Wright, Biblical Archaeology Today, BA, 1947, p. 14.

Delta during the 18th dynasty points to the 19th dynasty for the Hebrew construction of Pithom and Raamses (Exod. 1, 11)"; and elsewhere[5]: "The pharaohs of the 18th dynasty with their capital at Thebes did little building in the Delta. Israelite forced labor on royal projects in the Delta therefore could only have been in the 19th dynasty."

In his book on biblical archaeology Wright says about Tell Rotaba–Artabi (which has been identfied as the biblical Raamses), "No other royal building of an earlier Pharaoh was found there, so we must conclude on the basis of our present evidence that if the Israelites worked on royal projects, it must have been in the time of Rameses II."[6] However, if we accept that the land of Goshen was located in Upper Egypt, then for the reasons cited above the Exodus must have taken place at an earlier date. According to the biblical narrative, and certain historical and archaeological facts, this would be in the reign of Amenophis II, (Amenhotep II) (c. 1446 B. C.). There are many theories regarding the Exodus, its starting point, its date and the location of the Red Sea crossing. Yet, aside from the biblical account, there is no epigraphical evidence relating to it, and all scholars–irrespective of their conclusions–base their theories on the Bible, whether they accept its statements or not. The date of the Exodus is given in the Bible (1kn. 6: 1) as being 480 yearsbefore the fourth year of Solomon's reign. Given that the beginning of Solomon's reign dates to c. 970 B. C.[7] the Exodus would then have taken place in c. 1446 B. C. But. the LXX reads "the 440th " probably omitting the forty years' wandering. so virtually coinciding with the Hebrew. Josephus variously states the period as 592 years (Ant. VIII iii § 1 and X VIII § 6), and 612 years (Ant. XX. x § 1). So this specific biblical reading has been much questioned without any direct critical evidence. and is not accepted by most investigators, and indeed there are differing versions of the event. The Exodus never occurred (Nibuhr), there were two Exoduses (Albright, Gressman, Meek, Rowe and others) etc.; What I shall try to show in the following is that all these theories were INEVITABLY created and indeed had to come about because of an erroneous primary belief which scholars in the past as well as in the present have taken as the point of departure. The Bible states that the Israelites settled in Egypt in the land of Goshen (Gen. 47: 4: 6: 27) (also called the land of Raamses), and built the store cities Pithom and Raamses (Gen. 47: 4: 11 ; Ex. 1: 11) The mention of the name Raamses was considered by Brugsch, Naville and Bunsen as positive proof that Raamses II was the Pharaoh of the Oppression, and accordingly the Exodus took place in

---

5   Wright, Two Misunderstood Items etc. pp. 32—35.
     Barton, expresses the same opinion, Barton, The Habiri of The El–Amarna Tablets And The Hebrew Conquest of Palestine, JBL. (48), 1929, p. 144.
6   Wright. Biblical Archaeology, 1957, p. 58
7   Cook, CAH. p. 160; Peet, T.E., Egypt and the Old Testament, p. 112.

the days of his successor king Merneptah This belief prevails to this day.[8]. Once Raamses II was claimed to be the pharaoh of the Oppression this INEVITABLY led scholars to look for the land of Goshen in the region of Lower Egypt, seeing that during Raamses II's reign there was extensive building in this area, (though the monumental activity of the pharaohs of the 18th dynasty took place mainly in Upper Egypt). This have been cited by many scholars as proof that the oppression took place during the period of Raamses II[9] They ignore that this so–called proof is an outcome and consequence of their primary assertion that Raamses II was the king of the oppression Moreover from biblical statements such as: "...every shepherd is an abomination unto the Egyptians "(Gen. 46, 33–34), and "God led them not through the way of the land of the Philistines although that was near" (Ex. 13: 17), it was inferred that Goshen was a pasture region and its location must not be sought in Egypt itself, but on its borders near the land of the Philistines.[10] These statements were seen to corroborate the belief that Goshen was in Lower Egypt. Moreover since the building activity in this region was mainly during Raamses II reign, it was inferred once again that Raamses II was the Pharaoh of the Oppression. Today most if not all scholars tend to agree with Ebers, Lepsius, Petrie and Naville[11] and locate Goshen in the area

---

8   Naville, The Exodus and The Crossing of The Sea, p. 165. in: Illustrated Bible Treasury, edit. Wright, London, 1896.
     Naville. The Geography of The Exodus. J. E. A. p, 32.
     Lepsius, Letters From Egypt etc. p. 426
     Petrie, Palestine and Israel, p. 55. ; – Egypt and Israel, p. 37.
     Sayce, A. H., The "Higher Criticism", PP. 238–240.
     Barton, Archeology and The Bible, p. 26.
     Lods, Israel, p. 192.
     Burney, Israel Settlement In Canaan, p. 83.
     Wright, Two Misunderstood Items In The Exodus Conquest Cycle. BASOR. 86, 1942, p. 34;
     Biblical Archaeology, p. 60.
     Gardiner, The Geography of The Exodus, Recueil Champollion, pp. 204, 208.
     Oesterly and Robinson, A History Of Israel, p. 73
     Aharoni, Eretz Israel In Biblical Period, pp. 167, 168. (Hebrew). Brugsch, Hist. of Egypt, II, p. 353. See also Conder, Note On The Supposed Date of The Exodus, TEAT p. 191.
     Trumbull, Kadesh Barnea., p. 381.
9   See above notes no. 2. 3, 4, 5, 6.
10   See for example Trumbull, ibid, p. 381
     Naville, The Geography of The Exodus, JEA. (10), 1924, p. 32.
     Bourdon, La Route de L'Exode, RB. 1932, p. 371.
     Mallon, ibid. p. 93.
11   Naville, The Geography of The Exodus, JEA. (10), 1924, p. 32.
     Ebers, Egypt, English Trans. pp. 87–115.
     Petrie, Egypt and Israel, p. 29 ; Researches In Sinai p. 203.
     Lepsius, Letters From Egypt etc. pp. 410, 448–449
     Mallon, Les Hebreux En Egypte, Orientalia, 1921, p. 90.
     Bourdon, La Route De L'exode etc. RB. 1932, pp. 370–372.

between today's Seft–el–Henna and Ismailia, that is in the region of Zagazig–Wadi Tumilat. Naville in 1884 excavated in the area of Tell–el–Maskhuta which by Lepsius and Linant is identified with the biblical Raamses, and by Naville with the biblical Sukkot and with the name T. K. U mentioned in the Egyptian papyri (Papyrus Anastasi; V–VI)[12]. Among other objects, Naville found in this excavation a sphinx and the figure of a hawk, which he connects with the god Tumm. He also unearthed a few epigraphical and monumental finds that range in date exclusively from the period of Raamses II to the Roman period. These findings led him to ascribe this city to Raamses II.[13] In addition, he uncovered foundation courses which seemed to him the foundations of storehouses. In the Bible we read about the children of Israel: "And they built for Pharaoh store cities (Hebrew – מסכנות miskenot) Pithom and Raamses" (Ex. 1: 11). Naville following Delitsch accepts the interpretation of miskenot as 'stores', and accordingly sees complete agreement between his findings and the biblical narrative. This leads him to identify Tell–el–Maskhuta with the biblical Pithom,[14] and the entire region with T. K. U (to him TUKU), which according to him, is the biblical Sukkoth, of which Pithom is the district town[15] This is the accepted identification today. Petrie,

---

Kent, Biblical Geography And History, p. 108.

Renan, Histoire Du Peuple D'israel, p. 139.

Robinson, Biblical Research In Palestine, vol. I, pp. 76–78

Conder, The Exodus, PEP. 1883, pp. 83, 88.

Weld, The Route of The Exodus, PEP. 1883, p. 139.

Trumbull, Kadesh Barnea, pp. 382 – 383.

Lucas, The Route of The Exodus, p. 11

Javis, The Forty Years Wandering of The Israelites etc. PEQ. 1938, p. 28.

Clark–Smith, The Route of The Exodus, PEP. 1883, pp. 223 – 224.

Scarth, A Few Thoughts Upon The Route Of The Exodus, PEP. 1882, p. 237

Rowley, The Date of The Exodus, PEQ. 1941, p. 153

Watson, Egypt and Palestine, PEQ. 1915, p. 133.

Maspero, The Struggle of The Nations: Egypt, Syria and Assyria, p. 172.

12   The Egyptian hieroglyphic system did not provide for the notation of vowels, only for consonants. So T. K. U can be read Taku; Tuku; or Teku, and each scholar refers to it as best suits him.

13   Naville, The Geography of The Exodus, JEA, 1924, p. 35 ; see also: Servin, LA Tradition Judeo – Chretienne De L'exode, BIE, 1949, p. 326.
Sayce, A. H., The "Higher Criticism" pp. 240 – 245.

14   Gardiner likewise identifies Tell Maskhuta with T. K. U (mentioned in Papyrus Anastasi V), and Tel–Artabi he identifies with Pithom. Linant as quoted by Conder, identifies Tell Maskhuta with Raamses.
Brugsch equates Raamses with Zoan which he identifies with San. About this identification Mallon writes: "It is a pure hypothesis of poor consistency". Gardiner, The Geography of The Exodus, an answer to Prof. Naville and others, JEA, 1924, pp. 87–96.
Conder, The Exodus, PEP, 1883, p. 84.
Brugsch, Egypt Under The Pharaohs, 1891, p. 91.
Mallon, Les Hebreux En Egypte, Orientalia, 1921 (3), p. 165.

15   Naville, ibid. p. 34.

who excavated (1905–6) in Wadi Tumilat at the site of Tell Rotabah (Artabi; Rotab), found a granite stela with only its lower part preserved. The inscription on it may be interpreted in one way "...and building in cities upon which his name is to eternity".[16] This slight reference to building activity was seen by Petrie,[17] Naville,[18] and others as irrefutable proof that the inscription refers to Raamses II, and that Tell Rotaba is to be identified with Raamses–Goshen. Petrie also found a victory stela of king Merneptah. Its inscription reads, inter alia: "The kings are overthrown saying Salam; Not one raises his head among the Nine Bows; Vanquished are the Tahennu (Tehenu); the Khita (Hathi) are quieted, ravaged is Pa Kanana(Canaan) with all violence. Taken is Askadni (Ashkelon); seized is Kazmel(Gezer); Yenu of the Amu (Yenoam) is made as though it had not existed. The people of Isirar (Israel–N. G.) is spoiled; it hath no seed; Ruten (Hurru) has become as widow of the land of Egypt; all together are in peace."[19] As Raamses II has been considered the Pharaoh of the Oppression so Merneptah his successor is seen as the Pharaoh of the Exodus.[20] Petrie who agrees in this matter with Bunsen and Brugsch, regards the mention of Israel's defeat in this inscription as proof of its veracity; and he identifies it with the defeat at Horma (Nu. 21), which according to him took place in the fourth year of Merneptah's reign, and in the second year of the Exodus.[21] Therefore he believes that the entry into the land of Canaan took place in about 1186 B. C., i. e. during the reign of Raamses III.[22] Most other scholars agree with him. Brugsch,[23] Petrie,[24] Naville and others rely on the biblical mention of the name 'Raamses' as proof that Raamses II was the Pharaoh of the Oppression. Yet Jacob is said to have settled "in the land of Rameses" (Gen. 47: 11). Conder referring to this writes: "One of the chief arguments in favour of the date proposed by Egyptologists for the Exodus is founded on the mention of Rameses as the starting point (Exod. xii

---

16 Naville, ibid., p. 2
17 See Petrie, Egypt and Israel, p. 33; pp. 55, 63; –Hyksos And Israelite Cities, p. 2.
18 Naville, ibid., p. 32
19 Breasted, Records, vol. III, pp. 263, 616.
    Pritchard, ANET, 376–378. p. 231, Princeton 1973
    Conder, The Date of The Exodus, PEP. 1896, p. 255 (Translation by Petrie)
    Slouschz, Motzai Haivrim, p. 44 (Hebrew)
    Aharoni, Historical Geography, p. 163 (Hebrew)
20 Brugsch, Egypt Under The Pharaohs, p. 318.
    Conder, ibid., p. 255.
    Clarke, The Route of The Exodus, PEP. 1883, p. 318.
    Maspero, Histoire Ancienne Des Peuples de L'orient, p. 308
21 Petrie, Palestine and Israel, p. 67.
22 Petrie, ibid., p. 58.
23 Brugsch, Hist. Of Egypt, II, p. 353. See also Conder, Note On The Supposed Date Of The Exodus, TEAT p. 191.
24 Petrie, Egypt and Israel, p. 37; Palestine and Israel, p. 55.

37, Num. xxxiii 5), but the earliest mention of the land of Rameses in Genesis destroys much of the force of the argument for no critic has as yet proposed to make the descent of Jacob Into Egypt as late as the time of Miamoun the founder of Pi–Ramessu."[25]. And elsewhere[26] he notes: "If the conclusion is to be that Jacob therefore lived in or after the time of Rameses II the Exodus would be brought down to 250 or 400 years after his reign that is to say, to the time of David or Ahab. If the biblical statements are quoted at all it is impossible to argue on one to the exclusion of the other". In other words, what has become of the scientific approach and clear methodical thinking? Either the biblical mention of Raamses is seen as proof that the oppression in Egypt did not take place before his period, in which case one must go all the way and accept that Jacob also lived "not before Rameses" – an argument that no critic, as Conder states, has yet dared to propose; or one must regard the name 'Raamses' as an anachronism, as suggested by Hall, Jack, Dussaud, Lucas and others.[27] Anachronisms of this type are not unusual in the biblical context, where frequently a name is applied to a specific place in one period, while elsewhere in the text the same name refers to a later period. Abraham pursues Chedorlaomer "as far as Dan".[28] However, in the Bible the name of the city of Dan belongs to a much later period than Abraham's, namely the period of the conquest of Canaan.[29] Jacob on his way to Haran slept at Beth El, and the Bible[30] tells us: "And he called the name of that place Beth–El, but the name of the city was Luz at first". Yet we learn from the book of Judges (1: 22–27) that Luz continued to be the name of the city of Beth–El as late as the period of conquest. Now if one assumes that the Bible was edited (though not written) at a later period than the events it narrates, it will be evident that in order to give later readers a precise idea of the places where the narrated events occurred, the editor, or editors had to have recourse to the contemporary place names (i. e. the names of cities, etc. as current in the period in which the Bible was edited, which of course differed from those when the Israelites were in Egypt). Moreover we know that Raamses II annexed to himself activities of earlier pharaohs by erasing their names from

---

25 Conder, The Exodus, PEF. 1883, p. 84; Topography of The Exodus, PEF, 1880, p. 231.
    He expresses the same views elsewhere in his book, Syrian Stone Lore, pp. 52–53.
26 Conder, The Exodus, PEF. 1883, p. 84. see also: TEAT 1893. Appendix, p
27 Jack, The Date of The Exodus In The Light of External Evidence, pp. 24–25.
    Lucas, The Date of The Exodus, PEQ. 1941, pp. 110–112
    Dussaud, RHR. 109, 1934, 126.
    Redford, Exodus, I ii, VT., 1963, p. 401.
28 Gen. 14: 14.
29 Judges 18: 29 "And they called the name of the city Dan, after the name Dan their father howbeit the name of the city was Laish at the first."
30 Gen. 28: 19.

memorial stelea and inscribing his own name instead.[31] The belief which treats the biblical mention of 'Raamses' as evidence for the oppression of the Israelites in the time of Raamses II caused scholars to look for 'scientific' and archaeological documentation. This resulted in the finding of the Raamses stele at Tell Rotaba, also in Naville's excavations at Tell Maskhuta, as well as in the victory stele of Merneptah. On the excavation at Tell Rotaba (Artabi) Wright comments[32]: "...the finest structure on the site was the temple built by the great builder Rameses II (1290–1224 B. C.). No other royal building of an earlier Pharaoh was found there, so we must conclude on the basis of our present evidence, that if the Israelites worked on royal projects at the site, it must have been in the time of Rameses II." We quoted Wright in order to indicate an approach to the subject, which is not peculiar to this scholar only. It is based primarily on identifying Raamses II as the pharaoh of the Oppression, with the inevitable consequence that this particular region is then identified as the land of Goshen, and further that Tell Rotaba–Artabi is identified as the biblical Raamses. This identification leads willy–nilly to the conclusion "...that if the Israelites worked on Royal projects at the site, it must have been in the time of Rameses II", So here we have "proof" that the oppression took place during the rule of Raamses II and consequently the Exodus from Egypt took place in the period of Merneptah, his succesor. However this argument is based entirely on the assumption that Tell Rotaba is the biblical Raamses; and what proof is there for this, in fact a single line which tells of "building in cities upon which his name is to eternity." Is this sufficient evidence to show that this was indeed the site of biblical Raamses? Gardiner, the eminent Egyptologist, states: "Is there any serious evidence that Tell–er Retabah was ever called Raamses or was a royal residence at all? Certainly the stela of Raamses II on which Naville comments proves nothing of the kind."[33] Mallon states similarly: "It should be observed that this theory is scarcely more than a conjecture and does not attain any sort of certainty."[34] Naville in his statement bases himself on the excavations at Tell el Maskhuta where he supposedly found storehouses – a finding that according to him corroborates the biblical statement that the Israelites "built for Pharaoh treasure (Heb. miskenot) cities, Pithom and Raamses". (Ex. 1: 11) The word 'miskenot' was interpreted by him as 'stores'[35] and he claimed that the

---

31   Maspero, The Struggle of The Nations, Egypt, Syria and Assyria, p. 421.
       Histoire Ancienne Des Peuples de L'Orient, p. 270.

32   Wright, Biblical Archaeology, p. 58.

33   Gardiner, The Geography of The Exodus, etc., JEA. 1924, p. 8.

34   Mallon, Les Hebreux En Egypte, Orientalia, 1921, p. 9. ("Il est juste de remarquer que cette theorie ne depasse pas les limites d'une opinion et n'atteint aucun degré de certitude").

35   He follows Delitsch who translated "Verpflegungs Magazines"; see also Gesenius for the word "miskenot" – "מסכנות"; Redford, EXODUS 1: 11 VT. 1963, p. 407. Onkelos' – The Aramaic translation of the O. T. has "Beth–Otzarin"– treasure

foundations unearthed in his excavations were those of storehouses. Peet[36] objecting to Naville's identification claims that "the 'store chambers' which he unearthed, ...and which he assumed, on no evidence whatever, to extend 'over the greater part of the space surrounded by the enclosure', are probably nothing more than the foundation walls of a fortress precisely similar to those found at Naukratis and Daphnae." Gardiner[37] agrees with him. Wright[38] notes that "...the 'store chambers' which Naville discovered are actually the foundations of a large fortress which we know to have existed there."

As already stated, Naville claimed the ruins at Tell el Maskhuta to be those of a city built by Raamses II, since the findings from this site date exclusively to the time–span between Raamses II and the Roman period. On the other hand, Servin[39] disagrees with the view put forward by Naville: "The excavations of M. Naville were published in 1885. Twenty years later, in 1908, M. Cledat made an interesting discovery on the same site, which, however, remained unnoticed at the time. In a ditch about twenty meters from the temple's gate of Tell el Maskhuta, he found a cylindrical seal with the double cartouche of Mirinri and his brother Pepi II. This discovery recalls the passages in Ounis' inscription that refer to a series of campaigns which failed to expand the borders of the Kingdom in the direction of distant Palestine, but which led to the annexation of Wadi Tumilat to the Kingdom of Egypt, and most probably to the creation of an important administrative center at Tell el Maskhuta, from the VIth dynasty onwards. Naville's main argument in favour of locating Pithom at Tell Artabi is thus shown to be mistaken". The Arabic مسحوطة = mashuta (with its guttural sound ح), generally transliterated in Latin characters by scholars 'maskhuta'; which eventually produced the spelling 'maskuta', thus creating a phonetical resemblance to the biblical 'Sukot'. A similar approach is evident in words like Kheta, T. K. U, which appear in the Egyptian papyri. These also appear in variant spellings like Kheta–Khetam–Etam; Tuku –Tukut – Suku–Sukot, thus producing an illusory phonetic resemblance to the biblical names Etam and Succoth.[40] Phytian Adams, in his excellent article on the subject,[41] writes: "It is the prevailing fashion today to assume that the Exodus took place in the reign of Pharaoh Merneptah (1225–1215 B. C.) and so firmly has this idea been allowed to take root that it seems almost idle to plead for

---

house, Rabbi Saadia (892–942 A. D.) in his Arabic translation has "Makhazin" = Magasins.

36   Peet. Egypt and The Old Testament, p. 8, n. 2. p. 84, n. 1 ; Gardiner, ibid., p. 61.
37   Gardinr, ibid., p. 61.
38   Wright, ibid., p. 61.
39   Servin, La Tradition Judeo–Chretienne de L'exode, BIE. 1949, p. 327
40   See for example Sayce, The Early History of The Hebrews, pp. 155; 181.
41   Phytian Adams, Israelite Tradition and The Date of Joshua, PEQ. 1927, pp. 34–35.

an open mind on the subject. Yet it is of this hypothesis that Prof. Peet, who recently subjected the whole problem to a searching re–examination records the following considered judgement (Egypt and the Old Testament, 1922, p. 108); 'The evidence for the belief that Merneptah was the Pharaoh of the Exodus, nevertheless, can only be described as so flimsy that it is difficult to see how the belief can ever have arisen'. Those who will take the trouble to study that evidence for themselves with unbiased minds can hardly fail to agree with Prof. Peet as to filmsiness with which he charges this theory". Prof. G. Steindorff in an outline of ancient history of Egypt in Baedeker's Egypt writes: "Ramses II is frequently identified, but probably erroneosly, with the Pharaoh of the oppression".[42]

The belief of an Exodus during Merneptah's reign brings in its wake many discrepancies which require to be explained.:

1. How can we explain the date of the Exodus as given in 1Kn. 6: 1, which is completely at variance with the supposed date of an Exodus in the period of Mernephtah.

2. The El Amarna Tablets, which have been dated to the 14th century B. C, depict the destruction of cities in Canaan. On the other hand, the biblical account tells of their destruction by the incoming Israelites. Archae–ological evidence points to the destruction of the cities in about the c. 14th cent. B. C. Therefore an Exodus supposedly during Merneptah's reign inevitably leads us to the conclusion that the Israelites at their arrival in Canaan found those cities already destroyed.

3. In the Amarna letters we find mention of invaders named Habiru, which by most scholars were identified with the Hebrews, Yet how can we explain the invasion of the Hebrews into Canaan in the 14th century B. C. if we accept an Exodus during the reign of Merneptah (c. 1220 B. C.).

4. A triumphal stela of Seti I (c. 1303–1290 B. C.) includes a description of a victory over a tribe named Asaru settled in the north of Canaan in a region which according to the Bible was allotted to the tribe of Asher. Most scholars (following Miller) tend to see the name 'Asaru' as synonymous with 'Asher'. But the supposition that the Exodus took place during Merneptah's reign (c. 1220 B. C.) makes it difficult to explain the presence of
the tribe of Asher in Canaan as early as the period of Seti I.

5. According to the Bible the period of the Judges lasted about 380–400 years. However, acceptance of an Exodus during Mernephtah's reign shortens this to a period of about 180 years.

To explain these discrepancies various a posteriori theories were constructed:

---

42   Baedeker's Egypt. 6th edit. 1908, p. lxxxi

1. According to the biblical account (1 Kn. 6: 1) the Exodus took place 480 years before the fourth year of Solomon's reign, that is in c. 1446 B. C. This date agrees with archaeological findings and also with the views of Garstang, Newberry, Marston, Rowe and others concerning the destruction of Jericho, but contradicts the belief that the Exodus occurred during the period of Merneptah. The principal argument to overcome this contradiction, used by Wellhausen, Lepsius, Petrie, and followed by Burney, Rowley and others down to our day, states that we cannot accept uncritically the biblical statement, for the reason that 480 is an artificial and unfeasible number, and in fact is the result of the multiplication of the number 40 by 12.[43] The number 40 corresponds to the 40 years wandering In the desert, and in addition represents a conventional reckoning of the length of a generation Therefore, the biblical scribe used the number 480 in a symbolic sense to denote the duration of twelve generations (ie. 12 x 40=480) that elapsed from the time of the Exodus to the building of the Temple, and not in the actual sense of 480 years. As a consequence the Exodus did not take place in C. 1446 B. C. (i. e. 480 years before Solomon), but in c. 1170 B. C., which is approximately the period of Raamses–Merneptah. So, to all intents and purposes, this controversy supposedly has been settled, Yet curiously, though the number 40 is claimed to represent the length of a generation in the Bible, each individual scholar adopts the number that suits him best. Thus, for Lepsius it is 30 years, for Petrie 21 years, while for Burney it is 25 years. Again, for Rowley it is circa 50 years[44]; and there are also other estimates. To strengthen their argument scholars draw on certain dynastic lists in the O. T.[45]. Petrie on 1 Chr. 6 (4–47). Burney on 1 Chr. 6. (3–10) (In the Hebrew text it corresponds to 1 Chr. 5: 29ff.) Burney names twelve priests in consecutive order between Elazar, Aaron's son, and Azaria, the high priest in Solomon's time, who represent according to him twelve generations, he accepts each generation to be 40 years–equal to the number of years in the desert. Multiplying 40 by 12 we get 480; therefore in his opinion the text indeed refers to 12 generations. Petrie, for some reason, came to a different

---

43   See for example: Burney, Israel Settlement In Canaan, p. 4.
      Lods, Israel, p. 208.
      Albright, A Revision of Early Hebrew Chronology, JPOS. 1920–1921, p. 64 (note 1).
      Lepsius, Letters From Egypt, etc. pp. 403, 457, 460–470.
      Petrie, The Date of The Exodus, PEF. 1896, p. 335
      Bright, A History of Israel, p. 113.
      Aharoni, Eretz Israel In Biblical Period, p. 168. (Hebrew).
44   Petrie, Egypt and Israel, p. 56.
      Lepsius, ibid., pp. 457, 460–470.
      Rowley, From Joseph to Joshua, p. 161.
      Burney, ibid. p. 4
45   Petrie, Egypt and Israel, p. 56. Burney, Israel Settlement in Canaan. p. 4.

conclusion from Burney, namely that the duration of a generation is only 21 years, and that there were ten to eleven generations. The arguments produced by Petrie and Burney are misleading, and basically erroneous. In the dynastic lists on which they rely, we count from priest Aaron till Azaria (inclusive) fifteen names and not twelve. Why make an arbitrary cut–off and start the count only after Elazar? For the period of Elazar's priesthood began only at Mount Hor, that is a short time before the Israelites' entry into Israel, and he was also among those who settled in the country. On the other hand the number 480 mentioned in the Bible denotes the period of years that elapsed from the Exodus, that is we have to include in this period all the names in the dynastic list, including that of Aaron the priest, and not start the name–count only from the period after Elazar, though this fits in better with some theory. While it is possible to accept the idea that the biblical narrator considered 40 years as the span of one generation, it is not comprehensible why the same narrator, using the same criteria, should condense twelve generations into approximately 200 years (i. e. the time from Merneptah till king Solomon). Moreover, elsewhere in the Bible we find year counts that are not divisable by the number 40, as for instance: 38 years' journey from Kadesh–Barnea to the brook Zered (Deut. 2: 14); the children of Israel dwelling in Egypt during 430 years (Ex. 12: 40), 300 years from the conquest of the Jordan's east bank till Jephthah's time (Ju. 11: 26); etc. These numbers are not divided by the biblical narrator by 40 years ("one generation count"). If this indeed had been characteristic of him he would surely have applied the same system to these numbers also. Why then should he do so only in the instance of the 480 years following the Exodus?

It is mistaken to identify the 40 years wandering in the desert with the period of one generation, since in this context 40 years do not refer to one (full) generation. Scholars misunderstood the biblical text, which in regard to the 40 years wandering states clearly: "For the children of Israel walked forty years in the wilderness, till all the people that were men of war, which came out of Egypt, were consumed". (Jos. 5: 6)."Until all the generation of the men of war were wasted (consumed)" (Deut. 2: 14); The Vulgate reads "donec consumeratur omnis generatio huminum bellatorum de castris" (Deut. 2: 14). Thus the meaning as between "a period of one generation" and "until the generation... were wasted " or "till all the people. . were consumed", is not at all the same, for the one indicates a full generation, while the others – ("until all the generation was wasted"; "till all...were consumed") refer to only part of a generation. It is clear that the biblical scribe regards the 40 years in the desert as part of a generation. Elsewhere it may be inferred that the biblical narrator calls 'Dor (Heb. = generation) a period of one hundred years (i. e. a century): "Know of a surety that thy seed shall be a stranger in a land that is not theirs, and shall serve them, and they shall afflict them four hundred years... But in the fourth generation (Heb. =Dor (–דּוֹר‎ they shall come hither again". In other words, four generations denotes a period of 400 years, and any attempt to explain this as a later addition[46] is untenable. After all, no later addition which assumes a generation to be one hundred years is reasonable if at that time a generation was thought to be 20 or 25 years. The notion that the duration of a generation is 40 years seems to derive from Moore, citing Hecateus of Miletus who compiled the ancient chronology of the Greeks, based on dynastic genealogies that counted 40 years for each generation. Lagrange who similarly tries to explain the 480 years from the Exodus on the 40 years generation principle also relies on Moore. However, he notes referring to Mayer[47] that the alleged chronology is not found in the fragments of Hecateus cited in Dido's writings[48]. Nevertheless this does not prevent him from citing the number 480 as representing 12 generations[49]. In contrast, Lepsius, who likewise refers to Greek chronology, considers 30 years the length of a generation, basing himself on Eratosthenes, Apolodore and Diodorus.[50] However, if scholars consider a generation variously to be 20, 25, 30, etc. years they must be consistent all the way and agree that four generations' sojourn in Egypt adds up to respectively only 80, 100, 120 or 200 years. It follows therefore that the entry of the Israelites into Egypt happened only 80 or 100 etc., years before their leaving it. If so, how does this agree with the argument that the entry of the Hebrews into Egypt took place in the period of the Hyksos?

2. Most scholars agree that the reign of King David begins circa 1040 B. C. If therefore we accept the theory that the Exodus took place in the period of Merneptah (c. 1220 B. C.), it logically follows that after substracting the forty years wandering in the desert the entire period of the Judges lasted only about 180 years. However this conclusion blatantly contradicts the biblical narrative. Moreover the Bible states that three hundred years passed from the time of entry of the Israelites into the eastern part of Canaan till the period of Jephtah[51] In Acts (13. 20) the apostle Paul specifies the period of the Judges as 450 years. Thus 480 years from the Exodus to king Solomon seems a more reasonable period than 180 years.

Petrie[52] trying to explain this discrepancy claims that the individual

---

46 Rowley, From Joseph To Joshua, pp. 69–70.
47 E. Mayer, Forschungen, 1, p. 169ss.
48 Fr. Hist. Grec. I
49 Lagrange, Introduction Au Livre Des Juges, RB. 1902, p. 27. see there also note 1.; see also: Albright, Syria, The Philistines And Phoenicia, CAH Vol. Ii, Chap. 33. P. 39.
50 Lepsius, Letters From Egypt, Etc., P. 470.
51 Ju. 11: 27
52 Petrie, Egypt and Israel, pp. 54–55

judges ruled concurrently in their various districts; and thus condensed the period of the Judges into 120 years, rather then the 400 years indicated in the Bible. This idea prevails to this day. He, as well as his followers, disregard the explicit Biblical statements that the judges suceeded one another: "And Othniel the son of Kenaz died. And after him was Shamgar.. after Abimelech arose Tola ...and after him arose Jair... And after him Ibzan...and after him Elon. and after him Abdon the son of Hillel a Pirathonite ...When Ehud was dead and it came to pass as soon as Gideon was dead." (Ju. 3: 11; 3: 31; 10: 1; 10: 3; 12: 8; 12: 11; 12: 13; 4: 1 ; 8; 33). Thus even if we admit that the Judges ruled in different districts, it is clear from the Bible that the periods of their rule did not overlap.

3. For some reason scholars tend to specially point up the name "Isirar" on the Merneptah stela, while at the time ignoring the fact that this stela tells of the wars fought by Merneptah in Canaan but not in Egypt.[53] "Isirar" is taken as equivalent to the name 'Israel'; yet in order to have the stela serve as proof that the Exodus took place in Merneptah's reign, it is necessary for scholars to distort the biblical narrative and utterly disregard the forty years wandering in the desert, as also the time necessary for the wars of conquest in Canaan. How else could Merneptah's encounter with the people of Israel in Canaan be explained, seeing they were supposed to have left Egypt during his reign? Moreover this will also produce a discrepancy between the biblical chronology on the one hand and certain archaeological findings (Jericho, Ay, etc.) on the other. Petrie, attempting to resolve this discrepancy, has suggested two alternative explanations: One, that a certain number of Israelite families did not migrate to Egypt but remained in Canaan; and two, that a certain number of families left Egypt in advance of the main body[54]. This second explanation of two separate "Exoduses" (as will be seen below) gained a following in the studies of Burney, Rowton, Meek and Albright. The stela of Merneptah recounts his victories and destruction of the cities of Yenoam, Kazmel, Pakanana etc. (the precise identification of these cities is unimportant.) However, at the end of the list of cities the subject changes from the destruction of the cities to the destruction of a nation (people): "Ishirar is laid waste, his seed is not". The phrase "his seed is not" clarifies beyond doubt that that the subject is now the destruction of a nation. But why only in relation to Ishirar? The accepted explanation was first given by Petrie[55]: The Israelites had already infiltrated into Canaan but had not yet

---

53 Conder and Faulkner hold the same view.
   Conder, The Date of The Exodus, PEF. 1896, 255.
   Faulkner, Egypt from the Inception of The 19th Dynasty To The Death Of Raamses III,
   CAH. vol. II, Chap. xxiii, 1966
54 Petrie, Egypt and Israel, p. 35.
55 Wright, ibid., p. 71.

become a settled people in that country; therefore Merneptah refers to them as a people but not yet in connection with a specific place. Petrie alludes to the biblical verses (Nu. 14: 40–45) about the children of Israel who went up the hill and fought the Amalekites and Canaanites who came down and smote them. He also refers to the story of the Canaanite king of Arad who fought against Israel and took some of them captives (Nu. 21: 1). He interprets these as an attempt by some of the Israelites to invade Canaan from the south. The Merneptah stela is seen by him as a recounting of this attempted invasion, which in his view took place in the fourth year of Merneptah's reign and in the second year of the Exodus.[56] It is evident that this accepted interpretation a)disregards the biblical text, which speaks of a war by Canaanites and Amalekites and not by Egyptians b) disregards the extended period of many years before the Israelite tribes entered the central region of the land of Canaan c) disregards the fact that the Exodus must be considered an Israelite and not an Egyptian victory; d) does not make sense, for if Israel was (as supposed) a nomadic people which had not yet acquired a fixed place of settlement, it seems ridiculous that a king should boast of his victory over these nomads and record it on a stela, while his conquest of established cities such as Ashkelon, Gezer, Yenoam, etc. is mentioned offhandedly: "plundered is Canaan carried off is Ashkelon, seized upon is Gezer...". For in the very reference to "his seed is not" the author of the stele inscription expressed the importance he ascribes to Isirar. For some reasons it has been usual for scholars to cite only partially Merneptah's triumphal hymn, begining from: ..."The kings are overthrown saying Salam...", but if we view it in its entirety we obtain a totally different picture[57]. The hymn opens: "great joy has come to Egypt, rejoicing comes forth from the towns of Tomeri (Egypt). They converse of the victories which Merneptah has achieved AMONG THE TEHENU: 'How amiable is the victorious ruler, how magnified is the king among the gods. How fortunate is he, the commanding lord. Sit happily down and talk or walk far upon the way, (for) there is no fear in the heart of the people. The strongholds are left to themselves, the wells are opened (again)."(emphasis – N. G.) The hymn continues with a description of the peace and tranquillity that have returned to Egypt, and then goes on: "The kings are overthrown saying Salam..." etc.

From the outset we learn that this is a paean for the victory over the TEHENU; and the cities mentioned in it make up a list of the cities of the Tehenu. Therefore, the final line "Isirar is destroyed..." may be seen as

Virey, Note Sur Le Pharaon Meneptah Et Le Temps De L'exode, RB. 1900, p. 585.

56 ANET, p. 376; Petrie, Palestine And Israel, p. 67.

57 Breasted, Records, vol. III, p. 263 ; § 616
ANET, pp. 376 – 377

summing up the destruction of the country, that is having described the destruction of the land of the Tehenu the hymn proceeds to recall the destruction of its people. In the Bible (Nu. 26: 35–37) the name Tahan denotes a clan of the Ephraimite tribe, while the city of Gezer which on the Merneptah stela is of the Tehenu, is described as an Ephraimite city (Ju. 1: 29). The accepted explanation for the mention of Isirar in this hymn appears an unconvincing attempt to sustain the theory which places the Oppression in the reign of Raamses II. The belief that Raamses is the Pharaoh of the Oppression and therefore Merneptah the Pharaoh of the Exodus, though it lacks any logical basis and contradicts the biblical text as well as Josephus and several archaeological findings, is very deeply rooted and widely accepted. However, one may well agree with Prof. Peet that "If analysed impartially it amounts to nothing more than the facts that Pharaoh of the Oppression has generally been assumed to be Raamses II, and that Merneptah succeeded him. The identification of Raamses II with the Oppressor is based merely on the statement that under the Oppression the Israelites 'built for Pharaoh store cities, Pithom and Raamses'." (Peet, p. 108) Yet, this belief produces many contradictions, the most important of which are:

1. The stela of Merneptah recounts a victory over Isirar (Israel) in the land of the Tahanu (in Canaan), while the Exodus is depicted in the Bible as a victory of the Israelites over the Egyptians (in Egypt). If the stela refers, as Petrie suggests, to the war of the Israelites against the Amalekites and the Canaanite king of Arad (Nu. 14: 40–45), it should be recalled that the biblical narrative refers to Canaanites and not to Egyptians.

2. According to the biblical account the Children of Israel wandered forty years in the desert before they entered the land of Canaan and then they spent several years (as we have seen, approximately thirty one years) in wars before they finally settled in the country. If the stela of Merneptah is taken as contemporary evidence of the Exodus, it follows that the wanderings in the desert (including the period of wars in Canaan and of the settlement) lasted only one or two years. Indeed some scholars are content with this explanation. However, if we accept that the stela relates to the Exodus and likewise accept the bibical narrative concerning the forty years wandering plus the additional years before the settlement of the Israelites, it follows that the Exodus could not have taken place in the period of Merneptah but only in the reign of Raamses his predecessor. Indeed, Albright tries to argue along these lines, but his view involves a new contradiction of the biblical text, as this states that the Exodus took place when a new Pharaoh acceded to the throne (Ex. 2: 23).

3. According to Burckhardt[58] Merneptah reigned from 1235–1227 B.

---

58   Cited by Albright, who affirms this date: Albright, Archaeology And The Date Of The Hebrew Conquest Of Palestine, BASOR., 58, 1935

C., according to Breasted,[59] from 1225–1215 B. C. . These are the accepted dates today. On the other hand, Brugsch and Mahler date the beginning of Merneptah's reign outside these limits, the one to c. 1300 B. C. and the other c. 1190 B. C. Therefore, if we accept the theory that the Exodus took place in the reign of Merneptah we have to allow that the date of the Exodus is either 1235 B. C. or 1225 B. C. ; And if we accept the extreme chronologies of Brugsch and Mahler we can add to these dates also the years c. 1190 and c. 1300 B. C. Adding the forty years of wandering in the desert[60], we find therefore that the Israelites reached the land of Israel either in c. 1195 or in c. 1180 B. C. (or according to Brugsch and Mahler, either in c. 1260 or in c. 1150 B. C.). This means that the destruction of the cities of Jericho, Ay, etc., as described in the Bible, must have taken place within the limits of the above dates. But the archaeological findings contradict these dates. Watzinger, who excavated in Jericho, believed the city was destroyed in 1600 B. c., while Vincent thought this happened between 1600–1200 B. C.[61]. Wright[62] rejected Vincent's opinion and agreed with Garstang that the city was destroyed in c. 1407 B. C. Garstang who likewise excavated in Jericho, concluded that the cities of Hazor, Ai and Beth–El were also detroyed in the same period[63]. Accordingly he fixed the date of the Exodus in c. 1447 B. C., which coincides with biblical chronology. Newberry, who examined the scarabs from the tombs of Jericho, confirmed this dating of Garstang by showing that these scarabs dated to the Hyksos up to the time of Amenophis (Amenhotep) III. Moreover he found no objects that belonged to the period between Amenophis IV and the time of Raamses II. Sir Charles Marston draws on the researches of Garstang and Newberry, as well as on certain pottery types from the burnt strata of Jericho to prove that the city was destroyed by Joshua during the reign of Amenophis III. On the basis of this evidence he concludes that the Exodus took place in the beginning of Amenophis II's reign. i. e. c. 1447 B. C.[64]. Albright who disagrees with

---

59 Breasted, A History of Egypt, p. 597.

60 As already noted we refer to the Biblical text and not to scholarly theories which will be discussed later.

61 Vincent. L. H., The Chronology of Jericho, PEQ. 1931, pp. 104–105; Ceramique Et Chronologie, RB. 1932, pp. 269, 271; La Chronologie Des Ruines de Jericho, RB. 1930, p. 432. Chronique, L'aube De L'histoire A Jericho, RB. 1938, pp. 561–589; RB. 1939, pp. 91–107.
    see also: Lucas, The Date of The Exodus PEQ., 1941.

62 Wright, Two Misunderstood Items, etc., BASOR, 861942 ,. pp. 32–35.

63 Garstang, The Date of The Destruction of Jericho, PEQ, 1927, pp. 96–100; Jericho, PEQ, 1930, p. 132. ; The Story of Jericho, PEQ. 1941, pp. 168–171. The Ruins of Jericho, PEQ. 1936, p. 170. ; The Fall of Bronze Age Jericho, PEQ. 1935, p. 68. ; – Joshua – Judges, pp. 54–55; 225. – A Third Season At Jericho,
    City And Necropolis, PEQ. 1932, pp. 149–153.

64 Marston, The Bible Is True, 1934, p. 154.

Garstang believes that Jericho was conquered between 1360–1320 B. C.[65], and Beth–El and Ai between 1300–1250 B. C. Therefore, if the Israelites left Egypt during the reign of Merneptah, the inevitable conclusion is that when they reached Jericho, Beth–El, Ai and other cities they must have found them already destroyed. Many scholars refer to this argument[66], and we shall quote them in the course of our discussion.

4. Petrie, has suggested two possibilities: one, a certain number of the Israelite families did not migrate to Egypt but remained in Canaan and the other –a certain number of families left Egypt in advance of the main body, and remained in Canaan "during most, or all, of the time that the others were in Egypt". (Petrie. Egypt and Israel 1912, p. 35) Thus, inevitably, we witness the formation of a theory of two Exoduses. A succession of scholars ranging from Petrie, Steuernagel to Burney, Rowley, Meek and Albright, tried each in his own systematic way, to prove that there were two Exoduses (or two separate entries into Canaan), either of concubine tribes or of Leah or Rachel tribes (Steuernagel, Bohl, Barton and others), or Josephite and Levites tribes (Albright) or only of Caleb tribes (Gemoll)[67]. According to Rowley, during the el–Amarna period a group of Israelite tribes (Judah, Simeon, and Levy) joined by Kenites, Calibbites and others penetrated into Canaan from the south. A small group of the tribe of Levy migrated to Egypt, where it joined a group that had earlier arrived there. Four centuries later, i. e. in the Merneptah period the Exodus took place under the leadership of Moses Hence, Jericho, Ai and other cities were destroyed by the first wave which he

---

65 Albright, The Israelite Conquest of Canaan In The Light of Archaeology, BASOR, 1939, pp. 18–19; Archaeology and The Date of The Hebrew Conquest of Palestine, BASOR, 58, 1935, pp. 16–17.

66 Rowley, From Joseph To Joshua, p. 19; – The Date of The ExodusPEQ. 1941, p. 155.
   Phytian–Adams, Jericho, Ai And The Occupation of Mount Ephraim, PEQ. 1936, pp. 141–143.
   Wright, Epic of Conquest, BA. 1940 (3), p. 36. ; Biblical Archaeology, p. 80.
   Albright, The Israelite Conquest of Canaan In The Light of Archaeology, BASOR, 74, 1939, p. 16.
   Bright, A History Of Israel, pp. 118–119.
   Cook (S. A. C.), Notes on Excavation, PEQ. 1926, p. 208.
   Dussaud, Note Additionelle, SY. 16, 1935, p. 351. ; Notes, PEQ. 1936, p. 54.
   Meek, Hebrew Origins, p. 24.
   Aharoni, Eretz Israel In the Biblical Period, p. 107. (Hebrew).

67 According to Gemoll only Caleb sojourned in Egypt. Bohl believes that Rachel tribes were in Egypt whereas Leah tribes together with concubine tribes were already settled in Canaan Steuernagel identified the Habiru with Leah tribes, whom he believes conquered the south of Canaan, at c. 1400 B. C. Patton identified the Habiru with what he calls adult Leah tribes –Reuben, Simeon, Levy, Judah and a wave of young Leah tribes – Zebulun and Issaschar, whereas the Exodus concerns the Rachel tribes. According to him Gad, Asher and Zilpah were Canaanite tribes intermixed with Leah tribes, while Dan Naphtali and Bilha were Canaanite tribest intermixed with Rachel tribes.

identifies with the Habiru. But in the national consciousness the two waves of conquests merged into one. Albright believes that one Exodus came after the expulsion of the Hyksos from Egypt, this was an Exodus of "Josephites"; whom he identifies with the Habiru (14th century), who conquered Jericho. A second Exodus of "Levites" (Leha tribes and especially the tribe of Judah) under the leadership of Moses and Joshua took place c. 1260 B. C. Meek believes an invasion of Israelite tribes under the leadership of Joshua took place c. 1400 B. C., and one in c. 1200 B. C. under the leadership of Moses. Other scholars like Burney, Rowton etc. adopt a similar line of thought. Some scholars quote Josephus (Cont. Ap. I. 26), who cites Manethon to the effect that the Israelites left Egypt in the days of a king named Amenophis; and elsewhere Josephus (Cont. Ap. I, 15) says that the Israelites were driven out by Thutmosis and subsequently built Jerusalem. The name 'Amenophis' is explained by the scholars to be Manethon's corruption of the name Merneptah.[68]. All these ideas share several common features, 1) The belief that the Exodus took place in the Raamses–Merneptah period (c. 1200 B. C.). 2) Placing of Goshen in the Wadi Tumilat region 3) The assumption that the biblical text is a conflation and harmonisation of different traditions which are not to be trusted historically. This assumption is brought into play whenever a fact or a verse is problematic or contradictory. There were scholars (Nibuhr, for example) who went so far as to deny the story of the Exodus, and in the wake of this denial demolished a whole set of facts.

Having earlier discussed the factors which led to these assumptions we found them to be basically erroneous, and therefore there can be no substance to any of the views founded on them.

What can we learn from the Bible?

1. We have seen that on the basis of certain statements, (Gen. 46, 33–34; Ex. 13: 17 and others), it was rightly inferred that Goshen was located on the borders of Egypt. In Genesis (45: 10) we are told that Joseph invited his father to Egypt and informed him"... and thou shalt dwell in the land of Goshen, and thou shalt be near unto me." This means that Goshen was considered to be near Joseph's dwelling place. It is logical to assume that Joseph resided in the royal city, which at the time of Jacob's descent to Egypt was the city of On Moreover he marries Asenath, the daughter of Poti–phera priest of On. This implies that the land of Goshen was near the city of On. About the proximity of the royal residence to Goshen can also be learned from the biblical account of Moses' ark being found by Pharaoh's daughter; (Ex. 2: 5), as well as from the story of the Exodus. We read (Ex. 12: 31 ff) that Pharaoh summoned Moses and Aharon in the middle of the night and ordered them to leave Egypt; and on the same night they gathered together the Israelites and all of them left Egypt. This shows that the biblical narrator thought the distance

---

68   Conder, The Date of The Exodus, PEP. 1896, p. 256.

between Pharaoh's residence and the land of Goshen to be sufficiently short for all these activities to take place in one night. Elsewhere (Ex. 8: 25–27) Pharaoh tells Moses and Aaron: "...Go ye, sacrifice to your God in the land". And Moses answers him: "It is not meet so to do, for we shall sacrifice the abomination of the Egyptians before their eyes, and will they not stone us?" These verses indicate that the dwelling place of the Israelites was in the midst of the Egyptians and not at the border of Egypt, as is universally accepted. Also in the story of the ten plagues the emphasis is on the fact the plagues afflicted the Egyptians but left the Israelites unscathed: "And I will sever in that day the land of Goshen And I will put a division between my people and thy people" (Ex. 8: 22–23). This would be pointless if the Israelites had not lived among the Egyptians. Gardiner[69] states unequivocally that the Israelites lived in the capital. Clark[70] refers to the biblical story wherein the Israelites were ordered to mark their houses, so that the angel of God would pass them by, and sees this as evidence that the Israelites did indeed live among the Egyptians, for otherwise the order to mark the houses would be pointless. This too is the opinion of Robinson[71], who gives yet another reason, namely that the Israelites were ordered to borrow vessels of silver and gold from their Egyptian neighbours. (Ex. 11).

To sum up: The Bible indicates that the dwelling place of the Israelites was among the Egyptians, somewhere near Pharaoh's residence, AND AT THE SAME TIME ON THE BORDER OF EGYPT. At the time of Jacob's descent to Egypt the Royal Residence was in the city of On, and it follows that Goshen had to be in that region (i. e. today's Cairo). We thus return to Josephus' and the Septuagint who identify On with Goshen. As to the location of the Israelites' dwelling place on the borders of Egypt, the natural tendency is to apply modern territorial notions and not ancient ones. The term 'Land of Egypt' (Hebrew – ארץ מצרים Eretz mitzraim) is regarded by scholars as a territorial name, corresponding to Egypt's present–day geographical situation; however, in the Bible we read; "The land of Egypt is before thee; in the best of the land make thy father and brethren to dwell; in the land of Goshen let them dwell."(Gen. 47: 6)."And the sons of Israel dwelled. . in the land of Egypt, in the best of the land, in the land of Rameses..." (Gen. 47: 11). Clearly therefore the land of Goshen was located IN the land of Egypt. How can one land exist within another land? Perhaps the word "land" (Heb. eretz) is used in the Bible in a different sense from the modern? That this was indeed the case is confirmed by certain biblical passages containing the word "land" (Heb. eretz, ארץ) – as "gave him a house... and gave him land*" (1Kn.

---

69   Gardiner, ibid., p. 89
70   Clarke, The Exodus, PEF, 1883, p. 92
71   Robinson, Biblical Research In Palestine, Vol. I, p. 77
*   The Hebrew has: eretz – ארץ.

11: 18); "As for the earth,* out of it cometh bread" (Job. 28: 5); "...Pirathon in the land * of Ephraim " (Ju. 12: 15); "...in the land* of Benjamin." (Jer. 3, 33: 13); ". the land * of Shalisha, the land * of Shalim. . the land* of the Benjamites..." (1 Sam. 9: 44); "...the land * of the plain" (i. e. the region of Sodom – Gen. 19: 28); "Like worms of the earth * "(Mi. 7: 17); "mine hand also hath laid the foundation of the earth *...(Is. 48: 13); "and I will sever in that day the land * of Goshen in which my people dwell."(Ex. 8: 2 2) In the Hebrew text (Ex. 8: 18) it read –"ארץ גשן אשר עמי עמד עליה" literally translated "The land of Goshen whereon my people stands." It is clear therefore from the foregoing that the Hebrew word ארץ (eretz) has the double meaning of both "land"and 'earth', 'ground'... This also applies to all the other quoted verses. The equivalent Arabic word" ard "similarly means both 'ground' and 'land.'

From what is said above, 'eretz must be understood to mean 'ground', 'earth', and not 'state' or 'land'. Moreover in the past the word eretz was not applied to an extended area of territory but also to specific regions, such as "land (eretz) of the plain", "land of the Benjamites", etc. Accordingly "And Israel dwelt in the land * of Egypt in the country * of Goshen " is to be understood as meaning that the Israelites settled in the land of Egypt, in the land of Goshen, that is within the land of Egypt, in the territory of Goshen.

But what in fact is the land of Egypt?

About the Exodus we read: "...even the SELFSAME DAY it came to pass, that all the hosts of the Lord went out from the land of Egypt. It is a NIGHT to be much observed unto the Lord for bringing them out from the land of Egypt: This is THAT NIGHT of the Lord to be observed of all the children of Israel in their generations" (Ex. 12: 41–42. emphasis–N. G.) Evidently this narrative concerns only the night of the 14th of the month of Nissan[72], (i. e. the biblical date of the Exodus from Egypt). Yet according to the Bible story it took the Israe – lites another three days AFTER THE EXODUS at least, till they reached the Red Sea[73], generally regarded the border of Egyptian territory. However, the biblical text indicates the night of 14th Nissan as the date of the, Exodus, and even insists on this: "...this is that night of the Lord to be much observed..." etc. It is clear therefore that from the biblical viewpoint, the Land of Egypt – ERETZ MITZRAYIM –indicates merely the name of the location (town or region) – which the Israelites left on the night of 14th of Nissan, and does not denote the country of Egypt as whole. Hence it is evident that Egypt (–mitzrayim) was the name

---

72 See also: Ex. 12: 6, 18, 39, 51.

73 Josephus (Ant. II, 315) writes: "They took the road to Letopolis. Omitting the country by the shortest route, they arrived ON THE THIRD DAY, at Beelsephon, a place beside the Red Sea." (emphasis – N. G,)

of a district (and the district town), which eventually became the name of a more extensive territory (i. e. complete country) As has been noted the Bible places Goshen near Pharaoh's residence, which location In the time of Joseph's was the city of On . The city of Cairo (i. e. the region of ancient On) is called in modern spoken Arabic 'masr' = (Mitzrayim = Egypt), whilst Old Cairo (Fustat) is called 'MASR el ATTIKA'[74], with New Cairo known as 'MASR el GEDIDA' (or 'MASR el KAHIRAH')[75]; the entire country of Egypt is called today 'BALLAD MASR'.[76]. Accordingly this takes us back to Josephus and the Septuagint who identify Goshen–Raamses with Heliopolis (On), that is the area of present–day Cairo. According to Josephus the king then permitted him (Jacob) to live with his children in Heliopolis"[77].

To sum up: 'The Land of Egypt' (Heb. eretz–mizrayim) is meant to denote the land (i. e. area) of the district town Mitzrayim; and when told in the Bible that the Israelites dwell on the borders of Egypt, we are to understand that they lived at the edge of this district town, i. e. in its suburbs. Thus the biblical narrative which describes the Israelites as living amongst the Egyptians and at the same time on the border of Egypt, near the Egyptians is clarified. This district town is to be identified with Heliopolis (On), that is the area of present day Cairo.

In the following we shall review some of the theories underlying most arguments and views still current today: Like many other scholars Burney in his book "Israel Settlement in Canaan" claims that the Exodus took place in the time of Merneptah; moreover he asserts that the biblical statement about the Exodus occurring 480 years before the construction of the Temple. (1Kn. 6: 1.) cannot be accepted uncritically; the reason given for this is that 480 is an artificial number, in effect merely the result of multiplying 40 by 12. The number 40 corresponds to the 40 years wandering in the desert; and moreover denotes a conventional reckoning of the length of a generation.[78] This argument was fully discussed in an earlier chapter, and was shown

---

74 See for example maps: Murray's Handbook for Travellers, 8th. ed. pp. 161; 221;
   Baedeker's Egypt etc. 1908, pp. 40; 101
   Les quides bleus, Egypte p. 76. Hachette, paris 1956.
   Wright, The Illustrated Bible Treasury, London 1896, map, p. 166
75 See map of Egypt in "National Geographical Magazine", May, 1965.
76 Also in modern Arabic the word "medineh"(–state) means both "state" and "town".
77 Josephus, Ant. II, 183.
78 See for example: Burney, Israel Settlement In Canaan, p. 4.
   Lods, Israel, p. 208.
   Albright, A Revision of Early Hebrew Chronology, JPOS. 1920–1921, p. 64 (note 1).
   Lepsius, Letters From Egypt, etc. pp. 403, 457, 460–470.
   Petrie, The Date of The Exodus, PEF. 1896, p. 335
   Bright, A History o, . /f Israel, p. 113.
   Aharoni, Eretz Israel In Biblical Period, p. 168. (Hebrew).

to be basically misleading. Another argument of Burney that gained wide acceptance is one that assumes the books of Joshua and Judges "consist of a substratum of ancient narratives which frequently run parallel in presenting more or less variant traditions of the same series of events. These narratives have been utilized and combined by later editors" (ibid. p. 6). Burney also believes that "in dealing with this period of Israel settlement in Canaan we have to rely upon records which as written documents are undoubtedly much further removed from the handed down across a considerable period in the form of stories told and retold period with which they deal than are the records of the monarchy", and "Events have been round the camp fire and beside the well and have undergone (can we doubt it?) some amount of modification and embellishment in the process". Moreover Burney bases his theory on the seeming contradiction between the account of the conquest of Hebron and Jerusalem by Joshua on the one hand, and the conquest of these cities by Judah, Benjamin and Caleb on the other.[79] Accordingly he regards the story of the conquest as a synthesis of two versions. One version speaks of a quick and all–sweeping victory under Joshua's leadership, while the other depicts a slow, gradual penetration of the country by separate tribes. Yet Burney thinks that we have to accept the version of the conquest as described in the book of Judges: namely gradual penetration of the country by separate tribes, who mostly did not succeed in driving out the original inhabitants but had to be content with settling alongside them. In other words, the settlement was accomplished in the form of a gradual and peaceful infiltration[80]. He bases this view on the biblical statement that the tribes did not dispossess (Heb. lehorish– להוריש) the inhabitants of the country.[81] But, as already noted, the interpretation of lehorish as "dispossess" or "driving out" is utterly erroneous, and so equally is the conquest concept According to Burney the biblical narrative of Joshua's conquests may be divided into two campaigns: the first the conquest of the south of the land of Canaan, and the second – the war against Yavin king of Hazor and the conquest of the north of the land[82] Since in the Song of Deborah there is a "Jabin... who reigned in Hazor", he assumes that the Yavin who in Joshua xi is depicted as warring against Joshua is the same Yavin who fought against Deborah and Barak (Burney, p. 54). This leads him to conclude that the war in the north was conducted by the tribes of Naphtali and Zeb–ulun only. The verse "From Machir came down the commanders..." (Ju. 5: 13–15) in the Song of Deborah demonstrates

---

79   The conquest of these Canaanite cities as well as the conquest of Canaan overall has already been discussed earlier and it was clearly shown that the alleged contradiction is illusory.

80   Burney, ibid. pp. 24–28.

81   Burney, ibid. pp. 17, 18, 22.

82   Burney, ibid. p. 15.

to Burney that Machir was on the west side of the Jordan at the period of Deborah. However, this necessarily contradicts the statement in Joshua that the sons of Machir were in Gilead, east of the Jordan. To resolve this contradiction Burney, (pp. 33–34) argues that in the period of Deborah the sons of Machir were settled west of the Jordan and only afterwards migrated to the east of the river, and therefore the "settlement supposed to have been carried out under the direction of Joshua, really only took place later than the victory of Barak and Deborah. This later hypothesis is certainly to be preferred; AND, IF CORRECT, it forms a second illustration of the fact that our old Jnarrative of the settlement assigns to the direction of Joshua movements which were really undertaken independently of him, and at a different period." (Burney, p. 34 ; emphasis – N. G.)

The conquest of the south is reconstructed by Burney as follows: In Num. XXI, 1–3, we read: "And the Canaanite, the king of Arad who dwelt in the south, heard tell that Israel came by the way of Atharim; and he fought against Israel, and took some of them captives. And Israel vowed a vow unto Jehovah, and said, if thou wilt indeed deliver this people into my hand, then I will utterly destroy their cities. And Jehovah hearkened to the voice of Israel, and delivered up the Canaanites; and they utterly destroyed them and their cities, and the name of the place was called Horma" On the other hand in Ju. 1: 17 we read: "And Judah went with Simeon his brother and they smote the Canaanites that inhabited Zephat and utterly destroyed it. And the name of the city was called Horma." According to Burney these are two parallel narratives telling the same story (Burney, p. 28): "Adopting then the view that the position of the narrative as it stands in Numbers is the more correct, and that the conquest of Arad in the Negeb (here the conquest of Arad is an accomplished fact, because of his assumption that the two narratives tell the same story – N. G.) took place through a tribal movement northward from the neighbourhood of Kadesh, THE INFERENCE BECOMES PLAUSIBLE that this movement was effected, as related in Judges, by the tribes of Judah and Simeon in alliance with the Kenites". (Burney, pp. 29–30, emphasis – N. G.) Burney ignores the fact that the story in the book of Numbers deals with a number of cities; "I will utterly destroy their cities... and they utterly destroyed them and their cities, and the name of the place was called Horma", that is, the story tells of a number of cities in the region of Arad, whereas the book of Judges is concerned with only one specific city, namely Safad (Zephat). In fact, Burney seizes only on the word "Horma", which is enough for him to combine the two stories and develop an overarching theory. It should be noted that both biblical stories concern cities which, after being destroyed, are called "Horma". In Hebrew horma means 'absolute destruction', and one should therefore understand that Horma emphasizes the extent of utter destruction to the city (or cities) and does not signify a new name for a new city. The conquest of Caleb, as related in the book of Judges, seems to Burney to have a somewhat contradictory character which causes him to ask (Burney, p. 31): "Is it not, then, at least a plausible theory that the original Calibite story related that Caleb, after first spying out the Negeb, then proceeded to go up and conquer it? "He links this to his former theory about Arad, and sees it as proof that the tribes of Simeon and Judah, together with what he calls North Arabian clans advanced from Kadesh Barnea northward, conqu—ered Arad and from there advanced to a region which later became known as the hill country of Judah (Burney, pp. 31–32) "...IF THIS INFERENCE BE CORRECT," Burney continues, "it will help to explain to us a very striking fact in the later history, viz. the isolation of Judah and Simeon from the rest of the tribes." (pp. 31–32). (The fact that the tribes of Simeon and Judah are not mentioned in the Song of Deborah is sufficient reason for Burney to assume they were isolated from the other tribes). So on the strength of several completely unfounded assumptions, Burney reaches the conclusion that Joshua did not lead the Children of Israel across the Jordan but was only the leader of what he (Burney) calls the Joseph tribes, who gradually infiltrated into the country (Burney, p. 27). Yet the el Amarna Tablets mention the Habiru who are identified with the Hebrews. How, therefore, can this contradiction be explained from Burney's viewpoint? He leans on the fact that the Habiru are mentioned together with the 'Sa—Gaz', and these in their turn are mentioned together with 'Aziru' in 'his' wars in the north of the country. Since in Babylonian epigraphical findings the name 'Sa—Gaz' is supposedly mentioned, Burney concludes that the mention of the Habiru in the el Amarna Tablets in fact refers to an Aramaic invasion of northern Canaan (Land of Israel) (Burney, pp. 74–76). The Bible tells us that Jacob and his sons returned from Padan – Aram, and this story is enough for him to determine that the Habiru are merely tribes–the tribes of Jacob – who conquered the country while returning from Padan – Aram. According to him, they also conquered the town of 'Shechem' at the same time, (Burney, pp. 85–86), and moreover, this is proved by the story of the rape of Dina and the killing of the Shechem inhabitants by Levy and Simeon (Gen. 34). According to Burney "the story is one which beyond a doubt we are dealing with the doings of tribes under the guise of individuals. The small Israelite tribe of Dinah enters into terms of friendly alliance and intermarriage with the Bene – Hamor of Shechem. an event which excites the resentment of the tribes of Simeon and Levy. Under cover of friendly overtures these two latter tribes treacherously attack the Shechemites... and effect a general massacre" (Burney, p. 37). He presumes that the inhabitants of Shechem retaliated and eventually expelled and drove them out, greatly reducing their number (Burney, p. 46). The remnants of the two tribes settled in the desert region bordering on Egypt, and in due time, during the reign of Amenhotep II, also entered Egypt (Burney, p. 87). Why should a friendly alliance have led to resentment and war? This Burney does not explain, as he does not explain on what evidence he concludes that they were expelled from Shechem and entered Egypt. Indeed he states that "Available evidence is but slight, and is much obscured by accretions representing later points of view, and any such theory must therefore be largely tentative". (Burney, p. 46)

Furthermore, how can Burney's theory explain that in the time of the Joshua conquest Shechem did not remain in the hands of Simeon and Levy but was allotted to the sons of Joseph?

Burney finds the explanation in a phrase in Jacob's blessing; "There is an interesting but obscure allusion in Gen. Xl. VIII, 22 E, WHICH PROBABLY has a bearing on the question. Here, the aged Jacob is pictured as saying to his son Joseph: 'Moreover I have given to thee one mountain–slope (in the biblical text "portion"

Hebrew – שכם 'Shehem – lit. 'shoulder' – N.G.) above thy brethren, which I took from the hand of the Amorite with my sword and with my bow.'". He (Burney) construes שכם= shechem –not as shoulder but as the town of Shechem (pp. 43–44). Thus Burney arrives at the general conclusion that Hebrew tribes settled in Egypt together with the Hyksos and were later driven out. He finds an echo of this settlement in the biblical narrative of the descent of Abraham to Egypt and of his subsequent expulsion.[83] One of these tribes–Yacobel–dwelled in Israel at the time of Thotmes (Thutmosis) III. and was expelled by the Edomites; when the tribe returned from Padan–Aram it managed to conquer a part of the country. These are the Habiru conquests which were concentrated in the region of Shechem. Some of the conquerors (the tribes of Joseph, Simeon and Levy) went to Egypt in the period of Amenophis II, while the other Israelite tribes remained behind. Therefore, the name of the tribe of Asher is mentioned on the stelae of Seti I and Raamses II, and the name Ishirar on the stela of Merneptah. Phytian – Adams commenting on Burney's book concluded:[84] "Let us... note their most prominent characteristic, as revealed in the 60 pages of Burney's investigation. 'The inference becomes plausible' 'gains some support', 'we seem to be in the brink', 'if this inference be correct', 'it is not improbable that', 'we shall probably not be far wrong', 'we may reasonably conjecture'. These are only a few expressions culled from these pages at random, and they can hardly fail to impress the reader with the extreme tenuity of the structure upon which the thesis is based. Such speculative methods are of course quite legitimate provided that the 'conjectures' of one page do not become the 'facts' of another". These sentences of Phytian–Adams convey only a few of

---

83 The Bible does not refer to Abraham's expulsion from Egypt but to his leaving it.
84 Phytian–Adams, Mirage In The Wilderness, PEQ. 1935, pp. 69–78.

the multitude of speculative assumptions on which Burney bases his theories; these gained plausibility and support from the theories of Rowley and Meek, which seemingly are independent and self–sufficient but in fact are founded on Burney's ideas. Where for Burney the assumptions on one page become 'facts' on the next, for Meek and Rowley, Burney's assumptions have already become facts in support of their arguments. Rowley,[85] attempting to validate Burney's theories also starts from the assumption that the Exodus took place in the period of Raamses II–Merneptah, and that Goshen was located in Wadi Tumilat. Rowley argues that during the el–Amarna period (14th century B. C.) a group of Israelite tribes penetrated into Canaan from the south. This group included the tribes of Judah, Simeon and Levy, joined by non–Israelite elements: Kenites, Calibbites and others. At the same time more distantly related tribes settled in other parts of the country, that is what he calls "other Leah and concubine tribes" while from the first group Israelite elements separated and migrated to Egypt In a later period–the period of king Ikhnaton–one of the people of these elements gained power and became governor. Rowley believes that the group of Simeon, Levy and Judah penetrated the region of Shechem and conquered it, though they suffered heavy losses and even defeat. In consequence the Simeonites became absorbed in the tribe of Judah. Also a part of the tribe of Levy combined with the tribe of Judah, but the majority dispersed over the entire country. Simultaneously a small group of the Levites migrated to Egypt, where they joined the group that had earlier arrived there. Four centuries later, in Merneptah's period, the Exodus took place under the leadership of Moses, who on his mother's side was a Kenite. This group which made up the people of the Exodus was comprised mostly of the Joseph tribes and elements of the tribe of Levy; it was this group that penetrated under the leadership of Joshua into the central part of Canaan. Therefore Jericho, Ai and other cities were in fact destroyed by the first wave of the invasion which Rowley identifies with the Habiru. However in the national consciousness the two waves of conquest became merged into one. What then are the true facts and on what rests Rowley's theory?

Primarily it is the assumption that Goshen is in Wadi Tumilat, and accordingly he concludes: "...the fifteenth–century date for the Exodus (according to biblical chronology – N. G.) would make Thothmes III the Pharaoh of the Oppression. No known building operation of this Pharaoh took place in the Nile Delta region, and he is not known to have had a royal residence in the district. It is of the essence of the biblical tradition of the

---

85   Rowley, From Joseph To Joshua. He expresses the same ideas also in: The Exodus And The Settlement In Canaan, BASOR. 85, 1942. pp. 27–35. ; The Date of The Exodus, PEQ. 1941, pp. 152–157.
      Israel's Sojourn In Egyp

Exodus that the building operations on which the Israelites were engaged were close to the palace,... On the other hand, when the Israelites went into Egypt, they were assigned a district far from the court, "(Rowley, pp. 23–24; see also p. 77). Thus, according to Rowley we have to look for a period when Goshen at the time of the Israelites' entry into Egypt was far from the royal court and situated near it in the period of their exit from it. For this reason he is opposed to the suggestion that the Exodus took place in the 15th century B. C. and that the Israelites entered Egypt during the Hyksos period (Rowley, pp. 25–28): "For the Hyksos monarchs had their capital at Avaris, which has been identified with the Delta residence of Rameses II by recent writers. A descent in Hyksos period and Exodus in the thirteenth century B. C. would therefore mean that the proximity of the Hebrews to the court would be the same in both ages". (Rowley, p. 25.). Elsewhere (pp. 77–79; 89–90; 94) when referring to the biblical statement that the Exodus took place 480 years before king Solomon's reign, he (Rowley) claims this number to be a fictitious one. Moreover, he claims a generation to be "more than forty years "(Rowley, p. 161). However, as seen already in the case of Burney, this claim severely undermines his position, for accepting the notion of a 50 years generation inevitably means accepting the idea that the Israelites entered Egypt only 200 years before they left it, (i. e. four generations). Hence this renders his arguments invalid. Rowley's views are based chiefly on three assumptions, which he regards as indubitable and verified facts, namely:

1. Biblical Goshen located in Wadi–Tumilat.
2. The Israelites' entry into Egypt in the Hyksos period
3. Avaris = Pi–Ramesu= biblical Raamses.

The belief that the Israelites entered Egypt in the Hyksos period is shared by many scholars,[86] and though they rely on the biblical narrative for its corroboration, it is in fact contradicted by it, as was pointed out already by Yahuda and by Lucas,[87] They both refer to the biblical narrative about Joseph and his brothers: "...and said, set on bread. And they set on for him by himself, and for them by themselves, and for the Egyptians, which did eat with him, by themselves: because the Egyptians might not eat bread with the Hebrews; for that is an abomination unto the Egyptians". (Gen. 43: 31–32). Hence, they rightly concluded from the fact that the Egyptians would not eat with the Hebrews that the period of the biblical narrative was not that of the Hyksos, since there was nothing whatever to prevent the latter

---

86 For example: Meek, Hebrew Origins, p. 17; Albright, A Revision of Early Hebrew Chronology, JPOS, 1920, p. 65. Hall. H. R. The Ancient History of the Near East. 1913.

87 Yahuda, The Accuracy of The Bible, 1935, p. 46.

from eating with the Hebrews.[88] The same also arises from the biblical text: "that ye shall say, Thy servants' trade hath been about cattle...that ye may dwell in the land of Goshen; for every shepherd is an abomination unto the Egyptians." (Gen. 46: 34). Not only are the Hyksos not prevented from sitting with the Hebrews, but seeing their name is usually interpreted as "kings of the shepherds", it would be absurd to have them regard shepherds as an abomination. Speaking about Joseph, his brothers and the Egyptians: the Bible text reads: "for he spake unto them by an interpreter"[89] If this concerned the Hyksos period, why the need for an interpreter?

Rowley has yet another argument to oppose to a 15th century B. C. Exodus. If we accept the Exodus occurred in the 15th century it follows that Joshua's conquest coincides with the period of the el–Amarna Tablets, but according to Rowley, the wars described in the EAT. should not be linked with Joshua's wars, for the Tablets speak of wars by small groups whereas the book of Joshua describes a war by a united army (Rowley, pp. 39, 41)[90]. Moreover he maintains that the names of individuals mentioned in the Tablets and the names in the Bible (relating to the conquest period) bear no relation whatever to each other (pp. 41–42). Added support for his theory is found by Rowley in Albright, who places the destruction of the Canaanite cities in the 13th century. Altough the biblical mention of Raamses is regarded by Rowley as an anachronism, he nonetheless accepts that the Exodus took place in the days of Merneptah. However, because the Merneptah stele refers to the undeniable fact of wars in Canaan, Rowley argues: "Yet if Merneptah was the Pharaoh of the Exodus, then the Israelites traditions carry ample memory of their relation with him, and the non–mention of the activity as recorded on the stele is not seriously surprising. For there is no pretence to record every detail of history in the book of Judges and there can be no doubt that the event recorded on the stele was of trivial significance for Israel's history compared with the event of the Exodus." (Rowley, p. 31)

However, if the Merneptah stele is expected to serve as evidence of a war in Canaan fought by the group that left Egypt, one may well ask: How, two years after Merneptah came to power could there be a war in Canaan fought with a group which according to the biblical narrative had entered that country only after 40 years wandering in the desert? Rowley tries to overcome this problem by taking the Israelites straight to Kadesh–Barnea in three days; (Rowley, p. 104): "When the Israelites came out of Egypt we read that after crossing the Red Sea they went three days journey into the

---

88   This same argument was already pointed out by Yahuda in 1935. (ibid p. 47.). Lucas believes the Israelites entered Egypt in c. 1876 B. C
89   Gen. 42: 23.
90   His opinion here contradicts that of Burney, who believes Joshua's wars were conducted by the individual tribes.

wilderness without finding water (Ex. xv 22). We are not told the name of the place they then reached, BUT IT SEEMS PROBABLE that it was Kadesh. For they came to a place called Marah, where there were some bitter waters which Moses sweetened (ibid 25), and we read that after the sweetening of the waters God made for them statutes and ordinances, and there he tested them (ibid, 25). This would seem to refer to the testing which took place at Massah (ibid. xvii 1–7), which means 'testing'. But Massah is identified with Meribah (ibid. 7), and Meribah is elsewhere located at Kadesh (Num. xx 13; xxvii 14)" (Rowley p. 104). However, in a footnote Rowley states: "On the other hand Ex. xvii, 6f. would appear to associate Massah and Meribah with Horeb. BUT IT IS PROBABLE that there was some conflation here, and that these two verses come from separate sources". Thus he deliberately sidesteps the contradiction; and this allows him to conclude that the Israelites reached Kadesh Barnea in only three days, i. e. in time to be inscribed on Merneptah stele (Rowley p. 137)[91]. How could this body of people that included women, children and the aged, along with their flocks and herds be able to traverse the waterless desert and moreover cover the whole distance to Kadesh Barnea in only three days? Apparently only Rowley knows the answer. According to the Bible in order to get from Goshen to the Red Sea (Yam Suph) – a much smaller distance – (the true identification of these places is irrelevant here) – three days walking was needed. His theory of the three days trek to Kadesh, which was designed to explain the Exodus occurring in Merneptah's days, as well as the name Isirar inscribed on the Merneptah stele two years after his ascending to the throne, obliged Rowley to correlate these matters with the biblical account of the 40 years wandering in the Sinai desert; and so he explains: "It is likely, therefore, that two accounts of what happened after the Israelites came out of Egypt have been combined. According to the one they proceeded straight to Kadesh, and there offered sacrifice to Yahweh and received his statutes. They remained there for thirty – eight years and then advanced northwards into territory occupied by Judah. According to the other, they proceeded to the sacred mount of Sinai or Horeb, where they received the divine ordinances, and had a two years' period of wandering in the wilderness." (Rowley, pp. 105–106). From Rowley's text it is not clear; a) Why the Israelites remained in Kadesh thirty – eight years, if their brethren, the tribe of Judah, had already occupied the south of Canaan whom they joined after this prolonged delay? b) If they waited thirty – eight years at Kadesh, how then does it come about that the name Isirar appears on Merneptah's stele?

Rowley tries to get out of this dilemma by explaining (Rowley, p. 106): "We have to distinguish between the history behind the tradition and the

---

91 Baker – Green also believed the Israelites passed straight through Wadi et–Tieh, but he took them to Eilat and not to Kadesh.

tradition as it is modified by combination with the traditions of the various tribes. If the tribes all came out of Egypt and were all led by Moses, they cannot have gone first to Kadesh and also have gone first to Sinai and Horeb, and one of these traditions would have to be pronounced false. But if some of the tribes came out of Egypt and some did not, and if some were led by Moses and some were not, then it is equally possible that some went to Kadesh and some did not, and that some went to Sinai or Horeb and some did not" . But Rowley fails to explain how a tradition of 40 years wandering in the desert came about when one group is said by him to have traversed the Sinai desert in three days straight to Kadesh, whilst the other "had a two years' period of wandering in the wilderness". (Rowley, p. 106) Of course, given his opposition to the theory that the Exodus occurred in the 15th century B. C., there remains for him to explain the biblical statement that the Exodus took place 480 years before Solomon's reign. Rowley, in common with Wellhausen, Burney and others[92], regards this a fictitious number. However, he tries to bring "added proof" to Burney's presentation, namely the assumption that Balaam son of Beor who was summoned by Balak to curse the Israelites, is the same Bela son of Beor who is mentioned in the Bible as being the first king of Edom (Gen. 36: 32).

The Bible mentions eight kings who ruled in Edom before there reigned a king in Israel, and since in Rowley's opinion "an average of more than fifty years each for a succession of eight kings would be most remarkable, and it can scarcely be seriously maintained. An average of twenty–five years would seem more probable, and this would bring the period from the Exodus to the fourth year of Solomon to something in the neighbouring of 260 years". Elsewhere (ibid. p. 161) he holds a generation to be "somewhat more than forty years". Hence the number 480 is not for him a reliable one (p. 79).

According to Rowley an Exodus of all the tribes in the 13th century B. C. is inadmissible: "It can claim the support of Ex. 1, 11[93] and of the relevance of Egyptian conditions at the time of the Exodus, but it has to deny or explain away the earlier Egyptian references to Asher, and to overpress the philological difficulties in the equation of Habiru and Hebrews so as to dissociate the Amarna letters entirely from the biblical history and it is embarassed by the Merneptah stele. It is significant that Meek and Albright, no less than many older scholars, hold that there was a double entry into Palestine, even though their account of the double entry differs materially from that represented by Burney." (Rowley, p. 109)

Rowley, like Burney, distinguishes in the Amarna letters accounts of wars in the south and the north of Canaan which, in his opinion, reflect wars of the Hebrew tribes. This conclusion, he says, is made not on the ground of

92   Rowley, ibid. p. 94.
93   And they built for Pharaoh treasure cities, Pithom and Raamses

the philological equation of the names Habiru and Hebrews, but because of the evidence of identical activity. According to him the Hebrews, like the Habiru, made war in both the south and the north (Rowley, p. 110). Proof for his assertion he sees, like his predecessors Burney and others, in the biblical account of the unsuccessful attempt to attack Arad; in the story about Horma; and the non–mention of the names of the tribes of Judah and Simeon in the Song of Deborah (Rowley, pp. 102–103; 111). From this he concludes – like his predecessor Burney – that the Israelites entered from the south (Rowley, p. 11), whereas the war in the north he links with the biblical story about Simeon and Levy who killed the inhabitants of Shechem (Rowley, pp. 113–114).

It seems strange and surprising that these magnificent victories (assigned by him to the sons of Jacob), which find powerful expression in the Amarna letters, and refer to the conquest of a vast territory in the south and north, should be reflected in the biblical narratives by no more than two meagre allusions: one– the description of a failure and of an unsuccessful military attempt, in place of the celebration of a famous victory; and the other, an account of the massacre of the inhabitants of Shechem, and nothing beyond this. Admittedly, Rowley states elsewhere (pp. 3–4) that "it was believed that this was due to a harmonistic motive, and that really this was a separate movement in a different age ". Yet whatever this harmonistic motive aimed to achieve, it is illogical and difficult to believe that the intention was to turn victory into failure.

Thus in the way indicated above, Rowley constructs his theory of two separate invasions. However, as we have seen, the principal basis underlying this theory is the determination that the Exodus took place in the period of Raamses II and accordingly that Goshen was located in Wadi–Tumilat, for the reasons that no known building operation took place in the Nile delta prior to Raamses etc. There is also his desire to explain on the one hand, the stelea of Merneptah, Seti–I and Raamses II, and on the other hand, the destruction of Jericho in 1407 B. C. and the TEAT dating from the same period.

Meek,[94] whose main ideas are also derived from Burney, regards the biblical story of the descent into Egypt of Abraham, Isaac Joseph and Jacob, as connected with and reflecting successive waves of the Hyksos entering Egypt. He sees the story of the settlement in Goshen as reflecting (somehow) division of the land among the conquering Hyksos (p. 17), that is, according to him the entry of the Israelites into Egypt occurred in the Hyksos period (as stated above, the biblical narrative contradicts this belief). On the other hand, he sees the accounts of war in the EAT. as exactiy paralleling the biblical narrative of the conquest of Jericho and Canaan by Joshua, and consequently identifies

---

94   Meek, Hebrew Origins.

the Habiru with the Hebrews; (p. 21), However since the biblical narrative makes mention that the invading tribes did not evict[95] the inhabitants of the country he argues: "The so called 'conquest' was neither complete nor immediate. The Old Testament picture here, as so frequently elsewhere, is very much foreshortened. The 'conquest' was rather gradual infiltration of the Hebrews into the country by small groups or clans, and it must have continued over a century or more before they had made any considerable portion of the land their own." (pp. 22–23). But this view contradicts what is stated by the EAT., which, as stated, he sees as exactly paralleling the account of the Joshua wars. He therefore continues: "The account in the Tell el – Amarna letters marks the beginning of the movement, while the Old Testament account has to do largely with its final accomplishment, the end product. That the two accounts are not contemporaneous is indicated by the fact that the Canaanite kings mentioned in the two bear altogether different names and so cannot be of the same time." (p. 23). Meek fails to explain how in the two accounts different names came to be linked to the conquest of places with identical names. This points to anything but different periods. Also the archaeological evidence does not indicate that these cities were destroyed twice over within a short period of time. (People are liable to be killed during fighting and wars, hence the names of kings may well be different in the same period, but this hardly applies to place names).

Meek, who makes use also of Garstang's finding that Jericho was conquered in 1407 B. C. considers this date as evidence that Joshua invaded the country in the el–Amarna age (p. 23). Moreover, he quotes a number of additional facts to prove that Israelites were settled already in Canaan from the el–Amarna period. These are:

a. The stele of Seti – I, found at Beth–Shan (Beisan), which mentions the "Apiru" (identified with the Hebrews) (p. 23–24).

b. Inscriptions of Seti I and Raamses II mentioning the name of Isr (Asar), which applies to the inhabitants in the northern region of Israel (Canaan) Most scholars identify this name with the tribe of 'Asher' (p. 30).

c. Jephthah's words to the effect that Israel dwelt on the east bank of the Jordan "...in Heshbon and her towns, and in Aroer and her towns, and in all the cities that be along the coasts of Arnon, three hundred years" (Ju. 11: 26). (Meek, p. 30)

d. The story about Judah who married a Canaanite woman (Gen. 38) is seen by Meek as evidence of intermarriage with and assimilation to the Canaanites; he therefore considers that the Canaanites continued to live among the Israelites. (Meek, p. 30)

e. Merneptah's stele with its mention of a victory over Isirar proving

---

95   The Hebrew reads "lehorish" which, as explained earlier, was misunderstood and mistranslated as "drive out".

beyond any possibility of doubt that there were Israelites there at that time and the Exodus had not as yet taken place."(Meek, p. 31).

On the other hand, Meek takes the biblical mention of the names Pithom and Raamses as proof that Raamses II was the Pharaoh of the oppression; hence the Exodus could not have occurred earlier than his reign, c. 1290–1223 B. C. (Meek, p. 34). Yet he himself notes that: "A date as late as this, however, conflicts seriously with that of the fall of Jericho and continues: "Out of this dilemma there are only two avenues of escape, both of them quite drastic: either to deny the historicity of Ex. 1: 11, as some scholars do, or to assign the conquest of Jericho to an invasion that antedated the Exodus, as we have done, because the fall of Jericho cannot possibly be brought down to a date as late as Rameses II and there is no good reason to doubt the historicity of Exodus 1: 11. In that case Joshua has to be dissociated from Moses or from the capture of Jericho he cannot possibly be both the successor of Moses and the conqueror of Jericho if the Exodus occurred c. 1200 B. C. and the fall of Jericho c. 1400 B. C., as there is every reason to believe. He is so inextricably connected with Jericho that we have to dissociate him from Moses, and again we would account for the disorder in the Old Testament narratives by the fusion of the different sagas of the several groups that eventually coalesced to make the Hebrew people." (Meek, pp. 34–35). Meek does not consider the existence of a third possibility, namely that his basic assumptions that the oppression in Egypt took place in the days of Raamses II, and that the Exodus occurred during Merneptah's reign may be mistaken. Thus Meek concludes that there were two invasions of the country. One of these c. 1400 B. C. was of Israelite tribes under the leadership of Joshua. These tribes "were more natives than Hebrews", and included the tribes of Asher, Dan, Naphtali, Issachar and Zebulun. They entered from the east across the Jordan, and their conquests are in the north of the country (Meek, pp. 42– 44). The second invasion was of Jewish tribes in c. 1200 B. C. under the leadership of Moses It was accomplished from the south and concerns the tribes of Judah, Simeon, Caleb, Othniel and other related tribes. (Meek, pp. 44– 46). According to Meek, the biblical narrative of the conquest is a fusion of the stories of both invasions (p. 45). This he claims on the basis of the supposed disagreement between the Book of Joshua and the Book of Judges concerning the conquest of Debir and other cities, as we have already indicated in an earlier chapter.

The theory of two invasions demands an explanation of how the second group reached Egypt. This is already provided by Meek at the beginning of his book (p. 28), where he refers to the story of the Israelites' attempt to battle uphill (Num. 14: 39–45; Deut. 1: 41–44). Burney had already referred to the same story, but while Burney regards it as referring to a possible successful penetration into Canaan, Meek on the contrary infers from the same story that the Israelites failed and were driven back and that "some of the more venturesome spirits pushed their way to the very borders of Egypt and by the benevolent goverment they were allowed entrance into Wadi–Tumilat, the land of Goshen of the Old Testament." (p. 28). This group leaves Egypt c. 1200 B. C. under the leadership of Moses, and penetrates into Israel directly from the south without touching Jericho Moreover according to Meek, Bedouin tribes, called Habiru and mentioned in the EAT., came from the desert and invaded the region. From the main body of Habiru one group split off and under the leadership of Joshua penetrated into Israel from the south–east and conquered Jericho c. 1400 B. C. On the other hand, the main body of the Habiru continued to advance toward the eastern side of the Jordan. On their advance into the interior of the country ther groups separated from the main body of the Habiru and established the kingdoms of Amon, Moab and Edom, whilst another group, as mentioned, descended to Egypt, which they left c. 1200 B. C. under the leadership of Moses They were joined by other tribes from Sinai. This latter group penetrated Israel directly from the south and did not pass by Jericho at all. (p. 28ff). Albright trying to find a compromise between the various theories on this subject advances the hypothesis that there were two Exoduses. One Exodus came after the expulsion of the Hyksos from Egypt in c. 1550 B. C. but not before 1400 B. C. This was an Exodus of "Josephites" (whom he identifies with the Habiru), who conquered Jericho between c. 1375–1300 B. C. The second Exodus, under the leadership of Moses and Joshua, occurred in 1290 B. C.[96] that is midway in the reign of Raamses II was of "Levites" (Leah tribes and especially the tribe of Judah). Elsewhere he suggests c. 1260 B. C. as the date for the Exodus and c. 1230 B. C. as the year of entry into Israel[97]. According to Albright the Merneptah stele refers to a war fought in Canaan a short time before 1231 B. C.[98]. or c. 1225 B. C.[99].

Rowton,[100] also, agrees that an Exodus of "Levites" took place in c. 1125 B. C, that is in the period of Raamses III.

The common denominator of these theories that underlie most views today (not to say all) is the assumption that the oppression of the Israelites in Egypt took place in the period of Raamses II, the Exodus in the period of Raamses – Merneptah, and that the location of Goshen was in Wadi –

96   Albright, Archaeology and The Date of The Hebrew Conquest of Palestine, BASOR, 58, 1935, pp. 10–18.
   – The Israelite Conquest of Canaan In The Light of Archaeology, BASOR 74, 1939, pp. 11– 23;
   – A Revision of Early Hebrew Chronology, JPOS. 1920 – 21, pp. 68–79
97   Albright, A Revision of Early Hebrew Chronology, JPOS. 1920–21, p. 79
98   Albright, Archaeology and The Date of The Hebrew Conquest, BASOR. 58, 1935, p. 17.
99   Albright. A Revision of Early Hebrew Chronology, JPOS. 1920–1921, p. 79.
100   Rowton, The Problem of The Exodus, PEQ, 1953, p. 46.

Tumilat. All in complete disregard of the biblical narratives about the forty years wandering in the desert, and the 480 years that elapsed from the Exodus till king Solomon, etc. To these scholars the biblical narratives are but a gathering of traditions which were passed on orally until a later period when they were recorded in writing. Thus the story of a single, unified conquest of the whole country is but a fusion of different traditions about different conquests in different periods (Burney, Meek and others). The story of the conquest of Ai really refers to the conquest of the city of Beth–El, but the two conquests were mixed up by the Israelites as the story was passed down the generations. (Albright)[101]. According to these scholars the biblical stories do not belong to the realm of true historical facts, despite the biblical statement that Moses himself wrote about the wanderings of the Israelites – from the day they left Egypt till their arrival in Israel (Canaan), and about the law–giving, which it is difficult to imagine could have been preserved verbatim, had those laws been passed on orally from generation to generation. One of the main reasons for this approach seems to be that the beginning of phonetic writing was assigned to about 1000 B. C., hence it was thought, that the biblical narratives about the Exodus and the conquest had to be oral traditions. Moreover this explanation seemingly contributed to the clarification of some hitherto unsolved problems. Thus when the Protosinaitic inscriptions and the Ras Shamra tablets were discovered, the beginning of the phonetic script was advanced to the middle of the 15th century B. C; Accordingly there is nothing to debar us from accepting that events were recorded in writing –as indeed is attributed by the Bible to Moses and Joshua at the period of the Exodus and the conquest of Israel, Yet the change of conceptual attitude towards writing did not produce a parallel change of conceptual attitude to the biblical narratives, which are still thought to be based on oral traditions. It should be observed that the theories of Burney, Rowley, Meek Albright etc. lack all real basis in archaeology or the Bible. They serve merely to smooth out the contradictions occasioned by the view that the oppression took place in the reign of Raamses–II and that the Exodus occurred in the period of Merneptah. And this in complete disregard of the biblical text, or in Conder's words: "We know nothing of Hebrew history outside the Bible for this period, and the Bible discountenances such suppositions."[102]

The theory that Raamses was the Pharaoh of the oppression also extends to the identification of the place where the Israelites crossed the Red Sea. The Bible particularizes the route taken by the Israelites from the moment they left Goshen–Raamses until they reached Yam Suph (Red–Sea). Their second encampment after Goshen was Succoth, and thereafter "...they took

---

101 Albright, Archaeology and The Date of The Hebrew Conquest of Palestine, BASOR. 1935, p. 15.
102 The Date of The Exodus, PEP. 1896, p. 256

their journey from Succoth, and encamped in Etham, in the edge of the wilderness" (Ex. 13: 20), and here "...the Lord spake unto Moses, saying, Speak unto the children of Israel, that they turn and encamp before Pi–Hahiroth, between Migdol and the Sea, over against Baal–Zephon: before it shall ye encamp by the Sea" (Ex. 14: 1–3)

The journey from Goshen to Yam–Suph, as related in the Bible, took three days. This is confirmed by Josephus who writes: "Quitting the country by the shortest route they arrived on the third day at Beelsephon, a place beside the Red Sea."[103] Accordingly if we assume that Raamses–Goshen was really located in the Wadi–Tumilat area (and this assumption is compelling, once we accept that Raamses II was the Pharaoh of the oppression), it follows logically that the crossing place on Yam–Suph was about three days' walking distance from this area. (i. e. Wadi Tumilat) This has resulted in different theories regarding the crossing place on the Red Sea, corresponding to the different identifications of the places mentioned in the Bible: Succoth, Etham, Baal–Zephon, Migdol and Pi – Hahiroth. Thus Brugsch identified Yam–Suph with the Mediterranean, and he contends that the Israelites never crossed the Red Sea at all, but marched along a narrow strip of shore between the Serbonian lagoon and the Mediterranean.[104]

According to Trumbull[105] the theory of the israelites never crossing the Red Sea etc. was first suggested by Haas at the beginning of the 18th century, and subsequently revived from time to time, by Richter at the end of the same century (1778), by Tierbach (1830,) and by Schleiden (1858) and finally by Brugsch (1874) who supposedly found support for it in Egyptian monuments[106]. Subsequently many other scholars adopted this theory. Thus

---

103 Josephus, Ant. II, 315, Loeb Classical Library, London., MCML. (1950).
104 Brugsch, Egypt Under The Pharaohs, 1891, pp. 95–97; L'exode et Les Monuments Égyptiens, 1875, pp. 8, 12, 19–25.
Brugsch identified Goshen with Phacusa (Fakus), Raamses with Tanis, (San el Haggar), Etham with Kheta (of the Papyri) and with Tel Defneh, while Migdol he believes is the Migdol mentioned in the book of Antonin, situated 18 km. south of Pelusium, which he identifies with Tel Habooa (or Tel Samut) near Kantara. Pi–Hahirot he locates in the Serbonis, while Baal Zephon is placed by him in Mount Kasius in El Kelzeh. He identifies Succoth with T. K. U. of the Papyri. See also: Chester, A Journey To The Biblical Sites In Lower Egypt, PEF, 1880, p. 144.
Conder, The Exodus, PEF. 1883, pp. 85–86. Conder like Robertson Smith disagrees with the identification of Etham with Kheta of the Papyri (ibid. p. 85)
105 Trumbull, Kadesh Barnea, p. 403. See also: Lagrange E, L'itineraire Des Israelites etc. RB. 1900, p. 79
106 Trumbull, ibid. p. 403. See also: Brugsch, L'exode Et Les Monuments Egyptiens, Brugsch bases his belief on a passage from Papyrus Anastasi which tells about a chase after two escaped slaves, and that the pursuer reached T. K. U on the tenth day of the month and Kheta on the twelfth day. Brugsch who identified T. K. U. with Succoth, and Kheta with Etham insists however that the distance between

Noth[107] identifies Baal–Zephon with Mehmedia, Migdol with Tel–el–Hir and Yam–Suph with the Serbonian lake.

According to Eissfeldt the Israelites left Raamses (the site of which he does not identify) and from there went on to El–Gisr, there changing direction by turning through an angle of 90 to as much as 180 degrees, and then advancing toward the Mediterranean where they finally encamped near Pi–Hahiroth; this he does not identify, but places between Migdol – identified by him with Tel–el–Hir and the Mediterranean and Baal–Zephon, which he identifies with Casius in Mehmedia.

Chester traversed himself along the land–strip of the Serbonian lagoon and came to a point where it is cut off by the sea and does not permit passage by foot; and here is his comment: "The map. is a sheer invention and creation of Herr Brugsch's imagination... I now saw that it was so ...all communication with the mainland being here impracticable... the remark may be allowed that it was scarcely fair of Herr Brugsch to construct a map and publish it to the world without having himself visited the place depicted."[108]

Trumbull writes in a similar vein: "Brugsch is clearly at fault in his Exodus theory, and is at variance with positive declarations and exhibits of fact made by himself elsewhere in his writings. He has rearranged sites, changed directions, and mis–stated distances, as if for the purpose of conforming the facts to a preconceived theory of the Exodus." (Kadesh Barnea p. 404). Both Ebers and Renouf insist that Brugsch is entirely wrong in the location of Pi–Hahirot, with Renouf going to the extreme of saying that Brugsch's attempt to identify this site "involves the wrong reading of many words, a fatally erroneous and exploded system of ethymology and false theories of decipherment and language."[109]

Brugsch theory of a Mediterranean passage is completely at variance with the biblical account. Conder, drawing on the survey of the Royal British Engineers and on the Geography of Ptolemy (A. D. 147), concluded that the region of the Serbonian lake did not exist at the time of the Exodus[110]. He strongly disagrees with the views of Brugsch, Scarth and Chester (to be discussed later). Conder's disagreement is based inter alia on the fact that if Brugsch's and Chester's identifications of the places (of the Exodus route), are accepted. it becomes difficult to explain the distances which the Israelites had to traverse by foot. There is also the notion of Barton that in late geological times, the region north of Cairo was a bay of the Mediterranean[111]. About

---

these two places was only one day's walk.
107 Noth, Exodus, pp. 109–110.
108 Chester, ibid. pp. 154–155.
109 Trumbull, Kadesh Barnea, pp. 373–374; 405.
110 Conder, The Exodus, PEF, 1883, pp. 83, 86;
    Topography of The Exodus, PEF. 1880, pp. 231– 234
111 Barton, Archaeology and The Bible, p. 4

the crossing of Yam–Suph the biblical text reads: "Speak unto the children of Israel, that they turn and encamp before Pi–Hahiroth (Ex. 14: 2). The verb "turn" (Hebrew – יָשֻׁבוּ yashuvu) in this verse means in Hebrew a turning back, i. e. either an exact retracing of steps along 'the same track, or a return to the point of departure but not exactly along the same route. If we accept that the Israelites passed along the narrow land–strip of lake Serbonian, it follows on the basis of the biblical statement and of the topography of the region that when ordered to turn back they would have found themselves either at a fairly advanced place along the way to the land of Israel or on the way to the Port–Said region. of today. Indeed Chester has the Israelites advance in the direction of Port Said but then makes them turn back, probably in order to harmonize his theory with this particular biblical verse. Earlier already Conder had pointed to the contradictions and difficulties presented by this verse; and he therefore suggested an emendation; i. e. veyeshvu (=וישבו, abide, dwell, settle), instead of veyashuvu (return).[112] The two suggested solutions, one by Brugsch and the other by Chester, are both implausible and illogical. If the Israelites were already at an advanced point along the way to the Land of Israel, there was neither rhyme nor reason for them to turn back, so that they could cross the Serbonian lagoon, and strike the same path somewhat farther from where they had been when ordered to return? As to the Egyptians, it is hard to imagine they would be so stupid and foolhardy as to pursue the Israelites into this narrow strip of land which permits only a narrow column of people to pass along it? In these circumstances it would be possible to capture only a very few stragglers, at best. It is highly unlikely that the Egyptians were so ignorant of the topography of their own country not to know that this narrow strip of land extended to the other side of the shore? All that was required, therefore, was to send a small contingent of men to bar the Israelites' exit to the shore, and capture them all at one blow with no risk. Moreover, as it is generally agreed that the "Way of the Philistines" should be traced along the sea shore; and hence, since this route must have been known to the Egyptians, there was no reason, topographic or other, to prevent them from barring the way to the Israelites. Was it likely that the builders of the pyramids and conquerors of the East were so completely lacking in savoir faire? If Moses was capable of leading the Israelites out of Egypt, he most probably was familiar with the region, especially as he

---

112 Conder was not aware that "yeshiva"(staying) in biblical Hebrew means a long and not a short stay, as shown by such verses as: "Now the sojourning (Hebrew: moshav) of the children of Israel, who dwelt (Hebrew ; yashvu) in Egypt, was four hundred and thirty years". (Ex. 12: 40)."And Israel dwelt (Hebrew; vayeshev) in the land of Egypt, in the country of Goshen" (Gen. 47: 27). Moreover, if Conder's interpretation is taken as correct it makes little sense to repeat twice the same instruction, i. e. veyeshvu – "stay – (Conder's interpretation) and encamp"

is credited with knowing about a passage along a narrow land–strip of the Serbonian Lagoon. it is nonsense, therefore, to believe that Moses would lead the Israelites in the direction of Port Said, a swampy region in the past as it is today, if his real goal was the Land of Israel. Chester, like Brugsch, believes that the crossing of Yam–Suph was in the area of the Mediterranean, though not along the narrow land–strip of the Serbonian lake, because; "It is remarkable that throughout the direct narrative there is no mention of a Jam–suf or Sea of Reeds at all, the Jam, the sea alone, is spoken of. The Israelites were commanded to encamp not by the Sea of Reeds but by the sea which can scarcely be understood of any other body of water than the Mediterran –ean. In all this direct narrative not one word is said about any Jam–Suf or sea of reeds –the sea alone is spoken of, and that in a manner suitable to the physical features of the region between the Gelse Hemediyeh, the presumed Pi–Hahiroth and El Gelse, mount Cassius, the presumed Baal Zaphon."[113].

According to Chester, the children of Israel left Raamses–Goshen (identified by him as Tell Fakusa) and passed through Succoth to Etham, which he identifies with Tell Defneh; and from there went to Migdol–which he identifies with Tell–El–Hir[114] – and encamped before today's Gelseh–Hemediyeh (ibid. p. 107). As stated, he also "sends" the Israelites in the direction of Port Said and makes them turn back. Gardiner[115] likewise identifies Yam–Suph with the Mediterranean, but locates it in the area of lake Menzelah and not the Serbonian lake. According to him, Raamses (Goshen) was located in the area of Pellusium, Pithom he identifies with Tell–Rotaba and the biblical Migdol with Tell–El–Hir; whereas Baal–Zaphon he believes must be sought in the far north, though he does not state exactly where. He disagrees with the identification of Succoth with T. K. U. mentioned in the Egyptian Papyri. Gardiner's point of departure is that Raamses equals Pi–Ramesu, the Pharaonic city in the Delta; and he supposes that it was the northernmost city from which the Israelites were said to have made their Exodus.[116]

---

113 Chester, Notes on The Topography of The Exodus, PEP. 1881, p. 107.
 Brugsch, also, was of the opinion that the failure to mention Yam–Suph proves the crossing of the Mediterranean sea by the Israelites (L'exode et Les Monuments Egyptiens), p. 5.

114 Chester justifies this identification as follows: "My reasons for suggesting that Tell el Hir is the site of the Migdol of Exodus and the Magdolon of the Greeks are that at the point I found not only the remains of a city of large extent and evidently of considerable importance in ancient times, but that at the same place I found a massive square tower of crude brick, the remains of a strong and important frontier fortress." (ibid. p. 106; see also pp. 145–146)

115 Gardiner, The Geography of The Exodus etc. pp. 87–96
 –Tanis and Pi–Ramesse' A Retractation, JEA (19), 1933, pp. 122–128;
 –The Geography of The Exodus, Recueil Champollion, pp. 203–215.

116 Gardiner, The Geography of The Exodus, Recueil Champollion, p. 209.

According to the Anastasi Papyrus, Pi–Ramessu was located on the edge of the desert[117], whereas the Israelites had to travel some days before they reached Yam–Suph. Consequently Gardiner concludes that Yam–Suph is identical with lake Menzaleh, and that the biblical chronicler "have been ignorant of actual geographical facts and had wrongly identified Pi–Ramessu with Tanis, etc."[118] A view similar to Chester's based on the fact that in the biblical text the word YAM (sea) is frequently mentioned but YAM–SUPH (Sea of Reeds) only twice, is advanced by Scarth.[119] Notwithstanding the very fact that YAM–SUPH does appear in the text, if only twice, leads him to conclude that the crossing must have taken place in an area which on one side was bordered by the YAM–SUPH and on the other by the YAM i. e. the Mediterranean.[120] Indeed, it is hard to conceal one's impatience with these ideas and formulations –they are obviously the product of people not familiar with the Hebrew language for whom the biblical idiom is completely alien. Indeed, it is difficult to understand how they ever found adherents.[121] Admittedly in Exodus 14, the word YAM (sea) only is mentioned: "between Migdol and the sea"' "Encamp by the sea", etc. . However at the beginning of the narration in chapter 13 we read: "But God led the people about through the way of the wilderness of the Red Sea", (Heb. Yam–Suph) (Ex. 13: 18), and at the end of the same narrative, in the Song of the Sea (Heb. Yam–Suph) (Ex. 15: 4); "His chosen captains also are drowned in the Red Sea." Anyone conversant with the Hebrew language knows that the demands of stylistic variation make it unnecessary to repeated a name in full once it has been mentioned at the beginning of a narrative. A specific example is found in the book of Exodus; the Israelites have reached the "Wilderness of Sin" (Ex. 16: 1), but after its first full mention the name always appears in shortened form as "wilderness": "And the whole congregation of the children of Israel murmured against Moses and Aaron in the wilderness" (Ex. 16: 2); "into this wilderness" (Ex. 16: 3); "toward the wilderness" (Ex. 16: 10); "in the wilderness" (Ex. 19: 2). A more striking example perhaps is found in Ex. 19: 2: "For they were departed from Rephidim, and were come to the desert of

117 Gardiner, ibid. p. 210
118 Gardiner, ibid. pp. 210–213.
119 Scarth, A Few Thoughts Upon The Route of The Exodus, PEP. 1882, p. 244.
120 Snaith, (V. T. 1965, pp. 395–398), however, regards the expression of "the depths have covered them" (Ex. 15: 5) as proof that "The Yam Suph was the deep sea away to the south with its tides and great depths, all of it very different from the Mediterranean which was close at hand and the only sea they really knew".
121 Noth, Exodus, pp. 109–110.
Aharoni, Eretz Israel In The Biblical Period, pp. 169–170, (Hebrew), accepts the crossing of Yam Suph in the Serbonian lake and draws a map to correspond. See also Map of the Exodus in the Biblical Atlas (Heb.), Mazar – Shapira. Map in Toldot Eretz Israel etc. p. 142. Edit. Ministry of Defence Israel, 1980.

Sinai and had pitched in the wilderness; and there Israel camped before the Mount." The name of the mountain goes unmentioned and only in verse 11 does one read "Mount Sinai". Subsequently the site is referred to in the text NINE times as merely "mountain"and twice only as "Mount Sinai". Adopting the views of Chester, Brugsch and Scarth it would appear that whenever the word "mountain" is mentioned alone this refers to the mount of Moriah, and likewise the mention of 'desert' only, without addition, invariably refers to the Negev desert. Perhaps this can serve as "proof" that the Israelites never left Israel at all. The belief that the Israelites crossed the Mediterranean Sea because the name Yam–Suph does not appear in full is quite absurd. It so happens that the biblical text frequently mentions the Yam–Suph as the place of the crossing[122], and it is also mentioned similarly in the apocryphal writings[123] as well as in Acts.[124] The name "Yam–Suph" is commonly interpreted as "The Sea of Reeds". Since no reeds grow today on the banks of the Red Sea, this is seen by some scholars to imply that it should not be identified with the biblical Yam–Suph[125]. We shall not inquire here into the meaning of "Yam–Suph" or seek to find out if reeds did or did not grow on its banks, but simply try to learn from the Bible which sea is meant by Yam–Suph. In the account of the locust plague we read: "and the Lord brought an east Heb. – kadim – (קדים) wind upon the land all that day, and all that night; and when it was morning, the east wind brought the locust." (Ex. 1o: 13–14). And further in the same chapter, verse 19: "And the Lord turned a mighty strong west (Heb ים = yam = sea) wind, which took away the locusts, and cast them into the Red Sea; " It is evident from this account that the sea wind (in the A. V. translation: 'west wind') is the opposite to the wind from KEDEM, that is the wind from the east (Heb; kedem = קדם east). This sea wind carried the locusts to the Red Sea (Yam Suph). We conclude therefore:

1. Yam Suph is not to be identified with Yam (i. e. the Mediterranean)

2. Yam Suph must be identified with a sea located east of Egypt and opposite the Mediterranean (i. e. Yam), that is, today's Red Sea.

In contrast to the above ideas we have the views of many other scholars who claim that today's Red Sea is indeed the biblical Yam–Suph but suggest different identifications for the places–Pi–Hahiroth, Baal–Zephon etc. mentioned in the text; and therefore reach different conclusions regarding the place of crossing. Conder believes the crossing was made near Kantara, somewhere between Birket–Ballah and lake Menzaleh,[126] He identifies Pi–

---

122 Jos. 2: 10; 4: 23 ; 24: 6. Deut. 11: 3–5. Ps. 106: 9 ; 136: 3
123 Judith, 5: 13; I Maccabees 4: 10.
124 Acts 7: 36.
125 For example: Wright, Biblical Archaeology, p. 61.
     Javis, The Forty Years Wanderings of The Israelites, PEQ. 1938. pp. 24–2
126 Conder, Kadesh – Barnea, PEP. 1885, p. 25.

Hahiroth with Tell–el–Hir, and as to Baal–Zephon he looks for it somewhere east of Birket–Ballah. He disagrees with Brugsch's identification of Kheta of the Papyri with the biblical Etham, and sides with Robertson Smith who questions this identification.[127] Lucas thinks the place of the crossing was at Lake Timsah. Naville who identifies Pithom with Tell–el–Mashuta, Migdol with Serapeum, and locates Etham in the area of Lake Timsah, considers the crossing was at mid–point between the Bitter Lakes and Lake Timsah.[128] According to Trumper the Israelites made the crossing in the area of today's Bitter Lakes.[129] Petrie believes the crossing was at Serapeum between the Bitter Lakes and Lake Timsah,[130] while Gell claims it was near Shalufeh. He identifies Gebel–Gineffeh with Migdol, and locates Goshen in Wadi Tumilat.[131] Ali Bey Shafi[132] believes that Raamses was located in Kantir, and he identifies Succoth with the ruins of Salieh; Etham he locates in the desert of Salieh; Migdol he identifies with Tell el–Hir; Baal Zephon with Tell Defneh; consequently he argues that the crossing of Yam Suph was made in Lake Ballah. Bourdon places Goshen in Wadi—Tumilat near Seft–el–Henna; Succoth and Etham he identifies with T. K. U and Kheta of the Papyri; and Etham, according to him, should be identified with Serapeum. Moreover he believes that in the past the Red Sea was continuous with the Bitter Lakes, and consequently the crossing of Yam–Suph must have been near Gebel Gineffeh[133]. On the other hand, Stanley[134] claims the Israelites crossed in the region of today's Suez and he identifies Raamses with Tell Mashuta; Pi–Hahiroth with Ageroud, Baal Zaphon with Suez, and Migdol with the Muktalla hills. Ebers, as quoted by Trumbull,[135] identifies Pi–Hahiroth with Ageroud, and Baal Zaphon with Gebel Ataka. Mallon[136], like Gardiner, places Raamses in the Pelusiac region but disagrees with the identification of Succoth with T. K. U. and the Kheta of the Papyri. He also regards today's Red Sea as the biblical Yam Suph, and

–Topography of The Exodus, PEP. 1880, pp. 231–234.
–The Exodus, PEP. 1883, pp. 88–89.
127 Conder, Kadesh–Barnea, p. 24.
128 Lucas, The Route of The Exodus etc, p. 41
Naville, The Exodus and The Crossing of The Red Sea–article in p. 165 – Illustrated Bible Treasury, edited by Wright, London, 1896.
129 Trumper, The Route of The Exodus, PEQ, 1915, pp. 22–29. He identifies Pithom with Tell el Mashuta, and Baal Zaphon with Gebel Kabrit.
130 Petrie, Palestine and Israel, p. 65;
– Egypt and Israel, p. 39.
– Researches In Sinai p. 205.
131 Gell, The Exodus, PEP. 1883, pp. 97–98.
132 Gazelle, Les Localisations De L'exode etc. RB. 1955, p. 331.
133 Bourdon, La Route De L'exode De La Terre De Gesse' A Mara, RB. 1932, pp. 370–392, 538– 549.
134 Stanley, Sinai and Palestine, pp. 37–66.
135 Trumbull, Kadesh Barnea, pp. 406; 423.
136 Mallon, Les Hebreux En Egypte, pp. 162–175.

vehemently disagrees with identifying it as the Mediterranean. According to him this identification is a "Phantasy without any basis whatsoever".[137] Pi–Hahiroth he identifies with the plain south–east of Abu Haas, Migdol with the citadel of Abu–Haas (the tower of Seti I and of Raamses II); Baal Zaphon he identifies with Gebel Ataka. Therefore, according to him, the crossing was in the region of Gebel Ataka. According to Robinson[138] the Israelites crossed the sea south of today's Suez, which they reached from a point not far from the western edge of the Bitter Lakes. Servin[139] identifies Pithom with Tell el–Mashuta; Succoth with Gebel Miriam, south of Lake Timsah; while Etham, he believes, was near Deversoir. Pi–Hahiroth he identifies with Bir–Suis and Baal Zaphon with Erkady. According to him of ancient the Israelites crossed in the area of today's Suez. Hutchinson[140] believes the crossing took place in the region Clyoma – Clysma, while identifying Migdol with Gebel Ataka, Baal Zaphon with Gebel Abu Deraj and Pi–Hahiroth with a ford near Memphis. According to him Succoth has no relation whatever to any place name. According to Hull[141], Prof. Ritter believes that the place of crossing must be sought above Suez, in the region of the ancient bed of Yam Suph and he agrees with this view.

The common denominator to all these ideas is the assumption that Raamses – Goshen was located in Wadi–Tumilat. Having already discussed the factors which led to this assumption we have found it to be basically erroneous, and therefore there is no substance to any of the views founded on it. Now let us see what can be learned from the biblical text about the Exodus. For some reasons scholars believe that several routes led from Egypt to the Land of Israel[142], one along the sea shore–believed to be the "way of the sea" or the "way of the Philistines" mentioned in the Bible, and the second – the "way of Shur", which went from the Negev to the desert of Shur. The third route, which later on became the way for the Moslem pilgrims to Mecca, cut

137 Mallon, ibid, p. 174.
138 Robinson, Biblical Research In Palestine, Vol. I. pp. 84–86.
139 Servin, La Tradition Judeo–Chrétienne De L'exode, BIE, 1948–1949, pp. 315–355.
140 Hutchinson, The Exode, PEP, 1887, p. 244.
141 Hull, On The Relations of Land and Sea, etc. PEP, 1884, p. 139.
142 Clarke, The Exodus, PEP, 1883, p. 91.
      Kent, Biblical Geography And History, pp. 75–76.
      Meek, Hebrew Origins, p. 35.
      Hayness, The Route of The Exodus, PEP, 1896, p. 176
      Trumbull, Kadesh Barnea, pp. 337; 429.
      Bourdon, La Route De L'exode, RB. 1932, pp. 374–376.
      Servin, ibid, p. 319.
      Cassuto, (Heb.), Exegesis on The Book of Exodus, Magnes, Press 1965, pp. 106–107.
      Aharoni, (Heb.), Eretz Israel In Biblical Period., Historical Geography p. 34.

across today's Sinai desert.[143]

In keeping with this the verses in Exodus"...God led them not through the way of the land of the Philistines although that was near; ...But God led the people about, through the way of the wilderness of the Red Sea." (Ex. 13: 17–18)[144]. were interpreted to the effect that the Israelites did not go by the way of the sea shore, though this was the nearest way, but passed across the Sinai desert.[145] The belief that the land of the Philistines was situated on the sea coast is based, among other things, on the assumption that the Philistines are identical to the "Sea Peoples" mentioned in the Raamses III stela, and that they invaded the land of Israel and settled along its southern coastal plain.[146] Moreover there are those who believe that if the name "Philistines" is mentioned in the Exodus narrative, this proves that the Exodus took place in 1200 B. C. or thereabouts. But they conveniently forget that the name "Philistines"is mentioned earlier in connection with the period of Abraham, Isaac and Jacob. The Bible assigns the area of Philistine settlement in the patriarchal age to a more central region. Of Abraham, who dwells in Beer–Sheba, we read: "And Abraham sojourned in the Philistine's land many days" (Gen. 21: 32– 34). Also Isaac dwells at Gerar in the land of the Philistines (Gen. 26), and his slaves quarrel with the slaves of the Philistine king in the Negev region south of Beer–Sheba. Gerar is mentioned as being "between Kadesh and Shur" (Gen. 20: 1); Shur is said to be "Shur, that is before Egypt". (Gen. 25: 18). Josephus, referring to the verse, "And Shaul smote the Amalekites from Havila until thou comest Shur, that is over against Egypt" (ISam. 15: 7) speaks of "...conquering the whole district extending from Pelusium in Egypt to the Red Sea."[147] Elsewhere (Ant. II, 323) he writes: "The Philistines.... for their country was coterminous with that of the Egyptians". Therefore Gerar was located somewhere near today's Suez. I discovered that Bar–Deroma had already come to the same conclusion,[148] and among the points in support of his conclusion he also quotes the Samaritan version of the verse in Genesis; "And the border of the Canaanites was from Sidon, as thou comest to Gerar, unto Gaza, as thou goest unto Sodom, and Gomorrah, and Admah, and Zeboim, even unto Lasha." (Gen. 10: 19) and is: "From the great river, the river Prath until the last sea". In one place in the Bible the

---

143 Trumbull, ibid. pp. 337– 364.
144 Other versions read: ". . by the way of the land of the Philistines'...by the way of the wilderness by the Red Sea".
145 Hull, ibid. p. 138.
Servin, ibid. pp. 331, 319.
Palmer, Desert of The Exodus. pp. 35–36.
146 Hull, ibid. p. 138.
Palmer, ibid. pp. 35– 36.
147 Josephus, Ant. vi, 140.
148 Bar Deroma, (Heb.) Wezeh Gevul Haares, 1958, pp. 19–28.

Dead Sea is also called The Sea of the Philistines.[149] In other words, according to the Bible the land of the Philistines in the patriarchal age was not situated along the coast but mainly in the southern part of the country from Beer–Sheba towards the Sinai desert up to the Egyptian border.[150] During the period of the Judges and of King David we already read about Philistines in Ziklag, Timnath, Sorek and elsewhere. According to the Bible, Ziklag was situated in the region of the cities on the border of Edom in the Negev (Jos. 15: 20), while Timnath was in the mountainous region (Jos. 15: 57) Therefore, in antiquity, the "way of the land of the Philistines"was not necessarily a way that passed along the coast but a way that passed in the centre of the Negev. Confirmation of this may be found in the story of Jacob travelling to Egypt to visit his son Joseph, (Gen. 46: 1–5): "And Israel took his journey with all that he had, and came to Beer Sheba...And God spake unto Israel...fear not to go down into Egypt...". Thus in order to reach Egypt Jacob (Israel) first descended to Beer–Sheba, which, as we have seen, is in the land of the Philistines; and came to Egypt from there, and not by the way of the coast. That this indeed was the way to Egypt we learn from another verse (Gen. 26: 1–2): "...And Isaac went unto Abimelech King of the Philistines unto Gerar; and the Lord appeared unto him, and said, Go not down into Egypt; ". This warning tells us that Gerar was a station on the way to Egypt. But this Gerar was located in Philistine country, south of Beer–Sheba, between "Shur that is before Egypt" and Kadesh. It is said about Abraham: "And Abraham went up out of Egypt... into the south (Heb. – into the Negev) (Gen. 13: 1).

Therefore the way from Egypt leads Abraham to the south (Negev), but this way does not pass along the coast. Again in Genesis (50: 10–11) we read about Joseph who goes up to Hebron to bury his father in the Machpelah cave: "And they came to the threshing – floor of Atad, which is beyond Jordan and there they mourned...wherefore the name of it was called Abel–Mizraim which is beyond Jordan". Hence, in order to get from Egypt to Hebron Joseph did not go along the coast. Moreover it is reasonable to assume that if there had been a shorter way along the coast Abraham, Isaac, Jacob and Joseph would have chosen to take it rather than travel the longer way through a barren desert. For them the Philistines were no obstacle, and

---

149 Ex. 23: 31."And I will set thy bounds from the Red Sea even unto the sea of the Philistines, and from the desert unto the River."

150 In 1Sam. 31: 7, we read: "And when the men of Israel that were on the other side of the valley, and they that were on the other side of the Jordan, saw that the men of Israel fled, and that Saul and his sons were dead, they forsook the cities, and fled; AND THE PHILISTINES CAME AND DWELT IN THEM". (emphasis – N. G.). This verse alludes to the Philistines' expansion, after winning their battle against the Israelites, into the interior of the Country; similarly it may be supposed they also expanded their hold from the desert of the Negev to the cities of Gaza, Ashdod etc. on the sea shore.

anyway they unavoidably had to pass through Philistine territory in their descent to Egypt.

To summarize: The "Way of the Philistines" is identical to the "Way of Shur" and led to Egypt through Beer–Sheba, the Negev desert, Gerar and the Shur desert. This way did not pass along the coast because the region in the north of Egypt was full of impassable swamps.[151] One may note in this connection that Herodotus writes about Phanes the Halicarnasian who advised Cambyses on how to pass the desert into Egypt, for "the only entrance into Egypt is by this desert".[152] He specifically mentions only a single entrance into Egypt. Reverting to the biblical statements": ...that God led them not through the way of the land of the Philistines, although that was near; ...But God led the people about, through the way of the wilderness of the Red Sea."; on the basis which we may conclude that the way to the land of the Philistines led across the desert; though even if conceivably there existed an alternative way along the coast, this would also have to partly traverse the desert because of the geographic formation of the region. Why therefore the biblical emphasis on "through the way of the wilderness of the Red Sea"? The above verses from the book of Exodus (Ex. 13: 17–18) served many scholars in the past, and even today, as evidence that the Land of the Philistines was located where the Israelites dwelled. In support, these same scholars maintain that the Israelites were settled on the border of Egypt and not in Egypt itself, "for every shepherd is an abomination unto the Egyptians". As shown already, it may be presumed that what is termed in the Bible "the Land of Egypt" refers to the district town only. Further, it may be noted that in the verse: "that God led them not by the way of the Land of the Philistines although that was near...", the words"that was near" (Hebrew: – קרוב הוא karov hu) are in the masculine in Hebrew, and therefore refer to "way" (Heb. – דרך. derekh) and not to "Land" (of the Philistines). The word "land" (Heb. –ארץ eretz) is almost always in biblical Hebrew in the feminine (Is. 1: 2 ; 32: 1; Gen. 1: 2; Deut. 32: 1; Mi. 1: 2); whereas "derekh"(=way) is mostly in the masculine (Je. 31: 9; Deut. 28: 7; Ezk. 21: 24; 26; 23: 13; 47: 2; Ps. 101: 2 ; Pr. 12: 15; 14: 12; 2Kn. 6: 19 Is. 30: 21; 1Kn. 13: 10; 12)[153]. This means that

---

151 Trumbull, Kadesh Barnea, p. 347– quotes from an article in the Edinburgh Review (Jan. 1877), which states that this region of Egypt was as yet covered by water during the period of the Exodus. However, he does not agree with this statement.

152 Herodotus–III, 4–5: Rawlinson trans. p. 147; –de Sélincourt trans. ; Penguin Classics p. 155.

153 It should be noted that contrary to English, Hebrew employs different conjugations for masculine and feminine nouns. Eliezer Ben–Iehuda in his Thesaurus of the Hebrew Language (Hebrew) lists to the word "eretz" (land, earth) as exclusively in the feminine gender. Ibn Jannāh in his book "Sefer Harikma"(Hebrew) Chap. 39 (38) p. 386, writes that the word "Eretz" is rarely used in the masculine, as its prevailing gender is the feminine .

the WAY which leads to the land of the Philistines was near the settlement area of the Israelites (i. e. Goshen), but it does not imply that the land of the Philistines was in actual fact near the settlement area; on the contrary, it could be a considerable distance away. Josephus[154] even states: "He did not conduct his people by the direct route to Palestine.". Also he refers to "route" (way) and not to "land". Likewise Sforno, who explains: "because that route and its end was near to Egypt". Accordingly the verses: "that God led them not through the way of the Land of the Philistines, although that was near, for God said, lest per adventure the people repent when they see war, and they return to Egypt", should be understood to mean: the reason that Moses did not take the Israelites by the way that leads to the Land of the Philistines was not to avoid fighting against the Philistines, as is commonly believed[155], but that he wanted to avoid confronting the Egyptians right from the start of the Exodus. He feared that if the Israelites would have to engage in war immediately they would want to return to Egypt (Heb. – mitzraim), (i. e. not the land but the district town) without delay. Hence Moses avoids the main route which leads to the land of the Philistines, though it passes nearby, and leads his people through the desert, "But God led the people about through the way of the wilderness of the Red Sea". The Hebrew text reads: "vayasev elohim et haam derekh hamidbar yam suph ״ויסב אלהים את העם דרך המדבר״ –"ים סוף" by the way of the desert to Yam Suph; or in other words, God led the people through the desert in the direction of Yam Suph (Red Sea). In order to reach Yam–Suph the people of Israel had to cross the desert. It is unlikely that the biblical text here refers to a route leading to the desert as happened in connection with "the way of the Philistines". Philological examination rules out this possibility. Moreover, why should "Yam Suph" appear in this verse if it is presumed to refer to a route leading to the desert? . If it is claimed that the text meant to explain that the Israelites reached the desert of Sinai by way of the Red Sea, then why so much detail? This is entirely unnecessary since any conceivable land route from Egypt to Canaan must cross the desert, not excluding the route along the coast (if we grant that it existed). Moreover any such route has to traverse the Red Sea also, so the phrase: "...derekh hamidbar Yam–Suph" which must be translated: "by way of the wilderness to the Red Sea", is meant to show that the Israelites' goal was YAM–SUPH and that in order to reach it they had to traverse a desert. This is also brought out in Onkelus Aramaic translation, "vehaskhar adonai yat ama orakh midbara leyama de suph", (: And God led the people go round about by the way of the desert TO Yam– Suph"). Seadiah ben Joseph (Rabbi Saadia Gaon)(892–942

---

154 Ant. II, 323.
155 See for example: Hull, On The Relations of Land And Sea, etc. PEP. 1884, p. 138.

A. D.) translates (into Arabic) "tarik albar ili bakhar alkulzum", by the way of the wilderness to the Red sea.

Rashi interprets: "Yam Suph – as if to Yam Suph".[156] The Vulgata translates: "Per viam deserti quae est Iuxta mare Rubrum". Sforno explains: "That they will go to Yam Suf through the desert". The French translation reads as well[157]: "Mais dieu fit faire au peuple un detour par le chemin du desert VERS la mer, " i. e. through the desert TO Yam Suph (in both translations), meaning that the desert precedes Yam Suph. On the other hand, the standard English translation[158] reads: "But God led the people about, through the way of the wilderness of the Red Sea."[159] The English translators confused "through" with "by the way"; and where they should have translated "by the way of the wilderness to the Red Sea", they wrote "through the way...of..." etc., thus changing the sense of the phrase completely. The same mistake occurred in their translation of the verse "that God led them not through the way of the land of the Philistines although that was near". Instead of translating "by the way...to the land of the Philistines", they translated "through the way of the land of the Philistines". It seems to me that the faulty translation of these verses is one of the main reasons for the misunderstandings that have beset the subject of the Exodus. Many scholars of this period had a British academic background, and made use of the standard English Bible translation for understanding this verse.[160]

To sum up: To reach the Red Sea (Yam-Suph) the Israelites crossed a desert, and as stated in the biblical text, they travelled about three days till they reached "Etham in the edge of the wilderness". From Etham they went on to the Red Sea. For some reason most scholars believe that the phrase: "in the edge of the wilderness" means "at the beginning of the wilderness"; and therefore Etham was located at the beginning of the today's desert of Sinai.[161] But the Hebrew text reads, katze – in Hebrew the word katze = קצה

---

156 see Pentateuch with targum Onkelus etc. Rosenbaum–Silberman.
157 Translation L. Segond
158 London edit., The British and Foreign Bible Society.
159 In the American, (Gideons Bible) 1901, the translation reads: "By the way of the wilderness by the Red Sea".
160 For example: Conder, The Exodus, PEF. 1883, p. 89.
   Pickering – Clarke, The Exodus, PEF. 1883, pp. 90 – 91.
   Smith, The Route of The Exodus, PEF. 1883, p. 223.
   Wright, Biblical Archaeology, pp. 60–61.
   Gardiner, The Geography of The Exodus, Recueil Champollion, p. 205.
161 See Cassuto, (Hebrew) – Exegesis On The Book Of Exodus, p. 108; who writes: "They encamped in Etham at the edge of the desert, that is the last station in settled land near the desert See also: Hull, On The Relations of Land and Sea etc. PEP . 1884, p. 138.
   Trumper, The Route of The Exodus, PEQ, 1915, p. 25.
   Hutchinson, The Exode, PEP. 1887, p. 242.
   Servin, La Tradition Judeo–Chrétienne De L'exode, BIE. 1949, p. 332.

is derived from ketz ,קץ = meaning 'end' . Therefore this particular phrase means that Etham existed at the end of a desert and not at its beginning. Moreover Onkelus' Aramaic reads: "Etham bistar midbara" (Etham at the end of the desert). Seadiah ben Joseph (Saadia Gaon) translates (Arabic)"fi taraf al baria" (=At the end of the desert), and so does the Vulgate: "Etham in extremis finibus solitudinis."

I believe the prime causes of this mistaken understanding are: a) The inaccurate English translation of the Hebrew text of the Bible, used by many scholars writing on the subject. This particular translation reads "edge of the wilderness", which in English can mean in this context either 'the beginning of" or 'the end of ' the wilderness. b) "Etham" is also part of the compound name "desert of Etham", which is situated on the other (i. e. the eastern) side of the Red Sea. From this it has been inferred that "Etham" was a place at the beginning of the desert of Etham[162] c) As already demonstrated, the verse: "But God led the people about through the way of the wilderness " was mistranslated and therefore erroneously understood, which misunderstanding inexorably led to the belief that Etham was situated at the beginning of the desert.

If we examine the biblical text as written it will be seen that there is no room for any mistake. The Israelites crossed a desert which extended well inside Egyptian territory and not outside it. Only after they had crossed this desert did they reach Etham at the extreme end of it. AND ONLY AFTER THIS DID THEY REACH THE RED SEA. We read in Exodus: "For Pharaoh will say of the children of Israel, they are entangled in the land, the wilderness hath shut them in." (Ex. 14: 3). This is said about the Israelites while they are still near the Red Sea, AND BEFORE THEY CROSSED IT. This being so, what meaning must one attribute to the phrase: "the wilderness hath shut them in"? If indeed it referred to the desert behind the Sea, one would have to write, "the Sea hath shut them in", and not the desert, since obviously the sea was then the initial obstacle yet ahead of the desert. It was the crossing of the sea which the Israelites saw as the great miracle to be remembered over the generations and celebrated in the Song of Deliverance. If indeed the enormous obstacle of the desert was still before them, what is the rejoicing for? Accordingly Pharaoh's words and the disposition of the Israelites must

Chester, A Journey To The Biblical Sites In Lower Egypt, PEP. 1880, p. 145.
Naville, The Geography of The Exodus, JEA. 1924, p. 39.
Robinson, Biblical Research In Palestine, Vol. I, p. 80. writes: "On the second day they reached Etham 'in the edge of the wilderness', what wilderness? the Israelites, after passing the Red Sea are said in Exodus to have gone three days march into the desert of Shur but in Numbers the same track is called the desert of Etham, it hence follows that Etham probably lay on the edge of this eastern desert perhaps not far from the present head of the Gulf or Canal"
162 Nu. 33: 8.

be understood as follows: On one side was the sea (Yam Suph) which barred the way to the Israelites and on the other side extended a desert INSIDE THE TERRITORY OF EGYPT. And wherever there was an open passage, the Egyptians were stationed barring the way. Now we understand the tactics and the wonder attached to the crossing of Yam Suph. The Egyptians were confident they could trap the fugitives, since the net was spread all around them; and yet lo and behold, the Israelites cross the Sea and escape. This was not forseen by the Egyptians, since they had not considered it possible. Topographically there is only one desert in Egyptian territory which takes three days walking to traverse in order to reach Yam Suph, and that is the Arabian Desert which at its far end extends to the suburbs of present–day Cairo (ancient On). This means that the area through which the Israelites travelled to the Red Sea must be looked for south of Cairo and not north of it. South of Cairo a wadi cuts across the desert which today is called Wadi et–Tih. Hutchinson[163] calls it Wadi –Musa (Valley of Moses), and according to Bedouin tradition, the Israelites passed through it when they left Egypt. On a map in La Jonquiere's book (Napoleonic era), it is named "Vallee de L'Egarment"[164]. Et–Tih is today also the name of a desert in the region where according to the Bible the desert of Etham was located[165]: that is this name also appears on the other, eastern side of Yam Suph as happened also with the name Etham. Perhaps Et–tih is a corruption of Etham Hence, if we calculate that the Israelites crossed the Arabian desert in three days' walking, arriving on the third day at Yam Suph (as is also corroborated by Josephus)[166], their point of departure, Goshen, must have been somewhere near today's Cairo, that is in the region of On and Memphis. This conclusion also accords with the opinion of Josephus and the Septuagint.

It should be noted that the sites of the cities of On and Memphis contain remains from the periods of Thutmosis III and Raamses II. In the memorial inscriptions of Raamses III incised on the walls of the Temple of Medinet Habu inThebes, he is called Lord of On[167]. In a Temple inscription at Karnak the city of On is called "City of Tum"[168], that is "Pi–Tum". It is well known that Raamses III renamed places with his own name. He also erased from the memorial inscriptions the names of earlier kings and substituted his own.[169]

163 Hutchinson, The Exode, PEP. 1887, pp. 243–244.
164 C. de La Jonquiere, L'expedition D'egypte 1798–1801, Tome II. p. 472 (valley of the wanderings). see also Stanley, Sinai and Palestine, p. 28.: Baedeker's Egypt etc. 1908, p. 114.
165 This desert is called by de la Jonquiere p. 496, "Desert de Tieh ou de l'Egarement", namely the desert of the wanderings. Let us note that in Arabic today the word "Tieh" means desert.
166 Ant. II, 315.
167 Trumbull, Kadesh Barnea, p. 371; Rowley, From Joseph To Joshua, p. 26.
168 Breasted, Records, Vol. III, p. 241, § 576.
169 Maspero, The Struggle of The Nations, Egypt, Syria, And Assyria, 1910, p. 421

This may explain the biblical anachronism of using the name Raamses to designate Goshen. The story of the worship of the calf in the desert (and later also the worship of the calves at Dan and Beth El, which were intended to replace the religious center in Jerusalem), also points to the Israelites' stay in the region of On and Memphis. As is known, in these districts (nomuses), this cult was linked to the deities Apis and Mnevis which are represented in the form of a calf, unlike the cults in the nomuses of the delta region which were not linked to these deities. According to Naville, who identifies Pithom with Tell el–Mashuta, the deity emblems that were found in the Tell are of the Hawk and Sphinx.[170] After I had reached my own conclusions, I found that Hutchinson[171] had already anticipated me by suggesting that the Exodus from Egypt to Yam Suph was made by the way of the Arabian desert. But he based his belief on Bedouin tradition and not on the biblical text. Moreover he, like most scholars, claims that Goshen was in the region of Wadi Tumilat, and thus in order to have the Israelites pass across the Arabian desert, he 'leads' them from Wadi Tumilat to On, and from there he has them continue through the desert to Yam Suph. If they had come along this route (i. e. from Wadi Tumilat to Yam Suph) this would have meant a journey on foot of about eleven days, yet this is clearly contradicted by the biblical text, and also by Josephus. According to Lagrange[172], Sicard thought the Exodus started out from Memphis and that Yam Suph was crossed near Towarig.

The puzzle is why did the Egyptians wait till the Israelites reached the Red Sea, and only then follow after them. Strange they should allow three days to pass before the Israelites left Goshen, and only then engage them. I submit that the answer to this question provides the explanation to the entire episode of the Exodus. In the biblical account we read: "And it was told the king of Egypt that the people fled: and the heart of Pharaoh and of his servants was turned against the people, and they said, Why have we done this, that we have let Israel go from serving us?"[173].

When Pharaoh was told that the people had fled, his reaction was: "Why have we done this, that we have let Israel go?" There is no mention here of an escape of the Israelites but letting (them) go. About "letting go" we read elsewhere in the Bible: "And it came to pass, when Pharaoh had LET the people go,"[174] "Let my people go, that they may hold a feast unto me in the wilderness"[175]; "Yet will I bring one plague more upon Pharaoh, and upon Egypt; afterwards he will LET YOU GO hence: when he shall LET YOU

170 Naville, The Geography of The Exodus, JEA, 1924, p. 35.
171 Hutchinson, The Exode, PEP. 1887, pp. 235–250.
172 Lagrange, Itinéraire Des Israelites Du Pays De Gessen Aux Bord Du Jourdain, RB. 1900, (1), p. 79.
173 Ex. 14: 5.
174 Ex. 13: 17.
175 Ex. 5: 1.

GO, he shall surely thrust you out hence altogether."[176]. Pharaoh calls Moses and Aaron to him by night and tells them: "Rise up, and get you forth from among my people, both you and the children of Israel; and go, serve the Lord, as ye have said. Also take your flocks and your herds, as ye have said, and be gone; and bless me also."[177]These verses and many others do not indicate an escape of the Israelites but point to their being sent away, why then; "And it was told the king of Egypt that the people FLED"?

Let us return to the verses in Exodus 12: "Rise up, and get you forth from among my people... and go, serve the Lord, as ye have said. Also take your flocks and your herds, as ye have said". These verses will be understood in the light of the argument between Moses and Pharaoh reported in an earlier chapter of the Book of Exodus. When Moses addresses Pharaoh: "We will go THREE DAYS' journey INTO THE WILDERNESS, and sacrifice to the Lord our God" (Ex. 8: 27; In Heb. text 8: 23), and Pharaoh asks: "but who are they that shall go?" (Ex. 10: 8). To which Moses answers: "We will go with our young and with our old, with our sons and with our daughters, with our flocks and with our herds will we go; for we must hold a feast unto the Lord" (Ex. 10: 9). But Pharaoh opposes this and agrees only to let the men go: "Not so: go now ye that are men, and serve the Lord, for that ye did desire."(Ex. 10: 11). Then Egypt was smitten with the plagues of locusts and darkness, until Pharaoh agreed for all the people to leave but without their sheep and cattle."Go ye, serve the Lord; only let your flocks and your herds be stayed; let your little ones also go with you". (Ex. 10: 24). But Moses insists and argues with Pharaoh "...Thou must give us also sacrifices and burnt offerings that we may sacrifice unto the Lord our God. Our cattle also shall go with us."[178]. Again a number of plagues strike Pharaoh and his people till he agrees at last: "Rise up, and get you forth from among my people ...and go, serve the Lord, as ye have said. Also take your flocks and your herds, as ye have said". This verse should be understood as indicating the end of the negotiations between Moses and Pharaoh; and indeed three days later it is said; "and it was told the king of Egypt that the people fled: ...why have we done this that we have let Israel go...". From the biblical narrative it may be understood that Moses asks Pharaoh's permission for a temporary cessation of work so that he and his people can go and worship God in the desert, inside Egyptian territory proper (the area of today's Arabian desert). Moses gets Pharaoh's consent because the king does not suspect that the Israelites would ever think of escaping from a desert situated in the heart of Egyptian territory. Moses pretends that he is entering with the Israelites into the desert, that is, penetrating deeper into Egyptian territory, but in fact he crosses it

---

176 Ex, 11: 1
177 Ex. 12: 31–32
178 Ex. 10: 25–26.

transversely and comes out on its opposite side near the Red Sea (See Map). To carry out this mission about three days are needed, and hence Moses' request: "We will go three days' journey into the wilderness". This gives him a period of several days without having to face Egyptian intervention (at least six days –three days for going, and three for returning), and so he avoids a confrontation within the territory of Egypt itself. It is only after three days[179], when the Israelites emerge into the open on the opposite side of the desert, that the Egyptians grasp Moses' real aim "And it was told the king of Egypt that the people fled, "It is only then that Pharaoh sets out to pursue the escaping slaves in order to bring them back But Pharaoh's pursuit miscarries, or the escape of the Israelites though described as being made in haste, was meticulously planned down to the last detail, as we know from the biblical. account. Already on the tenth of the month, Moses informs the Israelites to be prepared for the fourteenth of that month. Why this particular date? Because of the fact that the Hebrew months are reckoned by the moon; Josephus also notes that the Israelites left Egypt "in the month of Xanticus on the fifteenth by lunar reckoning." (Ant. I, 318). Hence the Exodus from Raamses–Goshen took place at midnight between the 14th and the 15th of the month, when the moon was nearly full. It may be assumed that the Israelites arrived at their next stop Succoth, on the 15th of the month, at Etham on the 16th and that the Red Sea crossing was made on the night of the 17th of the month, when the moon is still full, that is to say, at the MAXIMUM TIDAL variation OF THE MONTH. Furthermore, the month is the spring month of Nissan, approximately equivalent to the months April–May, which in this part of the world is the period of MAXIMUM HIGH AND LOW TIDE OF THE YEAR. Moses can be expected to have been familiar with these variations of nature and exploited them to his purpose. This also arises from the biblical account of the Red Sea crossing: "The one came not near the other all the night... and the Lord caused the sea to go back by a strong east wind all that night."(Ex. 14: 20–22). From this follows that for most of the night the Israelites waited near the sea without crossing it, and did so only during the early hours of the morning, that is at the end of the second night watch, [180] "And it came to pass that in the morning watch the Lord looked unto the host of the Egyptians...And took their chariot wheels, that they drave them heavily." (Ex. 14: 24–25), and further on in the same chapter, verse 27: "...and the sea returned to its strength when the morning appeared". This means that the sea did not return to its strength all at once but only gradually, from the morning watch until the break of dawn (from about 2 o'clock to about 5–6 o'clock in the morning), that is during the

---

179 According to the Bible they left in the middle of the night; hence, till the first encampment they marched about one and a half days.
180 The night is divided into three watches.

period when high tide follows ebb tide. The problem constituted by high and low tides in this sea was dealt with earlier, inter alia, by Hutchinson[181] and Servin[182]. Hutchinson also dwells on the fact that there was a full moon when the Israelites left Egypt; but by assuming that Goshen was located in Wadi Tumilat, and allowing eleven days to pass for the Israelites to reach Yam Suph, he deprives this fact of much of its cogency. Servin, who bases his arguments on data from a number of hydrographic surveys, notably French and English, states there exist quantitative and qualitative differences in the tidal picture of the Mediterranean Sea compared to that of the Red Sea. The tides of the Mediterranean are diurnal and reach their peak at 10 a. m., their upper height being 40 cm., whereas the tides of the Red Sea are semi–diurnal and reach their peak at 6 a. m, their upper height being 2 meters. These data lead him to conclude that the biblical account of a sea crossing and drowning of the Egyptians is appropriate ONLY for the Yam Suph (Red sea), and not for the Mediterranean.

The Israelites probably crossed Yam Suph in an area where during the annual and monthly ebb tides the sea floor was exposed to view or the water shallow enough to permit passage. Assuming that in time part of the Red Sea would dry up then the place where the Israelites crossed presumably was the first to be dry. Hence there is no reason to look today for the place of crossing in the Sea, as most scholars do (Hutchinson, Trumper, Brugsch etc.). Hull[183], and also Coode,[184] note that modern scholars tend to believe that the topography of the area in the remote past was identical to what it is today; notwithstanding, they believe that Yam Suph (about 1. 6 km. wide and 6–7 meters deep) in the past extended to the Bitter Lakes. This is also borne out by the geology of the land region between the Suez Bay and the Bitter Lakes, which contains fossils of shells, corals as well as fossilized animals of the species still found in the gulf of Suez today. Naville, Crace, Trumper, Watson, Renan, Bourdon, Lagrange and others also share the above view.[185] Naville cites a survey conducted over many years by Le Pêre and Du

---

181 Hutchinson, ibid. p. 243
182 Servin, La Tradition Judeo–Chretienne de L'exode, BIE, 1944, pp. 344–345.
183 Hull, On The Relations of Land and Sea etc., PEP. 1884, pp. 137–141.
184 Coode, The Passage of The Israelites across The Red Sea, PEP. 1885, pp. 97–99.
185 Naville, ibid. p. 37.
      Crace, The Routeof The Exodus, PEQ. 1915, p. 64.
      Trumper, The Route of The Exodus From Pithom To Marah, PEQ. 1915, p. 23.
      Watson, Egypt and Palestine, PEQ. 1915, p. 133.
      Renan, Histoire Du Peuple D'israel, p. 163.
      Bourdon, La Route De L'exode, RB. 1932, pp. 378, 538.
      Lagrange, ibid. pp. 77, 80.
      Hull, ibid, p. 137.
      Javis, The Forty Years Wanderings of The Israelites, PEQ. 1938, pp. 25–41.

Bois Aymé which finally produced the same conclusion.[186] Herodotus (II, 5) holds that all of Egypt, except the Nomus (region) of Thebes, was a swampy area at the time of the founding of Memphis

Where did the crossing of Yam Suph take place? The Bible tells us the exact place: "And the Lord spake unto Moses, saying, Speak unto the children of Israel, that they turn and encamp before Pi–Hahiroth, between Migdol and the sea, over against Baal–Zephon: before it shall ye encamp by the sea. For Pharaoh will say of the children of Israel, they are entangled in the land, the wilderness hath shut them in." (Ex. 14: 1–3) Despite the many attempts to identify the places mentioned– Pi–Hahiroth, Baal–Zephon and Migdol there is as yet no unanimity of opinion. However, I believe, the identification problem if examined from an angle hitherto neglected, namely the"interrelational" angle, will make it possible to locate them exactly. The phrase "between Migdol and the sea" may be seen to refer either to the Israelites or to Pi–Hahiroth, that is: in one version: You the children of Israel will encamp between Migdol and the sea, before Pi–Hahiroth; or in the second version "you will encamp before Pi–Hahiroth", which is situated between Migdol and the Sea, However for some reason it was always understood to mean: 'the Israelites encamped between Migdol and the Sea[187]. But this disagrees with the text in Numbers (33: 7–8) "And they removed from Etham, and turned again unto Pi-Hahiroth, which is before Baal–Zephon: and they pitched before Migdol"; "before Migdol" is at variance with "between Migdol and the sea", especially when it already had been preceded by "before Pi–Hahiroth". Indeed there are scholars[188] who in their explanation of this difference have been tempted to take the easy way out by claiming that the books of Numbers and Exodus were not written in the same period, hence the disparity of the versions. But this explanation does not square with the biblical verses: "before ye shall encamp by the sea" or "but the Egyptians pursued after them...and overtook them encamping by the sea". (Ex. 14: 9), since these state that the Israelites were ordered to encamp on the sea shore[189] AND NOT between Migdol and the sea. And it was on the sea shore that the Israelites were overtaken by the Egyptians. Thus it may be understood from the foregoing that the Israelites were ordered to encamp on the sea shore, before Pi–Hahiroth, which is situated

---

Mallon, Les Hebreux En Egypte, Orientalia, 1921, p. 176.
Hayes, Most Ancient Egypt, JNES, 1964, p. 77.
186 Naville, ibid. pp. 36–37.
187 See for Example: Trumper, ibid. p. 27.
Conder, The Exodus, P.E.P. 1883, p. 86.
Noth, The Exodus, p. 110.
Cassuto, (Hebrew) Exegesis on The Book of Exodus, 1965, p. 110.
188 For example: Clarke, The Exodus, P.E.P, 1883, p. 95.
189 Compare with Ex. 15: 27, "and they encamped there by the waters".

between Migdol and the sea, and it logically follows therefore, that they also encamped before Migdol, (see Nu. 33: 7). This also agrees with the the Latin translation: "Pi–Hahiroth quae est inter Magdaloum et Mare."The fact that the phrase "between Migdol and the sea" had to be added to qualify Pi–Hahiroth indicates that the place of encampment was not a clearly defined site–and this qualifying addition came to define it more precisely. The meaning of the name Pi–Hahiroth is unclear. Gesenius believes it is derived from a Coptic word meaning "place of sedge", while Brugsch, for some reason, explains it as: "entrance to the Gulfs". Gardiner interprets it as: "Pi–Ḥthrt", that is, "House of Hator"[190]. Servin connects it with the name of the deity Ha. Seadiah ben Joseph (Rabbi Saadia Gaon) translates "fam alhirat". Onkelus, (Aramaic translation) translates pum hirata that is, both see the name derived from the Aramaic–Hebrew pe = mouth. Thus the name may perhaps be explained on the analogy of Hebrew expressions like pi – nahar (=river mouth); pi–yeor (Is. 19: 7) pi – pahat, etc. The prefix "pi" indicates that Pi Hahiroth denotes an entrance to something of long extension, like a river mouth, and therefore the addition "between Migdol and the sea" is meant to define the precise place of encampment It is possible that Pi–Hahirot means "Mouth of the Rocks", as interpreted by Rashi (Heb. pi-haselaim). Josephus too states that the Egyptians caught the Israelites in a narrow passage between the sea and the rocks (Ant. II, 324–325). Whether this interpretation is correct or not is of very little importance to my mind. Where was Pi – Hahiroth located and where was the site of the Israelites' encampment? According to Exodus (14: 1–4) the Israelites were orderd to encamp "before Pi–Hahiroth". According to Numbers (33: 7), they encamped "unto Pi–Hahiroth"(Hebrew: al pi hahiroth – על פי החירת) meaning "by Pi–Hahiroth" and the Egyptians "overtook them encamping by the sea beside Pi–Hahiroth before Baal–Zephon" (Ex. 14: 9). Taken together these verses tell us that the Israelites encamped somewhere before Pi–Hahiroth, yet very close to it, as is indeed Indicated by the Hebrew original "by Pi–Hahiroth" (Hebrew: al pi – hahiroth – (על פי החירת)[191]

In light of the biblical text the following may now be established:

a) Pi–Hahiroth is situated between Migdol and the sea;

b) The Israelites encamped on the sea shore before Pi–Hahiroth and very close to it.

c) The Israelites encamped before Baal–Zephon and over against it (Heb.: nokhah = נכח i. e. opposite it).[192]

---

190 Gardiner, The Geography of The Exodus, Recueil Champollion, p. 213.

191 Compare: "The top of the Pisgah, that is over against Jericho (Deut. 44: 1) (Heb: al pnei Jericho). "by Jordan near Jericho" (Heb. al yarden Jericho) (Nu. 33: 48); "And the Canaanites dwell by the sea"(Heb.: al hayam) (Nu. 13: 29); "And they encamped by the waters" (Heb: al – hamaim) (Ex. 15: 27)

192 Compare: "over against Jebus" (Ju. 19: 10) (Heb. נכח nokhah) ; "over against

d) It further emerges from the verses: "For Pharaoh will say of the children of Israel, they are entangled in the land, the wilderness hath shut them in." (Ex. 14: 3–4); that at one end within Egyptian territory the desert closed in on them. (i. e. on the Israelites)

A schematic picture of the topographical layout at the time of the crossing of the Red Sea shows: The Israelites (I) are encamped on the sea (S). shore. Before (in front) and very close to them is Pi–Hahiroth (P), which is located between Migdol (M) and the Sea (S). South of them (i. e. behind them) is the desert (D), whilst opposite and somewhat ahead of them is Baal–Zephon (B). Theoretically there are two alternatives to indicate that Baal–Zephon will be before Pi–Hahiroth, and at the same time the Israelites will be before Pi–Hahiroth and before Baal–Zephon and facing it. 1) Baal–Zephon, located on the same shore as the Israelites, but slightly to one side (B 1). and 2) Baal–Zephon, on the other side of the sea, slightly more forward (B 2) (See schema).

```
M  |   P   |   |
   |   B1  | S |   B2
   |   I   |   |
   |   D   |   |
```

The Israelites were ordered to encamp at a specific place along the sea shore. Since this place was in a sparsely settled area it could not be pinpointed exactly; this could only be done by reference to other places: Pi–Hahiroth, Baal–Zephon and Migdol, these are conspicuous landmarks that function in the same way as coordinates on modern maps. Thus "before Pi–Hahiroth, between Migdol and the sea" would function as the longitudonal and "over against Baal–Zephon, before it" as the latitudonal coordinate.

Our schematic picture shows the topographical relationships between the different places without considering distances. The precise identification of the places is really irrelevent, nor do we know what the distances between the places were in actual fact; but since they served as markers for latitude and longitude, they were necessarily near each other. For there could be no other reason for mentioning them, since obviously their function was to fix the place of encampment.

These topographical relationships must be borne in mind when we seek the place of the Red Sea crossing. An examination of the many different theories of the Red Sea crossing shows us that not one of them satisfies our topographical relationships, and therefore all are equally unacceptable. To my mind the only region that suits our schematic picture is the area that

---

Gibeah" (Ju. 20: 43)(Heb. nokhah); "over against Maale Adumim" (Jos. 18: 17) (Heb, nokhah) "over against the table" (Ex. 40: 24) (Heb. nokhah)

extends along the Suez Canal (Gebel Ataka; Ageroud, and the southern part of the Arabian desert).

After having dealt with the subject of the Exodus and the passage of the Red Sea, I will now attempt to round out the picture. Once they had crossed the Red Sea, the Israelites entered the desert of Etham: "And they departed from before Pi–Hahiroth, and passed through the midst of the sea into the wilderness, and went three days' journey in the wilderness of Etham, and pitched in Marah. And they removed from Marah, and came unto Elim; and in Elim were twelve fountains of water, and three score and ten palm trees; and they pitched there. And they removed from Elim and encamped by the Red Sea". (Nu. 33: 8–10). We learn from this that after crossing the Red Sea Moses and the people of Israel first entered into the desert and only afterwards they reached the Red Sea once more. They probably passed over today's Mitla pass, and then continued to the eastern branch of the Red Sea (today's Akaba); they turned either towards the western branch of the Red Sea making a detour to mislead the Egyptians or when there was no water for the people they changed direction and returned to the sea shore where sweet water was more easily available. In this region are found today wells of brackish water. From here Moses leads the people through the wadis where it is possible to sustain a scarce subsistence, so detouring the barren central part of the desert. Indeed some scholars[193] claim that the route taken in the Sinai desert was along the line leading straight to Kadesh–Barnea or Akaba, I will cite only one, though rather unusual, example of this kind of view, namely that of Javis[194], He claims that the phenomenon of bird migration is repeated unchangingly over the centuries, and that no such migration is observed today in the southern region of the Sinai desert. The Bible tells us however about the meat of quails eaten by the Israelites in the desert, and this being so, Javis concludes that this cannot be the region in question. I have no wish to dispute this ornithological law, but it seems to me that Javis paid insufficient attention to the biblical text: "And there went forth a wind from the Lord, and brought quails from the sea". (Nu. 11: 31), which clearly connects the quails with the sea, a fact which shows that a) The Israelites were in the vicinity of the sea; therefore a journey in the southern part of the Sinai desert is far more likely than the suggestion of a passage in the central region. b) Most likely the birds in question are sea and not land birds, and probably the = שליים salvim=quails of the Bible are really sea–gulls. It may be inferred from the verse: "Wherefore should the Egyptians speak ,and say, for mischief did he bring them out, to slay them in the mountains" (Ex. 32: 12). that the Israelites were in a mountainous region; and we know, of

---

193 Greene, The Route of The Exodus, PEF. 1884, pp. 230–237 ; –The Route Of The Exodus, PEF. 1885, pp. 67–73.
194 Javis, The Forty Years Wanderings etc., pp. 25–41.

course, that the mountains are in the south of today's Sinai while the plain covers its central and northern parts. One notes in this connection that most of today's Bedouin population in the Sinai is concentrated in the southern part, and not the central region, mainly because the southern part offers the best subsistence possibilities. Rothenberg, who recently surveyed the Sinai desert, revealed the existence of many Chalcolitic settlements especially in the southern part of this area.[195] Bar–Droma in his two excellent Hebrew books, "The Negev" and "Wezeh Gvul Haares" (This is the Border of the Land)[196] shows convincingly that what today is known as the Sinai desert is really the Negev region, that is the southern part of Judean territory, whereas the biblical Sinai desert should be seen in today's Arab peninsula.

The Exodus is mentioned many times in the Bible, thus: "out of the land of Egypt, from the house of bondage." (Deut 5: 6; 7; 8; 8: 14)"out of the house of servants"(Mi. 6: 4). Although most verses in the Bible about the Exodus refer to the redemption from the house of bondage, there are also some which refer to the coming out of the iron furnace (Heb. כור הברזל = iron mines). (Je. 11: 4; Deut. 4: 20) "the furnace of iron", (1Kn. 8: 51); and other verses.[197] The description of the bondage in Egypt reads as follows:". And they built for Pharaoh treasure cities, Pithom and Raamses...And the Egyptians made the children of Israel to serve with rigour: And they made their lives bitter with hard bondage, in mortar, and in brick, and in all manner of service in the field: all their service, wherein they made them serve, was with rigour." (Ex. 1: 11–15). This description fits especially a people wanting to escape from a house of bondage. Hence the two biblical quotations cited above seem to suggest the existance of two separate groups of the nation; the first, and major one, being the group that escaped from the house of bondage, while, the second, and minor one, stayed in the mines and subsequently joined the first group. The mines mentioned in the Bible may well have been the mines of Serabit el Khadem which most probably were encountered by the Israelites as they travelled through the desert in south Sinai and it was at this point in their journey that perhaps they were joined by the second group. One reads in the Bible: "And a mixed multitude (Heb. ערב רב – erev rav) went up also with them". (Ex. 12: 38). From the verse: "they separated from Israel all the mixed multitude." (Heb – הערב. ha–erev) (Ne. 13: 3), we have to understand that "erev" ערב – refers to non Israelite people.[198] It may therefore be assumed that the main body of the fugitives consisted of Hebrews, joined by many slaves of other races.

---

195 Rothenberg, An Archaeological Survey of South Sinai PEQ 1970, p. 4.
196 Bar–Droma, Wezeh Gvul Hhares, 1958; – Hanegev, Jerusalem . 1934. (Heb.)
197 Deut. 13: 6; Deut. 13: 11. etc.
198 Cassuto explains "erev – rav"– mixed multitude of non–Israelite origin. (Exegesis On The Book of Exodus, p. 101) (Hebrew).

To sum up: The Israelites crossed the Red Sea in the region between today's Suez and the Bitter Lakes at a point which most probably is dry land today. They arrived there from Goshen–a suburb of the city of Egypt (Mitzraim), On (Heliopolis) i. e. today's Cairo, after they had travelled three days in the southern desert (today's Arabian Desert).

When did this Exodus take place? With On as the point of departure, the Exodus had to take place during the 18th dynasty, and it has been shown by our reckoning, based on the biblical account, that the Exodus occurred about 1446 B. C., that is during the reign of Amenhotep II (Amenophis II), and this accords with what has been said so far. Moreover, the Pharaoh of the Oppression was clearly Thothmes III, while the entry of the Israelites into the land of Canaan dates approximately 1406 B. C. . These dates agree completely with the biblical chronology and the conclusions of Garstang, Rowe, Newberry, Marston, Jack and others[199]. They also agree with the statement of Manethon reported in Josephus (Cont. Ap. I, 26), that the Exodus took place in the reign of a king named Amenophis. This dating also explains why "Asaru" appears on the Seti I stela, and the name "Isirar" on the Merneptah stela[200]. Moreover, the date of entry of the Israelites into Egypt must be fixed according to the biblical text to 430 years before the Exodus,[201] that is in approximately 1876 B. C. This means that the entry of the Israelites into Egypt did not take place in the Hyksos period, as most scholars tend to assume[202] I already quoted Lucas in this matter and also the biblical passages which disagree with this belief.

---

199 Hayness, The Date of The Exodus, PEP, 1896, pp. 249, 252.
   Headlam, The Bible as An Historical Source, PEQ, 1931, p. 128.
   Garstang, The Story of Jericho, PEQ. 1941, pp. 168–171.
   Lucas, The Date of The Exodus, PEQ. 1941, pp. 110–112.
   Conder, The Date of The Exodus, PEP. 1896, pp. 255–258.
   Jack, The Date of The Exodus In The Light of External Evidence, p. 257.
200 Merneptah stela is generally thought to date to c. 1220 B. C. This date is contemporaneous in Israelite history to the period of Judge Shamgar the son of Anath. In reference to this period the Bible states: "In the days of Shamgar the son of Anath, in the days of Yael the highways were unoccupied and the travelers walked through byways" (Ju. 5: 6). These passages indicate that the period of Shamgar the son of Anath was a period of disturbances when the country was in upheaval. It is possible that this disturbed state of affairs reflects Merneptah's victory.
201 "Now the sojourning of the children of Israel, who dwelt in Egypt was four hundred and thirty years." (Ex. 12: 40).
202 Cf. Rowley, From Joseph To Joshua, pp. 23–26.
   Conder, Syrian Stone Lore, p. 53.

THE PHILISTINES AND THE "SEA PEOPLES" NOT THE SAME ENTITY

We have already indicated the opinion of Rowley and others[1] who believe that the mention of the Philistines in the Bible proves the Exodus occurred after the Philistines settled in the land. Since it is generally considered that they settled about the period of Raamses III,[2] we are accordingly obliged to date the Exodus about 1100 B. C. This dating condenses the whole period of the wandering in the desert, the conquest of Canaan the period of the judges as well as Saul's reign into a time–lapse of about 50–80 years[3]. Such an estimate is in complete contradiction with the biblical narrative. Some scholars try to settle this difficulty by stating that the Philistines settled in the land several generations after the Israelite conquest,[4] and their mention in the patriarchal period is anachronistic. Those scholars who so vehemently reject the possibility of anachronism when dealing with Raamses, are prepared without hesitation to accept such a possibility with the name "Philistines".

The view which holds that the Philistines Settlement occurred at a late historical period is based on various factors. The Bible calls "Caphtor' the original Philistine homeland, and regards them as being of Egyptian descent: "And Mizrayim (=Egypt) begot Ludim, and Anamim, and Lehavim and Naftuhim, and Patrusim and Kasluhim (out of whom came Pelishtim) and Kaftorim"(Gen. 10: 13–14). Elsewhere Caphtor is mentioned as "Iy – Caphtor" (אי כפתור Jer. 47: 4). The word "Iy – אי" is understood to signify

---

1   Petrie, Palestine and Israel, p. 56.
     Duncan, New Light on Hebrew Origins, p. 189.
     Rowley, From Joseph To Joshua, p. 23.
2   Wright, Philistine Coffins and Mercenaries, BA. 1959, (3), p. 63.
     Wainwright, Caphtor, Keftiu and Cappadocia, PEQ, 1931, p. 208.
     Headlam, Sixty–sixth Annual General Meeting, The Bible As An Historical Source, PEQ.
     1931, p. 130.
     Renan, Histoire du Peuple D'israel, p. 114, note 2.
     Albright, A Revision of Early Hebrew Chronology, JPOS, 1920–1921, p. 56; – Syria, The Philistines and Phoenicia, CAH II, ch. 33, p. 24. (Albright notes that the wars of the "sea peoples" occured at 1190 B. C.) Dotan, The Philistines And Their Material Culture, 1967, p. 5 (Hebrew)
3   The reign of king David is generally accepted as having begun c. 1040 B. C.
4   For example: Wainwright, Some Early Philistine History, VT. 1953, (9), p. 73.
     Hall, On The Philistines (Annual Meeting), PEQ. 1923, pp. 126–127.
     Aharoni, Eretz Israel Bitkufat Hamikra, p. 230 (Hebrew).

an island. and the Hebrew expression "Iy Caphtor" was therefore taken to be the island of Caphtor[5]. Hence reasons could be adduced for not linking Caphtor with Egypt, as the biblical text does, and the Philistines' land of origin was sought for among the islands But the verse in Gen. 10. states clearly that the Pelishtim came out of Kasluhim and not Kaftorim! In the books of Zephania and Ezekiel, the Philistines are referred to as "the nation of Kretim" (Heb: – goy kretim –"גוי כרתים") "Woe the inhabitants of the sea coast, the nation of Kretim, the word of the Lord is against you; O Kenaan, the land of Pelishtim"; (Ze. 2: 5); "Behold, I stretch out my hand upon the Pelishtim, and I will cut off the Keretim and destroy the remnant of the sea coast." (Ezek. 25: 16)[6]. It was thus inevitable that Caphtor would become identified with the island of Crete; and this is the accepted theory today.[7] For support scholars cite the names "Chreti and Plethi" mentioned in the Bible as being David's bodyguards. These names are considered a corrupt form of "Chereti and Pelishti"[8] (i. e. Philistine), and therefore are thought to

---

5   MacAlister, The Philistines, Their History and Civilisation, p. 5.
     The different biblical translations all read the same. The Vulgate translates: Reliquias Insulae Cappadociae; the French translation: ile de Caphtor.

6   Onkelus, (Aramaic translation), translates Goy Kretim–The nation that must be destroyed (dehayvin leishtezaa), he derives the name from the Hebrew verb karot = cut; destroy.

7   Albright. Syria, The Philistines etc. CAH. vol. II, ch. 33, p. 29
     – A Colony of Cretan Mercenaries on The Coast of The Negeb, JPOS. 1921, p. 188;
     – A Revision of Early Hebrew Chronology, JPOS, 1920–21, p. 57, note 2.
     Berard, Philistines et Préhellenes, RAr, 1951, (37), p. 129.
     Barnette, The Sea Peoples, CAH. Vol. II (68), Ch. 28, 1969, pp. 16; 18.
     Cullican, The First Merchant Venturers, p. 29.
     Gordon, The Role of The Philistines, Antiquity, 1956, p. 22.
     – Before The Bible, Am Oved, 1966, p. 31 (Hebrew trans.).
     Greenfield, The interpreter's Dictionary of the Bible, p. 791. entry Philistines.
     Lods, Israel, p. 81.
     MacAlister, The Philistines etc., pp. 13; 25.
     Maspero, Histoire Ancienne des Peuples de L'orient, pp. 368; 699. (notes 2–3)
     Prignaud, Caftorim et Keretim, RB. 1964, p. 425.
     Smith, The Religion of The Semites, p. 11.
     Renan, Histoire du Peuples d'Israel, Tome II, pp. 29; 124.
     Salama, What has Become of The Philistines, PEQ. 1925, p. 74.
     Virolleaud, Kaftor dans Les Poemes de Ras Shamra, R. E. S. 1937. (3). pp. 137; 140.
     Wright, Philistine Coffins and Mercenaries, BA. 1959, (3), p. 64.
     Wainwright, Caphtor – Cappadocia, VT. 1956, p. 199.
     Slouschz, Motzaei Haivrim, p. 44. (Heb.).
     Mazar, The Phoenicians on The Eastern Shore etc. article in Western Galilee and the coast of Galilee, p. 6 (Heb.)
     Dotan, The Philistines etc., pp. 15; 24 (Heb.).
     Aharoni, Eretz Israel Bitkufat Hamikra, p . 8. (Heb.).
     Biblical Encyclopedia, 1962, entries "Caphtor" "Kereti" (Heb.).
8   Maspero, ibid. p. 368.

reinforce the "link" between Crete and the Philistines. MacAlister explains Plethi–" Philistines" as follows:[9] "In other places the Chretites are alluded to as part of the bodyguard of the early Hebrew kings and are coupled invariably with the name – פלתי Pelethites. This is probably merely a modification of פלשתי(Heb: plishti–N. G.), the ordinary word of 'Philistine', the letter S being omitted in order to produce an assonance between the two names."[10] And he continues: "In three passages –2 Samuel XX, 23; 2 Kings XI, 4, 19, the name of the royal bodyguard of Cheretites appears as כרי (Heb :cari–N. G.) Carians'. If this happened only once it might be purely accidental due to the dropping of a) ת t –N. G.) by a copyist". (ibid p. 7). Moreover he notes that: "if this old explanation be not accepted, we should have to put the word 'Plethites' aside as hopelessly unintelligible" (ibid .p. 6.)

Following this assumption that the original homeland of the Philistines was Crete, scholars tried to find supporting evidence for linking the Philistines with Greece. This was presumably to be found in certain Egyptian tombs in Thebes (the tombs of Senmut, architect of queen Hatshepsut, Rekhmara, vizier of Thutmose III, and of Menkheperuseneb, son of Rekhmara). In these tombs, wall paintings with inscriptions were found, in which the name Keft or Keftiu is mentioned, For some reason or other the name Keftiu is regarded as synonymous with Caphtor. This identity was assumed by Birch in 1858. Brugsch accepted this identification and assumed that Caphtor – Keftiu – Cretans are identical names.[11] In the wake of this assumption scholars tried to point out similarities and analogies in details such as the shape of objects, people, hair styles, ornaments, etc. found depicted in these wall paintings, as well as objects etc found in Crete,[12] Later they attempted to demonstrate

---

Albright, Syria, the Philistines etc. CAH. II, 33, p. 29. – A Colony of Cretan Mercenaries, JPOS, 1921, p. 189.
Prignaud, ibid. pp. 226; 228.
Barrois, Manuel D'archaeologie Biblique, 1953, p. 97.
Conder, The Syrian Stone Lore, p. 56 (notes)
Gordon, Ibid. p. 23. ; – Before The Bible, p. 31 (Hebrew trans.).
Wainwright, Ibid. p. 140.
Virolleaud, ibid. p. 140. ;
Renan, ibid. p. 29.
Lods, Israel, p. 421.
MacAlister, ibid. pp. 5–7; 61.
Biblical Encyclopedia, article "Kreti" (Hebrew).

9   MacAlister, ibid. p. 6.
10   According to MacAlister (note p. 6.) this explanation was advanced at first in 1729 by Lakemacher: Lakemacher, Observation Philologique, II p. 38. And in 1827 by Ewald,
     Kritische Grammatik Der Hebraffschen Sprache, p. 297.
11   See: Hall, The Peoples of The Sea, Recueil Champollion 1922, pp. 299; 301. – Keftiu, And The Peoples of The Sea, BSA, 1901–2, p. 163.
12   For Example: Wainwright, Caphtor– Cappadocia, p. 200.
     Gordon, The Role of The Philistines, p. 24;

analogies between Mycenaean pottery and various types of vessels found in the land of Israel[13]. These so – called similarities were taken as conclusive proof that the Philistines originated from Crete, and in consequence their pottery was labelled 'Mycenaean' or 'Philistine'. On the other hand, in inscriptions and bas–reliefs found in a temple in Medinet–Habu (Egypt) dating from the period of Raamses III, there is mention of various peoples with whom the Egyptians were in a state of war such as[14]: P. R. S. T. (Przt); T. K. R (Tekeru, Tjeker, Takar, Zakara); D. N. N (Dananu, Danoi, Denyen, Danauna); M. S. S (Mashasha, Meshwesh); A. K. S (Akayusha, Ekwesh); V. S. S. (Weshasha, weshwesh, Uashasha, uashashe); R. K (Ruku, Ruka, Reka); M. S. (Masa), S. R. D. N (Sherdan, Shardan, Sirdan); T. R. S. (Teresh, Tursha,); Maona etc. Occasionaly the word "island" or "sea" is attached to some of these names, e. g. "in their isles"[15]; "Sardan from the sea"; "Teresh of the sea"[16]. Some of these names occur also in Harris Papyrus which appears to represent a sort of a summary for the wars of Raamses III. The papyrus also includes citations as "I slew the Denyen in their isles"; "The Thekel (T– kr) and the Peleset (Pw–r'–s'–ty) were made ashes, the Sherden and the Weshesh (W–ss) of the sea they were made as those that exist not"[17]. These nations were dubbed by scholars "the sea peoples".

Champollion[18] was the first to claim the name P. R. S. T. to be a transcription of the P. L. S. T. –Philistines. He maintained that the Egyptian script incorporates an interchange of the letters R and L, and he was followed in this by Osburn, Hincks, Brugsch, Lenormant and others[19]. With the

---

– Before The Bible, p. 94. (Heb. Trans.)

Evans, The Palace of Minos, Vol. II, 1928, pp. 559–654; 734–749

Hall, The Keftiu Fresco In The Tomb of Senmut, BSA, 1903–4, pp. 15 4–157.

– Keftiu and The Peoples of The Sea, BSA, 1901–1902, pp. 170–174

MacAlister, The Philistines, pp. 8–10.

13 Welch, The Influence of The Aegean Civilisation on South Palestine, PEQ. 1900, pp. 342 – 350. The same article appears also in BSA. 1899–1900.

Benson, A Problem In Orientalizing Cretan Birds Mycenean Or Philistine Prototypes, JNES, 1961 (20), (2), pp. 73–84

14 It may be noted that the hieroglyphic writing is composed of consonants only and omits all vowels. Therefore, the exact pronunciation of Egyptian words and names is unknown and each scholar transcribes the names as suits him best, resulting in multiple pronunciations of the same name. I have cited here the names (consonants) only as they appear in Egyptian inscriptions and I have added in brackets, pronunciations of them as thought fit by individual scholars.

15 See: Breasted, Records, Vol. IV, p. 37. § 64.

16 Breasted, Records, Vol. IV, p. 75. § 129.

17 Breasted, Records, Vol. IV, p. 201. § 403.

18 See: Champollion, Dictionnaire Hieroglyphique, Grammaire, pp. 151; 180.

Hall, The Peoples of The Sea, Recueil Champollion, 1922, p. 297

19 Maspero, The Struggle of The Nations, Egypt, Syria and Assyria, 1910, p. 463, note 1.

MacAlister, The Philistines etc., p. 24

identification of Caphtor with Keftiu and the island of Crete on the one hand, and the mention of the names P. R. S. T., S. R. D. N etc., (some of which were depicted as "from the isles of the sea", "in their isles", "of the sea")on the other hand, the tendency of scholars was to link them with one another and to regard this linking as proof of the Cretan origin of the Philistines, even though the name P. R. S. T. is not once mentioned in connection with the word "sea" and the like.

Today it is generally accepted (in accordance with the theory of Maspero)[20] that we are dealing here with different nations which migrated from the region of Crete or Asia Minor, and tried to infiltrate into Egypt. Repulsed by the Egyptians, the Philistines (P. R. S. T.) settled in the coastal area of Canaan, while the Tyrsenes, Sardanes, and others migrated to Italy, Sardinia and other places. In 1747 Fourmont tried to prove that the name "Philistine" was an erroneous form of the Greek "Pelasgi". His theory was accepted by Chabas[21], Hitzig and others who enlarged upon it. Maspero stated in this context: "The name 'Plishti' by itself sugests a foreign origin or long migrations and recalls that of the Pelasgi"[22].

The equation Plishti–Pelasgi is based solely on a supposedly phonetic similarity.

The name T. K. R was also identified on the basis of the interchange of the letters R and L, i. e. T. K. L. . However, since the T here is a weak form of the letter, and can be pronounced as S, the name finally emerged as S. K. L., pronounced, Sakala and Zakala. By changing its pronunciation scholars have found a similarity with the Philistine city of Ziklag[23].

Lauth, Chabas and Lenormant identified the T. K. R – Zakala with the Teucrians, while Unger and Brugsch identified them with the Zigrita in Lybia. Later on Brugsch recanted, and adopted their identification with the Teucrians[24]. Maspero identifies the Zakala with Siculo–Pelasgi, while Hall identifies them with the Cretans[25].

The multiplicity of these identifications derives from the fact that there is no mutual agreement concerning the morphology of interchanging

Hall, The Peoples of The Sea, Recueil Champollion, p. 299.
– Keftiu and The Peoples of The Sea, BSA. 1901–2, p. 182.

20 Maspero, Histoire Ancienne des Peuples De L'orient, pp. 261; 314–317.
21 According to Maspero Chabas was the first to form this identity, Maspero, The Struggle of the nations, Egypt, Syria And Assyria, p. 463 note 1.
22 Maspero, Histoire Ancienne Des Peuples de L'orient, p. 368
23 This similarity is suggested by Brugsch; See: Hall, The Peoples of The Sea, Recueil Champollion, p. 301 ; Wainwright, Some Early Philistine History, VT. IX 1953, p. 78.
    MacAlister, ibid. p. 89.
24 See: Maspero, The Struggle of the Nations, Egypt etc. p. 464, note 3. – Revue Critique, 1880, Vol. I, p. 110.
25 Hall, Keftiu and The Peoples of The Sea, BSA. 1901–2, p. 184.

consonants in the name T. K. R, S. K. R., S. K. L., etc. Albright[26] notes that: "The second (the Tjekker–N. G.) is perhaps to be identified with the Teucrians (or less probably with the Homeric Sikeloi, who occupied Sicily and gave their name to the island)" His attitude is: "Take hold of this, but do not withdraw thy hand from that either". If we are dealing with T. K. R. we have Teucroi but if S. K. L. is the name then we have the Siculians. Today there are scholars who already shy aside the name T. K. R. and refer only to Sikeli as if this was the original name.[27]

In the same manner as the P. R. S. T. were identified as P. L. S. T., namely by the interchanging of R and L, so De Rougé identified the R. K (Ruku, Reka, Ruka, etc) as Luku (Leka, Luka) and equated them with the Lycians[28]. The W. S. S. were identified by Chabas as Opici–Obsci = Oscanes (of ancient Roman History)[29]. Brugsch believed them to be Caucasians, but later on revised his opinon and saw them as settlers from Asia Minor[30]. According to Maspero they were inhabitants of Caria or Lycia[31].

The D. N. N. (Danyun, Denyen, Danauna, etc.) were identified by De Rougé with the Danaans (of Greek history), by Chabas with the Deunians in Italy, and by Brugsch with the Libyans[32].

The T. R. S. were identified by De Rougé and Champollion with the Etruscans. The M. S. (or Masa) were linked with the Mycenaeans, etc.

The widely held view that the Philistines were originally from Crete, and that their settlement in Israel took place in the 11th century B. C., raises a number of questions which remain unanswered

A. No Greek element is to be found in biblical Philistine names, whether those of cities or personal names. Gaza, Gat, Ziklag, Yishbi, Fichol, Abimelech, Achuzat, Dagon, Achish and others are not derived from the Greek, but are Semitic names.[33] Scholars have already referred to this fact[34]), including MacAlister[35] who regards Crete as the homeland of the Philistines. This fact

26   Albright, Syria, The Philistines and Phoenicia, CAH. Vol. II ch. 33, p. 25.
27   See for ex. Stern. E., When Canaanites Became Phoenician Sailors, B. A. R. vol. 19 no. 1. Jan/Feb. 1993, pp. 25, 26, 27.
28   See: Maspero, The Struggle of the Nations, Egypt etc. p. 359, and note 3 there.
29   Maspero, ibid. note 5, p. 464.
30   Brugsch, Egypt Under The Pharaohs. 1891, II, p. 124.
31   See: Maspero, ibid. p. 464, note 5.
32   Maspero, ibid., p. 360, note 1.
33   MacAlister, Bonfante and others try to link certain names to the Greek language. For example, Bonfante, Who Were The Philistines, AJA. 1946, pp. 251–262.
34   See for example: Dotan, The Philistines etc. p. 22. (Hebrew).
     Conder, Notes By, PEP. 1896, p. 341; –The Canaanites, PEP, 1887, pp. 227–231.
     Sayce, The early History of the Hebrews, 1899, 2nd edit. p. 294
     Smith, G. A., The Historical Geography etc. p. 127.
35   MacAlister, The Philistines etc., pp. 13; 81.

has driven scholars to believe that the Philistines were Semites although the conjecture is that they came from the Greek islands[36], or at least, that they adapted themselves to the Semitic–Canaanite way of life and religion[37]. Greenfield remarks in this connection that "All their gods known to us have a semitic name. The Philistines it may be surmised lost their language soon after coming to Palestine and spoke a Canaanite dialect which gradually gave way to Aramaic".[38]

Winckler as cited by MacAlister[39] notes: "As immigrants they naturally adopted the civilisation of the land they seized and with it the cultus also".

B. Scholars try to point out the similarities between so called Philistine garments, hair styles, pottery, etc. and those of the Cretans. But how are we to explain their presumably total preservation of such characteristics on the one hand, and the total abandonment of their "Greek autochtonous" culture in nearly all other spheres such as language, religion, personal names, deity names, idol forms etc. on the other. In all spheres, excluding art, the dominant characteristics of the Philistines are Semitic, while in the Arts – so we are told – they are Greek. Is it possible to become so integrated into the local population, and in such a very short period of time?

C. Philistine names such as Dagon, Beit–Dagon, Ashkelon, Gaza, Gath and others are linked in the Bible and to some extent also in the Tell el–Amarna and Ras–Shamra tablets to a period prior to Raamses III, before the appearance of those called "Sea peoples"; therefore if the mention of the name Philistines in the Bible before the period of Raamses III is considered anachronistic, we must also accept anachronism in the mention of the names of Philistine cities. But the appearance of these names in the el–Amarna and Ras–Shamra tablets indicate their existence in a prior period. Hence according to the accepted version, the Philistines must have settled in already existing cities, e. g. Ashkelon, Gaza. etc. How is it that scholars, therefore, try to explain these names as derivations from Greek?[40]

D. Archaeological findings considered as being Philistine were discovered in sites outside the region supposed to be Philistine, such as Tell Yehudieh in Egypt, Nebesha in the Nile delta, Aniba in Nubia, Sehab in Transjordan and others[41].

---

36 For example: Robertson Smith, The Religion of The Semites, p. 11.
37 For example: Dotan, ibid., p. 22. (Hebrew).
    MacAlister, ibid., p. 94.
    Wright, Philistine Coffins and Mercenaries, BA. 1959, (3)p. 64
    Barnette, c The Sea Peoples, CAH. (68), 1969, Vol. II, Ch. 28, p. 17.
38 Greenfield, The Interpreter's Dictionary of the Bible, p. 792 entry, Philistines.
39 MacAlister, ibid., p. 94.
40 About the name Ashkelon see: MacAlister, ibid., p. 72
    Bonfante, ibid., pp. 251–262.
41 See: Benson, A Problem In Orientalizing Cretan Birds, Mycenean Or Philistine Prototypes, JNES. 1961, XX. (2), p. 77.

E. So–called "Philistine" findings were discovered at sites in strata which were ascribed to periods antedating that of Raamses III (c. 1170–1139 B. C.), though there were unsuccessful attempts to link them to this period.[42]

In excavations at Tell el– Farah, Petrie discovered a cemetery containing "Philistine pottery" (cemetery 500). In one of the tombs (no. 552) he found an Egyptian scarab which bore the name of Raamses II (c. 1290–1224 B. C.) and therefore dated the tomb with its "Philistine" findings to the thirteenth century B. C.[43]. (Albright nevertheless tried to push the date forward to the period of Raamses III).

Hall notes that Petrie discovered at Abydos "Aegean" pottery in tombs of the first dynasty which "still remain difficult to explain".[44]

Anthropoid coffins inscribed with Egyptian hieroglyphs[45], found in a tomb at Lachish and ascribed to the Philistines, also point towards the 13th century B. C. . Speaking of the pottery found in them, Wright says: "Whether the pottery dates from the late 13th century (as I think probable) or from the early years of the twelfth, it still appears highly likely that the bodies in Lachish tomb 570 were Philistine. If so, they were newcomers in a Canaanite context using native pottery before their own particular variety was made in the country"[46].

F . Since the Philistines were supposed to have come from Crete, attempts were made to find a connection with various Greek names, and to link these in turn with names of the so–called "Sea Peoples" who were also considered to be Greek. Such interconnections resulted in many contradictions which were somehow completely overlooked.

1. The Greek peoples with whom the so–called "Sea Peoples" are linked came originally NOT FROM CRETE but from Asia Minor, Greece, Sardinia, Italy, Libya etc. What basis is there for the theory of a Cretan origin for the Philistines

2. The period of settlement of some of these Greek peoples does not correspond with that of the "Sea peoples". Herodotus (I, 94) states that[47]: "In the days of Atys the son of Manes, there was great scarcity through the whole land of Lydia. For some time the Lydians bore the affliction patiently, but finding that it did not pass away. the king determined to divide the nation

---

Wright, Philistine Coffins and Mercenaries, BA. 1959, (3) p. 54.

42 For example see: Vincent, Chronique, RB. 1922, p. 102. (Les Fouilles Anglaises D'ascalon) Wright, ibid., pp. 54–56; 58.
    Barnette, The Sea Peoples, CAH. 1969, Vol. II, Ch. 28, p. 17.

43 See above note No. 39.

44 Hall, Keftiu and The Peoples of The Sea, BSA. 1901–2, p. 160. see there also note 1.

45 Wright refers to "Crude Egyptian hieroglyphs which make no clear sense and which were certainly not written by an Egyptian" (ibid, p. 66)

46 Wright, ibid. p. 66.

47 Translation, Rawlinson . p. 37.

in half, and to make the two portions draw lots, the one to stay, the other to leave the land. He would continue the reign over those whose lot it should be to remain behind; the emigrants should have his son Tyrrenius for their leader. The lot was cast and they who have to emigrate went down to Smyrna, and built themselves ships, in which after they have put on board all needful stores, they sailed away in search of new homes and better sustenance.

After sailing past many countries they came to Umbria where they have built cities for themselves, and fixed their residence. Their former name of Lydians they laid aside, and called themselves after the name of the king's son, who led the colony Tyrrhenians".

According to Herodotus the Tyrrhenians moved to Umbria, and this emigration occurred about two generations before Raamses III. Maspero points out this discrepancy, but he discounts it and asserts that "Whatever Herodotus says, this migration was not accomplished at one single occasion and in one sole direction. It lasted for nearly two centuries"[48]. On what basis is this belief founded? There is no allusion to it whatever in Maspero's words, and there is nothing in his statement which can resolve the discrepancy.

3. The Lycians who are equated with the Ruku (or Reka) were not known by the name of Lycians, but, as mentioned by Herodotus, were called Termilae[49]. This contradiction has already been pointed out by Barnette.[50]

4. The Shardanes, whose name is linked with Sardinia, could not have come from Sardinia, as already pointed out by Maspero.[51]

G. Another point to be more fully discussed later should be emphasized here, namely the dates of destroyed cities and the findings unearthed at their sites were studied, recorded and collated on the assumption that the Exodus took place during the Raamses – Merneptah period (c. 1200 B. C.). But with an Exodus as shown in the preceding chapter dated in c. 1446 B. C, the conquest of the land of Canaan would have taken place at c. 1406 B. C. Accordingly the dates of the destruction of cities and the findings from their sites which had been attributed to a later period will now have to be advanced at least 200 years, which means that the conjectured date of the settlement of the Philistines in the period of Raamses III will not accord with the dates of most "Philistine" findings.

Why are the Keftiu equated with Caphtor? MacAlister, considered one of the foremost scholars in this field of study, summarizes this question in his book[52]: "The various lines of evidence which have been set forth in the preceding pages. indicate Crete or its neighbourhood as the probable land of

---

48   Maspero, Histoire Ancienne des Peuples de L'orient, p. 298.
49   Herodotus, VII; 92.
50   Barnette, The Sea Peoples, CAH. 1969, Vol. II, Ch. 28, p. 6.
51   Maspero, Struggle of The Nations, Egypt etc. p. 360, note 2.
52   MacAlister, The Philistines etc. pp. 25–26.

origin of this group of tribes[53]; they may be recapitulated: 1) The Philistines, or a branch of them, are sometimes called Cheretites or Cretans. 2) They are said to come from Caphtor, a name more like Keftiu than anything else, which certainly denotes a place where the Cretan civilisation was dominant. 3) the hieratic school–tablet mentions Akasou as a keftian name: it is also Philistine (Achish)." and elsewhere (p. 27) he writes: "As for Carpathos which Homer calls Crapathos is it too bold to hear in this classical name an echo of the pre – Hellenic word whatever it may have been, which the Egyptians corrupted to Keftiu and the Hebrews to Caphtor..."

Another source of information upon which MacAlister bases his conclusions are the wall paintings in the tombs of Senmut, Rekhmara and Menkheperuseneb: "in these wall paintings we see processions of persons, with non–Semitic European – looking faces; attired simply in highly embroidered loin cloths folded round their singularly slender waists, and in high boots or gaiters; with hair dressed in a distinctly non – Semitic manner; bearing vessels and other objects of certain definite types. The Tomb of Sen–mut is much injured, but the Cretan ornaments there drawn are unmistakeable." (ibid p. 8).

In other words the identification of Keftiu with Caphtor is based solely on phonetic similarity and has no scientific basis. Hall regards the name Keftiu as Egyptian meaning "Those beyond" (Ha–Nebu), namely the land of the Keftiu lying "back of beyond". According to him, it was initially the name given to the dwellers of the Delta swamps, but in time applied to all northern countries, i. e. Asia Minor, Rhodes, Crete, etc.[54] On the other hand, from the wall paintings in the tombs of Rekhmara, Puamra and others he draws the conclusion that: "The facial type of the Keftians, splendidly exemplified in Rekhmara's tomb and also in the earlier tomb of Puamra IS NOT ONLY NON – SEMITIC BUT IS DEFINITELY EUROPEAN. PUAMRA'S MAN HAS A ROMAN NOSE AND LOOKS RATHER LIKE AN ITALIAN; THE SECOND MAN IN REKHMARA'S TOMB IS ABSOLUTELY ITALIAN IN TYPE, and has a remarkable strong heavy–jawed, almost 'nut–cracker' face, evidently a portrait: ...the rest are more or less conventionalised types approaching the ideal Egyptians; the utter dissociation from anything even remotely resembling a Semitic type." (ibid. p. 164 emphasis –N. G.).

Another important 'scientific fact' that Hall refers to it is: "...in the tombs of Puamra Senmut, Rekhmara and Menkheperusenb ...their costume is as definitely non Semitic." (ibid. p. 164). Having determined this, Hall finds "an identity of similarity" between fresco paintings discovered by Evans in Knossos and the wall paintings in the Theban tombs. This he advances as proof

53   namely the so called "Sea Peoples".
54   See also: Hall, Keftiu and The Peoples of The Sea, BSA, Vol. VIII, 1901–2, pp. 159–163.

for the conjecture that the Keftiu came from Crete (ibid. p. 166). In fact, there is a certain difficulty with some Keftiu profiles which even according to Hall's criteria are 'Semitic' and with vases which are not of Mycenaean workmanship. Hall's explanation of this is: "Among the Mycenaean vases brought by the Keftians are also others which are not of Mycenaean workmanship. These are apparently Phoenician imitations of Egyptian work. Since in style they are more or less Egyptian, this fact compels us to believe that much of the commerce between the Keftian lands and Egypt filtered through Phoenician channels, and that the Keftian ambassadors quite possibly came via Phoenicia and in Phoenician ships...that this importation from Keftiu of Mycenaean objects and probably of Mycenaean ambassadors also by Phoenicians occasionaly led to some confusion in the minds of the Egyptians is natural and the result is that occasionaly we find Keftian tribute bearers represented as approximating to the Semitic type. No doubt the question may fairly be asked whether this is really a mistake and whether undetermined Semites from the far north (What place north is he refering to – is it Crete from which the Keftiu came according to him? – N. G.) were not sometimes included in the Keftian names as well as the Mycenaeans." (ibid. pp. 174–175).

He goes on to say: "The people from Keftiu are always depicted as Mycenaeans of the type of the Knossian cupbearers and the bull–catchers of the Vaphio cups. The representation of Keftians as Semites is unusual and only occurs when the subject is bearded: the influence of use and customs seem then to have inclined the artist's hand to approximate to the Semitic types. But when Mycenaeans are correctly represented they are always described as Keftians and bear no other name; it seems then that when the Egyptian artist represented Keftians as Semites he was simply making a mistake." (ibid. p. 175).

In other words, when the paintings do not correspond with Hall's theory it is only because the Egyptian artist simply made a mistake, It is amazing how the Egyptian artist "made a mistake" only in drawing the Semitic types, whereas he drew the others with the utmost accuracy (so at least we are told by Hall and others). If the artist "was inclined to make mistakes" is it not probable that "he made mistakes" also in drawing the "Mycenaean" objects? Or is it not rather Hall who is at fault here for regarding each bearded type as Semitic, and vice–versa, for seeing in each unbearded type a non–Semite.

This approach of Hall is shown again when he deals with those called "Sea Peoples": The T. K. R, D. N. N., etc. for he writes: "The features of the Philistines and of many of the Shardina at Medinet–Habu (in the wall paintings – N. G.) are of classical straight– nosed Greek type, and the Tchakaray are as has already been remarked European. In fact all WITH OCCASIONAL EXCEPTIONS are definitely EUROPEAN IN APPEARANCE, some with the moderately aquiline nose of the Italian, others with a decided snub. WE HAVE ONLY TO LOOK AT THEIR PORTRAIT TO SEE THAT THEY ALL COME FROM WEST OF TAURUS AND MANY NO DOUBT FROM EUROPE ITSELF.". (ibid. p. 185). Elsewhere he remarks that "the European types, especially of the Shardina and the Teresh are conspicuous, whereas the Shekelesh seem Semites".[55]

No doubt in the light of such "outweighing scientific facts": the "classical Greek and European face"and the "straight" or "moderately aquiline nose" – the sole conclusion to make is that we are dealing with Europeans. But Hall is not satisfied with these "facts", and so he tries to find other supporting evidence such as garments and the like: "Their costume points the same way. The Philistines, Tchakaray and Uashasha wear the distinctive feather headress which the Lycians wore in Salamis (Herodot. VII, 92)" (ibid. p. 185). He makes this explicit declaration merely on the basis of a vague phrase in Herodotus (VII, 92) which says that the Lycian sailors "wore an headress a hat encircled with plumes". This verse is sufficient for him to determine that there exists a similarity and resemblance between the two. According to Barnette there is no foundation for this surmise[56].

Evans, describing the wall paintings in the Theban tombs, also agrees that the form of the nose indicates the ethnic affinity of the painted figures, When one of the Keftiu is shown without "a classical Greek nose" he says: " The nose here is of a decidedly aquiline form, but this may have been partly taken over from the neighbouring Semitic profiles."[57] When Evans compares the garments drawn in the Theban wall paintings to those of Knossos, he discovers certain differences in the form of the garment, but he, like Hall, rejects this dissimilarity with the plea that the Egyptian artist made a mistake: "The Egyptian artist misled by Lybian arrangement with which no doubt he was better acquainted suggests that the whole was dependent on the front of the girdle." (ibid. p. 737).

Moreover his approach to comparable findings in the tomb of Rekhmara is similar. (ibid. p. 744). If Hall, Evans and their followers had troubled to examine more attentively ancient reliefs in overall, and the reliefs and paintings referred by them in particular without preconceived ideas, they could have discovered other "scientific evidence" such as "classical Greek" or "classical Italian" noses also featuring in the figures of exiled Jewish Semites depicted on Sargon's bas–reliefs. They also feature in other Semitic figures, especially in Egyptian reliefs, and appearance cannot be taken as "proof" that they are Greeks or Europeans. This so–called "scientific evidence" proves nothing, and rather should be regarded as the outcome of a certain

---

55   Hall, The Peoples of The Sea, recueil Champollion, pp. 314–315.
56   Barnette, ibid. p. 7.
57   Evans, ibid. p. 739.

education. The Egyptian paintings serve Hall and others as the basis for their theory of the reciprocal tendencies between the so–called "Sea Peoples" and Mycenaean culture. Yet these scholars somehow tend to disregard the common features evident between these "Sea Peoples" and their geographic locale. Evans[58] notes that some of the objects carried by the Keftiu "are well–known Egyptian fabrics" and that a certain sword "is also non–Cretan". But he fails to explain how it comes about that Keftiu people (i. e. would –be Cretans) carry Egyptian wares as presents to Egypt; and if some of these wares are not from Crete, is it not more likely that the other objects are not from Crete either? Evans alluding to the hair style of certain figures says: "The curls rising above the heads of several of these figures are very characteristic of the Minoan coiffure and the band of diadem is also found, though it is also a Semitic feature." (ibid. p. 741).

If we examine one of the reliefs (see drawing 1) we remark that the so–called "Sea Peoples" who are thought to be Philistines wear short girdles adorned with fringes and sometimes terminate in tassels. But exactly the same girdles are also worn by the Egyptians who fight them. The same style of dress is also found in the depictions of Canaanite settlers (see drawings 4, 5.), and on a stele of Baal (see drawing 5).

The oar–galleys of the so–called "Sea Peoples" closely resemble those of the Egyptians despite differences between them. The Egyptian vessels are more elaborate, with many oars and oarsmen as compared to the other vessels. However both the Egyptian vessels and the others have a central mast with a look–out post manned on top . From the top of the mast a pole curves downward to each end of the vessel. To this pole sail sheets are attached by ropes to the central mast. The place of the steersman is at the extreme end of the vessel. (see drawing 3).

Looking closely at drawing 3 considered to be of Philistines, we notice clearly that the figures depicted form a heterogenous group, some with negroid features. In drawing 2., which depicts a land battle between the Egyptian army of Raamses III and the so–called "Sea Peoples", the figures at the rear are seen to drive carts harnessed to oxen (and horses), yet these "Sea Peoples" are supposed to have come from Crete. How, then, could they have brought along the carts, oxen and horses? Let us not forget that we are dealing with a war for which a large number of carts, oxen and horses are needed. How were these carts with heavy chests (as depicted in the painting), oxen and horses conveyed to Egypt?

Were they shipped on the sailing vessels directly by sea from Crete to Egypt? Could they have been landed directly on Egyptian soil? Or perhaps were they brought by sea first to Canaan where they organised into formations before

---

58   Evans, ibid., p. 7

making their assault on the Egyptians? Was it at all possible to transport such a huge mass by sea vessels? Albright notes in this context: "The use of carts suggests a long overland journey but by no means proves it, since that may have been constructed after arrival in Palestine by sea" (Albright CAH. 1975, p. 508). If these "sea peoples" first came by sea to Canaan before going on to Egypt, how could they, in the short time available (as suggested apparently by the archaeological evidence) manage to get organised and trained to fight with carts? Or, perhaps, these "sea peoples" considered to be primarily sea warriors, had also superior skills in land fighting with carts? .

If they first came to Canaan (which must be assumed if we accept they made war with carts), what then becomes of the theory that they settled along the sea coast of Canaan after having being thrust out from Egypt by Raamses III. Is there the least shred of evidence that they made war and destroyed cities after arriving in Canaan and before they went to Egypt?

Furumark who made a searching study of the subject in a wide–ranging article[59], points to the contrasts and dissimilarities between the wall paintings in the tombs of Rekhmara, Senmut and Menkhepheruseneb, and the depictions related to Cretan culture. Furumark claims that the wares, hairstyles, etc. depicted in these tombs are of Asiatic origin and are not Cretan. (ibid. pp. 231–232). Garstang[60], who shares this view, writes that the goddess Anuket "wears a feather hairdress identical with that later worn by the Philistines", and elsewhere[61] he notes: "The Philistines were not like the Minoan Cretans nor Keftians either in dress or armor or facial type".

Furumark in reference to other Theban tombs such as that of Kenamoun (Amenhotep II, notes that in one of the paintings a figure of a prisoner said to be a Keftiu wears an Asiatic beard and short hair–cut (in contrast to the general depiction). In regard of another Keftiu represented on a dais in the tomb of Ineni (Amenhotep III) Furumark says: "It has been argued that these applications of the name Keftiu are erroneous (Davies – N. G.). This may very well be the case, since such labels can in some instances be shown to be inexact and since, as we have seen, both the pictures and the texts were created in a manner that inspires no great confidence in their value as historical documents. But it is an error of method to reject this evidence only for the reason that the men described as chiefs of Keftiu are not Cretans. For this would be to presume the very thing that one wants to prove, viz. that Keftiu is Crete."[62] Furumark continues – "Unfortunately this discussion (on Aegean elements in Egyptian tombs – N. G.) has been marred by much

---

59   Furumark, The Settlement at Ialysos and Aegean History c. 1550–1400 B. C., OA. VI, 1950, pp. 150–271.
60   Garstang, A Criticism on Albright, in PEQ. 1932, p. 227.
61   Garstang, Joshua – Judges, p. 311.
62   Furumark, ibid. p. 240.

prejudice and by a certain lack of precision. Most writers on the subject have been possessed by the preconceived notion that Keftiu is identical with Crete and when dealing with the pictorial representations they have allowed this idea to confuse the issue" (ibid. 223). And elsewhere: "there is nothing whatever in the Egyptian records referring to the Philistines (P. R. S. T.) that associates them with Crete and (sic). the same is true of the archaeological material assignable to them that has been found in Palestine" (ibid. p. 242).

It is worth citing here part of his general views about the Keftiu–Cretan relationship:

"The conviction that Keftiu means Crete would not have been so strong and persistent –and might, indeed, never have originated at all had it been based only on the Egyptian evidence now reviewed. The real reason for this equation (though this does not always seem to be clear to those who believe in it) is the assumption that the land of Kaphtor mentioned in the Bible is identical to Crete and that Kaphtor is the same thing as Keftiu. It is because of this that most writers on the subject have gone to such pains to make the Egyptian material fit into their theory.

Now already the linguistic equation Keftiu – Kaphtor presents serious difficulties and requires somewhat elaborate theories to become fairly acceptable. But granting that it is correct, what reason is there for identifying Kaphtor with Crete? In the Old Testament Kaphtor is mentioned as the original homeland of the Philistines (Amos 9: 7 Jer. 47: 4; Gen. 10: 14 ; 1Chr. 1: 12) In these passages there is nothing that suggests an identification with Crete (if we do not regard as a hint in that direction the expression שארית אי כפתור In Jeremiah 47: 4)[63]. And in reality this theory is based exclusively on the fact that in other connexion 'Cherethites' are mentioned together with 'Pelethites' or with Philistines[64]. The term 'Cherethites' and 'Pelethites' occurs seven times in the Old Testament and is traditionally considered to signify the life guard of David. According to a current view Pelethi should be explained as derived from 'Pelisti' either as a 'Volkstümlich Verstümmelung ' or as a modification in order to obtain an assonance with 'Krethi' . The first of these explanations is unacceptable, since it is phonetically impossible, and since no parallels to such a transformation exist, and the second is extremely far–fetched and dubious. There is indeed, no plausible reason at all for associating 'Pelethi' with 'Pelisti'. This time honoured equation is based exclusively on a similarity of sound and the same is true of the alleged identity of Kerethi with Cretans" (ibid., p. 241–243).

---

63 The text in brackets appears as a note in the original text. The Hebrew reads=Sheerit Iy Kaphtor =The remnant of the country of Caphtor. (A. V.)

64 It will be pointed out that in the Bible the Cherethites are never mentioned with Philistines but only with Pelethites.

Furumark is not alone in this view. In an article on Philistine ceramics[65] Saussey analyses among other topics, the different stages in the consolidation of the view that these ceramics are of Mycenaean manufacture[66]: "How is it – one asks – that the apogee of the Palestinian ceramics production is due to a population which is often imagined to have left few traces and voluntarily represented as a horde of warriors settled in a conquered land, which does not constitute a high presumption in favour of its intellectual and artistic superiority. Unless mistaken it is Tiersch who made an explicit determination (in 1908) of this term (i. e. of Mycenaean ceramics – N. G.) after he examined two sets of pottery of Mycenaean inspiration and considered one of them to be a genuine imported Mycenaean production, and concluded 'such a local category cannot be other than Philistine' . Watzinger and MacAlister accepted this view and so did Mackenzie who excavated in Ashkelon; and spoke about pseudo–Philistine ceramics...Dussaud[67] pointed out that most of the alleged pieces (of Mycenaean ceramics – N. G.) manifestly date back to beyond the date of the settlement of the Philistines in Palestine.[68] That is indeed what the discoverers themselves had to acknowledge from the nature of the excavation stratifications. MacAlister at first dated them to 1400 B. C. and when later he says that it was not obligatory to date them so far back, he does not furnish any reason for this retraction. We are justified to reject it, considering that the first impression acquired at the site of excavation is formulated without preconceived ideas, whereas the negation was produced under the influence of a theory to be validated". (ibid. p. 182). He continues by saying: "In the regions where they retained full autonomy the 'Philistine' ceramics is in full decadence less than two centuries after it was introduced by them. How are we to explain this fact, if the Philistines were really so gifted with original esthetic ingenuity so necessary for the creation and implantation of a certain form of Art, humble as it may be?" (ibid. pp. 183–4).

Elsewhere he remarks: "The decorations lead us to analogous conclusions. On the one hand, we are dealing with local elements, or at least very ancient ones, like the Bichromia in red and black which is considered today specifically Asiatic, or naturalistic decorative elements such as plants, stags, fish, birds (which have no connection with the Philistines)[69]. On the other hand certain motifs, such as snail–shapes, spiral designs centered around a Maltese cross, and the geometric patterns in general confirm the presence of Mycenaean and Cretan influence". (ibid., p. 184).

Saussey concludes: "The ceramics which we call 'Philistine' are not

---

65 Saussey, La Céramique Philistine, SY. V, 1924, pp. 169–185.
66 ibid. pp. 169–172.
67 Dussaud, Observations Sur La Céramique Du II Millenaire avant Notre Ère, SY. ix 1928, p. 145.
68 namely, as believed, about 1100 B. C.
69 The brackets in the original text.

Philistinian at all. but a further stage in the general developement of local pottery which has come under the influences of Mediterranean pottery. (Cretan, Mycenaean, Cycladic etc.)...These ceramics should not be attributed to the Philistines in any way whatsoever." (ibid. p. 185).

Furumark[70] claims that: "Both the spiral and the rosette are indeed old Asiatic motives and the attempts to derive them from Aegean sources must be regarded as ill founded" (ibid. p. 207).

Heurtly[71] also objects to naming this pottery "Philistine" and regards this label as "unfortunate" (ibid. p. 109). He disagrees with the inference that the Philistines brought this pottery with them, and also asserts "nor can we deduce from it where the Philistines came from" (ibid. p. 108).

Berard, too, disagrees with identifying the Keftiu as Cretans, and remarks,[72] citing Glotz, that the many findings of weights in Crete, based on the Chaldeo–Phoenician system, indicate that their use was widespread in Crete, and he asks how these weights were imposed upon the Cretans (ibid. II, p. 79). He notes also that a basin and a ewer were discovered in a sarcophagus in Byblos and were classified as Mycenaean, because the decoration on the basin was the same spiral network as in Mycenaean decoration. But the ewer that accompanies the basin is of quite a special form, such that at first Poittier acknowledged it was Levantine rather than Aegean. He maintained that this vessel had no name in Greek. However, he classified the ewer also as being of Mycenaean production, asserting that both vessels form one inseparable entity, and that if the basin is identified as Mycenaean production, so also must be the ewer. Dussaud in 1910 asserted that the Phoenicians were influenced by the Greeks, but in 1925 (SY. p. 195) he went back on this, and wrote that these vessels from Byblos were closely related to the ceramics in the first Babylonian dynasty and that the ewer found in our Phoenician tomb is a sample of these Babylonian ceramics (ibid. II. p. 181). Hence Berard inquires: "If the conclusion has been reached that the ewer is of Giblite manufacture, will not the basin found with it – the inseparable entity – be also Giblite? And if this basin with spiral decoration is Phoenician, is it from Egypt directly or is it from Phoenicia by stages that the Cretans and Mycenaeans received this decorating motif, or on the contrary, the spiral motif passed from Crete via Phoenicia to Egypt? But if such variability is to be expected in the relations between Crete and Egypt, what are we to think about most of archaeological determinations?" (ibid. Vol. II, p. 188). Elsewhere[73] Berard writes: "Let us observe the paintings in the Theban tombs, the gifts brought by the Keftians and their tributaries. If all these contributions are of Cretan

---

70   Furumark, ibid., p. 207.
71   Heurtly, "Philistine" and Mycenaean Pottery, QDAP. V. pp. 99–110.
72   Berard, V. Les Phéniciens Et L'odysée
73   Berard, V. ibid., Vol. II, pp. 312–314.

origin, how are we to explain the presence among them of salmon figures in gold and copper, metals that have never been produced in Crete, neither in the classical era nor in the modern one? Moreover, how are we to explain these elephant tusks – an animal that never existed in Crete, whether wild or domesticated? How especially are we to explain the fact that the other tributaries in the adjacent paintings bring the same tribute to the Pharaoh? – The archaeologists have in effect neglected to tell us that in the tomb of Khamait, for example, the wares which are supposed to be Aegean are in the hands or on the shoulders of envoys from Lotanu[74] and in those of Syrian tributaries, and that the garments, features, profile and their beards have nothing Minoan about them...Are we to conclude that these Syrians received from Crete the ivory vessels, the copper and the elephant tusks they brought to the Pharaoh? Or on the contrary, to adopt the old opinion of Helbig, that the Mycenaean objects and art are of Phoenician origin?"

As already noted, the biblical expression "Iy Caphtor" (אי כפתור) was understood as being the island of Crete. The word Iy (אי) was, and still is taken, to mean an island. But was this also its meaning in the past? In the biblical context the word Iy (אי) in its plural form occurs in verses like: "Jehovah reigneth let the earth rejoice. Let the multitude of ISLES be glad" (Ps. 97: 1) ; "Glorify ye Jehovah...in the ISLES. of the sea"(Is. 24: 15); "and men shall worship him...even[75] all the ISLES. of the nations" (Ze. 2: 11); "Keep silence before me O ISLANDS..." (Is. 41: 1); "...till he have set justice in the earth and the ISLES shall wait for his law" (Is. 42: 4); "Sing unto Jehovah a new song and his praise from the end of the earth; ye that go down to the sea, the ISLES. and the inhabitants thereof " (Is. 42: 10); "Let them give glory unto the Lord and declare his praise in the ISLANDS" (Is. 42: 12); "To the ISLANDS he will repay recompense" (Is. 59: 18); "the ISLES. have seen and fear" (Is. 41: 5). According to the accepted interpretation of Iy – אי as island, we must understand the above phrases to mean: only the islands will wait for the Lord's law; only the islands of the world will praise the Lord God of Israel; only the islands will receive recompense, etc. Is this the real meaning of these verses? And what about all the lands apart from the islands? It is evident that the accepted interpretation of the word Iy – אי In these verses is unacceptable, or perhaps "Iy" does not mean an island. One's scepticism as to the correctness of this interpretation increases in light of verses in which cities such as Sidon, Ashdod, and countries like Egypt, Israel, Greece, are also called "Iy": "Be still ye inhabitants of the isle, thou whom the merchants of Sidon, that pass over the sea, have replenished." (Is. 23: 2 A. V. The Gideon Bible reads: "inhabitants of this coast–land": The Hebrew

---

74   Lotanu–being the name given by the Egyptians to part of the land of Israel
75   The Hebrew text reads "all the isles"(without the word "even"). –כל איי "הגויים".

verse reads: "Domu yoshvei Iy sokher Sidon "דמו ישבי אי סחר צידון" "which literally translated is "Be still the inhabitants of the' Iy 'of Sidon"; "And the inhabitants of this coast– land (in Hebrew it reads Iy –"אי") shall say" (Is. 20: 6 A. V.). (In this verse the reference of Iy "–island" is to the land of Israel): "And I will set a sign among them, and I will send those that escape of them unto the nations to Tarshish, Pul and Lud, that draw the bow, to Tubal and Javan; to the isles afar off". (Is. 66: 19) The Hebrew verse reads: "...To Tubal and Javan (Greece–N. G.) the far off 'Iyiim ('islands')". In Jer. 25: 22 we read: "and the KINGS of the ISLES which are BEYOND the sea". (A. V.) (in the Hebrew text "Iy" is in the singular while Kings is in the plural i. e.: and the KINGS of the ISLAND which IS BEYOND the sea –see also the Gideon Bible). If Iy is to be understood as island, why does the text not refer to the island within the sea? Why "beyond the sea"? For beyond the sea lies the land again. Moreover, the Hebrew verse refers to kings in the plural whereas Iy is in the singular (so also translated in the gideons' bible). How are we to explain this unless the text refers to land and not island? The fact that the word "Iy" means "land" is proved by the phrase in Is. 42: 15: ושמתי נהרות לאיים ואגמים אוביש". (Vesamti neharot leiyim veagamim ovish). This was translated: "and I will make the rivers islands and I will dry up the pools". (A. V.) The Vulgate also translates "insulae"(islands). The Jerusalem bible: "turn rivers to pools and dry up lakes". However, we have here a linguistic parallelism and the end of the verse provides the clue to the meaning of its beginning, namely "I will dry up the pools" gives us to understand that the beginning of the verse: "and I will make the rivers islands means, I will make the rivers dry–land and not islands. We find the same parallelism in the verse: "that saith to the deep, be dry and I will dry up the rivers" (Jes. 44: 27). Hartom and Cassuto[76] also interpret "land" and not "islands", and we find the same in the French translation[77] "Je changerai les fleuves en terre ferme. Et je mettrai les etangs a sec". i. e."I will change the rivers into dry–land".

I believe that the word "Iy" is simply what the Greeks called "Ge" (Yñ – pronounced in Greek Iy – yee), namely – land, Earth. According to Greek mythology this was the name of the Phoenician earth goddess[78]. Most probably the letter א (Aleph) in the word "אי" (Iy) was transcribed into Greek as "G". A similar transcription may be presumed also for the Greek word "genos" which signifies the name of a Phoenician deity, namely the god of race[79]. This name corresponds to the biblical name Enosh – אנוש (Gen. 4: 26 in Hebrew spelled also with the letter Aleph) which also signifies the human

76   Hartom– Cassuto, Yavneh ed. 1960, Israel (Hebrew Bible).
77   French translation by Louis Segond, Paris, 1962,
78   Contenau, La Civilisation Phénicienne, p. 86.
79   Contenau, ibid. p. 86.
      Rawlinson, Phoenicia, p. 339.

race. Moreover, it is known that certain personal names written in Hebrew with the letter Ayin (ע) were transcribed in Greek by the letter gamma e. g. Aza –Gaza, Amora –Gomorrah, Dauel–Daguel, Athniel – Gothniel. The fact that the Hebrew letters A (Aleph –א) and A' (Ayin ע –) frequently interchange was already discussed earlier.

We may summarize by saying that the word "Iy"– אי in the Bible is invariably understood to mean "land", and not island, therefore "Iy Caphtor" simply means the land of Caphtor and nothing else. There is no basis whatever for the conjecture that Caphtor is an island, and hence there is no obstacle for connecting it with Egypt, as indeed we find in the Bible. Since, as stated, there is no reason whatever for considering Caphtor an island, the main argument for equating the island of Crete with Caphtor is completely invalidated,

As noted earlier, the mention of "Kerethites and Pelethites" in the Bible is taken as proof of their identification with Cretans, But as pointed out, it seems that the connection between Kerethi–Cretans and the island of Crete is solely one of assonance. From a rational point of view the fact that the "kerethi and pelethi" are mentioned together points to two different groups, as evidenced by the conjunctive letter waw (ו=and). If we grant that Pelethi means "plishti" (Philistines), then Kerethites and Philistines should not be equated since they are two distinct groups. If the Kerethites are presumed to be Cretans, then they too ought not be equated with Philistines. Yet, assuming the Philistines are the Kerethites, the question arises as to the need for this duplication and repetition in the same sentence.

Who are the Kerethites and Pelethites? We hear of the Krethites and Pelethites for the first time in King David's army: "And Benaiah the son of Jehoiada was over the Cherethites and over the Pelethites" (2 Sam. 20: 23). The Hebrew text reads: "And Benaiah the son of Jehoiada was over the KARI (כרי) and over the Pelethi". In other verses we read the Kerethi instead of the Kari: "and Benaiah the son of Jehoiada was over the Chrethites and the Pelethites" (2Sam. 8: 18)[80]. According to Josephus[81]: "To Benaiah son of Joados he (i. e. king David – N. G.) entrusted the command of the bodyguards, while his elder sons were in attendance on him and guarded his person".

From this passage it was understood that the Chrethites and Pelethites served as King David's bodyguard, and as already pointed out that they were considered "Cretans and Philistines".

In 2 Sam. 15: 18–19 we read about David who escapes from his son Absalom: "And all his servants passed on beside him; and all the Cherethites and all the Pelethites, and all the Gittites, six hundred men that came after

---

80   See also 1 Kn. 1: 38.
81   Josephus, Ant. VII, 110, Trans. Thackeray, Loeb Classical Libr.

him from Gath passed on before the king. Then said the king to Ittai the Gittite, wherefore goest thou also with us? return, and abide with the king; for thou art a foreigner and also an exile." It is plain from the verse "and all the Gittites, six hundred men that came...from Gath" that this number refers specifically to the Gittites and does not refer to the Cheretites and Pelethites, the supposed king's guards. The fact that the king addressed Ittai as a foreigner leads one to infer that the Cherethites and the Pelethites are not considered foreigners by him.

The fact, that the Cherethites and Pelethites are not to be considered foreigners is also indicated elsewhere, in a list of appointments by David (2Sam. 8: 17–18), we read:

"וצדוק בן־אחיטוב ואחימלך בן אביתר כהנים ושריה סופר ובניהו בן־יהוידע והכרתי והפלתי ובני דוד כהנים היו" which literally translated will read: "and Zadok the son of Ahitub and Ahimelech the son of Abiathar – priests (Hebrew :kohanim) AND Seraiah – scribe, AND Benayahu the son of Yehoiadah AND Chreti AND Plethi AND the sons of David were priests (Hebrew: kohanim)"[82]. The conjunctive letter waw (= and) between the different names in the last phrase: "and Benaiah...and the Chreti, and the Pelethi, and David's sons..." indicates that the end of the phrase "were kohanim" (i. e."were priests") applies to all the preceding names, that is to say, Benaiah, the Chreti, the Plethi, and the sons of David all were priests. As to Benaiah being a priest, this cannot be derived only from the above verse, but also is clearly stated in 1Chr. 27: 5–6; "The third captain of the host for the third month was Benaiah, the son of Jehoiadah the priest, chief...this is that Benaiah who was the mighty man of the thirty". This is also stated by Josephus (Ant. VII, 315); "The fifth was Banaios of priestly descent". Thus the final words "were priests" (kohanim) in the above verse quite obviously apply to Benaiah, as well as to the Chreti and the Pelethi and the sons of David.

As mentioned, Benaiah was set "over the Cari[83] and Pelethi" (2Sam. 20: 23). Of the Cari during Athaliah's reign we read: "And in the seventh year Jehoiadah sent and fetched the captains over hundreds of the Carites and of the guard (The Hebrew text reads ratzim רצים i. e. runners =couriers, not guards). and brought them to him into the house of Jehovah; and he made a covenant with them" (2Kn. 11: 4). This same episode is depicted with slight variations in the book of Chronicles (2 Chr. 23: 1): "And in the seventh year Jehoiadah strengthened himself and took the captains of hundreds, Azaria

---

82   This passage is wrongly translated in the A. V."and Zadok the son of Ahitub and Abimelech the son of Abiathar, were the priests; and Seraia was the scribe; and Benaiah the son of Jehoiadah was over both the Cherethites and the Pelethites; and David's sons were chief rulers. (alternative translation, "chief ministers". The Koren Bible translates thus: "and Benayahu the son of Yehoyada and the Kereti and the Peleti, and sons of David were ministers of state".

83   The Hebrew verse reads Cari (כרי) erroneously translated as Cherethites

the son of Jeroham, and Ishmael the son of Jehohanan and Azariah the son of Obed, and Maaseiah the son of Adaiah, and Elishaphat the son of Zichri, into covenant with him". It is therefore evident that in this second passage as compared to the first, there are listed specific Hebrew names instead of Carites and Ratzim (=Couriers). From this we may conclude that those called Carites were simply Hebrews[84]. (however, the Carites and Ratzim are also called Cherethites and Pelethites, and moreover scholars have even tried to link the Cherethites =Carites to Carians in Greece[85]. The fact that the Cherethi – Cari come out as Hebrew ethnics is consistent with the fact that the Cherethi and Pelethi and the sons of David were priests.[86]

We may now conclude as Furumark does that the similarity between Chereti and Crete is based on assonance alone. It is quite probable that the name Pelethi refers to people from the house of Peleth son of Jonathan from the sons of Jerahmeel of the tribe of Judah (1Chr. 2; 33). i. e. the Pelethites were people from David's own tribe. If we look carefully at the mighty people who surrounded David (1Chr. 11: 10 ff) we realise that most of them are his kinfolk or members of his tribe. Joab, Abishai and Asahel are the sons of Zeruiah – David's sister (1Chr. 2: 16). Jonathan his uncle was his counsellor (1Chr. 27: 32), Eleazar his cousin the Ahohite (1Chr. 11: 12), Elhanan his cousin[87] of Beth Lehem (1Chr. 11: 26). In the book of Samuel (2Sam. 21: 19) his name appears as "Elhanan the son of Jaare – Oregim the

---

84   Segal in commentary on 2sam 8.18 states that Gershonides (Levi ben gershon = Ralbag), and Kimhi David (=Radak) explain that kreti and pleti were israelite families.

85   MacAlister, The Philistines etc. p. 7.
Gordon, The Role of The Philistines, Antiquity, XXX, 1956, p. 23 note 5.
Maspero, Histoire Ancienne des Peuples de L'orient, p. 368.
Renan, Histoire du Peuple D'israel, tome II, p. 30.

86   My friend S. Regulant drew my attention to the verse in Is. 16: 1."שלחו כר" "משל־ארץ" Shilhu car moshel eretz" translated "send ye the lamb to the ruler of the land". "car" is translated – lamb. But in the Hebrew text car כר is vocalised by pathah = פתח (a short a'), therefore it points to being a gemmate verb; whereas "to the cari2 (לכרי) ("–kn 11: 4) is written with a qamatz (long a) a fact that strengthens the assumption of it being a gemmate verb (a consonant strengthened by a Dagesh before a guttural consonant R) i. e. the verb is כרר = Krr (karar=carar). In Arabic the verb karar is linked with runing "kurur el ayam" = in the long run. Hence the cari will be explained "the runners"= courriers, and indeed in 2 Kn. 11: 4, the cari are mentioned dovetailed with runners (in the Hebrew text = לכרי ולרצים of the Cari and the runners), hence the verse in Is. 16: 1, must be explained "Send a courrier..."and not a lamb. It is noteworthy too that in Latin languages the word for runnning is phonetically identical to the Semitic stem "karar"; Latin –Currere, Italian – correre; Spanish and Portugese – correr, French – courir.

87   The Hebrew text reads "Ben Dodo" which literally means son of his uncle = cousin. But it was translated as son of Dodo. The same applies to Elhanan of Beth Lehem who we learn elsewhere was the son of Jaare – Oregim (and not the son of Dodo).

Beth–Lehemite" (this verifies that Ben Dodo must be understood as "his cousin"). Benaiah son of Jehoiadah of Kabzeel (1Chr. 11: 22), Ira the Ithrite, Gareb the Ithrite (1Chr. 11: 40), Mahari the Netophatite, Heled the son of Bannah the Netophatite (1 Chr. 11: 30). Kabzeel is one of the cities of the tribe of Judah (Jo. 15: 21). The family of the Ithri (יתרי) is related to the families of Kiriath–Yearim in the tribe of Judah, whereas Jether (יתר) the Ishmaelite is the father of Amasa son of Abigail – David's sister (1 Chr. 2: 17; 53). The Netophatites are one of the families of Beth – Lehem (1Chr. 2: 54) etc., moreover we have already mentioned the passages in Josephus relating that David's sons served as his bodyguards. It is obvious then that David's retinue consisted mainly of members of his family or tribe, that is their make up was a tribal one, as is the custom still prevalent among Beduin tribes today. It is highly unreasonable to assume that within such a tribal formation an outside group made up of foreigners who were completely alien to the native environment would be introduced. So it is evident that we are definitely not dealing here not with foreigners, but with Hebrews – most probably from the house of the Jerahmeelites of Judah's tribe.

It is noteworthy that Phytian–Adams regards the Greek name "Aiguptos" (Egypt) as a combination of Ai = Iy and Kept which name he identifies with the biblical Iy–Caphtor. Kept or Kebt he identifies with the nomus (region) of Kept or Kopt. Basing himself on Herodotus who stated that the Greeks applied the name Aegyptos exclusively to the region of the Delta, he concludes ithat Iy– Caphtor was in fact the name of the Delta region[88].

Since Philistine origins are generally accepted as being Cretan, and connected with the so–called "sea peoples", scholars have tried to link the names of these people with Greek names. As shown, the Philistines cannot be equated with Cretans and therefore it becomes necessary to reconsider our approach to the so–called "sea peoples".

Below some comments on the subject:

A. – Various scholars try to elucidate the names of the "sea peoples" by analogy with Greek names, stressing mainly assonantal i. e. phonetic similarities. Yet in the process they create a completely distorted picture, though in their search for names with similar sounds they take in a large range of geographical regions – Libya, Asia Minor (Cilicia etc.), Rome, Sardinia, the Aegean islands, Sicily, etc; they yet utterly fail to answer the implied question: How is one to explain that a variety of different peoples from totally different geographical regions assembled together for the one purpose of migrating to the same geographical region? How could this migration of different peoples from such disparate geographical regions be successfully coordinated? Be it remembered that we are dealing here not with the 20th

---

88   Phytian – Adams, Aiguptos – A Derivation and Some Suggestions, JPOS. 1922, pp. 94–100.

century, with its abundant resources of modern transport, but with an era in which the distance between Crete and Greece or Sardinia was enormous by prevailing standards, as shown, inter alia, by the descriptions of voyages in the Iliad and Odyssey.

B. – In Papyrus Harris[89] we read: " I slew the Denyen (D'ynywn') in their isles". Assuming the D. N. N. represent the Danayans, how are we to explain the conquest of their "isles", seeing that Raamses III never reached the Greek islands? However if the text is assumed to refer to their "new" settlements in Canaan, then the expression of "isles" has nothing to do with Greece but rather with the shores of Canaan.

Similarly we read[90]: "I made for thee numerous lands in the new isles in the southern and northern districts". Again, if "isles" is taken to refer to the region of Greece, this implies that Raamses III conquered the isles of Greece, which we know is not the case. But if on the other hand the text does not refer to the Greek islands, then the word "isles" obviously should not be linked to Greece, as has been done by most scholars .

In the inscriptions on relief sculptures Raamses boasts that "the Peleset (Pw'r'st) are hung up in their towns"[91], which is to say that the P. R. S. T. were attacked in their towns. What becomes then of the theory that the P. R. S. T. supposedly Philistines, came to Egypt after they migrated from the isles of Greece before they settled in towns? .

C. – As noted earlier, the T. K. R were identified as T. K. L. Since the T is weak and pronounced like S or Z the T. K. L. became Sakal – Zakal, and from Zakal it was changed to Zakala. Scholars have seen in this name a resemblance to Siculians – Sicilians, and also to the Philistine city of Ziklag. Since the Philistines were considered Cretans, here was yet another proof of the "Myceanisation" of the Philistines and the "sea peoples". There are some scholars today who refer to Sikeli as if this was the original name written in Wen Amon's letter and Raamses III' inscriptions[92]. A number of scholars believe that the T. K. R. are identical with Teucrians. T. K. R. is found in Egyptian inscriptions also as an element in the name Tkr–Baal[93]. T. K. R. is equated by scholars with T. K. L. – S. K. L–Sakal–Sikel etc. as mentioned above, while "T. kr– Baal " is transcribed BY ALL SCHOLARS as Zakar–Baal[94]

---

89   Breasted, Records, Vol. IV, . § 403, p. 201.

90   Breasted, Records, Vol. IV, § 265, p. 146.

91   Breasted, Records, Vol. IV. § 69, p. 41.

92   Stern E., When Canaanites Became Phoenician Sailors. B. A. R. 1993. vol. 19 no. 1, pp. 25; 26, 27.

93   breasted, Records, Vol. IV. § 567, p. 279; §. 574, p. 281

94   For example: Breasted, Records, Vol. IV, §. 567, p. 279.
      MacAlister, The Philistines etc. pp. 30 – 38.
      Pritchard, ANE. Princeton, paperback reprint, 1973, Vol. I. p. 17.
      Mazar, The Philistines and... The Kingdoms of Israel and Tyre. 1966, p. 2–3 (Hebr.).

and not Sakal–Baal. Why the change? There is no reason for this change, for we are dealing with EXACTLY THE SAME NAME.

D. – In the name Takar–Baal the element "Baal" is undoubtedly Semitic. How can this element be linked to people who are thought to be Siculians–Sicilians? We should remember that these names refer to the period when they are supposed to have entered the region, which implies that the name Tkr–Baal was evidently an original and not an adopted name, for it is hardly likely that they adopted it in the short time available.

E. – The name T. K. R is also found in the letter of Wen–Amon (dated first half of the 11th century B. C.): "I reached Dor, a town of the Tjeker".[95]. Here we have clear evidence that the city of Dor belonged to the T. K. R. Since the T is weak and is pronouncd like S (as most scholars maintain) one might read S. K. R. As seen in earlier chapters, the date of the Israelite conquest of Canaan precedes the date of the letter of Wen–Amon. Who, one may ask, were the inhabitants of the city of Dor? .

In Joshua 17: 11 we read: "And Manasseh had in Issachar and in Asher Beth–Shean and its towns, and Ibleam and its towns, and the inhabitants of Dor and its towns...". It is obvious that the city of Dor was in the inheritance of Issachar, but was the property of Manasseh. The Simeonite tribe was of the same status (Jos. 19: 1–10): "their inheritance was in the midst of the inheritance of the children of Judah, and they had for their inheritance Beer–sheba or Sheba, and Molada..."etc. But all the names of the towns of the Simeonite tribe within the inheritance of the tribe of Judah appear also in exact detail in the inheritance of the tribe of Judah itself (see Jos. 15: 20–37). Thus although these towns were given to the Simeonites, they were grouped under the inheritance of Judah. It must therefore be supposed that the same also applied with regard to the city of Dor, which is listed under the name of Issachar.

As seen earlier the city of Dor is called in Wen – Amon's letter a city of the T. K. R (S. K. R.); moreover the phonetic resemblance between Skr and Issachar is inescapable the more especially as both are supposed to have owned the same town. Actually I believe the two names are identical with one another[96].

Pernigotti, Phoenicians and Egyptians p. 526 in The Phoenicians, edit. Bompiani 1988.

Bondi Sandro Filippo, The course of History p. 39 in The Phoenicians, Bompiani 1988.

Lemaire, Divinités Egyptiennes etc . pp. 89–90, STU. PH. 1986.

Sabatino Moscati, The world of the Phoenicians p. 10. weidenfeld & nicolson1968.

95 Breasted, Records, Vol. IV, §. 565, p. 278; ANE. ibid. Vol. I, p. 17.

96 As known the name Issachar according to the Bible, derives from "Yesh – Sachar" namely there is a hire (reward) (Gen. 30: 18). Sachar is the main composite of the name.

F. – In the name D. N. N. (Danayun etc.) De Rougé recognises an affinity with the Greek mythological hero Danaos, and this leads him to identify them with the Danaeans. But according to Greek mythology Danaos came from Egypt to Greece and not vice versa; so this name could not have been foreign to the region of Egypt.

G, – The name D. N. N. is present also in the Tel el Amarna tablets which means they were in the region already in the 14th century B. C. Also Hall points out that in the el Amarna period they were already settled on the coast of Canaan[97]. This however contradicts the inference, based upon the Egyptian inscriptions, which equates them with the

Danaeans. Hall tries to overcome this contradiction by stating that the D. N. N. who are mentioned in the el Amarna tablets are Danaeans who settled in Canaan during the el Amarna period, whereas the Danaeans mentioned in the Egyptian inscriptions represent a new wave of Daneans[98]. However he discounts the fact that about 300 years separate the el Amarna period from that of Raamses III[99].

H. – The name "Iy" (understood as isle), linked to the D. N. N., should be seen as referring to their places in Canaan and not Greece; hence the D. N. N. cannot be Daneans. The name D. N. N. is found also in the form D. N. (Danu), as was pointed out already by Maspero and others[100]. It is therefore more plausible to regard them as sons of the tribe of Dan who settled on the sea shore in Canaan on the 14th century B. C.

I . – The R. K (Ruku, or Reka etc.) were identified as Luku (Luka Leka etc.) and equated with Lycians. However, the Ruku are also mentioned in the el Amarna tablets[101], (circa three hundred years prior to the Raamses III period). According to Herodotus[102], the Lycians were called Termili, only in later years came to be known as Lycians.

J. – The Ekwesh (this name also is vocalised by different scholars in different ways–Akawasha, Akayusha, Akayaousha etc.) were identified by De Rougé as Achaeans. Yet the surprising fact is that in the Egyptian inscriptions they are depicted as circumcised people, a custom that was not practiced by the Greek peoples. Barnette[103] notes this circumstance, and expresse his incomprehension. Astour (according to Barnette) sees in these particular

---

97   Hall, Keftiu and The Peoples of The Sea, BSA. 1901–2, p. 1

98   Hall, ibid. p. 183.

99   This solution reminds us the one employed to explain the Exodus.

100 Maspero, The Struggle of The Nations; Egypt, Syria and Assyria, 1910, p. 462, note 1.

101 See: Hall, ibid, p. 182.
     Hall, The Peoples of The Sea, Rec. Champollion, 1922, p. 304.

102 Herodotus, VII, 92. See also Barnette, The Sea Peoples, CAH. Vol. II, Ch. 28, 1966, p. 6.

103 Barnette, ibid., p. 11.

depictions evidence of the Semitic character of the Mycenaean culture,[104] while on the other hand most scholars discount it.

K. . The "Tahanu[105] are mentioned several times together with the T. K. R Breasted saw them as Libyans[106]. About these Tahanu we read: "The land of the Meshwesh is desolated at one time the Libyans (Tahanu) and the Seped are destroyed, their seed is not"[107]. and of the Mashasha it is said that Raamses III destroyes "the names of the Asiatic lands...repelling the nine bows taking captives the Meshwesh"[108]. Evidently the Tahanu and the Mashasha are to be linked to the Asiatic lands. As to the link between the Mashasha, Tahanu, and the nine bows we learn from several inscriptions.[109] In the Merneptah Stele which refers to a war in Canaan we read: "No one raises his head among the Nine Bows, Desolation is for Tehenu, Hatti is pacified, plundered is Canaan " etc. When the Tahanu are mentioned it is in connection with the Canaanite region. This connection negates the identification of the Tahanu with Libyans and links them with Canaan. Breasted already noted the strange coincidence in the time of the wars (with the Libyans and in Amurru) and it is hardly feasible that two wars took place simultaneously, one with the "Libyans" and one in the Amorite region.[110].

Seeing that the T. K. R are often mentioned together with the Tahanu, and in the light of our identification of the T. K. R. with the tribe of Issachar, perhaps some hint of the Tahanu may be gleaned from the Bible.

In Numbers (26: 35–37) one reads: "These are the sons of Ephraim after their families: of Shutelah, the family of the Shutelahites; of Becher, the family of the Becherites; of TAHAN, the family of the TAHANITES " (emphasis– N. G.). In Chr. 7: 21 we read about the clan of Zabad in the tribe of Ephraim. The names of these two Ephraimite clans, Tahan and Zabad are phonetically identical with the names Tahanu and Sephed[111] in the Egyptian inscriptions. In the Merneptah Stele (See above p. 57) which depicts a victory over the Tahanu, there is a mention of the city of Gezer, which is known to have been an Ephraimite city.[112].

Together with the Mashasha we also meet with the name Khepher: "Mashasha son of Khepher"[113] or "Khepher came to salam, he laid down

---

104 Barnette, ibid., p. 11, note 6. Astour, Helleno Semitica, Leiden, 1965
105 Breasted, Records, Vol. IV, §. 78, p. 46.
106 For example see: Breasted, Records, Vol. IV, . § 35, pp. 83; 85.
107 Breasted, Records, Vol. IV §. 91, p. 55.
108 Breasted, Records, Vol. IV. § 103, p. 60.
109 For example see: Breasted, Records, Vol. IV, §37, p. 20; §38, p. 21; §49, p. 27; § 52, p. 29
110 Breasted Records, Vol. IV. § 133, pp. 78–79.
111 Concerning the interchange of the letters P and B and the letters S and Z, I believe discussion is superflous, since this is a well known fact.
112 See: Jos. 16: 3; Jos. 21: 21; Ju. 1: 29.
113 Breasted, Records, Vol. IV, §. 90, p. 53.

his arms together with his soldiers"[114] Khepher is mentioned in the Bible as the name of clan of the Manasseh tribe "and of Khepher, the family of the Khepherite"[115]. Perhaqps the name Mashasha is merely a corrupt form of the name Manasseh.

The tribe of Zebulun includes a clan by the name of Sered: "of Sered, the family of Sardi[116].

Other names with a phonetic resemblance to those in the Egyptian inscriptions are "Tiria" a family in the tribe of Judah of the sons of Caleb (1chr. 4: 16) = Tyr'yw'. Masa and Tema of the Ismaelite tribes: = M. S. ; Masa, (Records Vol. III. 306, p. 136; Temeh (Vol. IV. 91, p. 54; 50. p. 28). Perez –of the Perezite family in the tribe of Judah; the famillies of Mushi and Ishvi in the tribe of Asher; Recha (1Chr. 4: 12)and Lecha (1Chr. 4: 21) of the sons of Shela son of Judah (names phonetically identical to R. K–Reka Leka etc.).

Apart from the phonetic resemblance, there is no certainty that some of these names are identical to those of the Egyptian inscriptions. They are mentioned here solely to point out that within the regional area a sufficient number of names can be found of identical phonetic value to those in the Egyptian inscriptions, so making it unnecessary to search among the Greek islands and in Europe for like sounding names. Leaving aside the many contradictions involved in such identifications, these can only be made plausible by a series of distorsions and unpleasing modifications of the original Egyptian names.[117]

---

114 Breasted, Records, Vol. IV § 97. p. 57.
115 Nu. 26: 32
116 Nu. 26: 26.
117 One may mention in this context the commandement given to the Israelites: "that they make them fringes in the borders of their garments throughout their generations, and that they put upon the fringes of the borders a riband of blue" (Nu. 15: 38). Compare this to the tassels and the hems in the clothing of the so called "sea people"

WHO WERE THE HABIRU

Dating the Exodus to the Amenhotep II period implies that the el–Amarna period overlaps with the period of the Israelite conquest of Canaan. In the literature on Canaan it is common practice to identify the Hebrews or the sons of Israel with an infiltrating horde called the Habiru, mentioned in the el–Amarna tablets. The inevitable question then arises: Who are the Habiru?

In the el–Amarna tablets the name "Habiru" appears in the letters of Abdi–hiba of Jerusalem, either as Habiru or in the third person genitive and accusative plural Habiri, as well as in gentilic or adjectival form Habira. When the letters were made public, attention was drawn to this name. Some scholars regarded it as an appellation from the West Semitic (Hebrew) root hbr meaning confederate, ally, companion, i. e. people from different races who were allied, together to fight the Egyptians (Sayce, Kraeling, D'horme)[1]. Other scholars (Hommel, Jastrow) derived it from the clan name Heber (Hebrew – Hever – חבר), in the tribe of Asher. Halevi, Hillbrecht and others took them to be Elamites. In contrast to this, Conder, Knudtzon and others[2] identified the Habiru with the Hebrews, firstly on the basis of the assonance of the two names, and secondly on the grounds of similarity between the description of the Habiru wars in the el–Amarna letters and that of the Israelite conquest as depicted in the Bible. This conjecture first raised by Conder was contested by other scholars because the Habiru wars were mentioned only in the letters from Jerusalem, while the conquest depicted in the Bible referred to the whole of Canaan. Attention was therefore turned to another group mentioned in the letters as having invaded large areas of Canaan: the Sa Gaz group. On grounds of identical activity, Winckler equated the Sa Gaz with the Habiru and by doing so forged another link in the chain connecting the Habiru with the Hebrews. For if the Habiru are equated with the Sa Gaz this implies that they fought not only in the region of Jerusalem but throughout the country.

---

1   See: D'horme, Les Nouvelles Tablettes D'El Amarna, RB, 1924, (33), p. 15.
Les Habiru et Les Hebreux, JPOS, 1924, p. 166.
Kraeling, Aram and Israel, 1966, p. 34. elsewhere: (Light From Ugarit On The Habiru, BASOR, 77, 1940, pp. 32–33) kraeling rejects the ethymology from br Hbr hhr (notes).

2   Conder, Monumental Notice of Hebrew Victories, PEF, 1890, 326 – 329; TEAT, p. 141; Notes, PEF, 1891, p. 72
Knudtzon, TEAT, p. 48; Mercer, TEAT, 1939. Excursus VII, p. 84

Sayce derived the name Sa Gaz from the Assyrian Sagāsu and explained this as meaning "murderers", "executioners". Delitzche in 1896 explained it as meaning "plunderers". According to him the name derives from the Akkadian Ḥabbātu, and altough he himself expressed doubts on the matter and refrained from ruling upon it, his explanation won wide acceptance.[3] Today Sa Gaz is Regarded as a pseudo–ideogram for Sagāssu – Ḥabbātu.[4]

Granted that the name Sa Gaz is an appellative for murderers, plunderers, etc. the fact that the Sa Gaz is equated with Habiru and the Hebrews implies that another connotation must also be given to the definitions of Hebrew and Habiru. Scholars have thus begun to regard the terms Hebrew and Habiru also as appellatives instead of as proper names. Spiegelberg was the first to see in these names an appellative for wanderers which had originally been applied to all wanderers in the area as a whole, and only later came to be restricted in reference solely to the Israelites (Ibri). Landesberger derived the name Habiru from Ḥaver (Hebrew for ally, friend), and explained Haver as meaning – "going in one group" i. e. plunderers living in groups (or gangs). Hence this name has no ethnic root, but denotes people without family living outside the tribe (outcasts)[5]. Winckler[6] believed the Sa Gaz meant robbers, and according to him, the Ḥabiru, whom he believes to be the invading Hebrews, were beduins, and "beduines are notorious for their robbery and pillage". He therefore concluded that so long as the Hebrews lived a nomadic life they were called Habiru which corresponds to the appellative plunderer (Sa Gaz – Ḥabbātu). This view of Winckler's became widely accepted even though the Sa Gaz are not depicted at all as plunderers in the el–Amarna tablets, and in spite of the inaccuracies caused by such a conjecture (already referred to by Knudtzon)[7].

The deeper scholars delved into the Ḥabiru question the more they searched for and pointed out the name occurring in texts from different places such as Nuzi, Boghazköi, Alalaḥ, Ras Shamra (Ugarit), Mari etc. With the interpretation of these new texts a change took place in the approach to the Ḥabiru and Sa Gaz in general, and to the meaning of their appellatives in

---

3 In his book the Ḥab/piru Greenberg notes: "However there would seem to be a difficulty in the fact that Akkadian Šaggāšu ('destroyer murderer') is far too strong for the normal character of the group. It ill accords with such legitimate and recognized social clsses as the Sa. Gaz were at Larsa, Boghazköi, Alalaḥ or Ugarit". (ibid. p. 89).

4 See for example: D'horme, Les Pays Bibliques Au Temps D'el Amarna, RB, 1909, Greenberg, The Ḥab/Piru, p. 88;
De–Vaud, Les Patriarches Hebreux et Les Documents Modernes, RB, 1948, p. 340. Albright, The Amarna Letters From Palestine, CAH, Vol II, Chap. 20, p. 16.

5 Bottero, Le Problem des Ḥabiru – a' la rencontre assyriologique internationale, pp. XIII; XVII.

6 Knudtzon, TEAT, pp. 45 – 51.

7 See Greenberg, ibid. p. 4.

particular. Some regarded them as an ethnically heterogenous group composed of different races, Semites and others, and not a distinct tribal unit[8] "aliens who were willing to place their services at the disposal of the country into which they immigrated". strangers in their places (Lewy), slaves, refugees (Bottero), fugitives without families or a tribe (Landesberger), persons of dependent status (Alt), nomads and villagers (D'horme), etc. Chierra, in the light of data from Nuzi, interpreted the term Ḥabiru as "foreign enemies"– war prisoners. According to him, the name Ḥabiru was a term of contempt which the people of the land called these enemies until in time the name was finally accepted by the invaders themselves. According to Chierra "thus we probably have the first historical instance of a name originally used in contempt later coming to be accepted as an official designation"[9]. Alt regards the Ḥabiru–Ibri as a legal term denoting persons who depend on others, namely people who had sold themselves into slavery (self enslaved). Parzen and De Vaux think along the same lines as Chierra, but go one step further in claiming that the term "Hebrews" is also a term of contempt. Parzen[10] claims that the biblical name Ivrim – עברים = Hebrews means barbarians with an overtone of contempt, and that the Hebrews themselves became labelled in time by this appellation (the same argument being used here as Chierra did with the Ḥabiru and since Ḥabiru and Hebrews are identified with each other hence their arguments). De Vaux[11] defines the Hebrews as "a people who do not enjoy the liberty of a free citizen in his own free country" (p. 338) and the term IBRIM "Is an ancient name that the foreigners were familiar with, and employed it in a sense of contempt, but the Israelites did not apply it voluntarily to themselves. The name could have originated outside Israel (ibid p. 338). He bases these conclusions on certain biblical verses such as: "Be strong, and quit yourselves like men, O ye Philistines, that ye be not servants unto the Hebrews" (1Sam. 4: 9); "...See, he hath brought in an Hebrew unto us to mock us" (Gen. 43: 32), and many other verses.[12] I have looked up all the verses he cites in support of his conjecture but have not succeeded in finding a hint of contempt in any one of them. I have quoted the most salient of these verses in full above as examples, but even in these can find no support for his conclusions which seem to have been based rather on preconceived notions.

---

8   See: Speiser, Ethnic Movements In The Near East etc. AASOR, XIII, 1931–32, p. 34.

9   See: Chierra, Habiru and Hebrews, AJSL, (XLIX), 1932–33, pp. 118; 123–124.

10   See: Parzen, The Problem of The Ibrim (Hebrews) In The Bible, AJSL, 1932–33, PP. 254–261.

11   See: De Vaux, ibid, pp. 321– 347.

12   Gen. 39: 17; 40: 15; 43: 32; 1 Sam, 16: 19; 2: 6, 7, 11, 13; 3: 18; 5, 3; 7: 16; 9: 1. 1Sam 4: 6; 13: 3, 19; 14: 11, 21; Deut . 15: 12 (ibid. 338).

Having confirmed himself in whatever views he might hold regarding the term Hebrews, De Vaux goes on to discuss the Ḥabiru, trying to prove that the Ḥabiru and the Hebrews were both treated in the same manner. As he puts it: "Everywhere the Ḥabiru appear as strangers; the environment is inimical to them, does not accept them unless on special terms. They cannot form a nation (Jirku's view). Hence we are dealing either with a very large nation which inhabits an extensive area in the Middle East, or with a small nation wandering very curiously" (ibid. p. 340). According to him it is improbable that we are dealing with a large nation, He therefore concludes that we must be dealing with an ethnic term,[13] "and if the Ḥabiru is not an ethnic term – than the name must be an adjective which describes a way of life or a social term" (ibid p. 340).

From a multitude of ideas concerning the Ḥabiru, there crystallised a more or less unified view, which is the current one today, that the Ḥabiru is not an ethnic term but an appellative for a way of life or a term which denotes a low social status, riffraff from different nations and lands.

On the other hand, Egyptian texts from the period of Queen Hatsepsut (c. 1486–1468 B. C.), Thutmose III and Raamses II and IV refer to names such as 'pr, 'pr. w,' prjw.[14] These 'pr were slaves that laboured in quarries, built temples etc. Some scholars tried to see in them some analogy with the Hebrew slaves in Egypt. This conjecture was first made by Chabas in 1862 and was accepted now and again, although many scholars opposed it. But matters changed in 1930 when Rowe made public the finding of the stele of Seti I (c. 1318–1301) found in Beit–Shan in Israel In this stele 'pr. w is mentioned in the land of Israel. For reasons of similarity between the Ḥabiru and the 'pr. w and the proximity of place, scholars inclined towards equating the Ḥabiru with the 'pr. w. But since the Ḥabiru were identified with the Hebrews, the result of this equation was inevitably the establishment of the first consonant) ח Heb. kheth) of Ḥabiru as ע (Ain) namely Abiru (עבירו). This was regarded as proof that that the name Ḥabiru is derived from Ever (עבר) and the view that that it derives from Heber (חבר) was therefore rejected. In the word 'pr. w the' was taken to represent the letter Ain (ע) and the pr as br, namely Eber (עבר) The change from P to B was accounted for on the basis of dialectal changes in Egyptian, Akkadian or Hebrew.[15]

In 1939 Virolleaud publicised a equation he found in the Ugarit tablets in which a list of cities was given in the Akkadian and Ugarit alphabets.

---

13 This is also Parzen's approach. Parzen, ibid, p. 258
14 See Gunn in Speiser, ibid, p. 38
15 See: Speiser, ibid, p: 39
    Rowley, Ras Shamra and The Habiru Question, PEQ, 1940, p. 92
    Jack, New Light on The Habiru – Hebrew Question, PEQ, 1940, p. 98
    De Vaux, Les Patriarches Hebreux etc., RB, 1948, p. 342
    Cazelles, Hebrew – Ubru et Ḥabiru, SY. 35, 1958, P. 211

In this list there appears five times the name of the city Ḥalb (Aleppo); Akkadian–: "alu Ḥalbi lu mes SAG GAZ". Ugarit– "Ḥalb 'prm". As Jack[16] notes in connection with this, "it is not clear whether we have five diferrent towns all named Ḥalbi in the above references, or only one under different forms".

Virolleaud identified the 'prm with the 'pr. w from the Egyptian texts, and since he believed that there is a complete and clear identity between the Ḥabiru and Sa Gaz mentioned in the el–Amarna tablets and the Sa Gaz and 'prm in the Ugarit tablets, he equates the 'prm with the Ḥabiru. He thereupon concludes that 'prm must be rendered Iprim or Apirim which in his view is the plural form of Ḥeber. Hence the name is not Ḥabiru but Ḥapiru, and Iprim has nothing to do with Ibrim (= Hebrews).[17]

His view was widely accepted and most scholars today refer to Ḥapiru and not Ḥabiru.[18] Langhe and others adjusted themselves to this supposition referring to the name Ḥapiru with a P and even deriving it from Apar (not Ḥeber) which they link with the Hebrew word Afar – עפר = sand. and explained that the Ḥabiru are "sand people" namely desert people. D'horme who first derives Ḥabiru from Ḥaver, changed his view to Ḥapiru – Apar with the additional connotation of "human dust" ("poussiereux"). It should be noted here that sand is pronounced in Hebrew Afar and not Apar, and rendering it so is merely an artificial means of reconciling the pronunciation with that of the Ḥapiru. Albright[19] believes the name is Ḥabiru – Ḥapiru denoting Apiru and this last derives from the biblical name of Epher (עפר) which according to him is a corrupt form of the name Eber (עבר) "The most probable explanation of the relationship between Apiru and Ibri is that 'Apiru had the by form ipru >Epher like middle Canaanite Milku 'king' beside proto hebrew Malku later Melekh. the change from ipr to ibr is the simplest kind of partial assimilation of the voiceless b to the following voicedr."[20] In citing the Amarna letters Albright already permits himself to alter the original texts and writes Apiru instead of Ḥabiru,[21] and by doing so regards the Ḥabiru Problem as solved.

Reviewing the various ideas about the Ḥabiru, one cannot ignore

16   See for example: Jack, ibid, p. 97
17   Virolleaud, Comptes Rendus (mai – juin), 1939, p. 329, see: Jack, ibid, p. 98; De Vaux, ibid, p. 341
18   Greenberg, The Ḥab/Piru, p. 11.
19   See: Meek, Hebrew Origins, p. 11
     Albright, The Smaller Beth – Shan Stele of Sethos I, BASOR. (125), 1952, p. 24–32.
20   See: Meek, Hebrew Origins, p. 11
     Albright, The Smaller Beth – Shan Stele of Sethos I, BASOR. (125), 1952, p. 24–32.
21   See: Albright, The Amarna Letters From Palestine, CAH, II, Chap. 20, pp. 17–20

D'horme's words that[22]: "the correspondence between Ḥabiru and עבר (Ever) can only persuade those influenced by the transcription of the word עברי (ivri) into our occidental languages in the forms Hebreux, Hebrews, Hebraes etc." When scholars point out the similarity between Ḥabiru – Apiru and עברים (Ivrim) they refer to the name as it appears in the latin languages: Ibri, Ibrim, Eber etc.[23] with a hard–voiced consonant (The Hebrew letter – ב beth with a point = dagesh) which is pronounced like the English letter B. Yet the name in the Bible (Gen. 10: 25) never once appears with a hard–voiced consonant (B ב) – but only with a voiceless one – ב (The letter beth without a point – dagesh) which is pronounced as the English letter V. The name in Hebrew is phonetically pronounced Ever, Ivrim and any attempt to change its pronunciation to Eber and Ibrim is artificial with the intention of producing phonetic similarity between the name Ḥabiru (with a guttural letter Ḥ=ח) and Ivrim (with the letter ain – ע) which is transcribed in occidental languages as Hebrews, Hebreux etc.[24]

Guillaume[25] remarks that: "the genealogical tables in Genesis make it plain that the eponymous ancestor of the Hebrews was 'Eber' which it would be less confusing to write Heber". These names are written in a foreign language and the Hebrew name – עבר Ever easily changes into "Eber", and then he quite simply decides that "it would be less confusing to write Heber", the result being a name resembling the name Ḥabiru. This is as far as Guillaume goes in dealing with the similarity between the Ḥabiru and the Hebrews. But when he makes another assumption, that the Arabs are descendants of the Ḥabiru, Guillaume then turns the tables upside down and writes: "Thus if we are right in believing that the Ḥabiru were nomad Arabs, we have ground for conjecturing that the older name Abiru was slowly changed to Aribu and lastly to Arabu, the name which the Arabs have borne ever since". (ibid. p. 85) The name Ḥabiru he already varies as Abiru, since such variation in the pronunciation of Ḥ and A in latin languages is nearly indistinguishable, whereas these letters here represent the guttural consonants Ḥ (Kheth ח) and

---

22   See: D'horme, Les Ḥabiru et Les Hebreux, JPOS, 1924, p. 167.
23   For example: Jack, The Date of The Exodus In The Light of External Evidence, p. 130; pp. 97–102.
      Cazelles, ibid, p. 211
      De Vaux, Le Problem des Hapiru Apres Quinze Annees, JNES, 1968, p. 225.
      Lods, Israel, pp. 58, 59.
      Meek, ibid, pp. 7, 11; The Israelite Conquest of Ephraim, BASOR, 61, 1936, pp. 17–19.
      Speiser, ibid, p. 40.
      Albright, The Smaller Beth – Shan Stele, BASOR. (125), 1952, pp. 24–32.
24   Indeed in the biblical translations into foreign occidental languages, we read the transcription "Eber" for the name "Ever" עבר But it is a translator's error in an attempt to reconcile it with the Greek – Latin name Ebraios. However this is not the original pronunciation of the name.
25   See: Guillaume, The Ḥabiru, Hebrews and The Arabs, PEQ, 1946, p. 64.

'a (Ayin **ע**) which are pronounced quite differently in Semitic languages. Guillaume's approach is one example of how scholars shift from Ḥabiru to Arabu, as well as from Habiru to Hapiru, Apiru, Abiru, Ibrim.

As mentioned earlier, Virolleaud claims that Habiru equals Iprim or Apirim, yet such an assumption is unfounded. Having tried at all costs to prove that Iprim – apirim – Apiru – Ḥapiru–Ḥabiru are one and the same, he thereupon chooses to read it as Iprim.

Since 'prm is known as denoting consonants only, it might well be pronounced Iprim, Oprim, Oparim, Apirim etc. with a strong P, (**פ**) or with a voiceless P–(**פ**= f) Afirim, Ifrim, Ofarim, Efrim and even Efraim, as in the tribal name Ephraim (the name in Hebrew is written with the letter Aleph– **א** which interchanges with the letter Ayin – **ע**.[26]

The same is true of the names 'prw, 'pr, etc. in the Egyptian texts. Egyptian writing, as with Ancient Hebrew, records only consonants without any vowel notation, so that 'prw,' pr, may be pronounced in a variety of ways, e. g. Apriu, Aperu, Eperu, Apuri, Apuriu etc.[27] and indeed each scholar refers to the name as best suits him[28].

Virolleaud claims that Ḥabiru equals 'prm based on the equation Ḥalb Sa Gaz– Ḥalb 'Prm which he considers interchangeable. Since the Amarna letters show the Sa Gaz and the Ḥabiru to be interchangeable he considers them identical. It is true that such interchangeability can be found in the Amarna tablets: in several letters the writer opens with the term Sa Gaz and concludes with the Ḥabiru and vice versa. Yet in many other letters the writer likewise begins with Sa Gaz and ends up with Abd Ashera or Aziru and vice versa.[29] Are the names 'prm and Aziru therefore identical, or 'prm and Abd Ashera? The sole conclusion we may draw is that a certain connection exists between them, nothing more. The names Israelites, Hebrews and Jews may indicate, for example, the same people, yet this does not mean that these

---

26 About the interchange of letters Aleph and Ayin see: Gesenius, Hebrew Grammar, 2nd English edit., § 6r, p. 35. Wright, Lectures on The Comparative Grammar of The Semite Languages. Cambridge university press, 1890, p. 48f. Harris, A Grammar of The Phoenician Language, 1936, p. 18.

27 Yeivin, Toldot Haktav Haivri, (The History of the Jewish Script). Library of Palestinology, 1938, pp. 11–12 (Hebrew).
    Gunn by Speiser, Speiser, Ethnic Movements In The Near East, AASOR. (13), 1931–1932, p. 38; note 93.

28 For example: Speiser, ibid, p. 38 – Apuru; Petrie, Palestine And Israel, p. 41(21) –Apuiru Rowley, Israel Sojourn In Egypt, p. 22, – Aperu; Ras Shamra And The Ḥabiru Question, PEQ 1940, p. 90; – Aperu; Wilson, The Eperu of The Egyptian Inscriptions, AJSL, 1932– 33, p. 275; Mercer. TEAT, Excursus, VII, p. 839.
    – Eperu. Hall, PEQ, 1923, p. 131. Aperiu; Brugsch, Egypt Under The Pharaohs, 1891, p. 318, Apura, Aperiu, Aper.

29 See examples in next pages.

three names are synonymous. Gunn[30] vehemently rejects the identification of Ḥabiru with Apiru because: "no instance is known of transliterating ḥor ḥby'." Poesner makes similar claims: "in the transcription of Semitic words to Egyptian, the Egyptian is used solely to render the Semitic Ayin."[31] For unexplained reasons these arguments are shunted aside and disregarded, perhaps because of the embarrassment they create. Jack who refers to the views of Meek, Chierra and Others justifiably asks: "...Thus, heterogenous diversified horde, belonging to various nationalities, coalesced by and by, probably in a short time into one united harmonious whole: From being a mixed lot of different races, they speedily became one and the same race. This is surely the most extraordinary transformation in history. Besides, how could these invaders, with their methods of violence and subjugation possibly be 'foreign servants'."[32] Such questions receive greater amplification once we realise that the period of the Exodus and the conquest of Israel is the same period as that of the el–Amarna tablets.

In addition to Jack's questions, other problens arise as indicated by Reuveni in his book KADMUT HAIVRIM (in Hebrew):[33] "If the name Habiru is an appellative for a special sort of people how could such an appellation persist so many generations later and in different countries" (p. 159). "One must take notice of this revealing fact that none of the scholars who held conjectures about 'social status' or 'profession' were able either to explain or to clarify what the Habiru status or profession might finally be." (ibid. p. 172). We may add to such questions by asking: If we are dealing with an appellative, how is it that in different countries and in different languages an identical appellative was formed in order to denote the same status, often in the very same period? Why should the name Apiru – Abiru – Ibrim be written as Ḥabiru in a region where phonetically there is no impediment or difficulty whatsoever in pronouncing guttural consonants such as Ayin (ע) There is no reason for changing the letter Ayin into Ḥ–Kheth. We might perhaps accept such a change by the Egyptians, But not in Canaan or Syria or Mesopotamia where the Hebrews were integrated even before the Ḥabiru invasion in the Amarna period.

Greenberg summarizes the Habiru–Apiru question as follows:[34] "The proposed equation of 'Apiru with the Biblical Hebrews' involves problems of a philological, ethnic–social, and historical nature.... The philological side of the equation may be summed up thus: On the face of it 'apiru and 'ibri

---

30   Gunn by Speiser, Ibid, p. 38. See also Mercer, Excursus VII, TEAT p. 839.
31   See: Poesner, Textes Egyptiennes, p. 165. in booklet: Le Problem De Habiru, Cahiers de la Societe' Assiatique, par J. Bottero.
32   See: Jack, New Light on The Ḥabiru – Hebrew Question, PEQ. 1940, pp. 114–115.
33   Reuveni, Kadmut Haivrim (Hebrew).
34   Greenberg, The Hab/Piru, pp. 91–92.

differ both in derivation as well as morphology. 'Apiru is a verbal adjective from 'pr;' ibri is agentilic of the substantive base 'eber from 'br. But eber < 'br may possibly go back to 'abir, so that the gentilic and the verbal adjective may ultimately be derived from the same base,"[35]

To sum up, the tendency to equate the Ḥabiru with the Hebrews raises philological and historical problems, and is confronted by a series of objections. Or, as Bottero put it in 1954: "Thus after sixty five years of findings, research, discussion and hypotheses on the problem of the Ḥabiru, it seems that the only evidence that still remains outstanding today is that quote capita tot sententiae or nearly so"[36].

Having realised that the el–Amarna period overlaps with the period of the conquest of the land of Canaan by the Israelites, let us now try and see whether we can find any allusion to the Ḥabiru in the Bible.[37]

In the book of Numbers[38] we read that Balaam the son of Beor is sent to curse the Israelites: "And he looked on the Kenites, and took up his parable and said...". Who were these Kenites? . In Num. 10: 29–32 we read: "And Moses said unto Hobab, the son of Raguel (in Hebrew–Reuel) the Midianite, Moses' father–in–law, we are journeying unto the place of which the Lord said, I will give it you: Come thou with us, and we will do thee good: for the Lord hath spoken good concerning Israel And he said (Hobab – N. G) unto him, I will not go; but I will depart to my own land, and to my kindred. And he said (Moses –N. G.), leave us not, I pray thee; forasmuch as thou knowest how we are to encamp in the wilderness, and thou mayest be to us instead of eyes". This dialogue between Moses and Hobab is abruptly cut, and the subsequent verses do not inform us if Hobab agreed or not to travel with the Israelites. But the answer to this can be found in Judges,[39] in the story of Sisera, the captain of Jabin's army, and Yael "the wife of Ḥeber the Kenite" which goes as follows: "Now Ḥeber the Kenite, which was of the children of Hobab the father–in–law of Moses, had severed himself from the Kenites and pitched his tent unto the plain of Zaanaim, which is by Kedes ". From this statement it is evident that Ḥeber is a son of Ken (Hebrew Kayin– קִין) and that Ken is a son of Hobab, Moses' father–in–law. But since the text

---

35 Let us note here that this argument is based on the analogy with the words Melekh and Malik (=king). (See Speiser, ibid, p. 40; Greenberg, ibid, p. 91). Perhaps the morphology of Melekh–Malik differs, but semantically they are identical, Whereas Ever (Eber) and Avir (Abir) are completely different in meaning.

36 As many heads so many opinions. (Bottero, ibid, p. XXVIII).

37 The following section about Ḥeber the Kenite which continues till the end of the chapter has already been published in booklet form under the title "who were the phoenicians?", first appearing in Geneva, 1952 and then in Israel, 1962.

38 Num. 24, 21.

39 Judges, 4, 11.

informs us that Balaam sees the Kenite we can infer that Hobab did not go with the Israelites to show them their way in the desert. For had they done so, the text would have referred to them under the name of Hobab and not 'Kenite' according to the name Kayin (Ken), Hobab's son. This inference is corroborated by the verse in the book of Samuel[40]: "And Saul came to a city of Amalek, and laid wait in the valley, and Saul said unto the Kenites, go, depart, get you down from among the Amalekites, lest I destroy you with them: FOR YE SHEWED KINDNESS TO ALL THE CHILDREN OF ISRAEL, WHEN THEY CAME UP OUT OF EGYPT" (My emphasis – N. G.). The Hebrew text reads "Asita khesed "עשית חסד"which is really: "You have done a favour–benevolence" instead of merely showing kindness.

From the above we understand that the favour they did "TO ALL" the children of Israel was in showing them the way through the desert after they left Egypt. Josephus also states: "They gave also the descendants of Jethro, the Midianite, the father–in–law of Moses, territory for habitation; for quitting their native country they had followed the Hebrews and companied with them in the wilderness."[41]

On the other hand we read that: "...the children of the Kenite, Moses' father–in–law, went up out of the city of palm trees with the children of Judah into the wilderness of Judah, which lieth in the south of Arad; and they went and dwelt among the people."[42]

From the above verses we see that the Kenites are actually the "children of the kenite" Although Hobab did not agree to join the sons of Israel, a large clan (Balaam speaks of them as a group apart) from among the sons of the Kenite (Ken – Kayin), but not Kayin himself, left their tribe and joined the Israelites to show their way through the desert. The name of this clan is not mentioned in the Bible, but from the verses in Judges that: "...Heber the Kenite had severed himself from the Kenites..." it is quite clear that the name of this clan is "Heber the Kenite".[43]

Most scholars see the name "Heber the Kenite" as a proper name because of the reference to "Yael the wife of Heber the Kenite" (יעל אשת חבר הקיני) They assume that Yael was the wife of a man with such a name.[44] Yet in the Bible we often come across phrases such as "Ish Yehuda" "Ish Levy", "Ish

---

40   1Sam. 15, 5–6.

41   Ant. V–127.

42   Ju. 1, 16.

43   The verse in Hebrew informs us that Heber the Kenite separated from Kayin and not from the sons of Kayin;" "...וחבר הקיני נפרד מקין מבני חבב חתן משה, –"and Heber the Kenite separated from Kayin of the sons of Hobab, Moses' father–in–law". (Ju. 4: 11).

44   See for example: "Heber" in The Jewish Encyclopedia; Garstang, Joshua – Judges, p. 301.

Israel" etc.[45] which gives the word "man" (Hebrew – Ish) in conjunction with the tribal or the nation's name. The meaning of such verses is: "a man from the tribe of Judah "or" "a man from the tribe of Levy" etc. The same principle applies when we refer to a woman from a certain tribe. In such cases we would have to use the conjunctive of "Isha" (=woman) i. e. Eshet (= אשת wife of). Thus, in verses such as the above, we would have the combination "Eshet Yehuda" (the wife of Judah" ,"(Eshet Levy" (the wife of Levy) etc. really meaning a woman from the tribe of Judah, Levy etc., and not to be explained as referring to the wife of a certain man named Judah, nor the wife of a certain man called Levy, etc. This also applies in the verse referring to "Jael the wife of Heber the Kenite" (Hebrew –"Yael Eshet Heber Hakeni), i. e. Yael is a woman of the tribe of Heber the Kenite. Josephus (Ant. V; 207) also refers to "one kenite woman named Yael."

Scholars thought that Heber was not a clan name, since the Bible mentions only twelve tribes, and Heber the Kenite was not included as a tribe amongst the twelve. In spite of their coexistence with the Israelites, they were not considered as part of them, and they acquired their share of the land together with that of the tribe of Judah. The Bible mentions this in connection with the lots assigned to each tribe, as quoted above: "...the children of the Kenite, Moses' father–in–law, went up out of the city of palm trees with the children of Judah into the wilderness of Judah, which lieth in the south of Arad; and they went and dwelt among the people" (Ju. 1, 16). Hence their lot was included with that of Judah, and their conquests were made together with that tribe.

The conquests of the Ḥabiru mentioned in the el–Amarna tablets refer to a region of Jerusalem which, according to the Bible, was, part of the lot of the tribe of Judah. This fact confirms the assumption that the Ḥabiru are simply the clan of Heber the Kenite which had followed the Israelites to show them their way in the desert.

In many of the el–Amarna tablets there is mention of attacks by Sa–Gaz people. Sometimes they are termed Sabe Gaz and at other times as Sa Gaz or just Gaz. D'horme states that: "it therefore implies that the essential element is represented by Gaz".[46]

We have previously examined, among other things, the accepted view about the connection and identification between the Sa Gaz and the Ḥabiru, and the explanation given to this name. We have seen that the period of the wars mentioned in the el–Amarna letters is identical with the period of the Israelite entry and conquest of Canaan. We noted that Aziru mentioned in the Tablets can be equated with the tribe of Asher, and have now learned

---

45   Ju., 19, 1; 2Sam 20, 1; 1Sam, 17, 24 and others. We refer to the Hebrew text and not to the translations.
46   See: D'horme, La Question des Ḥabiri, RHR, 1938, p. 173.

that the Habiru is to be identified with the tribe of Heber the Kenite. Who, therefore, are the Sa Gaz?

As already indicated, the Sa Gaz is regarded as a pseudo–ideogram for Sagassu (Ḥabbātu–destroyers–plunderers) etc. Some regard them as a group connected with the Ḥabiru without being identical with them, (Knudtzon)[47], Whereas others (Winckler, Weber, Mercer, Cook, Virolleaud et al) believe them to be identical with the Ḥabiru, and this later view holds today.[48] It is also widely accepted that Abd–Ashera (Ashirta) and Aziru were connected with them.

If we turn to the el–Amarna tablets we realise that in many letters "Aziru" is mentioned concurrently with Sa Gaz. For example, in letter 117[49] (sent by Rib Adi, king of Gubla) Rib Adi asks the Egyptian king for help against Aziru (ibid ff. 32– 40). By the end of the letter (ff. 54–59) the subject suddenly changes into Sa Gaz: "If in this year there are no archers than all lands will belong to the Gaz people." One gets the impression that according to the writer of the letter, Aziru is the same as the Gaz people. On the other hand, in letter 116[50], Rib Adi announces the fall of the city of Sumura: "...for the sons of Abdi–Asirta have conquered it...all my cities have united with the Gaz people." In contrast to the former letter cited, the subject of this letter is the "sons of Abdi Ashirta" which changes at the end into "the Gaz people". One may therefore assert that the writer of the letter regarded the sons of Abdi Ashirta and the Gaz people as identical.

In another tablet[51] Rib Adi informs the king that "All my cities, that are in the mountains and on the sea shore have united with the Gaz people. Gubla with two cities is left to me, and behold now Abdi Asirta has taken Sigata to himself."

Here, too, the letter starts with the "Gaz people" and ends with Abdi Ashirta, showing once again that the letter writer identified Abdi Ashirta (Abdi Ashera) with the Sa Gaz.

Similar instances occur in a great number of tablets[52] where the writer opens with Sa Gaz and closes with Aziru or Abdi Asirta or sons of Abdi Asirta and vice versa. Greenberg points out that:[53] "The analysis of the relation of the Gaz to Abdi–Ashirta is complicated by the evidently free interchange of

---

47 See: Preface, Knudtzon, TEAT, pp. 45–52.
48 See: De–Vaux, Le Problem des Hapiru Apres Quinze Annees, JNES, 1968, p. 22; D'horme, ibid, pp. 170–187
49 Mercer, Knudtzon, TEAT.
50 Mercer, Knudtzon, TEAT.
51 Mercer, TEAT, no. 74, L. 19–24.
52 52. See for example: letter 79 (Mercer), compare lines 19–21, 25–26, to lines 38–47. Letter 81 (Mercer); compare line 12 to the begining of the letter and its end. Letter 104 (Mercer) compare it to its ending. See letters 41, 69, 88 and more.
53 See: Greenberg, The Hab/Piru, p. 71.

the two. We note, in the first place, that the conquests of each are identical: Sumur has gone over to the Gaz (71: 34ff), or to Abdi–Ashirta (84: 11ff); ...all the lands are joining the Gaz (72: 26ff), or Abdi–Ashirta (73: 39ff). The solution to Rib Addi's troubles is the despatch of archers to drive out the Gaz (72: 22ff), or Abdi–Ashirta (77: 79ff) etc."

It may therefore be assumed that Aziru, Abdi–Ashirta (Abd Ashera), Gaz people and sons of Abd Ashera are synonymous. Mercer actually believed that there were three invasions of Rib Addi's cities – one by the Gaz people, a second by Abd Ashera and a third by Aziru.[54] Adopting such a supposition inevitably forces us to assume that these three invasions took place in the same cities during the same period of time. Such a coincidence of events is extremely unlikely

As with the name of Aziru, the name Gaz appears in the singular form: "this Gaz man".[55] We have already noted that Abd–Ashera (Abdi Ashirta) and "sons of Abd Ashera" are surnames of Aziru. And in speaking of Aziru we also mentioned the fact that the Amorite letter Z transcribes to Sh (Hebrew letter Shin). This principle might also be applied to the name "Gaz" from which we get the name Gash, phonetically resembling the Hebrew name Goshen. I therefore suggest taking the name Gash–Gaz as a form of Goshen, which makes the "Gaz people" – Goshen people, i. e. a surname given the Israelites who came from Goshen. Occasionally we read about Sabe Gaz or Sa Gaz: perhaps the word Sabe stands for the semitic word "Zava" which means Army – soldiers, i. e. the army or soldiers of Goshen, with "Sa" being the abbreviated form. The author of a certain booklet[56] I chanced to find, links the name Goshen with the Arabic word "Gish"[57] meaning grass that grows by rain water only, i. e. pasture–land. It may be that Goshen was at first a name which meant a type of soil, namely pasture–land, which is why we have a recurrence of this name in the southern part of Israel (Jos. 10: 41): "And Joshua smote them from Kadesh Barnea even unto Gaza, and all the country of Goshen".

Rabbi Saadia translated Land of Goshen as "Balad el Sedir" meaning land of grass or "grass soil". In Arabic "Sider"and "Gish" are synonymous, both meaning grass, the difference being that the first means ordinary grass, while the second means grass whose growth is conditioned by rain water, namely, "pasture land" grass. The word Gez is found in the book of Psalms signifying grass[58]: "He shall come down like rain upon mown grass" (in Hebrew –"Yered kamatar al Gez" – ירד כמטר על גז).

---

54   See: Mercer, TEAT, p. 836.
55   See: Knudtzon, TEAT, 71/L. 24; 91/L. 3–5; 112.
56   Moyal. D., Or Mimizrah (Hebrew).
57   غِبش
58   Ps. 72, 6.

It is reasonable to suppose that the name Gaz is synonymous with Goshen and probably the name Gaz originally meant an appellative not for people of a certain specific geoghraphical region but for herdsmen in general.

To summarise: The Israelites are surnamed "Gaz people" and sometimes Sabe Gaz = Gaz soldiers. It is interesting to note that near the city of On Heliopolis mentioned in the previous chapter, with Goshen located in its suburbs, there is a place called Gizeh where the famous pyramids are to be found. The name Gizeh resembles Gaz phonetically, and Josephus attributes the building of Pyramids to the Israelites when he says[59]" and with the rearing of pyramid after pyramid they exhausted our race".

If we accept this conjecture that Gaz equals Goshen, then the difficulties mentioned throughout the discussion are thereby resolved. The Habiru is the tribe of Heber the Kenite, but at the same time they are linked to the soldiers of Goshen (the sons of Israel). They are a part of the Israelites but also have their own name. Aziru is the tribe of Asher, but they are also one of the tribes of Goshen. Abd–Ashera is an appellative for the Israelites (Ashera worshippers) who are also called Sabe–Gaz = army of Goshen. It is therefore obvious that there were not three invasions of Rib Addi's land during the same period, but only one invasion by the tribe of Asher (Aziru) whose people were sometimes called "Aziru" (Ashiru), sometimes Abd Ashera (Asirta–Asratu) or sons of Abdi–Asirta, and sometimes people of Goshen or army of Goshen.

---

59   Ant. II –203.

THE PERIOD OF THE JUDGES

As stated earlier, the Exodus took place c. 1446 B. C. and the conquest of the land began c. 1406 B. C. According to the Bible, the region of Sidon was conquered by the tribe of Asher, identified with 'Aziru' mentioned in the el–Amarna tablets as having conquered this region. We may conclude that according both these sources, the region of Sidon must have been an Israelite one. Yet the Bible appears to contradict our conclusion by its narratives about Hiram king of Zor (Tyre) and Ahab who marries Jezebel, the daughter of Etbaal, king of the Sidonians; about David and Solomon and others who" reigned over all Israel", excluding Sidon.

It is puzzling that after the war waged by Asher in the region of Sidon (mentioned in the book of Judges), the Bible does not mention any other war between the Tyrians or Sidonians and the Israelites, whereas many wars of the Israelite tribes against the Philistines, Amorites, Moabites, etc. are mentioned repeatedly. Moreover, when David ascends the throne, a strong friendship develop between Sidon and Israel David is depicted in the Bible as an ambitious man, a warrior and a conqueror, a man whom God does not choose to build the Temple because his hands "shed blood abundantly".[1] It is strange that such a man does not go to war against Tyre and Sidon in spite of the fact that these were two important and rich harbour cities. Furthermore, he is a personal friend of king Hiram, and Solomon his successor even enlarges upon this friendship.

On the face of it, the Biblical narrative of Saul's coronation[2] gives the impression that Saul was the first Israelite king, and that until his election to the throne there were only judges. The term 'Judges' was taken to mean 'saviours' 'deliverers', on the basis of certain verses in the book of Judges: "...the Lord raised up judges, which delivered them out of the hand of those that spoiled them" (Ju. 2; 16)."And when the Lord raised them up judges, then the Lord was with the judge, and delivered them out of the hand of their enemies all the days of the judge" (Ju. 2; 18), "And after him was Shamgar, the son of Anath, which slew of the Philistines...and he also delivered Israel" (Ju. 3; 31) Garstang[3] in his book Joshua – Judges remarks that "the Hebrew

---

1   See: 1Chr. 22; 7–8.
2   See: 1Sam. chp. 8, 9.
3   Garstang, Joshua– Judges, pp. 265–266.

word for judge shofet is not in this case to be interpreted in the English sense of law giver or arbitrator. but rather as deliverer". This view which links judges with deliverers in general and the verse above" and after him was Shamgar, the son of Anath...and he also delivered..." In particular, do not accord with what is said in the song of Deborah:[4] "in the days of Shamgar the son of Anath, in the days of Jael, the highways were unoccupied, and the travellers walked through byways". Shamgar was a judge, and if the highways were unoccupied in his time because of troubles in the country, how can he be a deliverer? The version in the Song of Deborah must be the more authentic one since it forms an integral part of some ancient song retained without emendation in the biblical narrative. It is evident that Judge is a term of authority paralleling that of a king; as shown in the book of Samuel:[5] "make us a king to judge us like all the nations". In the book of Judges (9: 1–2) we read that after the death of Jerubaal, his son Abimelech came to Shechem, to his mother's brethren and tells them: "Speak, I pray you, in the ears of all the men of Shechem, whether is better for you, either that all the sons of Jerubaal, which are threescore and ten persons, reign over you, or that one reign over you?". Further on, (7; 6) in the same chapter, we read: "And all the men of Shechem gathered together, and all the house of Milo, and went and made Abimelech king..."

We can therefore conclude from this verse that Abimelech, already before Saul, was crowned king in Israel Despite this we read concerning him "Vayasar" = "וישר" (ruled; commanded – ibid. 22) and not "Vayimloch" – ("וימלוך" reigned), even though the English translation reads "reigned". In the Ugarit tablets, however, the name "sar" is synonymous with king.[6]

When Abimelech addresses the Shechemites with the words: "Whether is better for you, either that all the sons of Jerubaal...reign over you..." it seems the Shechemites had expected that in the natural course of things authority would pass by inheritance to seventy people. We may safely assume then that Jerubaal himself was already king. In Chapter 8 of the book of Judges concerning Jerubaal's pursuit of Zebah and Zalmuna, the Midianite kings: we read[7] "Then said he unto Zebah and Zalmuna, what manner of men were they whom ye slew at Tabor, And they answered, as thou art, so were they; each one resembled the children of a king. And he said, They were my brethren." If we take this verse literally, it may imply that Jerubaal was a king's son, and that Joash his father, was a king. After Jerubaal's death, his title passes by inheritance to his sons, one of whom, Abimelech, was

---

4   Ju. 5; 6.
5   1Sam. 8: 5, 20.
6   For example: Cazelles, Essai Sur Le Pouvoir de La Divinité a' Ugarit et en Israel, Ugaritica VI, Paris, 1969, p. 25.
7   verses 18–19.

eventually crowned king. These facts put together indicate that there were kings in Israel, if only to mention Abimelech, before Saul was crowned. The verses recurring: "in those days there was no king in Israel" (Ju. ch. 18: 19) which were brought as evidence that no king had reigned before Saul, may be explained as referring to those days, when a PARTICULAR event related in that SPECIFIC chapter occurred. Such acts as the villainous outrage in Gibeah (Ju. ch. 19), and the destruction of Laish by the tribe of Dan, of "a people that were at quiet and secure" (Ju. ch. 18) were possible because there was no one at the time to prevent such incidents happening, i. e."in those days there was no king in Israel, but every man did that which was right in his own eyes." (Ju. 17; 6).

In 1Sam. 12: 11 the prophet reproves the Israelites: "And the Lord sent Jerubaal, and Bedan, and Jephtah and Samuel, and delivered you out of the hand of your enemies", whereas in the Song of Deborah (Ju. 5; 6) we read: "in the days of Shamgar the son of Anath, in the days of Yael, the highways were unoccupied...". Shamgar ben Anath, Jephtah, Jerubaal, and Samuel are mentioned elsewhere in the Bible as Judges, while Bedan, Yael, are names only casually mentioned here. From the above, we may assume that the book of Judges, for one reason or another, does not give a full account of Israelite history at that period, and we shall return to this issue later. Let us merely note here that the Book of Chronicles does not mention the period of the Judges at all, and opens directly with the period of King David.

Occasionally we read verses such as: "he (David–N. G.) reigned...over all Israel" (2Sam. 5: 4), which leads us to assume that David ruled over all Israel and that there were no other kings ruling over Israel in his time. But in the Book of Chronicles we read that David sends ministers to all the Israelite tribes. When we number them, we find only ten listed: the two tribes to whom he does not send ministers are the tribe of Asher and the tribe of Gad. (1 Chr. 27; 16–22). This is significant in the light of what has been already demonstrated, that the tribe of Asher conquered the region of Tyre and Sidon, that Hiram, king of Tyre, reigned in David's time, that there had been kings before Saul who ruled over certain areas in Israel even though they are not called kings. From this we may assume that Hiram was an Israelite king who reigned over the tribe of Asher, or part of it. This explains the close ties of friendship between David and Solomon and the king of Tyre.

If we recall that Solomon asked for Hiram's help in the construction of the Temple, surely it would be sacreligious to request help with such a holy building from a foreign ruler. If even David was not permitted to construct the Temple, a minori ad majus, a foreigner.

Yet if Hiram is a king of an Israelite tribe, why is it not written that Hiram is the king of the Asher tribe, rather than the king of Tyre. The answer to this may be found in the Bible.

In 1 Sam. 31 we read that the Philistines fastened Saul's body to the wall of Beth–Shan, and that the inhabitants of Jabesh–Gilead took down Saul's body and buried it. The text does not indicate, even by allusion, whether these inhabitants of Jabesh–Gilead were Israelites or not. But in 1 Sam. (11; 1–3) the people of Jabesh–Gilead are mentioned: "Then Nahash the Ammonite came up and encamped against Jabesh–Gilead: and all the men of Jabesh said to Nahash, make a covenant with us, and we will serve thee. And Nahash the Ammonite answered them, on this condition will I make a covenant with you, that I may thrust out all your right eyes, and LAY IT FOR A REPROACH UPON ALL ISRAEL. And the elders of Jabesh said unto him, Give us seven days despite, that we may send messengers unto ALL THE COASTS OF ISRAEL and then, if there be no man to save us, we will come out to thee." (My emphasis–N. G.).

We read about them again in Judges[8], where we are told that the Israelites repented killing most of the Benjamite tribe and try to save it. But since the Israelites swore not to marry the Benjamites they searched for those Israelites who had not participated in this war, and were therefore free from the vow made: "And they said, what one is there OF THE TRIBES OF ISRAEL that came not up to Mizpeh to the Lord? And, Behold, there came none to the camp from Jabesh–Gilead." It is evident, therefore, that the people of Jabesh–Gilead were Israelites. Nevertheless the Bible calls them by their city and not by their tribal name. Similarly we read in the Book of Samuel[9] that David wants to count the number of Israelites: "Then they came to Gilead, and to the land of Tahtim–hodshi; and they came to Dan–jaan, and about to Zidon. And came to the stronghold of Tyre, and to all the cities of the Hivites, and of the Canaanites: and they went out to the south of Judah, even to Beer–sheba". Here, too, we get the city names and not the tribal ones. In the Book of Judges, Ch. 18, we are told that the tribe of Dan looking for an inheritance: "...came to Laish unto a people that were at quiet and secure, and they smote them with the edge of the sword...And there was no deliverer because it was far from Zidon."[10] It is obvious from the way the story is told that a villainous act was done to the people of Laish, for Dan "came unto a people that were at quiet and secure" etc.

In the Bible we read about Moses who commands the Israelites to destroy the Canaanites, and forbids them to make peace with the Canaanite population. Assimilation with them is considered an abomination. It is amazing, therefore, that instead of depicting the victory over the people of Laish, "the Sidonians", the Bible describes it as a villainous deed. Furthermore,

8   Ju. 21; 8
9   2Sam. 24; 6–7
10   Ju. 18: 7; 27–28.

the narrative commences with the phrase "In those days there was no king in Israel"

As we have seen, it was the tribe of Asher which had conquered the region of Tyre and Sidon. If so, the people of Laish must have been Israelites. Therefore the description as a villainous deed, and the explanation that such an act took place because "in those days there was no king in Israel".

From the biblical narrative we must conclude that the narrow tribal framework existed up until the Israelites began settling in the land, but once they were established there, and settled down, they began to be named after their cities. The Israelites did not give new names to conquered cities, and kept the original names existing before the conquest – Gezer fell, and Gezer was rebuilt, Sidon fell and Sidon was rebuilt, Jaffa fell and Jaffa was rebuilt. David sent out to all the Hittite and Canaanite cities to count the Israelites. Hence in the course of time, an Israelite from Sidon was called a "Sidonian" after the name of the city. However, since the Canaanites were not entirely destroyed, a Sidonian Canaanite would also be called a Sidonian. The same is true with Tyrians etc. A parallel can be drawn from our own times, with cities like Jaffa, or Ramle which were inhabited previously by Arabs, and are now also inhabited by Jews, without the name being changed. Until recently, the name 'Jaffaite' was synonymous with "an Arab from Jaffa", but nowadays it refers to either a Jew or an Arab residing in Jaffa.

In 1 Kings (7: 13–14) we read: "And king Solomon sent and fetched Hiram out of Tyre. He was a widow's son of the tribe of Naphtali, and his father was a man of Tyre." It is also told there that this Hiram constructs the Temple. The same story, with slight variations, is found in the Book of Chronicles,[11] where Hiram king of Tyre sends an experienced man to king Solomon to help him build the Temple: "And now I have sent a cunning man, endued with understanding, of Huram my father's. The son of a woman of the daughters of Dan, and his father was a man of Tyre". The name of this man is mentioned only in chapter 4 verse 11: "And Huram made the pots and the shovels and the basins. And Huram finished the work that he was to make for king Solomon for the house of God". We have here the same narrative, with slight variations, With The same name (Hiram – Huram) in both verses, referring to the same construction, (the Temple). But on one point they seem to contradict each other: the Book of Kings speaks of Hiram as "a widow's son of the tribe of Naphtali and his father was a man of Tyre", whereas the book of Chronicles speaks of him as "the son of a woman of the daughters of Dan and his father was a man of Tyre". From both these verses scholars assumed as if Hiram was an israelite only on his mother's side while his father was a Canaanite–Tyrian[12] and that in the names Dan and Naphtali

---

11   2Chr. 2: 13–14.

12   See for example: Slouschz, Hebreo – Phéniciens et Judeo Berbères, Archives

an error was. introduced by a copyist. It was also concluded that the Israelite Temple was copied from Phoenician temple construction.

As a matter of fact, there is no contradiction between these two verses: in the Hebrew text the one verse reads "Ben isha min bnot Dan בן אשה מן בנות דן" = "son of a woman of the daughters of Dan". The name Dan refers to the word "isha"– woman, i. e. Hiram's mother is from the tribe of Dan (as so translated into English); in the second verse the Hebrew text reads "Ben isha almana hoo mimate Naphtali "בן אשה אלמנה הוא משבט נפתלי" translated "he was a widow's son of the tribe of Naphtali" but the name Naphtali in the Hebrew text refers to the word" Hoo–= הוא= he, i. e. Hiram himself is from the tribe of Naphtali, and not the widow. In other words, Hiram is from the tribe of Naphtali, while his mother is from the tribe of Dan. It must be remembered that tribal affiliation was by the house of the father[13]. Hence Hiram was from the tribe of Naphtali by the house of his father, whereas his mother was from the tribe of Dan. When the text adds: "And his father was a man of Tyre", this is to inform the reader that although his father was of the tribe of Naphtali, he resided in Tyre. Why was it necessary to make this remark? because it was the tribe of Asher which had conquered Tyre and settled there, and not the tribe of Naphtali.

Rashi (rabbi shlomo Itzhaki) and Redag (david kimhi) comment these verses the same.

Hiram is then an Israelite both on his father's and on his mother's side. Josephus[14] writes about Hiram "who was of Naphtalite descent on his mother's side – for she was of that tribe – and whose father was Urias, an Israelite by race." This means he regards him as an Israelite on both sides, except that he substitutes the tribe of Dan with the tribe of Naphtali on the mother's side. To sum up, names such as Sidonian or Tyrian do not indicate that the intention is non – Israelites. They are by no means synonymous with Canaanites as most scholars seem to believe. The Hiram that built the Temple was an Israelite, and his name is identical with that of Hiram, king of Tyre. Why should we see this as a foreign name?[15]

There is reason to assume that the tribal formation existed for a certain period of time after the entry to Canaan. to be changed later to local sovereignties which existed in Israel even before Saul (like Abimelech, Jerubaal) . Since the tribe of Asher was the one to conquer the region of Tyre and Sidon, we must inevitably accept the fact that Hiram, king of Tyre, was an Israelite king who ruled over the tribe of Asher (or part of it), remaining

---

Marocaines, 1908, p. 65; p. 7, note 6.
Rawlinson, Phoenicia, 2nd edit. pp. 96–97.
Sayce. The early history of the Hebrews 2nd edit. p. 464.
13   Nu. 26: 2; 1: 2: 18: 24 ; 4: 2: 22: 40: 42 ; 3: 15: 20.
14   Ant. VIII: 76
15   Perhaps it is a distortion of the Biblical name Ahiram (Nu. 6: 39)

outside the general framework of the Israelite nation, and did not unite with the other tribes under one government – that of Saul and David. (There is reason to believe that also the tribe of Gad remained apart).

WHO WERE THE PHOENICIANS ACCORDING TO HERODOTUS AND DIODORUS SICULUS?

We have seen that Aziru mentioned in the el–Amarna tablets is the Israelite tribe of Asher, and that this tribe conquered the region of Sidon. We have shown that the Exodus occurred in c. 1446 B. C. Therefore the invasion of Canaan by the Israelites (the destruction of Jericho) began c. 1406 B. C., while the beginning of the separate tribal wars was c. 1376 B. C., namely in the period of the el–Amarna tablets. The region of Sidon, which is considered a Canaanite–Phoenician region, since the Israelites had supposedly not succeeded in conquering it, became in fact an Israelite region during the el–Amarna period. Hence, if the Greeks called this region "Phoenicia", and as seen above, this must have been after the conquest of Aziru – Asher, then this name refers to an Israelite region and Israelite inhabitants.

Herodotus–the earliest of historians (484–425 B. C.) in his writings on the ancient east, also indicates, here and there, certain borderlines between countries. In his book (IV, 39) we read about the lands that extend between Persia and Egypt: "But the second (peninsula–N. G.) beginning with Persia stretches to the Red Sea being the Persian land, and next the neighbouring country of Assyria, and after Assyria, Arabia; this peninsula ends (yet not truly but only by common consent) at the Arabian Gulf, whereunto Darius brought a canal from the Nile. Now from the Persian country to Phoenice there is a wide and great tract of land; and from Phoenice – this peninsula runs beside our sea by the way of the Syrian Palestine and Egypt, which is at the end of it. In this peninsula there are but three nations."[1] Hence according to Herodotus only three nations inhabit the area from Persia to Egypt, namely: the Syrian – Palestinians, the Phoenicians, and the Arabians. In another paragraph[2], Herodotus tells us about the tribute paid to the Persians by the nations subject to them: "The country reaching from the city of Posideium built by Amphilochus, son of Amphiaraus, on the confines of Syria and Cilicia, to the borders of Egypt, excluding therefrom a district which belonged to Arabia, and was free from tax, paid a tribute of three hundred and fifty talents. All Phoenicia, Palestine Syria, and Cyprus, were herein contained."

---

1   Herodotus, Translation by Godley, Loeb Classical Library. see also de Sélincourt–Penguin edit. p. 254. and G. Rawlinson p. 216.

2   Herodotus, III – 91, p. 181, Translation by Rawlinson. see also de Sélincourt p. 214.

In these two paragraphs as in others,[3] Herodotus tells about the Israelite region without mentioning the name of the Israelite nation. Herodotus describes in full detail the entire region from the Persian Gulf to Egypt (including the region of Israel) without once pronouncing the name of the Israelite nation–this is curious: Or does he, perhaps, mention them, but under some other name?

According to Herodotus, the lands that extend between Persia and Egypt are Syria–Palestine, Phoenicia and the Arabian region. Therefore, if Herodotus mentions the Israelites under another name, then it might be either under that of Syria–Palestine, or that of Phoenicia. Josephus[4] tends to believe that Herodotus mentions the Israelites under the term Syrian–Palestinians – and this is the generally accepted belief today. We will see whether Josephus was correct in his assumption further on. In the meantime, let us try to understand what Herodotus himself meant by Syria–Palestine, and who, according to him, were the Phoenicians?

Herodotus relates in Chapter III, paragraphs 4–5 that: "Now it happened that Cambyses was meditating his attack on Egypt, and doubting how he might best pass the desert, when Phanes arrived, and not only told him all the secrets of Amasis, but advised him also how the desert might be crossed. He counselled him to send an ambassador to the king of the Arabs, and ask him for safe–conduct through the region. Now the only entrance into Egypt is by this desert: the country from Phoenicia to the borders of the city of Cadytis belongs to the people called the Palaestine Syrians; from Cadytis, which it appears to me is a city almost as large as Sardis, the marts upon the coast till you reach Jenysus are the Arabian king's; after Jenysus the Syrians again come in, and extend to lake Serbonis, near the place where Mount Casius juts into the sea. At lake Serbonis where the tale goes that Typhon hid himself, Egypt begins[5].

From Phoenicia till Cadytis the land belongs to the Syrians called Palestinians. From Jenysus till the Serbonian marsh the inhabitants of the country are "the Syrian again", and from the Serbonian marsh the country is Egypt. From the phrase that "The Syrian again come in" it is obvious that it refers to the Syrians mentioned at the beginning of the paragraph, i. e. The Syrians called Palestinians. Herodotus' paragraph is therefore to be understood as follows: Phoenicia borders the country of the Syrian–Palestinians . From Phoenicia till Cadytis the land is that of the Syrian–Palestinians, Then a certain part of the country is inhabited by the Arabians, and then down to the borders of Egypt there are the Syrian–Palestinians again. We have no notion

---

3   VII – 89.
4   Ant. VIII – 260.
5   Rawlinson Translation, The History of Herodotus. pp. 147–148.

where Cadytis was[6], but it is irrelevant to our purpose. What is important for us to note is that the region of the Syrian–Palestinians extend as far as the borders of Egypt. Corroboration of this fact is found in Herodotus' elsewhere[7]: "This part of Syria, and all the region extending from hence to Egypt is known by the name of Palestine".

Speaking of the Scythians who marched against Egypt Herodotus writes[8]: "When they had reached Palestine, however, Psammetichus the Egyptian king met them with gifts and prayers, and prevailed on them to advance no further. On their return, passing through Ascalon a city of Syria, the greater part of them went their way without doing any damage; but some few who lagged behind pillaged the temple of Celestial Venus. I have inquired and find that the temple of Ascalon is the most ancient of all the temples to this goddess; for the one in Cyprus, as the Cyprian themselves admit, was built in imitation of it; and that in Cythera was erected by the Phoenicians, who belong to this part of Syria." The Scytians on their way BACK from Syria–Palestine were in Ascalon, and in Ascalon there were "Phoenicians, who belong to this part of Syria". It is therefore evident that Syria Palestine must extend at least from Ascalon southward in the direction of Egypt, and as we have already seen above, even as far as the borders of Egypt. According to the Bible this region which extended to the borders of Egypt was the abode of the Philistines, and not of the Israelites. Therefore, if we put together all the above evidence, the Syrian Palestinians of Herodotus are in effect the biblical Philistines. Thus having eliminated one possibility, it remains for us to conclude that Herodotus most probably includes the Israelites under the term "Phoenicians".

According to Herodotus (Vii – 89) "These Phoenicians dwelt in old time, as they say, by the Red Sea, Passing over from thence, they now inhabit the sea coast of Syria."[9] Which sea does Herodotus call the Red Sea? In his writings we find that the river Euphrates flows from Armenia and empties into the Red Sea,[10] and that the Tigris also flows into the Red Sea.[11] We are led to assume that Herodotus' Red Sea is today's Persian Gulf, and there are scholars who believe this to be so.[12]

---

6   There are several theories, one is that Cadytis is the biblical Kadesh.

7   VII – 89. Rawlinson Translation (p. 383)

8   I–105. Rawlinson's, Translation p. 41.

9   Godley's Translation, Loeb Classical Library, see also Rawlinson's Translation, p. 383. and: I–1.

10   I–180. In Rawlinson's Translation, p. 67.

11   I –189; In Rawlinson's Translation, p. 70.

12   See: Driver, Semitic Writing From Pictograph to Alphabeth, P. 195. Driver accepts that the Phoenicians came from the Persian Gulf, and cites Herodotus in support; Contenau, La Civilisation Phénicienne, p. 284.
     Chipiez – Perrot, History of Art In Phoenicia, etc., p. 11
     The reason for this belief is based also on a paragraph from Strabo, which was

Yet we also read[13] "Lybia shows clearly that it is encompassed by the sea, save only where it borders on Asia; and this was proved first (as far as we know) by Necos king of Egypt. He, when he had made an end of digging the canal which leads from the Nile to the Arabian Gulf, sent Phoenicians in ships charging them to sail on their return voyage past the pillars of Heracles (today's Gibraltar–N. G.) till they should come into the northern sea and so to Egypt. So the Phoenicians set out from the Red Sea and sailed to the southern Sea". In Book II, Par. 158 we read: "It was he (Necos – N. G.) who began the making of the canal into the Red Sea".

In another paragraph[14] Herodotus tells us that: "This is a sea by itself (i. e. the Caspian sea –N. G.) not joined to the other sea. For that whereon the Greeks sail, and the sea beyond the pillars of Heracles, which they call the Atlantic, and the Red Sea are all one.". We have already noted the paragraph: ". the second (peninsula–N. G.) beginning with Persia stretches to the Red Sea..." (Iv 39).

It is evident from the above paragraphs that by "Red Sea" or "Southern Sea" (Rawlinson translates "Erythraean Sea") Herodotus means the sea around the Arabian peninsula, i. e. today's Persian Gulf and Red Sea. If, according to him, the Phoenicians came from the Red Sea, we may assume that they could have come from any place along it, i. e. from Egypt to the Persian Gulf.[15]

As already noted, if Herodotus includes the Israelites under another name (and this must be assumed since he specifies the nations living in th entire region) then it could only be under that of Phoenicians. According to him, the Phoenicians came from the Red Sea area which we have seen he includes both the Red Sea and the Persian Gulf areas of today, whereas the Bible clearly states the Israelites came to Canaan from the desert of Sinai where they had gone after the Exodus. These statements taken together appear to corroborate our assumption that Herodotus refers to the Israelites by the term Phoenicians.[16]

---

understood to imply that there existed two cities in the Persian Gulf called Tyros and Aradus parallel to Tyre and Arad in Phoenicia. However, Pliny already registered his astonishment at Strabo's assertion, and points out that the name of the city is Tylos and not Tyros.

13   IV–42, Godley's Translation, Loeb Classical Library.

14   I – 202.

15   According to the Ras Shamra tablets (which will be discussed later) the Phoenicians came to Canaan from a region near today's Red Sea.

16   Dussaud, who equates Phoenicians with Canaanites, firmly believes the Israelites and the Canaanites had the same original homeland before settling in the country. Ras – Shamra, AAA, 1934, pp. 93–98.
      Virolleaud believes the Phoenicians came from the Red Sea region together with the Hebrews. He gets support for his view in the Ras Shamra tablets wherein Zebulun Asher and Terah tribes. are mentioned See: Contenau, Manuel d'Archéologie Orientale, P. 75. ; Barton, Archeology And The Bible, p. 139

In an interesting aside Herodotus (II, 104) notes that: "The Colchians and Egyptians and Ethiopians are the only nations that have from the first practised circumcision. The Phoenicians and the Syrians of Palestine acknowledge of themselves that they learnt the custom from the Egyptians... Those Phoenicians who hold intercourse with Hellas cease to imitate the Egyptians in this matter and do not circumcise their children".

We may conclude therefore, that Herodotus envisaged two kinds of Phoenicians 1. Those who hold intercourse with the Greeks and do not imitate the Egyptians. 2. The other Phoenicians who do imitate the Egyptians, but do not hold intercourse with the Greeks.

Diodorus (XI. 3) writes: "Now that we are about to record the war against the Jews, we consider it appropriate to give first a summary account of the establishment of the nation, from the origins, and of the practices observed among them. When in ancient times a pestilence arose in Egypt, the common people ascribed their troubles to the workings of a divine agency; for indeed with many strangers of all sorts dwelling in their midst and practising different rites of religion and sacrifice, their own traditional observances in honour of the gods had fallen into disuse. Hence the natives of the land surmised that unless they removed the foreigners, their troubles would never be resolved. At once, therefore, the aliens were driven from the country, and the most outstanding and active among them banded together and, as some say, were cast ashore to Greece and certain other regions; their leaders were notable men, chief among them being Danaus and Cadmus. But the greater number were driven into what is now called Judaea, which is not far distant from Egypt and was at that time utterly uninhabited. The colony was headed by a man called Moses" Elsewhere (V, 74), referring to the alphabetic letters he writes: "the Phoenicians having learned them from the Syrians and then passed them on to the Greeks, and that these Phoenicians are those who sailed to Europe together with Cadmus..."[17].

In this account he draws our attention in fact to his statement (XI, 3) about the group of aliens who left Egypt (not Phoenicia) with Cadmus. By stressing that "these Phoenicians are those who sailed..."etc. he differentiates them from those Phoenicians who did not sail with Cadmus and remained behind in Egypt (not Phoenicia). As Diodorus tells it those Phoenicians who sailed with Cadmus were "the most outstanding and active among them..." (i. e. the aliens – N. G.). It is obvious, therefore, that the Phoenicians who did not sail with Cadmus and remained in Egypt were "the greater number" of the aliens who according to Diodorus were led by Moses to Judaea. Let us not forget that Diodorus tells us this as a "summary account of the establishment of the nation (Jewish –N. G) from the origins".

We have already discussed in previous chapters the indubitable

---

17   Diodorus Siculus, Walton's Translation edit. Heinemann, London.

conclusion, based on the el–Amarna tablets and the Bible, that the region of Sidon, generally accepted as a "Phoenician" region, was conquered by the tribe of Asher. It was shown that names such as Tyrian and Sidonian do not specifically mean Canaanites. Any citizen of Tyre or Sidon was called Tyrian or Sidonian, and these names cannot be equated with the term Canaanite, as accepted today. We have now seen that if Herodotus tells us anything about the Israelites it must be looked for under the term "Phoenicians". When Diodorus gives a summary account of the Jewish origins, he describes them as aliens in Egypt, of whom "the most outstanding and active among them" are referred to as Phoenicians. We may therefore definitely conclude that the term "Phoenicians" is the Greek name for the nation of Israel

If the Phoenicians and the Israelites are one and the same, why are they regarded today as two different nations? Why have historians, including Josephus who was himself a Jew, written about the Phoenicians and the Israelites as two distinct nations?

To answer this question and to understand this chapter in history, we have to go back over Israelite history from the time of Israel's formation as a nation, and to trace its political and religious development. Only then will we be able to understand the reasons and causes that brought about the present–day differentiation between Phoenicians and Israelites.

THE RELIGIOUS EVOLUTION IN THE ISRAELITE NATION

In an earlier chapter, when we discussed the meaning of the name Israel, we assumed it to have been "Asera – El (Ashera El)". We stressed that there was reason to suppose the Israelites had worshipped the Ashera, i. e. the trees Ela and Alon (Terebinth and Oak). From the verse "...I am the Lord; And I appeared unto Abraham, unto Isaac and unto Jacob, by the name of God Almighty (in the Hebrew verse El–Shaddai – אל שדי N. G.) but by my name JEHOVAH was I not known to them"[1]. We ascertain that El–Shaddai was the name of the Israelite deity till their descent into Egypt, and its meaning is, as we have seen, "God of the fields". The Bible tells us that the Israelites were in Egypt for 430 years[2]. They leave Egypt under the leadership of Moses, who gives them a monotheistic religion. The Bible depicts the Israelites as a wandering nation, herdsmen like the Bedouines of our day until their descent into Egypt they worshipped trees, which means they were at the level of fetishism – a low level of religious development, from which they were suddenly transferred to monotheism, a very high level in religious development. All this is done without telling us about any evolution towards it. This nation "jumps" from a state of being "on the verge " of development to a state of being nearly at the highest peak of religious development, overtaking the Egyptians who were known to have achieved a high cultural level. We cannot, therefore, explain such a development unless we assume that this monotheistic conception was not originally evolved in the Israelite nation, but was brought to them from the outside.

According to the Bible, Moses, who was the founder of monotheism, was a Hebrew brought up in the house of the Pharaoh, and when reaching the age of eighty years, (Ex. 7: 7) returned to his own people. Freud in his book "Moses and Monotheism"[3] conjectures that Moses was an Egyptian, and believes that the aim of the narrative about Moses being saved from the waters of the Nile by the daughter of the Pharaoh, and brought up by her till he returns to his people, comes to mask the Egyptian origin of Moses[4]

---

1   Ex. 6: 2 – 3. (El – Shaddai was translated God Almighty)
2   Ex. 12: 40.
3   See: Freud, Moise et Monotheism.
4   The belief that Moses is an Egyptian name, is not exclusive to Freud. Renan, Breasted and others alredy referred to it.
    Renan, Histoire Du Peuple D'israel, pp. 159–160.

According to Freud, Moses, who was an Egyptian, gave the Israelites an Egyptian religion. It is known that Akhenathon (Amenhotep IV) enforced in Egypt the worship of a god by the name Aten. Because of the phonetical resemblance between the names Aten, Adon – Adonai, and because of the similarity between the principles of the religion of Aten and that of Adonai, Freud assumed that the monotheistic religion that Moses gave to the Israelites was the religion of Aten, and he accordingly fixed the date of the Exodus after the Akhenaton period.

As the Biblical narrative goes, Moses demanded that the king of Egypt let the Israelites go out of his country. From this narrative we get the impression that Moses stands firmly upon the fulfilment of his demand. Moses addresses the Pharaoh demanding "Let my people go, that they may serve me, And if thou refuse to let them go, behold, I will smite all thy borders...".[5] The king of Egypt refuses and then the ten plagues are brought upon him and his people until at last he agrees to let the people go. At one stage, the Pharaoh agrees to send the people, but without their flocks. Moses, instead of "jumping" at the chance and accepting the offer (the logical reaction of any man who is supposed to be under slavery) refuses to leave Egypt, and remains firmly upon his resolve. Moreover, his answer to the Pharaoh is that not only will they not leave without their flocks, but "Thou must give us also sacrifices and burnt offerings that we may sacrifice unto the Lord our God"[6]. How amazing is the language which the Bible ascribes to Moses, e. g. "but let not Pharaoh deal deceitfully any more in not letting the people go"[7], or the commanding language "Let my people go...For if thou refuse..." (Ex. 9: 1–2), or his impertinence in telling the Pharaoh "Thou must give us also sacrifices.' etc. When the Pharaoh loses patience and tells Moses "Get thee from me, take heed to thyself, see my face no more; for in that day thou seest my face thou shalt die" (Ex. 10: 28), Moses answers that he is leaving, but that a day would come when "all these thy servants shall come down unto me, and bow down themselves unto me saying, Get thee out, and all the people that follow thee; and after that I will go out. And he went out from Pharaoh in a great anger".[8] These harsh words, so highly mortifying, are ascribed to Moses who is considered a member of the slave families. This is quite extraordinary,

---

Griffith, The Egyptian Derivation of The Name Moses, JNES, XII, 1953, pp. 225–231.

Conder, The Syrian Stone Lore, p. 121 (notes).

Lods, ISREL, p. 192.

Albright, A Revision of Early Hebrew Chronology, JPOS, 920–1921, p. 67.

Cassuto, U., A commentary on the Book of Exodus, p. 11. (Hebrew).

5   Ex. 8: 1–2 (In the Hebrew text Ex. 7: 26–27)

6   Ex. 10: 24–26.

7   Ex. 8: 29 (In the Hebrew text Ex. 8: 25)

8   Ex. 11: 8

and goes against common sense. In fact, what prevents Pharaoh from killing Moses? No doubt, we may explain the biblical text quite simply by saying that this narrative in the Bible is a merely a fine legend. In order to glorify its hero, the Israelite nation ascribes to Moses a wonderfully divine power which permitted him to speak to the Pharaoh as an equal. Such was the approach of many scholars who did not give much value to the biblical narratives.

But can the facts be explained otherwise?

We saw in a previous chapter[9] that the Exodus occurred in c. 1446 B. C. According to the Bible Moses was eighty years old at the time of the Exodus.[10] We can therefore fix Moses birth c. 1526 B. C. If Moses is the son of the daughter of the Pharaoh as might be assumed from Freud's theory, then most probably the Pharaoh who reigned at about 1526 B. C. was Moses grandfather. As we know, during this period Thutmose I reigned as Pharaoh[11], and his daughter was the queen Hatsepsut. It is customary in the orient to name the grandchild after his grandfather[12]. Most probably Moses name was at first Thutmose, and the prefix Thut was later dropped. This assumption explains the narrative of the Exodus in the Bible.

Before the reign of Amenhotep II, Thutmose III reigned as Pharaoh, persecuting many of the royal house and those related to the queen Hatsepsut. To cite Breasted: "no doubt those who did not flee were surely sorry for it".[13] Most probably Moses also ran away, to Midian according to the Bible, and became a shepherd of the flocks of Yithro the Midianite priest. It seems that during this period of loneliness he developed his personal monotheistic philosophy. With the death of Thutmose III and the ascent of Amenhotep II (Amenophis II), Moses returns to Egypt. He is the grandchild of Thutmose I, i. e. the uncle of Amenhotep II, king of Egypt, and therefore has rights to the throne as well. Just as anyone with a philosophical idea would do, Moses is interested in propagating his monotheistic religion. He most probably relinquishes his rights to the throne, but instead demands possession of the slaves in whom he finds large scope for the propagation of his creed . Then begins a bargaining between Amenhotep II and Moses, and we can now understand the resolute language ascribed to Moses speaking to the Pharaoh, and why the Pharaoh does not harm him since he is his uncle. Indeed, the Bible itself states that: "...the man Moses was very great in the land of Egypt,

---

9   Chapter 2.

10   Ex. 7: 7 "And Moses was fourscore years old... when they spake unto pharaoh."

11   According to Petrie Thutmose I reigned 1541–1516. B. C. According to Breasted 1557–1501. B. C.

12   See for ex: Ganneau, Hiram, King of Tyre, PEF, 1880, pp. 174–181

13   See: Pere Bouvier, La pierre et P. Jouquet, Precis de L'histoire, p. 141

in the sight of Pharaoh's servants, and in the sight of the people".[14] without enlarging in what sense he is great[15].

In his book "Moses and Monotheism", Freud remarks that circumcision was an Egyptian custom, and the reason for enforcing this custom on the Israelites was, according to him, that Moses himself was an Egyptian.

Let us add to this the existence of two laws in the Bible which are ascribed to Moses: 1) "An Ammonite or Moabite shall not enter into the congregation of the Lord; even to their tenth generation shall they not enter into the congregation of the Lord for ever: Because they met you not with bread and with water in the way, when ye came forth out of Egypt; ...thou shalt not seek their peace nor their prosperity all thy days for ever"[16]. 2) "Thou shalt not abhor an Egyptian, because thou wast a stranger in his land. The children that are begotten of them shall enter into the congregation of the Lord in their third generation."[17] The strange peculiarity of these two laws is that the Ammonites and Moabites who are, according to the Bible, racially related to the Israelites – being descendants of Lot, Abraham's nephew – are not allowed to enter into the congregation FOR EVER, because they did not offer the Israelites bread and water when they came out of Egypt.

On the other hand, the Egyptians who had imposed forced labour upon the Israelites for decades, embittered their lives, and had commanded that "Every son that is born ye shall cast into the river"[18] These Egyptians are permitted to enter the congregation in the third generation, and the explanation offered in the Bible for this law is very odd and even ridiculous: "because thou wast a stranger in his land". But if Moses himself was an Egyptian and the Israelite nation also included Egyptian elements, then such a law is explicable.

Let us assume that Moses was not an Egyptian, but as the Bible describes him – a Hebrew saved from the waters of the Nile by Pharaoh's daughter, and brought up in the house of the Pharaoh. Grown old at eighty (Ex. 7: 7), he returns to his people – the Hebrew one. Yet in Pharaoh's house – was he brought up as a Hebrew or as an Egyptian? It is self–evident that even if we accept the biblical version, we must agree that Moses' education was an Egyptian one.

Whether he was a Hebrew, as in the biblical version, or an Egyptian as in Freud's version, his whole outlook and knowledge was Egyptian, and we have to assume that the religion he gave the Israelites must have been based

---

14   Ex. 11: 3.
15   Let us note that Manetho, by Josephus (Contra Apion. I–26), says that Moses was an Egyptian priest by the name of Asarsif. However he points out (ibid. 16), that this remark is made according to hearsay alone.
16   Deut. 23: 3–6
17   Deut. 23: 7–8 (In the Hebrew text 8–9)
18   Ex. 1: 22

on Egyptian culture. There is reason to assume, with Freud, that this religion resembles the religion of Aten. But Freud was in error when he fixed the date of the Exodus immediately after the Akhenathon period. The grounds for his mistake lies in his assuming that Akhenathon established this religion. Let us not forget that only about seventy years elapsed from the time of the Exodus till the accession to the throne by Akhenathon. This religion probably leaves a strong impression on him, and when he ascends the throne, he enforces this religion of the God Aten Adon[19]on Egypt. With the Israelite people, he believes in the same religion and in the same God, and there is an identity of religious interests between him and the Israelite people. Most probably this is also the reason why he did not come to the rescue of the Canaanite kings in their war against the Israelites[20].

With the Exodus a new era commences for the Israelites – the period of the worship of one God Adon. But when they received this new religion, did they stop worshipping the Ashera? From the verse "Thou shalt not plant thee a grove of any trees (in Hebrew–Ashera any tree אשרה כל עץ)near unto the altar of the Lord thy God, which thou shalt make thee"[21]. We can conclude that they linked their old deity with the new one, and formed a combination of the two, making it necessary to issue this warning commandment.

The Israelites sojourned in Egypt for 430 years[22]. Reason demands that in such a long period of time they came under the influence of the Egyptians and learned their ways. The narrative about the worship of the golden calf in the desert proves how deeply they were influenced by the Egyptians. We find support for this in the following verses "...and made myself known unto them in the land of Egypt...Then said I unto them, cast ye away every man the abomination of his eyes, and defile not yourselves with the idols of Egypt...But they rebelled against me, and would not hearken unto me: they did not every man cast away the abominations of their eyes, neither did they forsake the idols of Egypt."[23] "Neither left she her whoredoms brought from Egypt: for in her youth they lay with her."[24] "Because they have done that

---

19   There are scholars who consider "Jehovah" the name of the Israelite God. This will be discussed later, and meanwhile we shall continue to call the Israelite God "Adon".

20   The accepted belief is that Akhenathon did not come to the help of the Canaanite kings in the el–Amarna period because he was occupied in establishing his monotheistic religion and therefore did not pay attention to his political affairs and the events in Canaan.

21   Deut. 16: 21. The Hebrew verse reads: "Lo tita lekha Ashera kol etz ezel mizbakh adonai elohekha" – " לא־תטע לך אשרה כל־עץ אצל מזבח יהוה אלהיך"

22   Ex. 12: 40

23   Ezk. 20: 5–8

24   Ezk. 23: 8

which was evil in my sight, and have provoked me to anger, since that day their fathers came forth out of Egypt, even unto this day."[25]

The Israelites leave Egypt with the religion of their deity Adon, given them by Moses Because of the novelty of this religion it seems that part of the people – probably a very large part – still continues to worship the Ashera, as they used to do before. They also continue to worship the calf (bull) and perhaps also other Egyptian deities which they had adopted during their long stay in Egypt. Moses who professes a new religion, his own creation, fights against these elements. This much can be learnt from the biblical narratives. Following the golden calf episode Moses calls "Who is on the Lord's side? Let him come unto me". The people divide into two parts, with one part killing the other which had worshipped the calf.[26] Similar events occur in the Baal – Peor, Korah, and other incidents.[27]

In this connection it is worth adding the words spoken about Joshua when he was appointed as leader: "And they answered Joshua saying, All that thou commanded us we will do, and whithersoever thou sendest us, we will go. According as we hearkened unto Moses in all things, so will we hearken unto thee: only the Lord thy God be with thee, as he was with Moses WHOSOEVER HE BE THAT DOTH REBEL AGAINST THY COMMANDMENT, AND WILL NOT HEARKEN UNTO THY WORDS in all that thou commandest him, HE SHALL BE PUT TO DEATH: only be strong and of a good courage." (My emphasis – N. G.)[28] This line of thought can be found in Moses words also: "For I know thy rebellion, and thy stiff neck: behold while I am yet alive with you this day, ye have been rebellious against the Lord; and how much more after my death?" (Deut. 31: 27). i. e. if while I am alive and have been so stern with you, you are rebellious what shall I expect after my death?

Moses in the desert is a strong, firm leader, resolute about the strict observance of his ideas, and the performance of his commands. Anyone who rebels against him, such as Korah, or the calf worshippers, is killed. During this period of the wandering in the desert, the religion of the God of Israel is kept in its full monotheistic form, because Moses cares about its observance and enforcement. With the death of Moses the people of Israel enter a new era – the era of the conquest of the land of Canaan and the settlement in the land. Moses is dead. During his lifetime he had to act firmly with the people to keep faith with his ideas. We must assume therefore that without the presence of someone who would stand firmly on the observance of the monotheistic religion, the people were liable to return to the worship of their

---

25   2Kn. 21: 15
26   Ex. 32
27   Nu. 25 ; 11 ; 15: 32– 36 ; 16; 17
28   Jos. 1: 16 –18

former deities – the Ashera, the calf and the other deities they worshipped in Egypt. This in fact is what we learn from the Bible. Joshua speaks to the people and demands: "Now therefore fear the Lord, and serve him in sincerity and in truth, and put away the gods which your fathers served on the other side of the flood, and in Egypt; and serve ye the Lord. And if it seems evil unto you to serve the Lord, choose you this day whom ye will serve; whether the gods which your fathers served that were on the other side of the flood, or the gods of the Amorites, in whose land you dwell; but as for me and my house, we will serve the Lord."[29]; "Now therefore put away, said he, the strange gods which are among you"[30].

Such is the situation during Joshua's time, and there is reason to assume that it deteriorated after his death and the death of the Elders. The people then resume worshipping the Ashera etc."And Israel served the Lord all the days of Joshua, and all the days of the elders that over lived Joshua, and which had known all the works of the Lord, that he did for Israel. . And there arose another generation after them, which knew not the Lord, nor yet the works which he had done for Israel."[31]

It seems, however, that the efforts of Moses were not in vain: the welding furnace of the desert and Joshua's lifetime succeeded in implanting the monotheistic "creed of Adon" within a part of the nation. Therefore, when the nation of Israel settled in the land, we read in the Bible that they worship the God Adon – Adonai, besides the Ashera the Bull and other deities. When the prophet Samuel addresses the Israelites to return unto the Lord, he emphsizes "and serve him only". (1Sam. 7, 3.). The worship of multitude of deities including Adon does not accord with the monotheistic principles of the Adon religion, and cannot coexist with it. So it was quite natural that the God Adon had to descend from his high monotheistic level to a henotheistic level. By force of circumstance, the God Adon becomes a henotheistic god in the land of Israel, taking its place at the head of the deities in the Israelite Pantheon. From this, I believe, the word "Adon" in Hebrew eventually aquired the meaning of "Master" or "Head" e. g. Adon Haolam – Master (Ruler)of the world, Adon habait – Head of the household, etc. Because of their Ashera worship they are called the "sons of Ashera El " (i. e. the sons of the God Ashera) or the "sons of Israel".

---

29 Jos. 24: 14 – 16
30 Jos. 24: 23
31 Ju. 2: 7–11; see also Jos. 24: 31.

THE WORSHIP OF THE BAAL

During the Israelite period of settlement in the land of Canaan, the people worshipped among other deities those called "Baalim". The name "Baal" is encountered in Sidonian inscriptions, in the Ugarit (Ras Shamra) tablets, and in the Bible. It is the name of a deity and forms a composite in proper nouns such as: Baalia, Jerubaal, Hanibaal, Azdrubaal, etc. In many instances this name is synonymous with the word Adon (Master, Lord), and is encountered in the plural form "Baalim" as well. Accordingly the name Baal was understood as meaning Adon – Master – Lord."Baal Isha" (Isha in Hebrew = woman) meant "master of the woman" i. e. husband."Baal Nahala" (Nahala in Hebrew = estate) meant master of the estate". Thus the Baal deity was taken to be the Master (possessor) of a locality or district[1] e. g. Baal Zaphon or Baal Peor, Baal of Lebanon etc. The worship of these deities is depicted in the Bible as one accompanied by orgiastic rites[2]. From certain verses in the Bible[3] it would seem that the Israelites learnt how to worship the Baal deity from the Canaanites who remained in the country[4]. As pointed out, the name Baal is very common in Phoenician inscriptions. Since many scholars identify "Phoenicians" with "Canaanites", it is commonly accepted among scholars that the worship of the Baal was foreign to the Israelites and that they borrowed it from the Canaanites. Schaeffer even remarks that: "The Baal did not figure in the original Pantheon of the Semitic Canaanites. He was

---

1   Kapelrud, The Ras Shamra Discoveries and The O. T., pp. 30 – 31
    Perrot –Chipiez, History of Art In Phoenicia etc. p. 67
    Wright, Biblical Archeology, p. 107
    Robertson Smith. The Religion of The Semites, pp. 93–94.
    Lods, Israel, p. 138
    Contenau, La Civilisation Phénicienne, p. 90.
    Maspero, The struggle of the Nations, Egypt, Syria And Assyria, pp. 154, 167
    Weill, Phoenicia and Western Asia, etc. pp 68–69.
    Oesterley and Robinso, Hebrew Religion, pp. 57–58
    Cassuto, Biblical Encyclopedia, entry Baal. (Hebrew)
    Klausner, Kitvei Kodshenu, p. 188 in New Investigations and OLD SOURCES, Massada, 1957. (heb.)
    Ribichini, Beliefs and Religious Life p. 106 in "The Phoenicians", Bompiani, 1988.
2   See Baal Peor narrative. (Nu. 25: 1–4).
3   For ex. 1kng. 16: 31; Ju. 2: 11–13
4   For ex. Rawlinson, Phoenicia, pp. 109 –113
    Lods, Les Prophètes D'israël et les Débuts Du Judaism, p. 74

only added to it when the latter penetrated into northern Syria."[5] According to Gray: "Hadad is of course the deity who became Baal par excellence in Canaan".[6] Contenau notes[7] that: "In the Tell–el– Amarna letters...there are no proper nouns compounded with Baal but a great many with Addu (a form of Hadad, the Syrian god of mountain – tops and storms who wields the lightning and rides upright on a bull). On the other hand, when we look at Phoenician inscriptions, these same names have Baal as a compound term". Hence the Baal was not an original deity of the Canaanites, but was introduced into the region known as Phoenicia only in the el – Amarna period, or immediately after it, i. e. after the conquest of the country by the Israelites.

It may be assumed that the origin of the name Baal (בעל) is not derived from the name of a deity but from the combination of the adjectival term "Baal Isha" (בעל אשה) above mentioned. The term derives from two Hebrew words "Ba – Al Isha" (in Hebrew Ba–al – בא–על means to "come over" "Isha" = woman) which is a primitively picturesque way of describing the act of coupling.[8] In time these two words combined together to form an adjective Baal (באעל) Because of the juxtaposition of two guttural sounds the weaker one (Alephא) fell, and the adjective remained in its present form Baal (בעל). The verb Ba – El (בא אל) is encountered in the Bible in connection with the act of coupling. Jacob for example, says to Laban: "...give me my wife...that I may go in unto her"[9] (In the Hebrew text "vehavoha eleha" ואבואה אליה – future tense of Ba el); "...he took Leha his daughter, and brought her to him; and he went in unto her"[10] (in the Hebrew text " va–yavo eleha "ויבא אליה – future tense of Ba – el). The verb Ba El (בא אל) in the sense of coupling recurs often in the Bible[11]. The interchange of EL with AL is quite common in the Bible.[12]: "And Hezekiah sent TO all Israel... TO Ephraim..."[13]; "unto the people of Jerusalem...against the God of Jerusalem" (2Chr. 32: 18–20). (In the Hebrew text, the words "to" are alternatively El and Al). We may therefore assume that the verb Ba – El which means coupling was originally Ba– Al. The verb Ba – Al in the sense of coupling can be found in the Bible,

---

5   Schaeffer, The Cuneiform Texts of Ras Shamra, p. 8
6   Gray, The Legacy of Canaan, VT, 1957, p. 114
7   Contenau, Ibid., p. 97
8   Compare with the description in Job. (31: 9–10) If mine heart have been deceived by a woman...Then let my wife grind unto another and let others bow down upon her.
9   Gen. 29: 21.
10   Gen. 29: 23.
11   Gen. 29: 30 ; Gen. 30: 3 ; Gen. 16: 2; Jer. 1: 7 and more.
12   See (the Hebrew text) also: Is. 36: 7; 2Kn. 22: 8 ; Job. 1: 6 In 1962, in a booklet entitled "who were the Phoenicians". I have already discussed the interchange of El with Al.
13   2Chr. 30: 1.

although more rarely. For example, in the story of Lot's daughters: "...our father is old and there is not a man in the earth to come in unto us (in Hebrew" lavo alenu ...לבא עלינו‎ future from the verb Ba– Al. N. G.) after the manner of all earth; Come, let us make our father drink wine, and we will lie with him."[14] Another instance is: "her husband's brother shall go unto her"[15] (in Hebrew uba Aleah –ובא עליה–‎ – and He will come on her from the verb Ba – Al).

The following verses in the book of Deuteronomy clears up the doubt over the meaning of the name "Baal" and the verbs "Ba Al" and "Ba – El": "When a man hath taken a wife, and married her (the Hebrew text reads Ube'ala – (ובעלה‎) and it come to pass that she find no favor in his eyes..."[16] The second verse reads: "If any man take a wife and go in unto her (Hebrew text – uva eleha –ובא אליה‎) and hate her..."[17]

These two verses are identical and their context is the same, but they vary in style: in the first we read ube'ala ובעלה‎ – and he will husband her, and in the second uva–eleha ובא אליה‎ – and he will come to her

We may therefore conclude without hesitation that Be'ala (בעלה‎) is identical with Ba–eleha (בא אליה‎) which in turn can be equated as shown above, with Ba – aleha (בא עליה‎) and with Ba–ala (בעלה‎). This brings us back to the point of departure with the adjective "Baal" being derived from the two words Ba Al meaning "comes over" which is a primitive description of the sexual act of coupling. The verb Ba–al did not remain in the language except in isolated cases in the Bible[18]. most probably because of its primitive form. However, Ba–el, Ba–Al, and Baal are one and the same in meaning. The adjective Baal was at first the term used for a man coupling with a woman, i. e. the man who came over (in Hebrew – Ba – Al) the woman was her "Baal". Eventually, this word acquired a wider significance. In ancient primitive times man was the dominant partner of the two and master of the woman so that this term became synonymous with Master (in Hebrew – Adon). In time, this name was ascribed to deities and it meant a deity who was considered master of a certain locality such as Baal–Peor, Baal Zaphon, Baal Sidon etc. Later on the term was used more generally to signify anyone who held or was master of something: the master of the estate, the master of the household, the master of the cart were called Baal of the estate, Baal of the house, Baal of the cart etc. In Hosea we read:[19] "And it shall be that day, saith the Lord, that thou shalt call me Ishi; and shalt call me no more Baali".

---

14 Gen. 19: 31.
15 Deut. 25: 5.
16 Deut. 24: 1.
17 Deut. 22: 13.
18 Shulhan 'Arukh (Heb.), ch. 4 (19) "A heathen and a slave if they 'came over' an Israelite girl...".
19 Hosea, 2: 16 (in the Hebrew text – 2: 18).

This verse is explained as meaning: "You will call me Ishi and not Baali (my Baal – N. G.) as you called the Baalim you worshipped."[20]. However, in the light of our interpretation of the name "Baal" we can understand the verse otherwise: " You will call me Ishi (the Hebrew term means "my man" – husband) and you will not call me Ba–Alai (coming over me) any longer.". Hosea portrays the nation as a prostitute and he marries a prostitute to give more validity to this simile, with the above verse as a continuance of the image: the nation of Israel will cease to act like a prostitute and will not refer to the Lord as Ba–al namely, as to a lover who comes to couple from time to time, but the relationship between Israel and the Lord will be much more constant and intimate. The new tie will be expressed by addressing the Lord as Ishi and not simply as Ba – Alai. Such an explanation ties in very well with the next verse: "And I will betroth thee unto me for ever; yea, I will betroth thee unto me in righteousness...".[21]

The Bible relates that during the period in the wilderness an event occurs which brings war among brothers: the golden calf episode. In the Book of Exodus this is depicted in full: "...And Aaron made proclamation, and said, Tomorrow is a feast to the Lord. And they rose up early on the morrow, and offered burnt offerings and brought peace offerings, and the people sat down to eat and to drink and rose up to play."[22] (the Hebrew text reads: Lezakhek–לצחק).) What is the meaning of "lezakhek"? As we see above, the English translation is "to play" and this is the meaning given the word today. In the Book of Genesis[23] we read: "And Sarah saw the son of Hagar the Egyptian, which she had born unto Abraham, MOCKING (the Hebrew text reads: metzakhek – מצחק) Wherefore she said unto Abraham, cast out this bondswoman and her son And the thing was very grievous in Abraham's sight because of his son". In this verse too, the verb "letzakhek" was read as meaning "play" (the English translation reads "mocking"). Abraham casts his son out with his mother, and all because a thirteen year old boy was supposedly "playing" (or mocking). What was so horrifying in this act of playing as to merit such punishment? . Elsewhere in the Book of Genesis[24] we read: "And it came to pass...that Abimelech king of the Philistines looked out at a window, and saw, and, behold Isaac Was sporting (the Hebrew text reads: mezakhek– = מצחק – "playing") with Rebekah his wife: And Abimelech called Isaac and said, Behold of a surety she is thy wife: and how saidst thou, She is my sister? ...one of the people might lightly have lien with thy wife, ..." We meet with the verb "lezakhek" – to play, again in the narrative about

---

20   For example see different translations to the Bible.
21   Hosea, 2: 19 (in the Hebrew text –2: 21).
22   Ex. 32: 4–6.
23   Gen. 21: 9–17
24   Gen. 26: 8–11.

Potiphar's wife:[25] "The Hebrew servant ...came in unto me to mock me" (the Hebrew text reads: lezakhek – לצחק – to play). Abimelech understands that Rebekah is Isaac's wife for he sees him "playing" with her. Potiphar gets angry at Joseph, to the extent of imprisoning him because Joseph had supposedly "played" with his wife. From the above verses it is obvious that to play –"lezakhek" – means "love–play", i. e. to flirt, and not simply playing. Sarah sees Ishmael "play" i. e. to masturbate, which explains why Abraham was so grieved over his son. Also the description of the golden calf episode "and they sat down to eat and to drink, and rose up to play" (in Hebrew lezakhek) we now understand that they aroused themselves with "love play" i. e. the orgiastic rites which accompanied the worship of the Baal.

Thus the term Baal is derived from a Hebrew root,[26] and the orgiastic rites in the worship of the Baal were not foreign to the Israelites even before they entered Canaan. We may then regard the names such as Hanibal, Jerubaal, and Others composed with the adjective "Baal" as Hebrew names.

---

25 Gen. 39: 17.
26 Indeed, names as Baal Peor, Baal Zephon and alike are referred in the Bible to non Israelite sites, but this must be regarded as the use of an Hebrew adjective to designate a non Israelite deity.

JUDAH AND BENJAMIN— A NEW ENTITY

To sum up: In the religious evolution of the Israelite nation, we have to differentiate between certain periods each of a distinct nature:

1. The period of the Israelites in Canaan before descending into Egypt. This is the period of fetishism, the worship of the Ashera – tree worship, the worship of El Shaddai – god of the fields.

2. The period of slavery and assimilation in Egypt which ends with the Exodus.

3. The desert period – from the Exodus until the beginning of the settlement in Canaan and receiving of a new monotheistic religion of the God – Adon – Adonai. This is the period of pure monotheism and worship of the one God – Adonai.

4. The settlement period by the tribes in Canaan after the death of Moses, Joshua. and the elders During this period the nation returns to the worship of a multitude of idols and deities such as the Ashera – El Shaddai, the bull – calf, various Egyptian deities and Baal deities – masters of localities (cities). The nation assimilates with the inhabitants of the land and adopts their deities as well. It is obvious that the deities which the Israelites add to their worship are adapted to their own needs, and are merged with their own. The need for the command: "thou shalt not plant thee a grove of any trees near unto the altar of the Lord thy God"[1]). (the Hebrew text reads. . כל אשרה עץ... – = Ashera any tree...) points to the fact that the Israelites have merged the Ashera, their primary deity, with the monotheistic God Adon. Therefore we may assume that such merging took place not only with Ashera – Adon but with other deities as well.

This period of polytheism continues, as the Bible shows, for as long as the Israelites remained settled on their land, until they were taken into captivity and exiled. From the biblical narratives it is certain that the Israelite nation did not forget the God Adon, but continued worshipping him together with other deities at the same time. Such worship was in complete contradiction to the main principles of this monotheistic religion. The God Adon must have had to descend from his monotheistic heights, and there is reason to believe that the Israelite nation accept him as a national henotheistic god standing at the head of the other deities. Actually there do exist certain forces which work to restore Adon to its pure monotheistic position held before,

---

1   Deut. 16: 21.

which find their echo in the writings of the prophets in the Bible, showing how the struggle over the monotheistic tradition lasts for a long period until the nation goes into exile.

5. with the captivity and exile, a new period begins which proves to be a crucial one for the Israelite nation. It must be assumed that the people going into captivity, adhere to all the deities they have been accustomed to worship before. Yet all these deities being masters (possessors) of localities or districts, i. e: territorial. In captivity they are no longer significant since there is no connection whatsoever between them and the new localities. With such disconnection from their native land, they become devoid of content. the God Adon – the Monotheistic god – is the only one who can provide for the nation's needs even in the diaspora, outside the boundaries of the land of Israel Thus by sheer force of circumstance they return to the acknowledgement of the God Adon. According to the Bible, this process attains the summit in the days of Ezra the scribe who had most probably formed a new monotheistic creed based on the old monotheistic religion of Moses So it was in the land of captivity that Adon – the monotheistic god that had become a henotheistic god in the land of Israel, reverted to being monotheistic. Presumably, Ezra does not restore the crown to its original glory, but adds certain novel aspects to the religion of Moses. He regards the name of the God as a mere symbol, and any name– Ehye Asher Ehye – ("אהיה אשר אהיה" Ex. 3: 14) =I shall be Whoever I shall be (translated: I am that I am) can symbolise the deity, i. e. God is the main principle, and not his name. Altough Ezra's creed is based on the religion of Adon – an already existing name for the monotheistic god believed in by the people, and retained by Ezra, he most probably adds to it the four letters (the Tetragrammaton) JEHOVA (יהוה) that may had already been used before as an adjective for Adon. This deity then receives a more universal, abstract conception: the basis of this creed is that of Moses, but it becomes a different religion. A group of people form around Ezra the scribe, propagating his ideas, and disseminating them. Just as any reformer and as Moses did in his time, so Ezra in his own time wants his views accepted. He realizes that most probably his creed will not take root in captivity because of the many external influences against which he, as a foreigner, cannot fight. But if he returns to the land of Israel it would be easier to fight for the preservation of his teachings (Torah–תורה)

Let us not forget that this process takes place only in captivity. What has happened with the remaining people who did not go into captivity?[2].

In 2Sam. 24 we read about king David counting the number of Israelites: "And there were in Israel eight hundred thousand valiant men that drew the sword and the men of Judah were five hundred thousand men "(ibid. v. 9).

According to 1Chr. 21: 5 the number was: "All they of Israel were a

---

2   See for example: Neh. 13: 24 ; Ez. 9: 1–2

thousand thousand and an hundred thousand men that drew the sword; and Judah was four hundred threescore and ten thousand men that drew sword" i. e. one million and five hundred and seventy thousand men altogether in Judah and in Israel that "drew sword ". Hence the total population at the time of David must have numbered about four and a half million people – assuming that about 30% of the population were potential soldiers.

According to the Bible Tiglath – Pileser King of Assyria carried, as captives to Assyria, all the Land of Naphtali alone (2Kn. 15: 29). Shalmaneser carried away only the Israelites from the town of Samaria (2 Kn. 17: 6). In an inscription in Chorasbad, Sargon II informs us that he "led away prisoners 27, 900 inhabitants of it"[3]. The deportees to Babylon in Jehoiachin's days included only ten thousand people (2Kn. 24: 14 ff.). The deportees carried away by Nebuchadnezzar in the days of king Zedekiah is solely from the city of Jerusalem, and according to the Book of Jeremiah (52: 30) "all the persons were four thousand and six hundred". The number of deportees from Israel and Judah altogether did not, therefore, attain even half a milion persons. According to May,[4] the number of Israelites deported could not have been more than one– twentieth to one–fiftieth of the total population, and he therefore concludes that the ten tribes of Israel were never lost "because they were never deported". Lods[5] estimates that about three–quarters of the Israelite population remained in the land. He assumes that the number of deportees from Judah in the years 581, 586, 597 B. C. were at most about 20,000 persons, whereas the total population must have numbered about 90,000. This he based on an estimate of 30 inhabitants to one square km. in an area of about 3000 sq. km. Among others, he cites Guth who believes that the deportees did not number an eighth of the total population. As mentioned above, in David's time the population of Israel and Judah must have numbered about four and a half million, and this number could not have changed significantly by the time of the captivity. What had then become of the remaining people? What was their fate from a religious point of view? . It is understandable that the remaining population continued to worship the various deities which they had worshipped before the captivity, since these deities – lords and masters of localities and cities did not lose their significance in the eyes of those still living in the country. For them, the link with their particular locality still remained.

The deportees who returned led by Ezra believed in the monotheistic creed while that part of the nation which remained in the land and did not

3   See: According to Botta, in Pritchard, ANET, Princeton 1950, p. 136. ; ANE, paperback printing 1973, p. 195.
     Barton, Archeology and The Bible, p. 466 (according to Winckler).
4   May, TheTen Lost Tribes, BA, VI (3), 1943, pp. 55–60.
5   Lods, Les Prophètes D'israëL et Le Débuts Du Judaism, pp. 196–197.

go into captivity continued to worship the multitude of deities among whom they also worshipped Adon. But this is no longer the creed of Moses, nor is it that which the deportees bring back with them, although they do have a common basis. Two such contradictory movements could not have existed together and must have come into collision with each other. The Books of Ezra and Nehemiah depict precisely this state of affairs. Ezra, like Moses before him, acts firmly to quash the beliefs prevalent in the country so as to preserve the existence of his own creed. In his struggle he is assisted by Nehemiah, the commissioner to Judah. Since Nehemiah's authority is only valid for the district of Jerusalem and Judah, he drives out the disobedient only from this district.[6] But in places where Ezra and Nehemiah were without power, the inhabitants must have continued to worship their deities as they had before. The monotheistic movement which Ezra and Nehemiah tell us about concerns ONLY THOSE WHO RETURNED FROM CAPTIVITY, and takes place ONLY IN JUDAH WITH REFERENCE TO THE TRIBES OF JUDAH AND BENJAMIN ALONE: "Then rose up the chief of the fathers of JUDAH and BENJAMIN, and the priests and Levites, with all them whose spirit God had raised to go up to build the house of the Lord which is in Jerusalem "(Ez. 1: 5). In this Book of Ezra we read: "And they made proclamation throughout Judah and Jerusalem unto all the CHILDREN OF THE CAPTIVITY (בני הגולה) that they should gather themselves together unto Jerusalem.... Then all the men of JUDAH and BENJAMIN gathered themselves together"[7]. "...When the adversaries of JUDAH and BENJAMIN heard that THE CHILDREN OF THE CAPTIVITY builded the temple unto the Lord God of Israel"[8]. "And the CHILDREN OF THE CAPTIVITY kept the passover... and killed the passover for all the CHILDREN OF THE CAPTIVITY, ...And the children of Israel which were COME AGAIN OUT OF CAPTIVITY, AND ALL SUCH AS HAD SEPARATED THEMSELVES UNTO THEM from the filthiness of the heathen of the land, to seek the Lord God of Israel, did eat."[9] i. e. the religious movement is of those who came back out of captivity from among the tribes of Judah and Benjamin together with those who "had separated themselves from the filthiness of the heathen of the land". It is obvious then, that there were also those who did not separate themselves "from the filthiness of the heathen of the land". and they were the majority of the nation. These surely were not accepted by the reformed group which had returned from the captivity, as we may read: "...The people of Israel, and the priests and the Levites have not separated themselves from the people of the lands, doing according to their abominations even of

---

6   See: Neh13: 25 ; 28 ; 30 ; Ez. 9: 12
7   Ez. 10: 7–9 (My emphasis).
8   Ez. 4: 1 (My emphasis).
9   Ez. 6: 19–22. (My emphasis).

the Canaanites, the Hittites, the Perizzites, the Jebusites, the Ammonites, the Moabites, the Egyptians, and the Amorites...Now therefore give not your daughters unto their sons, neither take their daughters unto your sons, nor seek their peace or their wealth FOR EVER..."[10].

From the fact that this reform movement takes place in Judah alone, we must conclude that in the other districts of he land the Israelites did not separate themselves from the filthiness of the heathen of the land. Therefore we must assume that two groups of completely different standards are formed: The first were those who separated themselves from the filthiness of the heathen. It included those who returned from captivity together with people of the land who separated themselves from the filthiness of the heathen of the land. The second group were those who did not separate themselves from the filthiness of the heaten of the land and it included the whole country of Israel except the district of Judah and Benjamin (namely: ten tribes), yet there exists a very strong tie between them. Both these groups with different trends in religious outlook have a common past, possess the same language and are part of the same culture and tradition. This fact in itself endangered the creed of Ezra, and in the natural course of things might have led to the assimilation of those who returned from captivity with the heathen majority.

Ezra therefore erects a protective barrier around those who returned from captivity, enforcing their isolation in Jerusalem and Judah, and not allowing them to come into contact with the outside world. Such isolation could not be a lasting solution, for with the death of Ezra and Nehemiah the people would break out of this isolation forced upon them. In order to prevent this and the resulting assimilation of the two trends of religious belief the only solution Ezra can resort to is the destruction of those points of contact bridging the two: i. e. language, culture and tradition.

In the Talmud[11] we read: "Rabi Yosi says: it was fitting for Ezra to have given the Torah (tables of the covenant), if Moses had not anticipated him. It was said about Moses that he ascended (Mount Sinai – N. G.), so it was said about Ezra that he ascended (immigrated to Israel – N. G.)...and despite the fact that he did not give the Torah, he did change the script, AND ALSO HE RECEIVED (gave) A SCRIPT AND LANGUAGE"(My emphasis – N. G.). The same idea differently expressed can be found in the Jerusalem Talmud, Megilla A 8 (71; 72, etc.). and in the Babylonian Talmud, Sanhedrin (21; 72; etc.) where we read: "In the beginning the Torah (The five Books of Moses) was given to Israel in the Hebrew script and in the Holy language. It was again given to them in the days of Ezra in Assyrian script and Aramaic language. Israel chose Assyrian script and Holy language and left for the layman the Hebrew script and Aramaic language."

---

10   Ez. 9: 1; 12 (My emphasis).
11   Tosephta Sanhedrin 4, 7.

The Talmud ascribes to Ezra the change of the script from the Ancient Hebrew to the Assyrian. According to Prof. Tur – Sinai[12] the meaning of the word "script" (ketav –כתב) in the above verses is a "form" and he concludes that Ezra brought with him from Babylon a new form of the Torah, different from the one that existed in Israel The term "Labonaha" which was given to the ancient Hebrew script he explains as meaning "forged", and finds it astonishing that the language and script were changed at all. Tur Sinai asks:[13] "...and indeed this belief that the Tanaim referred to the change from the ancient Canaanite alphabet to the Assyrian script encounters many difficulties, some of which are quite obvious. The Canaanite script was not only given names without acceptable explanation, being called the scripts of Daatz, Raatz, or the Labonaha script – Why should there be such strange sounding terms for the national script, the traditional script inherited from the forefathers? ...and there is no question here even of beauty, since the Ancient Hebrew – Canaanite script, as discovered in the Lachish letters especially, is far more beautiful than the later script in all its forms known to us till today".

Evidently the change of script and language by Ezra was a vital factor in the preservation of his creed. Therefore, by branding the ancient script as Labonaha script i. e. forged script, he diverts the people's mind from the ancient script and advocates his own.

Every nation creates its culture on the basis of its past inheritance. The creed of Ezra, in order to be accepted by the people, must take its roots in the nation's past. But this past is filled with pagan culture. Ezra cannot wipe out such a past with one stroke, nor can he deny facts well known to everyone. Yet he cannot build upon a past which stands in complete contradiction to a monotheistic outlook. Ezra was faced with a problem for which there was only one solution: to leave the past as it was but to interpret it in the light most convenient for him. He gives the past a color and character which serve his own views. He collects together all the cultural legacy (or part of them) and like Akhenaton in his time[14] who had tried to establish the creed of Aten in his country, by erasing the names of deities from all steles and engraving the name of Aten; or like Raamses II who had erased the names of preceeding kings from memorial inscriptions and put his own name instead – so here, Ezra abolishes the names of the different Baalim and deities, and substitutes the name Jehovah instead, or sometimes "Adonai – Jehovah" to whom he ascribes all the properties and titles of the deities which the nation ever knew. For example El–Melech, El–Elion, El–Olam, El–Shamayim, El–Zedec etc.

---

12   Halashon Vehasefer, vol. I, 1954. ch. 7 – Ktav Hatorah. (Heb.)

13   Ibid. p. 124.

14   The Egyptian king Akhenaton instituted in Egypt the worship to one god – Aten – Aton, the sun disc.

(God the king, The Supreme God, God of the Universe, God of the Heavens, God of Righteousness). In many instances he also gives new explanations for names and events connected with idol names, e. g. Israel, which is the name of the nation derived from Ashera–tree worship. A new meaning is given to the name by bringing the story of Jacob who fought against God and men, and has prevailed (Gen. 32: 2–28). The same is done with the name Jerubaal, deriving from Baal, Benjamin (Ben – Oni) deriving most probably from Ben–On–son of On, etc. Ezra lends the heritage of the past a new look and the characteristics of a monotheistic religion. To allow the God – Adonai – Jehovah and the monotheistic outlook to take root within the nation's consciousness, Ezra creates the impression that it had originated in Abraham's period already. He gives a monotheistic interpretation to all events occurring in the world and in Israelite history. All the political and economic changes, in Israel or in the entire world, are explained from a religious monotheistic point of view. Everything is done by the will of "Adonai–Jehovah" – he lowers and raises kings, his glory fills the earth. He is the force which rules over the universe and all creatures do his wish alone. Every event is an act of his; whoever worships him is good, and whoever does not is wicked. A good king is the one who worships him, whereas a bad king is one who does not do so. Ahab, Omri and others were bad kings because they "worked wickedness in the sight of the Lord" whereas David, Solomon and others are good kings because they have done good deeds in the sight of the Lord. The Israelite nation was driven out of Israel not because it was defeated in battle but because they "worked wickedness in the sight of the Lord ". The king of Assyria or the king of Egypt won the battle with the Israelites because they are the scourge of justice in the hands of God and fulfil his wishes: he sent them to punish Israel This entire complex of cultural legacy and national history, granted a religious monotheistic colouring by Ezra, and perpetuated by others, sets the foundation for the composition of the Bible.

Ezra does not recount Israelite history, only Jewish history i. e. the history of the district of Judah. The history of the rest of the nation is not related in the Bible and only mentioned incidently when it is connected with Judaean history. There is reason to believe that this is why the Bible gives the impression that Saul is the first king in Israel For the same reason Hiram, Ethbaal and others are not mentioned as Israelite tribal kings, and are referred to only in connection with David and Solomon, and their liasons with them, as kings of Tyre and Sidon. The same applies to the fact that the Book of Judges is deficient in details, and that the Book of Chronicles begins with the events dating from King Saul.

In spite of the religious monotheistic character given by Ezra to Israelite history, he does not meddle with historical facts, since it would be impossible to do so with what was common knowledge. But because of the changes made in their colouring, discrepancies occur between various factual statements. These have caused, and still cause many scholars to reject the Bible as a reliable historical reference.

By editing the Bible and changing the ancient Hebrew script with that for the Assyrian script, Ezra demolishes the bridges between the two halves of the nation, forming a spiritual barrier substantial enough to last for generations after his death, and which will prevent the people of Judah from assimilating with the other half of the nation and other peoples surrounding them in general, as well as ensuring the continued existence and survival of the monotheistic creed of Adonai – Jehovah in particular. In the light of what has been said here, it can more easily be understood why Ezra is spoken of so highly: "It was fitting for Ezra to have given the Torah..."etc. Moses gave the Israelite nation the monotheistic creed of the God Adon, whereas Ezra developed this creed and gave it much wider and more universal significance. He founded the monotheistic creed of Adon Jehovah – this being the new version of the religion of Moses which Ezra had brought back from captivity.

THE MEANING OF "THEOPHORIC NAMES

In the Bible personal names such as Adoniya, Zidkiya, Ovadya, Yedidya, Yehoyakim and the like are mentioned. Such names are generally regarded as theophoric, derived from the name Yehova (Jehovah). i. e. Adoniya is explained "Adon – ya" (Ya =Yehovah is Adon = master), Zidkiya; Zadik–Ya (Ya=Yehovah is Zadik = righteous); Ovadya, Ovad –Ya (Ovad = worshipper of Ya =Yehova); Yedidya, Yedid – Ya (=a friend to Ya –Yehovah), the composite "Ya" being taken by scholars to be an abbreviation of the name Yehovah. According to such explanation with names such as Ovadya, Yedidya etc. the holder of the name is the active agent i. e. Ovadya – worshipper of Ya; Yedidya – friend to Ya, whereas in names such as Zidkiya, Adoniya – Ya is the active agent and not the holder of the name, i. e. Ya is the righteous (Zadik), Ya is the Master (Adon) etc.

We have said that Yehovah (Jehovah), though may had already been used before, is a name that Ezra links to the name of the God "Adon". If Ezra adds this name how is it that names supposedly derived from the name Yehovah (Jehovah) already existed a long time before the period of Ezra and the religious movement of those returning from the Exile?

To answer this question let us examine the meaning of these names and that of the name Yehovah.

The exact original pronunciation and etymology of the name is uncertain. In the fourth century B. C. we encounter the form Yahve (Jahve) and according to Theodorus this is the way the name is pronounced by the Samaritans. St – Epiphanes accepts this form, whereas St–Jerome adopts the form of pronunciation Yaho (Jaho). Clement of Alexandria adopts the form Yahove (Jahove). The pronunciation as Yehova (Jehovah) is in use already from the beginning of the 17th century. It is generally accepted as the name of the God of the Israelites. Innumerable attempts were made to explain its meaning. The traditional one is that according to the biblical account in Exodus 3: 14: ("Ehye Asher Ehye – = "אהיה אשר אהיה I will be whoever I will be), and therefore it derives from the Hebrew verb היה (Hayo = to be). This verse is erroneously translated "I am that I am ": "and God said unto Moses, I am that I am."

Gardner explains it as "he loves", Robertson Smith believes Jehovah means "he overthrows" (lightning). Wellhausen explains "he blows" or "he falls". Driver believes that the name developed from "a primeval interjection

– a god cry yah"[1], Duhm[2] sees in the name an extension of the word Hue (הוא –he), namely "he the unnameable". Some scholars went as far as to see in Yehovah a name of foreign deity, that the Israelites adapted from another nation, whether a kenite deity (Rowley, Tiele, Sado), or Canaanite (Land, Dussaud, Virroleaud) etc. Today names like Shefatya ((שפטיה Yehoshafat – (יהושפט)a cognate form, etc, are regarded as theophoric names i. e. derived from the god's name Yehovah (Jehovah), and that "Ya" is taken to be an abbreviation of Yehova. It must be noted here that the name Yehovah never occurs as a composite in "theophoric" names[3]. Many contrasting views exist regarding this dimminutive. Some argue that it is impossible to have a sacred name such as the deity's abbreviated, and we never find any other semitic nation that uses a diminutive form for the names of his deities.[4] Despite these arguments, "Ya" is generally accepted today as the diminutive form of "Yehovah". Here we should mention the peculiar fact that the name "Yehovah" appears in the Bible either alone, or in conjunction with the word "Adonai" i. e."Adonai – Yehovah"[5]. The Jews when reading the Bible avoid pronouncing the name "Yehovah" and substitute the name "Adonai", but when the text reads "Adonai Yehovah" they read instead "Adonai Elohim" (=Adonai the God; Adonai is the God). Referring to this custom Maclaurin remarks[6]: "If the name YHWH were too sacred to pronounce – so sacred that even the numerals 15, 16, were avoided because being YH; YW they could be taken as abbreviation of YAWH, why was Yah used in theophoric names. and more seriously why was Yah used independently as noted above as the name of God? "(p. 447)."the principle seems to be fairly clear–YHWH is not usually unaccompanied and where it has company the Tetragrammaton is often a secondary insertion, it has been customary to regard the other form as secondary, inserted to protect the divine name, but it seems expedient now to enquire whether the other terms are not to be regarded as primary and YHWH an insertion for doctrinal or political reasons. This will lead us to enquire whether Adon really is a reverential periphrasis for YHWH or whether it is in fact earlier in time and preferable in use. The position we

---

1   See: Driver, ZAW, 1928, p. 24
2   As brought by Raymond, The Divine Name Yahweh, JBL, 1961, p. 321, note 19.
3   See: Geheman, Manuscripts of The Old Testament In Hebrew, BA, (8), 1945, P. 100.
     Meek, Hebrew Origins, p. 106.
     Maclaurin, Y. H. W. H. ; The Origin of The Tetragammaton, VT. 1962, (12), p. 446.
     Lods, Israel, p. 372.
4   Driver, Jehovah, EB. 1929, edit.
5   Translated into English: "God Almighty".
6   Maclaurin, Ibid.

have established concerning YHWH is not what one would expect of a sacred name. a) It is not ancient. b) it is not pronounced "(ibid. p. 449).

Herewith we will see why it is impossible to accept the conjecture that the names assumed theophoric derive from the name 'Yehova' (the Tetragrammaton) and then we will discuss the meaning of the names themselves.

We have already noted that in the assumed theophoric names the active component shifts, sometimes it is the bearer of the name, at others it is "Ya", How to explain this fact? .

Such personal names are met not only in Israelite personal names, but also in gentile ones, like Uriya the Hittite, Tuvya the Ammonite, Nergal – ya, Niniv–Ya (namely in connection with foreign deities as Nergal and Niniv).[7] If we are to accept their derivation from the name "Yehovah" then how are we to explain the fact that these names are found also among gentiles, and in connection with foreign deities? .

In the book of Kings,[8] we read that the Pharaoh Nechoh; king of Egypt, enthrones Elyakim (Eliakim), the son of Joshia instead of his father and changes his name to Yehoiakim (Jehoiakim). If we accept the derivation of this name from Yehovah, it seems quite strange that a foreign Egyptian king calls an Israelite king by a name composed of the Israelite deity "Yehovah", and by this act apparently elevates him in position, when it is more logical that a foreign Egyptian king would call the subjugated king by a name that leaves him in a degraded position. In the Bible we also find the name Baalya (Bealiah – son of king David),[9] which according to the accepted explanation must be interpreted "Ya is Baal = Yehovah is Baal", such an explanation is paradoxical, and any attempt to explain – as it is done – that Baal means Adon = Master and therefore, Baalya means "Ya is master", and that this name is not to be connected with Baal is merely argumentative.[10]

Let us note here that the part considered theophoric namely "Ya" or "Yahu" may come either as a suffix or as a prefix of the name such as Zedkiyahu (Zedekiahau–צדקיהו) or Yehozadak (Jehozadak–יהוצדק), Yeshayahu–ישעיהו– (Isaiah) or Yehoshua – יהושע – (Joshua) etc. The name Yeshayahu (ישעיהו) according to the accepted explanation will mean "Yesha is Ya " = Deliverer – Salvation is Ya (Yehovah). The same meaning is given also to Yehoshua[11] יהושע except that with the later the part considered theophoric is in the prefix of the name, while with the name Yeshayahu it is in the suffix. But let us turn to the Book of Numbers (13: 16): "...And Moses called Oshea the son of Nun

7   See: Conder, The Syrian Stone Lore, p. 74; Neh. 3: 35; 2Sam. 11: 3
8   2Kn. 23: 34
9   1Chr. 12:
10   For exaple see this explanation by Koifman, TOLDOT HAEMUNA HAISRAELIT (Hebrew); Driver, EB 1929, entry: Jehovah.
11   See also: Wright W. Illustrated Bible treasure, pp. 522; 529.

Jehoshua – משה להושע בן־נון ויקרא יהושע" This verse informs us that in the beginning the name was "Oshea (הושע) "and Moses adds only one letter, the letter Yod=י (Y) and so changes the name to Yehoshua .(יהושע) Therefore in the name Yehoshua (Joshua) the letter Yod is additional and between it and the letters "HO" that folllow, there is no indivisible theophoric connection, deriving from the name "Yehovah".

On the other hand the name Yehoshua and Yeshayahu are one and the same, the only difference being in the position of the part "Yahu". in the prefix in the first and in the suffix in the second. We must therefore conclude that even in the name Yeshayahu (Isaiah), the part "Yahu" must not be regarded as separate entity representing a theophoric part: such a conclusion gets added support when we see names like Yehoseph (יהוסף – Ps. 81: 6), Yehonathan (יהונתן – 1 Sam. 19: 1)[12]; Yehonadav (Jehonadab) (2Kn. 10: 23); Yehoash (Jehoash 2) (יהואש Kn. 12: 1); Yehoyakim (Jehoiakim) (2Chr. 36: 4); Yehoram (Jehoram) (2Kn. 1: 17); Yehozadak (Jehozadak) (1 Chr. 6: 15)[13]; Yehohanan (Ez. 10: 28) etc (with the letter – ה –H). who appear also in an abbreviated form: Yoseph (Joseph יוסף, Yonathan (Jonathan 1) (יונתן Sam. 20: 1); Yonadav (Jonadab) (Jer. 35: 8); Yoash (Joash 2) (יואש Kn. 14: 1); Yoyakim (Joiakim) (Neh. 12: 10); Yoram (Joram) (2Kn. 8: 28) ; Yozadak (Jozadak) (Ez. 10: 18); Yohanan (Johanan) (1Chr. 3: 24). etc. (without the letter H– ה). The name Uzziya Uzzia – (עזיה) appears also in the form עזיא (Uzzia) – with the letter A – Aleph (א) instead of the letter Heh1) (ה) Chr. 11: 44)[14]

Such "Theophoric" names appear also in two forms such as Yermiya (Jeremiah) – Yermiyahu, Zidkiya (Zedekiah) – Zidkiyahu etc.[15].

We realise that in all these supposedly theophoric names, the part "Yahu" is not conserved as one integral unit. Moreover if we accept the explanation that "Ya" derives from "Yehovah", then names like Antothija, (ענתותיה). Shehariah, (שחריה) Sheariah, (שעריה) Rephaiah, (רפיה) Neariah(נעריה). Dalaiah (דליה)[16], which in Hebrew we will have to explain Ya (Yehovah) is Antothi = comes from Anatoth (a name of place near Jerusalem); Shehariah – we will have to explain Ya is shahor = black; Nehariah –(נעריה) Ya is Nahar =youngster; Rephaiah – Ya is Rafee = weak, feeble. The absurdity of such explanations is obvious.

Let us see if we can understand and explain these names otherwise. Names like Shefatya (שפטיה) Yirmiya – (ירמיה – Jeremiah), Zidkiya (צדקיה – – Zedekiah), Eliya – (אליה Eliah) and alike appear in the Bible in a more full form as Shefatyahu,(שפטיהו) Yirmiyahu (ירמיהו) Zidkiyahu (צדקיהו) Eliyahu

---

12 Yehoseph and Yehonathan appear only in the Hebrew text.
13 In the Hebrew text 1Chr. 5: 40.
14 Seen only in the Hebrew Text.
15 The two forms are only in the Hebrew text. In the English translation they are transcribed as one form.
16 1Chr 8: 24 (in the Hebrew text 25): 26: 38; 3: 21: 22: 24.

(אליהו) etc.[17] We can conclude that the suffix in these names is "Yahu" and not "ya" and "ya" is but a diminutive of "yahu". What does this added part Yahu (יהו) means? . Because of its final pronunciation it is reasonable to conjecture that originally it had the letter (Aleph) which was omitted in writing because it was superfluous in pronunciation. Similarly we see in other Hebrew words such as Haleluhu (הללוהו), Shabhuhu (שבחוהו) and alike that originaly were Halelu –Hue, (הללו הוא) Shabhu–Hue.(שבחו הוא)Meaning praise him, glorify him (הוא – Hue in Hebrew means He – him). There is place to assume that also the word Yahu – יהו, was originally Yahue–(יהוא with the letter Aleph א – at its suffix). In the Bible we find the name Yehue (Jehu – יהוא) (with the letter aleph) by itself. And also names like Elihu (אליהו), Avihu (אביהו) without the letter Aleph at their end, that appear in the form of Elihue(אליהוא) Avihue (אביהוא) with a letter Aleph at their end[18]. These forms with the letter Aleph must be regarded as the more ancient ones. Therefore names like Shefatyahu etc. must have been originally Shefatyahu (שפטי הוא) Zedekyahue (צדקיהוא) etc. (with an Aleph in their end) It is obvious that in these names the end part "Yahue" derives from the word "Hue"(הוא = he) preceded by the letter Y (Yod– י) And we have already seen that even in the name Yehoshua (Joshua) the letter y (Yod) was added afterwards "And Moses called Oshea the son of Nun Jehoshua." (Nu. 13: 16). In Hebrew the consonant (letter) yod (י) before the stem often represents the word Yihye (יהיה = will be) namely it is the conjunction in third person of the verb to be (hayo – היה) – If we apply the same rule also to Hebrew nouns (non verbs) that are prefixed by the consonant y (י) we realise that many words are thus rendered comprehensible.[19] For example, the Hebrew word yahad (יחד)= together, might be considered as yihye (will be) – had (= ehad =one), i. e. some objects group together to form one unit.[20]

In the book of Job (3: 6) we read: "As for that night, Let darkness seize upon it; let it not be joined unto the days of the year" (In Hebrew: Halayla hahu yikaheu ofel al yihad bi'yme shana". "הלילה ההוא יקחהו אפל אל־יחד בימי שנה" we can construe the word "yihad" as yihye had = will be one i. e, that night will not be one of the days of the year[21]. This rendering conforms with the succeding verse: "let it not come into the number of months" ("במספר ירחים אל־יבא.")

---

17   1Chr. 12: 5; 27: 16 ; 2Chr. 21: 2 ; 1Kn. 17: 1 etc. See note 85 above.
18   Job. 35: 1; 36: 1; 32: 4–5; 34: 1; 1Chr. 12: 20; 27: 18; 26: 7; 2Chr. 13: 20 –21; Le. 10: 1; Nu. 3: 2.
19   In the original Hebrew book i brought several examples but to alleviate the english reader only a few examples were brought in the english edition.
20   compare Ezk. 33: 30 "Vediber Had el Ehad" (Heb.) (Tran. A. V."and speak one to another").
21   Ibn Genah regards the word "Yihad" as derived from "Yahad (together). Cassuto explains "let no joy be in this day".

In Exodus (18: 8 – 9) we read that Moses told his father–In–law Jethro "all that the Lord had done to Pharaoh" etc."and Jethro rejoiced (in Hebrew Va –yihad – (ויחד for all the goodness which the Lord had done to Israel". We can explain "Vayihad" as "va–yihye had ,(ויהיה חד) "i. e. that Jethro was one (unanimous) with Moses, namely he agreed with Moses about the goodness, the wonders the Lord bestowed on Israel We see here words which apparently differ from one another, basically derived from one and the same root.

Another such group may be seen in the hebrew words "yasaf" (יסף) and "yasuf .(יסוף) "Yasaf is used many times in the connotation of ; to terminate, finish; cease. For example: "They prophesied and did not cease" (Nu. 11: 25). As for the word "Yasuf" it is used in the sense of to disappear; vanish. For example, "Lo yasuf zichro leolam vaed (לא יסוף זכרו לעולם ועד) "i. e. his memory will not vanish (will persist) forever. (See Esther 9: 28 – "nor the memorial of them perish" – in Heb. "Yasuf – from their seed"). If in these two words we consider the letter yod (י) as the abbreviation of yihye, we will understand that Yasaf and Yasuf derive from "yihye sof", i. e."There will be an end". Therefore "vayitnabu velo yasafu"(Nu: 11: 25) means "they prophesied and there was no end . .", their words did not reach an end, i. e. did cease. Whereas his memory will not "yasuf" forever – his memory will not have an end i. e. his memory will remain forever = will not perish. The verb "yarosh" (ירש) = to inherit, might be seen as "yihye Rosh" (yihye = to be, Rosh = head). namely: "to take the head" of the estate, house etc. i. e, to inherit. Another example might be seen in the verse (Eccl. 11: 3) "and if the tree fall toward the south or toward the north, in the place where the tree falleth there it shall be" (in Heb. sham yehue – "יהוא" namely sham yihye hue – שם יהיה הוא – there it shall be – remain.)

In the light of what was said above we may see the letter Y (י=Yod) in the suffix "Yahue" as the abbreviation of the word Yihye = יהיה = will be, and therefore Yahue will be Yihye Hue יהיה הוא – He will be; therefore names like Shefatyahu ,שפטיהו – Zedkiyahu צדקיהו – etc. (that in their origin were Shefatyahue ,שפטיהוא – Zedkiyahue צדקיהוא – etc. – with a letter Aleph in their end), are but Shofet yihye hue =a judge he will be, Zadik yihye hue =a just man he will be. El yihye hue = God he will be[22] etc.

In the words "Yihye hue "(=he will be) the reference is to the bearer of the name himself. When giving names to their children, the parents expressed their wishes and what they hoped to see in their children, or what they expected to find in them. and this was done by adding the suffix "Yahue"

22　Compare with Ex. 4: 16 "...he shall be to thee a mouth, and thou shalt be to him as God ".
　　The Hebrew text reads "a God" (אלהים) and Ex. 7: 1" I made thee as God to Pharaoh "The Hebrew text reads "I made thee God to pharaoh." (נתתיך אלהים לפרעה).

(יהוא) meaning "Yihye Hue "(He will be) to a certain name or verb. It was not only the parents that gave names to their children, but occasionally names were given later in life. For instance, Pharaoh Nechoh changes the name Elyakim to Yehoyakim, Solomon at first was called Yedidya, and Matanya –Zedekiah. The adding of "Yahue (יהוא) "or in its abbreviated form "Yahu" or "Yah" (The letter Aleph has been dropped most propably for being voiceless and not pronounced) could be added either in the suffix of a name or at its prefix. Like Shefatyahu – Yehoshafat, Zedekyau –Yehozadak etc. But the meaning remains the same. In the course of time, also these names have been abbreviated Yehozadak to Yozadak, Yehonathan to Yonathan, etc. Now we can understand that names like Uriah the Hittite, Tuvia the Ammonite, Baalya, or Nergalya their meaning is Ur (Or) = light– illumination will he be, Tov Yihye Hue – טוב יהיה הוא = Good may he be, Baal yihye Hue – He will be a Baal (The same as El will he be) –namely a priest to Baal he will be, and the same Nergal he will be. Such an explanation answers all the questions regarding such names. Now we can understand why Moses calls Oseah son of Nun–Yehoshua. Osheah means to save – but before entering the land of Canaan, Moses passes on to Joshua the leadership over the people of Israel, He therefore changes his name to Yehoshua (Joshua) namely: "He will be the saviour" i. e. he will save the people of Israel. We understand now names like Antotiya, Sheharia, Dlaya, Refaya, etc. which mean: He will be an Antoti, he will be dark coloured, he will be hirsute, he will be feeble etc. And the reference is always to the bearer of the name alone. In all such names the active component is always the bearer of the name. Such names are also met as women's names like Yehoad, Yehotal, Yehoshawa, Yehochan.[23]

Let us note here that in the light of the said above, there is reason for seeing the name Yoseph (Joseph) or Yehoseph as "yihye hue Saf" – He will be Saf. The meaning of Saf is unknown to us, perhaps it derives from the Hebrew word Sof=end, and the name then will mean; "he will be the end, " namely he will be the last. Rachel probably had hard labour and wishes he will be the last.[24] The name Saf by itself is found in the Bible "then Sibbechai the Hushathite slew Saph, which was of the sons of the giant".[25]

It is worth mentioning that Yoseph is called by the Pharaoh Zafhnath-

---

23   See: Lachish Letters. Let us add here that Stolper (BASOR, 227, 1976), refers to a name "Hu-u-na-tan in the Murasu texts that cannot be explained as a simple scribal lapse since it occurs in precisely the same form three times in the text. Instead, it must be inferred that in the language of personal names in 5th century Babylonia. Hu was current and acceptable as a shortened form of yahu. "

24   The traditional explanation is: "The Lord shall add to me another son " (Gen. 30: 24).

25   2Sam. 21: 18.

paaneah[26] The first syllable Zaf equals to Saf.[27] which forms the name Yoseph, perhaps therefore we can see Zafhnath – paaneah as Saf–Nath–paaneah, or Saf Nat Fanh – (voiceless p). The explanation of the name I leave to the Egyptologists, but it is interesting to note the similarity between Paaneah and Fan'h from the papyruses, which Sethe regards as equal to the name Phoenicians and on the other hand the similarity between Zaf – Saf which is part of the name Yoseph.[28]

---

26   Gen. 41: 45.
27   In Hebrew the letters S (Samech) and Z (zadek) interchenge. see the Hebrew text Job. 30 13: ("natsu"– for "natzu"); Ps. 71: 4 ("hometz" for "homes"); Is. 1: 17 ("hamotz" "hamos"; Tosephta, Avoda zara 5 (6) (Parsufot for Partzufot); Alatz – Alas; Karas – Karatz, See Gesenius (Hebrew Grammar. 19a). In Hebrew; Mitzrayim; Zidon. In Arabic – Masr; Saida Such an interchange is to be found also in ancient "phoenician" inscriptions, Slouschz (Otzar Haketovot afenikiyot, 1942, p. 24–Hebrew) mentions such interchange in the words "Samdat – Zemed" See these words also in Lidzbarski –Handbuch der Nordsemitische epigraphik, I – text 1962.
28   Let us note here that the name Zaphnath –paaneah is accepted by scholars to be an Egyptian name, and many interpretations were given to it. Mallon explains: "God say he is alive" ("Dieu dit il est vivant") – Les Hebreux en Egypte, Orientalia, 1921, (3), p. 75., So believes Spiegelberg as cited by Naville. Whereas Naville explains: "Head of the sacred college" – Naville –The Egyptian name of Joseph, JEA, 1926, pp. 16 – 18. Engelbach suggests "that the word צפנת– Safnat is a metathesis for צתנף (Zatnaf) meaning: "Joseph called Paneh". Engelbach, The Egyptian name of Joseph, JEA, 1924, p. 205.
Brugsch explains: "The governor of the residential district of he who lives" – ("Le gouverneur du district du domicile de celui qui vit"); Brugsch – L'Exode et les monuments Egyptiens, Leipzig 1875, p. 17.

THE MEANING OF THE NAME YEHOVAH (JEHOVAH)

The name Yehovah (Jehovah) is made up of three syllables Ye –ho – va. יהוה (four consonants – Tetragrammaton). If we draw analogies between this name and names such as Zedekyahu and the like. the first sylable represented by the letter Y – (Yod) will be an abbreviation for the Hebrew word "Yihye" (יהיה will be). The remaining syllables "Hova" have a striking resemblance to the Hebrew words "Hovee" and "Hava". it seems to us that the two are also simply abbreviations of words. The syllable "HO" represented by the letter) ה = H) seems to represent the Hebrew word הוה(Hovee = is ; exists), and the syllable "Va" represents the Hebrew word הוה(Hava – Hawah = was). The name Yehovah is merely the combination of the three words Yihye, Hovee. Hava. (will be, is, Was)[1]. The words Hove and Hava, resemble each other phonetically as to their consonants and differ only in their vocalisation. The letter He (ה – H) from the word "Hovee"and the letters "Va (וה)" from the word Hava were combined to form the two syllables "Hova". We can now understand why in the Bible the name Yehovah appears after the name Adonai namely, Adonai Yehovah. which means Adonai Yihye, Adonai Hovee, Adonai Hava. Which is: The God Adon; he will be, he is, and he was. This name comprises the essential credo of the Jewish religion and of any monotheistic religion, namely, the eternity of God. This principle is expressed in a different way in the Jewish book of prayers: "Adonai melech, Adonai malach, Adonai yimloch leolam vaed". (Heb.) "Adonai rules (is king), Adonai ruled, Adonai will rule for eternity", and "Vehu Haya, vehu Hovee, vehu Yihye betifhara"(Heb.)."and he was, and he is, and he will be in splendor".[2] It becomes clear that the name of the Israelite God is indeed Adon as conjectured before, and that the name "Yehovah" which Ezra (most probably) adds is only a surname for Adon–Adonai. The Jews do not pronounce the name "Yehovah" by its syllables, because Yehovah is simply an

---

1   Lately I found that Spinoza expressed the same idea writing: "If anyone considers without prejudice the recorded opinions of Moses, he will plainly see that Moses concieved the Deity as a Being Who has always existed, does exist, and always will exist and for this cause he calls Him by the name Jehovah which in Hebrew signifies these three phases of existence", (Tractatus theologico politicus – II, 380–of prophets) . English translation p. 288 the philosophy of spinoza, edited by J. Ratner the world's popular classics. Books, inc. new york.

2   Prayer "Adon Olam Asher Malach". (Heb.)

appellation of the God Adon – Adonai, Whenever the name Yehova appears by itself, the Jews read Adonai, but when it follows Adonai, they read "Adonai Elohim" – Adonai the God, to prevent duplication.

In the Book of Ezekiel (1: 1–2), the date of the time of his prophecy is indicated as follows; "Now it came to pass in the thirtieth year, in the fourth month in the fifth day of the month...which was the fifth year of king Jehoiachin's captivity" If we count back the given number of years (thirty) we realise that this calculation dates from the eighteenth year of Joshiah's reign, the year in which he started with his religious reformation in Jerusalem. (2Kn. Chap. 22–23). Of king Joshiah it is said: "And like unto him was there no king before him, that turned to the Lord with all his heart, and with all his soul, and with all his might. according to all the law of Moses; neither after him arose there any like him". (2Kn. 23: 25). Therefore if this year was used as a basis for chronology, it must have been an important date marking a fundamental turning point for reorientation. As pointed out, according to the Book of Kings this change consisted of a religious reformation. Perhaps it should be taken as the beginning of a processs which reached its climax with Ezra.

To sum up, names such as Shefatyahu Zedkiyahu and the like, have no theophoric connection whatsoever, with the name Yehovah. The only link between them is the verb Yihye (future tense of to be), which is common to both of them.

THE JEWISH NATION IN JUDAH

We have seen previously that Ezra creates a barrier between those who returned from the exile and that part of the nation which did not go into captivity, by confining the people within Judah, introducing fundamental changes in the interpretation of past culture (and values), and by changing the Hebrew script. In the course of time because of this enforced confinement a new nation is formed – The Jewish nation. Which is isolated from the rest of the nation of Israel and comprises mostly the tribes of Judah and Benjamin. But what became of the other remaining part of the nation which did not join the movement of Ezra and Nehemiah? Since no change befell them, we must assume that they continued to worship the idols they had worshipped before then, and that their cultural and linguistic heritage remmained as in the past, distinct from those of the people abiding in the region of Judah. In the course of time the ties linking the two parts are severed completely. Moreover, the rejected part profoundly hates the Jewish part for their rejection, and so two different nations emerge from the one stem of Israel[1]. Some generations later the people living in Judah emerge from their narrow boundaries. They call themselves Judeans, and their country Judah. It must be assumed that historians were faced with two facts: 1. The names "Phoenicia and Phoenicians" given by their predecessors to this region and its inhabitants.

2. The names "Judah and Judeans" which is the name given to a part of this same region and its inhabitants.

Being aware from their predecessors (Homer and others) that cities like Sidon and Tyre are in Phoenicia they continue calling the regions of Tyre and Sidon "Phoenicia". Since the inhabitants of these regions use a different script and their culture is different from that of the Judeans, therefore the name "Phoenicia" continues to be applied only to a part of the former land of Israel while the other part is called Judah. In other words: a part of former Phoenicia (= Israel) they call Judah and the name Phoenicia remains attached only to the remaining partThus a division is formed between Judeans and "Phoenicians" which grows deeper and deeper with the passing of time. ALTHOUGH THE NAME "PHOENICIANS" WAS ORIGINALLY

---

1   Such a division may have taken place also in the rejected part. Those neighbouring Judah accepted some values from the Judeans without departing from former values therefore were not accepted by the Judeans and formed The Samaritans.

THE APPELLATION GIVEN BY THE GREEKS TO THE ISRAELITE
NATION AS A WHOLE. The Jewish people and the subsequent generations
were confronted by a queer situation. According to tradition there were twelve
Israelite tribes, two tribes (Judah and Benjamin) form the Judean (Jewish)
nation. Where therefore are the ten other tribes? To answer this question, a
legend is woven about the ten lost tribes, which an angel of God led out of
the country etc. Later Jewish historians, like Josephus, for example, already
speak of Sidonians and Tyrians as of another nation having nothing to do
with the Israelites. However, Josephus in his writings is bewildered about
certain facts which he cannot explain satisfactorily[2]. Herodotus[3] remarks
that: "The Colchians and Egyptians and Ethiopians are the only nations that
have from the first practised circumcision. The Phoenicians and the Syrians
of Palestine acknowledge of themselves that they learnt the custom from
the Egyptians...Those Phoenicians who hold intercourse with Hellas cease to
imitate the Egyptians in this matter and do not circumcise their children".

Therefore, according to Herodotus we can conclude that there are two
kinds of Phoenicians. 1. Those who hold intercourse with the Greeks and
they do not imitate the Egyptians. 2. The other Phoenicians who do imitate
the Egyptians, but do not hold intercourse with the Greeks. Herodotus lived
about 400 B. C., Whereas the period of the differentiation of those who
returned from Exile from the other Israelites, occurred in the time of Ezra
and Nehemiah, i. e. in the same period, Therefore Herodotus must have
written his words when the difference between the two parts of the nation
had already been formed, though the ties were still not completely cut. He
therefore writes about two kinds of Phoenicians and not about two different
nations.

To sum up: The Israelite nation was surnamed by the Greeks "Phoenicians".
Because of a religious – cultural division two religious trends were formed,
which in time became two political entities, One receiving a new name,
i. e. Judah and Judeans (Jews), Whereas the name "Phoenicians" remained
attached to the people of the other entity which continued with their
idolatrous worship. Yet the name Phoenicians was originally applied to the
whole of the nation of Israel before the differentiation.

---

2   For example: Ant. VIII, 260 ; Cont. Ap. I, 22.
3   Herodotus II, 104. See: Trans. by Rawlinson, p. 115; Trans.: Godley, Loeb
    Classical Library.

THE MEANING OF THE NAME PHOENICIANS

The name Phoenicians (Phoinix) originally appears in Greek Literature with Homer. Most scholars saw the term as a Greek appellation, and tried to find an explanation for it in the Greek language.[1] Many scholars derive the name "Phoinix" from the Greek word "Phoinos" meaning–"blood red". Why were they called so? The explanations are various. 1. The Phoenician sailors that arrived to Greece after a long journey in the sea were spoken of as "red men" because of their sun–burnt skin (Pietschman, Evans, Fick)[2]. 2. The land of the Phoenicians like Caria was noted for its red skies in the morning (Beloch).[3] 3. The Phoenicians were experts in the extraction of red purple dye from Murex shells (Myer).[4] 4. They were so named because of their origins from the Red Sea area (Speiser).[5] 5. The torrential waters hurling down

---

1   Speiser, The Name Phoinikes, p. 324
     Contenau, La Civilisation Phénicienne, p. 288.
     Autran, Phéniciens, p. 52.
     Dunand, Byblia Grammata, p. 7.
     Harden, The Phoenicians, p. 22
     Slouschz, Hebreo – Phéniciens et Judeo – Berbères, p. 41.
     Astour, The Origin of The Terms, Canaan, Phoenician and Purple, JNES, 1965, p. 348.
     Kaperlud, Phoenicia, the interpreters Dictionary of the Bible.
     Muhly, Homer and The Phoenicians, Berytus, (19), 1970, p. 19.
     Bonfante, The Name of The Phoenicians, Classical Philology, (36), 1941, pp. 9–10.
     Evans, The Palace of Minos at Knossos, Macmillan, 1921, vol. I. p. 9.
     Berard, Les Phéniciens et L'odysée, vol. II, pp. 12, 33.
     Moscati, The World of The Phoenicians, London, 1968, p. 3.
     Whitaker, Motya – A Phoenician Colony In Sicily, p. 8.
     Wathelet P., Les Phéniciens et La Tradition Homèrique, pp. 235 – 236; STU. PH. II, 1983.
     Baurain, c., Portées chronologique et geographique du terme "phénicien" pp. 13; 25. STU. PH.
     IV, Namur1986.
     Vandersleyen, c. ; L'etymologie de phoinix, "phénicien". P. 20, STU. PH. V.
2   See: Evans, ibid. p. 9.
     Pietschman – Geschichte der Phöenizer, p. 107 as cited by Speiser, ibid. p. 325.
     Fick – Griech. Orten. p. 123, as cited by Berard, ibid. II. p. 35
3   Beloch, Griechische Geschichte I. 2 p. 70 as cited by Speiser, ibid. p. 325
4   Myer. Op. Cit. Geschichte des Altertum, I. 2 1. 97; 2, 66, as cited by Speiser, ibid. p. 325.
5   Speiser. ibid. p. 331.

to the sea is made red by iron laden soil.[6] 6. The country of origin of the Phoenicians being Edom.[7] etc. Such explanations are perhaps etymologically possible but are not logically tenable. A nickname is usually given to someone with a distinctive trait (characteristic) peculiar to him and exceptional for the environment. We will never call someone "dark skinned" or "red skinned" if our own skin is identical to his, dark or red. Geographically Greece is not far from Sidon and the climate of Greece does not differ much from the Sidonian climate, Hence there is no reason whatsoever for the skin colour of the Sidonians to be conspicous. Moreover, a man who becomes sunburnt has reddened skin only for the first days, but then it takes on a bronzed tan. Phoenician sailors arriving to Greece after a journey of several months by sea, could not possibly have remained red skinned, and it would be ridiculous for the Greeks to refer to their bronzed tan as being of red colour, especially so when their own skin tan was the same.

Regarding the conjectures that the name Phoenicia derives from the red colour of the sky in Phoenicia, or the colour of torrential waters, it seems that such conjectures were devised, with great effort to explain the "blood Red". Surely it is incomprehensible that the Greek people would give a surname referring to phenomena not seen with their own eyes, occuring in a far off country. Also are such phenomena of red skies, or red torrential waters peculiar only to the region of Tyre and Sidon? Are they not seen over the entire Middle East? Why would the Greeks specifically call the region of Tyre and Sidon Phoenicia? According to Vandersleyen there is no linquistic basis whatsoever to regard "phoinix" as derived from "phoinos".[8]

A certain conjecture links the name Phoinix with the Egyptian name"PNH", which Sethe believes refers to the region of Israel and Syria. According to Brugsch the name Fanhu was later associated with the Red colour. Countering this Speiser[9] asks: "Why the Greeks should have combed Egypt in search of a suitable designation for the Phoenicians? ". Myers also objects to equating Phoinix with Fanhu.[10]

1. When we examine the name "Phoenicians " in the light of its transcriptions into Latin languages we may realise from whence it derives. In French the Phoenicians are called "Phéniciens", in English –"Phoenicians", in German "Phöenizien", in Latin "Phoenices", and in ancient Greek "Phoinix". The pronunciation of the name in Greek and Latin is Pho. Whereas in the other languages we mentioned, though the pronunciation is Phe the

---

6   See: Contenau, ibid. p. 288.
7   Berard, ibid. vol. II, p. 37.
8   Vandersleyen, LÉtymologie de Phoinix, "phénicien" pp. 19–22 in Studia Phoenicia, V.
     Leuven, 1983.
9   Speiser, ibid. p. 327
10   Ed. Myer, Geschichte des Altertums, 4th Auflage, Berlin, 1921, p. 210,

letter "O" still remains and therefore indicates that the name was originally pronounced Pho and not Phe. Let us therefore use this pronunciation of Pho in these languages. We get in French – Phoniciens, in English – Phonicians etc. i. e. we get words for which the explanation in all these languages will be "Phoneticians", namely their derivation is from "Phoné (Φωνή)" which in Greek means Syllable – Voice. If we remember that the Phoenicians are considered as being the inventors of the phonetic script and its introduction to Europe. and that this writing constituted then a novelty for the Greeks and for the world in general, we will understand why the Phoenicians were so nicknamed.

We have already seen that the Israelites must have been the nation the Greeks surnamed Phoenicians. Therefore it results that the Israelites are those supposed to have invented the alphabetic writing.

THE ALPHABET – ITS INVENTION AND LETTER NAMES

Much has been written about the alphabet its letters, meaning and inventors; yet general agreement on this subject has so far eluded investigators. Most Greek and Latin writers in antiquity ascribed its invention to the Phoenicians; Herodotus, followed by Lucan, Pliny, Pomponius Mela, Clement of Alexandria and Diodorus Siculus present this belief. Eusebius quotes a fragment from Sanchoniathon who claims that "Thoth the Egyptian was the teacher of the Phoenicians in the art of writing". This belief is accepted by Plato, Plutarch. And Diodorus Siculus. Tacitus[1] notes that the alphabetic letters were brought to Phoenicia from Egypt. Herodotus (V. 58 – 60), claims that the Alphabet was brought to Greece by a Phoenician named Kadmos, and that the Greek Alphabetic letters were therefore called Kadmea Grammata, or Kadmon Tipoi. He himself refers to them as Phoinikea Grammata. In fact, although the belief that the Phoenicians invented the alphabet is common to most Greek and Latin writers in antiquity some quote traditions which were understood to refer its invention variously to Orpheus, Hermes, Linus etc.[2] According to Diodorus Siculus: "...when Kadmos brought from Phoenicia the letters, as they are called, Linus was again the first to transfer them into the Greek language, to give a name to each character, and to fix its shape."[3] Another tradition ascribed the invention of the Greek script to Palamedes and says of him that he adapted the Phoenician letters to the needs of the Greek language. Some of the ancient critics tend to mediate between the different versions by stating that the first alphabet of Kadmos contained only sixteen letters and that Palamedes added new ones[4].

Tacitus[5] states: "...the tradition runs that it was Cadmus arriving with a phoenician fleet, who taught the art to the still uncivilized Greek people. Others relate that Cecrops of Athens (or Linus of Thebes) and in the Trojan era, Palamedes of Argos, invented sixteen letters, the rest being added by

---

1   Annals, XI, 14.
2   Cohen, La Grande Invention de L'ecriture et son Evolution, p. 144.
    Diringer, The Alphabet a Key To History of Mankind, pp. 450 – 451
    Lenormant, Alphabetum In, Dictionnaire Des Antiquitès etc. pp. 188 – 218.
3   Diod. Sic. III – 67.
4   Lenormant, ibid. p. 206.
5   Tacitus, Annals, XI–14, Loeb Classical Library.

different authors, particularly Simonides.". Pliny[6] writes: "Gellinus hold that it was invented in Egypt by Mercury, while others think it was discovered in Syria, both schools of thought believe that Cadmus imported an alphabeth of sixteen letters into Greece from Phoenicia and that to these Palamedes at the time of the Trojan war added the four characters Z, ψ, Φ, X, and after him Simonides the Lyric poet added another four Y, Ξ, Ω, θ".

Caius Julius Higginus[7] records "that the fates invented the seven letters Alpha (onicron), Upsilon, Eta, Iota, Beta, and Tau, or alternatively that Mercury invented them after watching the flight of cranes which make letters as they fly. That Palamedes, son of Nauplius, invented eleven others, that Epicharmos of Sicily added Theta and Chi (or Psi and Pi). That Simonides added: Omega, Epsilon, Zeta and Phi."

On the face of it these traditions seem to contradict each other but according to Higginus Mercury invented the letters "after watching the flight of cranes which make letters as they fly"; obviously this means that he is referring to the form of the letters only, that is, to their signs and not to their names. Accordingly all the different traditions must be taken as referring to the invention of the letter signs and their modification but not the invention of the alphabet itself nor to its letter names. This is also to be understood from Herodotus who notes[8]: "And originally they shaped their letters exactly like all the other Phoenicians, but afterwards, in course of time, they changed by degrees their language, and together with it the form likewise of their characters...the Phoenician letters were accordingly adopted by them, but with some variation in the shape of a few.". He does not refer to any change whatsoever in the letter names. This is to be understood also from the Tacitus and Pliny references cited above. Lenormant reached the same conclusion by another route and writes; "All such traditions do not refer to the prime introduction of the Phoenician alphabet to the Greeks, but to the work of modifcation that the Greek inhabitants did to the alphabet brought by the Canaanite sailors, so to adapt it to their language and pronunciation."[9]

In modern times various theories concerning the origin of the alphabet have been advanced[10]; one general theory connects the origin of the alphabet

---

6   Pliny, Natural History, VII – 56 (192).

7   Hygini Fabulae 277. H. I. Rose, Lvgdvni Batavorum, 1933, Leyden. Translation quoted from R. Graves, The White Goddess, p. 224.

8   V– 58, Translation G. Rawlinson, The History of Herodotus, New York, 1947. p. 284.

9   Lenormant, ibid. p. 205."Toute cette categorie de traditions se rapporte non a la premiere introduction de L'Alphabet Phénicienne chez les habitants de la Grece, mais au travaille de modification que ces habitants firent subir a l'Alphabet apporte' par les navigateurs Chananeen pour l'appliquer a leur langue et a leur organe."

10   See: Em. de Rougé, Memoire sur L'origine Égyptienne De L'alphabet Phénicien.

with Egyptian writing, and this theory may be divided into three sub
– theories according to whichever stage in the development of this script
scholars took as their starting – point.

Hieroglyphic–advanced by Champollion, Salvolini, Lenormant, Halevi
etc.

Hieratic–Luzato, De – Rougé, Taylor, Kiele, Mallon, Montet, Ronzevale,
and others.

Demotic – Bauer.

Other theories try to connect the invention of the alphabet with the
cuneiform script (Sumeric, Babylonian, Assyrian etc.)

Evans (in 1909)[11] followed by Reinach, Dussaud and Macalister,
developed the theory that the alphabet was taken from Crete to Canaan by
the Philistines (believed to be natives of Crete) and from them borrowed by
the Phoenicians who in their turn diffused it. This theory is referred to by
Gardiner as "mere paradox.[12]

Within the context of the Greek language no explanation for the names
of the individual letters could be found, whereas it was possible to explain
most of them in the Hebrew language, for this reason scholars were inclined
to look for the alphabet origin in semitic languages and in the area of former
Canaan.[13]

In 1905 several inscriptions written in an alphabetic script with strong
hieroglyphic leanings were found by Petrie in the region of Serabit el
Khadem in Sinai. These inscriptions were ascribed by him to the period of
Thotmes III and Queen Hatsepsut (c. 1500 B. C.)[14]. A few years later other
inscriptions of this type were found in the same region (by Lake and Blake
of Harvard University).[15] These inscriptions, eventually called by Leibovitz
Proto–Sinaitic, were studied by the Egyptologist Alan Gardiner. At a meeting
of the British Archaeological Society held in Manchester in 1915, Gardiner
first advanced the theory that the Sinai inscriptions should be considered
an intermediate form of writing between the Egyptian hieroglyphs and the
Semitic alphabet. In his view, the Sinai script showed clear evidence of its
derivation from the Egyptian hieratic, and at the same time represented the
Greco–Phoenician alphabet at a stage when its individual characters still

Dunand, Byblia Grammata, Tome II, p. 173.
Diringer, The Origins of The Alphabet, Antiquity, 1943, pp. 77–90.
– The Alphabet, A Key to History Of Mankind, pp. 195 –197.
MacAlister, The Philistines etc. pp. 126–130.
11   Evans, Scripta Minoa. p. 2.
12   Gardiner, The Egyptian Origin of The Semitic Alphabet, JEA. 1916, p. 14.
13   Atkinson, Alphabet, EB. 1929, 14th Edit. p. 679b
14   Petrie, Researces In Sinai pp. 130–131. Gardiner, ibid. p. 13.
      Cowley, The Origin of The Semitic Alphabet, JEA. 1916. p. 17.
15   In the course of time, some inscriptions were found also in Israel

showed a close resemblance to the objects signified by their Semitic letter–names.[16]

Thus Gardiner came to regard the alphabetic script as originating from the Proto–Sinaitic writing, and moreover, he followed Nöldeke and Gesenius, in maintaining that the names of the alphabetic letters were derived acrophonically, i. e., "The forms of the letters originally represent the rude outlines of perceptible objects, the names of which, respectively, begin with the consonant represented "thus the sign of the letter Alpha (Aleph) (𐤀) is regarded as representing the form of an ox's head (in Hebrew Ox = אלוף Aluph); from here the name Alpha (or Aleph), where the first consonant A (א) is the one represented by the sign. The form of the sign of the letter Beta (or Bet.) (𐤁) is considered to resemble a house in Hebrew Bait – (בית), hence the name that begins with the consonant represented ב (B). Gamma (𐤂) Gammal = Camel; Delta (Δ) Delet=door. The same applies to all the other letters[17]). Gardiner published his views in 1916 (in the Journal of Egyptian Archaeology), at the same time with the views of Sayce and Cowley (1916), followed by Sethe (1917), Buttin (1928) and others.

The theory which sees the proto–Sinaitic Script as the origin of the phonetic alphabet and its letters as acrophonically derived is the most widely accepted and popular today.[18]

It is mostly Gesenius who gave this theory its widespread and enlarged popularity. However, it should be noted that there were scholars who strongly disagreed with it, including Lenormant, Dunand, Bauer Halevi and Diringer.[19]

On the other hand, many of the letters cannot be explained in this way, and for some of them the existing explanations are more imaginative than real. The form of the letter Gamma (𐤂) (Gimel), supposed to signify a Camel, does not resemble either the outlines of a Camel, or its hump. May be the ancients were primitive, but we can assume that at least they knew how to draw a camel. As Halevi writes: "Aleph ne rappelle en rien une tete de boeuf; Bet ne resemble pas a une maison, pas meme a une tente; Gimmel n'est pas plus un chameau que Daleth n'est une porte, etc. ("Aleph does not remind

---

16   Gardiner, The Sinai Script And The Origin of The Alphabet, PEQ. 1929, pp. 48–55.
      The Egyptian Origin of The Semitic Alphabet, JEA, 1916, pp. 1–16.

17   See: Gesenius, The Hebrew Grammar, pp. 27–28.
      Lidzbarski, Alphabet–The Hebrew, The Jewish Encyclopedia. 1916, p. 439
      The reference is to the ancient forms of the letters. For the forms and names of letters see Pl. x.

18   However Dunand claims that the Proto–Sinaitic inscriptions are not proved to be either Semitic nor Alphabetic. Dunand, Byblia Grammata, p. 172.

19   Diringer, The Story of The Alephbeth, p. 39.
      – The Alephbeth – A Key To History of Mankind, pp. 200; 219–220.
      Montet, L'origine Égyptienne De L'alphabeth Phénicien, pp. 294–305.

one at all of an ox's head; Bet bears no resemblance to a house or even a tent; Gimmel is no more a Camel than Daleth is a door").[20]

Yeivin notes[21]: "We cannot disregard the fact that for many letters it is difficult to find a pictorial resemblance even if we extend our imagination to its limits".

Acceptance of the acrophonic principle thus logically involves accepting the proposition that the letter–name is derived in each case from an object–name whose ideogram also stands as sign for the initial sound of this same object–name. However in the heat of the discussion on the merits and demerits of acrophony, scholars have tended to lose sight of the main point, namely that in their very nature these initial sounds are designed to reflect and convey the basic natural sounds which anatomically a human being is capable of producing; and that in the formation of the alphabet these sounds preceded both the letter–names and the object–names from which, in the acrophonic theory, the letters are said to be derived. In other words: one should never forget that the natural anatomic sounds came first– and that the phonetic script intended to perpetuate and convey these sounds and not their names. This proposition constitutes the fundamental basis and in it abides the uniqueness of any phonetic script designed to cover the whole gamut of anatomo – phonetic possibilities.

Accordingly, the anatomic sounds which make the initial consonant of the letter– names inevitably had to be the nuclear and key elements in the formation of the phonetic alphabet and they had to precede the formation of the letter– names and of their signs – and not the other way round. It is the anatomic sounds that were expressed by the names, and not the names by the sounds. Yet if the acrophonic principle is to remain valid, the object–names would have to form the basis for the determination of the initial sound (consonant) and its adaptation to the object–names and not the reverse. This, of course, contradicts all logic.

The champions of the acrophonic principle attempt to offer explanations for the letter–names, yet they do not give reasons why these specific names were chosen to represent the basic anatomic sounds, why, for instance, the name Aleph (or Alpha) and not Adam or Abir etc. – after all, the latter two

---

20   Halevi, Nouvelles Considerations Sur L'origine De L'alphabeth, RS. 1904 (IX), p. 366.

21   Yeivin, On Problems of The Origin of The Alphabeth Leshonenu, 17, B–C, p. 69. (Heb.)
     See also: Jean, Les Hyksos Sont Ils Les Inventeurs De L'alphabeth?, SY. IX, 1928, pp. 278–299.
     Garbini, The question of the Alphabet, in 'The Phoenicians', Bompiani, pp101–102.
     Sabatino Moscati, The world of the Phoenicians. p. 90. weidenfeld & nicolson 1968.
     They express a similar belief.

also articulate the basic anatomic sound A (א) Yet suppose one grants the acrophonic principle, one still will be puzzled why there should be a difference between the letter–names and the object– names, from which the latter are said to be derived. Why were the letter–names not straightaway Aluph, Baith, Gammal, Delet, etc., i. e. congruent with the object–names said to be contained in the symbols? Why the need to change these names to Alpha, Beta, Gamma, etc. or Aleph, Beth, Gimmel etc.? If an identity between the letter–names and the object–names existed, not only would the acrophonic principle be unaffected, but from the mnemotechnic viewpoint it would be much easier to memorize the letters because of the lack of duplication. And if it be claimed that such an identity existed in the past but was lost with the passage of time, how then explain that the working of time did not disturb the order of the letters yet completely changed their names?

One may also note Tur–Sinai's claim that the acrophonic principle is incapable of explaining why the order of the letters is the same in different languages.

What arises from the preceding is that even if we admit the acrophonic principle for the letter–names, it is evident that acrophony could have been established only after the letter– names already existed. At most one may regard the object– names as having been adapted to the corresponding letter–names, and not vice cersa, as the accepted version of the acrophonic theory would have it; hence, the explanation for the letter – names must be sought in some other principle than acrophony.

The Talmud explains the alphabetic letters by connecting them not with pictures (ideograms) but with a mnemonic verse: "The Rabbis told R. Joshua, R. Levi: Children have come to the Beth Hamidrash (Rabbinic school – N. G.) and said things (in the original Milei = words. N. G) the like of which was not said even in the days of Joshua son of Nun (thus) alef beth, (means) learn wisdom (alef Binah), gimmel daleth, show kindness to the poor (gemol dalim) etc."[22]

The phrase "the like of which was not said even in the days of Joshua son of Nun" warrants the inference, made by Tur– Sinai that already at that early stage in the history of Israel, in the days of Joshua, the alphabet was also taught by means of a mnemonic verse, though it went differently. The mnemonic method of teaching the alphabet is known amongst yemenite and Italian Jews as among many peoples. Tur–Sinai maintains that "the alphabetic letters are not connected with any pictures (Ideograms) but they were combined into a mnemonic verse which allowed the order, form and names of the letters to be learned and memorized; and eventually the whole alphabet– the letters, their names and order– passed into the Greek language sphere . It is thus

---

22   Babylonian Talmud, Tractate Shabbat, Ch. 12 "Ha–Boneh" (Soncino translation)

pointless to look for an explanation of this or that specific letter but one must endeavour to find an answer to the general question of the constituent whole of the verse, of which each letter forms only a small phonetic unit. After all, for the purpose of learning and memorizing the alphabeth it was unnecessary that there should be a series of intelligible names with objects represented, since any device will serve that facilitates memorizing, such as the juxtaposing of syllables which in isolation are quite meaningless but read together simulate a meaningful sentence whose alliterative and assonantal qualities make it stay in the memory."[23] As Tur–Sinai states: "Only by postulating a verse embracing all the alphabetic letters, which Later would be repeated simply PHONETICALLY, is one able to explain the otherwise perplexing fact that the alphabeth retained its Canaanite letter– names and sequence when it was transmitted to Greece. Along with the written list of characters, THE GREEKS LEARNT BY ROTE FASHION ALSO THE MNEMONIC VERSE, WHICH LATER SEEMED TO THEM A LIST OF REAL NAMES – ESPECIALLY AS IN THE NEW LANGUAGE SPHERE THE MEANING OF THE ORIGINAL VERSE WAS NO LONGER UNDERSTOOD."[24]

Tur–Sinai basing himself on the Talmud, Yemenite tradition, Testimony of the fathers of the Church (Hieronymus, Eusebius, St. Ambrose and others), attempted to reconstruct this verse, (in Hebrew) as follows: Aleph Binah, Gomel Dalim Hu Vehu Zan Khai Tov Yado, Kaph Lemad Mimenu, Smokh Ani Pi Tzedek Kaph Rosh Sim Tav.[25]. According to him, "even with all the doubts as to details, it is evident even from the words maintained in the variety of this tradition, that we have here not an exclusive mnemonic verse, but as in the Talmudic and Yemenite traditions, a verse that summarizes and teaches religious and moral doctrines...accordingly the Alphabetic tablet that passed to the Canaanite cities, was a religious document summarizing the principal moral attributes of the one and only God, a document which is difficult to detach from a major event."

The ideas of Tur–Sinai prompted me to think along similar lines. His theory is very plausible and I essentially agree with it; yet it seems to me that it is not without contradictions in its details. According to Tur–Sinai the alphabet was nothing other than mnemonic hebrew verse, which was meaningful in its original language, and in this form was passed on to the Greeks and other peoples, WHO LEARNT IT IN ROTE FASHION ENTIRELY BY

---

23   ur– Sinai article Alphabet in Encyclopedia Mikrait, I. 1955, Jerusalem, pp. 402, 404 (Hebrew). He expresses the same view in a somewhat different form in the chapter "Mereshit Torat Yisrael bemasoret haalephbet", Halashon Vehasefer" Vol. Hasefer, Jerusalem, 1959, pp. 150–190 (Hebrew).
24   Mereshit Torat Yisrael bemasoret Haalephbet, Vol Hasefer, pp. 170–171. (Hebrew)
25   Tur–Sinai ibid. p. 186.

ITS SOUND, so that eventually it "seemed to them a list of real names – ESPECIALLY AS IN THE NEW LANGUAGE SPHERE THE MEANING OF THE ORIGINAL VERSE WAS NO LONGER UNDERSTOOD". Now if one accepts this theory, it inevitably follows that the Greek alphabet names phonetically represent complete or fragmentary Hebrew words from a mnemonic Hebrew verse; this means that any Greek letter–names, such as Beta or Delta, must necessrily form elements of this same verse (unless these names were subject to change over the ages). Or in other words, it is required that the phonemes making up the Greek letter– names, Alpha, Beta, Gamma, etc. should be identified with the original mnemonic Hebrew verse. Yet in the version offered by Tur–Sinai no sounds equivalent to Alpha, Beta, etc. can be discovered; instead we have "Binah", "Dalim", etc. which have nothing in common with the corresponding letters in the Greek alphabet.

To summarize thus far: Tur– Sinai theory that the alphabet was learnt as a mnemonic Hebrew verse (as also inferred from the Talmud), should be considered plausible in its essentials; yet, his suggested reconstruction of this verse does not correspond to his theory and thus must be rejected.

With this theory as our guide, we shall now attempt to reconstruct the mnemonic Hebrew verse as it must have been originally.

As already stated, it is inferred by Tur Sinai in the wake of the Talmud, that even in the days of Joshua son of Nun the alphabet was originally taught as a mnemonic Hebrew verse, that in this form it passed on to the Greeks who learnt it in rote fashion entirely by its sound, "so that eventually it seemed to them a list of real names". It follows from this that the Greek alphabetic names must necessarily be elements of a Hebrew verse, that is to say, these elements phonetically represent complete or fragmentary Hebrew words which, juxtaposed, form a meaningful Hebrew sentence.

Insofar as we are aware, the Greek letter names did not undergo any significant changes at any time in their history, and this is also confirmed by the findings of most scholars in the field.[26] According to Halevi, Diringer

---

26   Dunand, Byblia Grammata, p. 170.
      S. E. Loewenstamm, New Light On The History of The Alphabet, IES., 16, 1951–52, 3–4, pp. 32–36, (Hebrew)
      D. Diringer, The Alphabet, New York, 2nd edit. 1953, pp. 218–219
      Lenormant, article "Alphabetum" in Dictionnaire des Antiquités etc. Ed, Daremberg et Saglio,
      Paris, 1877.
      Th. Gaster, The Chronology of Palestinian Epigraphy, PEQ. 1937, pp. 43–58.
      Albright, Some Important Recent Discoveries – Alphabetic Origins, BASOR, 118, 1949, pp. 12–13
      F. Moore Cross Jr., The Origin and Early Evolution of The Alphabet, in: Western Galilee and Coast of Galilee. Jerusalem, 1965, p. 17 (Hebrew).
      Atkinson and Whatmough, article "Alphabet", in EB. ed. 1968, p. 664.
      Atkinson, Article, "Alphabet", EB. ed. 1929.

and others, the alphabetic letter–names existed already in the 2nd Millenium B. C.[27]

Herodotus mentions (V–58) that "as time went on the sound and the form of the letters were changed", but he does not refer to any changes in the letter– names. Indeed, as noted at the outset, the ancient traditions which speak of changes in the Greek alphabet are really concerned with changes in its signs and not in its names. Admittedly Herodotus also mentions that "the letter Sigma was called San by the Dorians", and that "The Ionian dialect, in contrast to the Dorian, included the additional letters Upsilon, Phi, Khi, Psi, Omega". Yet this is not to be seen as a reference to any changes in letter–names, rather it points to a difference between two dialects Similarly when it is said about Linus that he determined the letter– names, this does not imply that he changed them in any way. Moreover, the answer of how linus came to determine the letter– names is implied in our acceptance of Tur–Sinai's theory, since it is exceedingly plausible that this determination was made in the way the theory states, viz. that the letter–names were derived from the existing mnemonic Hebrew verse. Nor does this import any contradiction with the ancient tradition; for it must always be remembered that our arguments are not concerned with the Greek letter– signs, which in fact did undergo certain changes, but solely with the Greek letter–names.

In contrast to the Greek alphabet, the Hebrew letters did undergo certain changes (e. g. the substitution of the script by Ezra); we cannot exclude the possibiity that some letters were added or changed by this substitution. Thus in view of the greater continuity of the Greek letter–names, it would seem more logical to use that alphabet as the basis for reconstructing the original mnemonic verse, rather than the existing Hebrew alphabet on which Tur–Sinai based his attempted restoration.

In keeping with our preceding argument, all that is required of us to arrive at the original mnemonic verse (supposed Hebrew) is to supply the Hebrew completions to the Greek alphabetic names that is, to supply the missing syllables needed to turn the fragmentary Hebrew words represented by the Greek names into complete Hebrew words.

Two implications, to be regarded as inescapable principles, follow inevitably from the above:

1. If it is assumed that the Greeks learned the alphabet from a mnemonic Hebrew verse in rote fashion entirely by its sound, hence each Greek letter– name phonetically represents a complete or fragmentary word from the Hebrew verse, it necessarily follows that these letter–names will be

---

27   Diringer, Op. cit., p. 219. See also: Gardiner, The Egyptian Origin of The Semitic Alphabet, JEA.
1916, p. 5.
Albright, BASOR. 118., 1950, p. 12 ; BASOR. 119, pp. 23–24.

rediscovered IN THEIR ENTIRETY in the original Hebrew verse we are trying to reconstruct. For instance, the letter– name "Beta" is a fragment of a word from the original Hebrew verse which also included the other alphabetic names, and hence it must appear unchanged in that verse, viz."beta", and not "Beti", "Ba'it", etc. and the completion of the looked– for word must supply the final sound of the Greek letter– name. For instance, the word fragment "Beta" along with its complementary part can appear in Hebrew only as – בֵּיתָךְ Beta–kh, — בֵּיתָה beta, or בֵּיתָם– beta – m; otherwise its phonetic agreement with the Greek letter– name will be lacking.

For practical purpose it here is taken for granted that the Greek letter–names represented only fragmentary hebrew words and not complete ones

2. It has been assumed that the alphabet was taught as a mnemonic Hebrew verse, and in this form it passed on to the Greeks etc. ; and this requires that each Greek letter–name is a fragment of a Hebrew word which, in its reconstructed form, must begin with the corresponding Hebrew letter represented in the Greek alphabet. Alpha corresponds to the Hebrew letter Aleph, and accordingly the letter Alpha, in the reconstructed Hebrew verse, will form part of a word beginning with the Hebrew letter א (Aleph); the Greek Eta corresponds in the alphabet sequence to the Hebrew letter Heth, and in the reconstruction will thus form part of a word beginning with the Hebrew letter ח; (Heth) similarly the letter Omicron, in the reconstructed verse will form part of a word beginning with the letter – ע Ayin; and so forth.

It is noteworthy that many of the Greek letter– names end with the vowel "a" (Alpha, Beta, Gamma, etc.) and this terminal vowel is considered by many scholars either a Greek addition unrelated to the original name, or a vestigial Aramaic root. Likewise the letters Omicron and Omega are often thought to be Greek words signifying small–O and big–O respectively.[28] As these are purely theoretical notions, lacking any epigraphical basis, we shall postpone commenting on them until after we have reconstructed the mnemonic verse; in the interim, we shall treat the Greek alphabet sequence as an integral

---

28 Diringer, ibid, pp. 218–219.
    Gardiner, ibid. p. 5
    Contenau, La Civilisation Phénicienne, p. 258.
    Cohen, La Grande Invention De L'écriture etc. p. 136.
    Atkinson, Alphabet, EB. 1929 edit.
    Atkinson and Whatmough, Alphabet, EB. 1968 edit. p. 664
    Taylor, History Of The Alphabet, 1883, II, p. 27, quoted by Atkinson in EB. Alphabet.
    Petrie, The Formation of The Alphabeth, p. 19.
    Tur–Sinai "Mereshit Torat Israel Bemasoret Haalephbet", Halashon Vehasefer, Vol. Hasefer, p. 184(Hebrew). See also note 7, p. 153
    Garbini, The Question of The Alphabet, p. 102 in'The Phoenicians' Bompiani, 1988

unit. The Greek alphabet we shall be concerned with is the Ionic, which is considered more ancient and widespread than either the Doric or Aeolic; and this is also confirmed by Herodotus: "...it was the Ionians who first learnt the alphabet from the Phoenicians" (V– 58).

The sequence of letters in the Ionic alphabet is as follows: Alpha, Beta, Gamma, Delta, Epsilon, Zeta, Eta, Teta, Iota, Kappa, Lambda, Mu, Nu, Ksi, Omicron, Pi, Ro, Sigma, Tau, Upsilon, Phi, Khi, Psi, Omega.[29]

The first letter of this sequence is Alpha, and in accordance with our basic principles, the Hebrew reconstructed verse must preserve these phonemes and begin with the corresponding letter in the Hebrew alphabet viz. א (Aleph). We must thus get the word fragment אַלְפָ... (Alpha). Now in Hebrew there is only one word to which this fragment can be connected, and that is the verb אַלֵף (Aleph), which means "to teach[30]. However, since the sound we require is alpha and the verb (אלף Aleph) assumes this sound only in its second person singular imperative form אַלְפָה (Alpha), it follows that our word fragment can be completed only as אַלְפָה (Alpha), meaning: "Teach thou"

The next letter Beta, in keeping with the same basic principles, will appear in the Hebrew reconstruction as בֵּיתָ (Beta). Immediately one is struck by the resemblance of this word fragment to the Hebrew word בַּיִת (Bayit = house), which makes it plausible to assume that the former was derived from the latter. However, the word בית (Bayit) assumes the sound of BETA in the third person singular feminine form בֵּיתָה (Beta – her house): plural בֵּיתָם (Betam – their house–masculine) בֵּיתָן; (Betan – their house–feminine); in the second person singular feminine or in the archaic second person singular masculine בֵּיתָך, (Betakh – your house)[31]. As the word before this letter name is Alpha ("Teach thou") which grammatically is second person singular masculine, it would seem appropriate to complete the word fragment to בֵּיתָך (Betakh) which is also a second person singular masculine form.

The third letter is Gamma, transcribes in Hebrew... גַמָ (gamma) The corresponding letter is called in Hebrew Gimmel, in syro – Aramaic, Gammal, and in Ethiopian Gamml. As we can see, in each of these languages there is an additional final "L" (Lamed), thus making it reasonable to assume that the original form of the letter- name was as in Syro – Aramaic גְמָל (Gammal). The meaning of this name will be dealt with further on. Passing on to the next

---

29 An aspirative letter, Digamma, representing the w sound (vau), is supposed to have existed in the Greek alphabet But its origin is obscure, and it disappeared entirely in Attic and Ionic at an early period therefore we did not refer to it.

30 Cf. Pr. 22– 25, "Make no friendship with a man that is given to anger; and with a wrathful man thou shalt not go; lest thou learn (Hebrew – Te ELAPH) his ways. Job. 33: 33.
"Hold thy peace, and I shall teach thee (Hebrew–Va–Aalephkha) wisdom".

31 See Gesenius, op. cit. p. 156. par. 58g. cf. Gen. 6: 18–19 "with thee" (Hebrew – Itakh) ; See also: Lev. 25: 39.

letter Delta, which in Hebrew transcription yields the word fragment...)דָלֶת Delta), we discover that the only Hebrew word that can be accommodated phonetically to this is דלת (Delet = door). We recall that the first word of our reconstructed verse, ALPHA (teach thou), is in the second person singular, and correspondingly also its second word BETAKH. With this in mind, we can now complete the word fragment דלת (Delta) to דלתָךְ (DELTAKH – your door), also an archaic second singular form. Writing these four Hebrew words together, we now get the following: ALPHA BETAKH GAMMAL DELTAKH...If this passage is read with a mind to its phonetic values only, it will be apparent that the word גָמֶל (Gammal) is really only a compound of the two Hebrew words גַם עַל (Gam – Al = also on). The letter מ (M-mem), which is vowelless in Hebrew, took its vowel from the succeeding ע (Ain); and in consequence the Ayin was elided in speaking and reading. The beginning of our mnemonic verse now reads as follows: "ALPHA BETAKH GAM-AL DELTAKH..."

Continuing with the next letter Epsilon, we obtain in Hebrew transcription the word fragment... הפסילונ (Epsilon). Admittedly no such word exists in the Hebrew language, but the Greek alphabet includes a very similar letter – name, viz. Upsilon. These two words differ only in their respective first letters, U(ו) and E, (ה) whereas the main part of the word is the same in both: Psilon. We are thus safe in assuming that the two letters E and U were added to the original word. Moreover there is a remarkable phonetic resemblance between Psilon and the Hebrew word פסל (PESEL=idol–figurine), in its plural form פְּסִילִים (PSILIM), or in the Aramaicized plural (פסילין PSILIN).[32] Accordingly we consider that the name Epsilon should be regarded as a part of the Hebrew word (plural form) הפסילונים (HE–PSILONIM – The idols)[33], where the letter ה (Heh) is the Heh of the definite article; similarly the letter–name Upsilon should be regarded as a part of the Hebrewופסילונים (U–Psilonim) where the "mutated" letter (waw=u) represents the conjunction "and ."

We now arrive at the letter Zeta, which in Hebrew transcription can appear either as. זת (Zeta with Tav –weak "t"), or) זט Zetta – with Tet – strong "t"). The latter can not be reconstructed in Hebrew, whether as an independent word or as a word fragment that may be completed, whereas the form... זת (ZETA) phonetically resembles only two Hebrew words זית (:Zayit –olive) and זאת (ZOT–this).

---

32 Cf."But he himself turned back from the idols (Hebrew–Ha–PSILIM) " (Jud. 3: 19); and "And served their graven images (Hebrew– PSILEHEM)". (2Kn. 17: 41) See also (the Hebrew text)
Is. 30: 22 ; Ho. 11: 2; Deut. 7: 5.

33 The suffix ון (on) is encountered in the Bible, like Zelem–Zalmon ; Talmon; Kedem–Kadmon; Sahar– Saharon, Adom–Admon; Hazor– Hezron etc.

ZAYIT can in no way be made to fit the context of our reconstructed verse, and thus we are left with the word זאת (ZOT), which in keeping with Greek phonetics will appear זאת (ZOTA)

The next letter ETA corresponds in the alphabet sequence to the Hebrew letter ח (ḤETH), and accordingly in its Hebrew transcription it must begin with this letter, while its second letter may be either ת (Tav – weak "t") or ט (Tet– strong "t"). This means that the original Hebrew word fragment could have been either ...חַת; ...(HETA) or... חַט (HETTA). Now the fragment חת... (HETA) cannot be fitted meaningfully into the context of the reconstructed verse; on the other hand the form חַט (HETTA) phonetically resembles the word חֵטְא (HETT = sin), in its archaic Hebrew form חטאה (HeTTAA)[34] or חטאה (HATTAA)[34] This word logically connects in our context with the word הפסילונים (HE–PSILONIM = the idols) which preceeds it, thus making it a safe assumption that originally the complete word was חטאה (HETTAA). The reconstruction of our mnemonic verse thus far reads: ALPHA BETAKH GAM–AL DELTAKH HE–PSILONIM ZOTA HETAA...

If we read this fragment of the mnemonic verse, paying attention only to its phonetical values, (for it is assumed that the Greeks learned the Alphabet in rote fashion entirely by its sound), It will be immediately apparent that the word ...זאת (ZOTA) is a combination of זאת־ה (ZOT – A), where the final Syllable TA got its vowel from the definite article ה (Heh = the) which belongs to the following word חטאה (HETTAA) but which came to be elided in speaking and reading.

The next letter Teta, in keeping with our basic principles, produces the Hebrew word fragment... טת (TTETA) or טט... (TTETTA). Again the first of these alternative syllables ...טת (TTETA) cannot be accommodated to any Hebrew word, but taking the second alternative טט... (TTETTA) we are justified, in view of a general drift of the mnemonic verse so far, "HE–PSILONIM ZOT–A ḤETTAA ...(= the idols this sin. .), in reading the original word as טְטַהֵר (TTETTAHER – "thou shalt purify")[35]. With this

---

34 Cf. for instance, "And let his prayer be turned into sin (Hebrew: Le–HETTAA) (Ps. 109: 7) ; and "For she hath sinned (Heb. HETTAA) against the Lord., (JE. 50: 14); Gesenius notes also "Hatiaa" (after C. I. S. 2–224).

35 In certain cases there is a interchange of the letters ת (Tav) and ט (Teth) as: נטש־נתש (Natosh = abandon) ;תפל־טפל ,(Tafel = Lacking flavour ,תעה־טעה; (Taoh = err) ;חרת־חרט; (Kharot=engrave) ,רתת־רטט Rettet = Tremble); See: Hoshea 13: 1; Je. 49: 24. See these words רתת־רטט in Gesenius, Hebrew And English Lexicon of The Old Testament; Hebräisches Und Chaldäisches Handwörterbuch., Hebrew Chaldee Lexicon to the Old Testament.
In the Book of Daniel (3: 7; 3: 10) we find "Psantherin" in both Tav and Teth פסנתרין ;פסנטרין In Mesha inscription we find Attarott עטרט (with Teth) instead of Attarot עטרת (with Tav); See Gibson, textbook of Syrian semitic inscriptions, p. 75. L. 11. Possibly the substitution of the Tav by the Teth may be explained by the principle of assimilation, where the Teth from the preceding Hettaa was

word added our verse now reads: ALPHA BETAKH GAM – AL DELTAKH HE– PSILONIM ZOT HA – HETAA TETTAHER...

Iota, the next letter in the Greek alphabet corresponds to the Hebrew letter יוד (Yod), which is phoneticaly identical with the first part of Iota (In the Slavonic languages pronounced YOT). Hence we may assume that the original Hebrew word was... יוֹד (YODA).

After the Iota comes Kapa which transcribes... כַּף (Kappa). Its corresponding Hebrew letter–name is – כף (Kaph), which may be construed "palm (of the hand)". Kaph (palm) in its plural form is כפיים KAPPAIM. Here the initial Syllables Kappa are phonetically identical with the Greek letter–name, thus making it reasonable to assume that this name is a fragment of the word כַּפיים(KAPPAIM) The next letter Lambda (pronounced Lahm-thah) appears in its Hebrew transcription as... לַמְד (LAMDA...). The obvious origin of this word fragment is the verb למד (LAMED – "to teach"). Already at the beginning of our reconstruction we saw that its first word ALPHA ("teach thou") is in the second person masculine, and evidently its other verbs will have to be in the same grammatical form. We may thus complete our fragment to – לַמְדָה (Lamda = Learn thou), which is also in the second person masculine.

Lamda is followed by... מוּ (MU). We recall that a common expression in Hebrew is לְלַמֵּד מוּסָר (LE – LAMED MUSAR = "to teach morals") ; it is thus reasonable to suppose that the two letter names.

Lambda and Mu are really a truncated form of לַמְדָה מוּסָר (LAMDA MUSAR). If we join these two words to what has gone before, we now get the phrase יוֹדַ...כַּפיים לַמְדָה מוּסָר. (YOD–A KAPPAIM LAMDA MUSAR). in amended form יודע כפיים למדה מוסר (YODA KAPPAIM LAMDA MUSAR). We shall deal with the meaning of this phrase further on.

The next letter Nu transcribes into the word fragment נוּ... (NU), its corresponding letter in Hebrew, Arabic and Syriac alphabets is נוּן (NUN). one observes that these two letter–names, Nu and NUN, not only occupy the same place in the alphabet sequence but are also identical phonetically; and it is thus a safe assumption that the final N – sound of this letter–name existed originally in Greek as well. As it happens the only Hebrew word that starts with the sound NUN is the word נוּן (NUN) itself, of which the meaning is "to flourish, to grow up".[36]

The next letter in the Greek alphabet is Ksi, which is supposed to represent the Hebrew letter name Samekh, but for some reason starts with another consonant, as also happens with the word – חטאה (HETTAA), and its initial

attracted to the next word. (see Gesenius, p. 149. par. 54), or perhaps this also started with another letter, namely Heh.

36 Compare "his name shall be continued (in Hebrew Yinon – N. G) as long as the sun"; ps. 72: 17.

and determining sound "S", follows in the second place. Though lacking an explanation of this phenomenon, we are safe in transcribing this name as... כ סִי (with Kaph, i. e. weak "k") or – קסִי ...(with Koph, i. e. strong "k"). In its second spelling, (with Koph), this fragment cannot be accommodated to any Hebrew word, but the first spelling ...כּסִי (Ksi with kaph) recalls the word כּסִיל (Ksil – witless, fool, simpleton). Since this word makes sense in the context of the verse, it has been incorporated in this form.

Following the Ksi is the letter Omicron, which in the alphabet sequence corresponds to the Hebrew letter ע (AYIN). Transcribed into Hebrew this name will appear as עוֹמִיכרוֹן (OMICRON – with Kaph) or עוֹמִיקרוֹן (OMIKRON – with Koph). No word of either spelling or with this initial sounds exists in the Hebrew language, but the first two syllables עוֹמִי (OMI) recall the word עַמִי (AMI). Bearing in mind the original assumption that the mnemonic verse was learnt in rote fashion by its sound only, it appears plausible that the syllable cluster עומיקרון – עומיכרון (OMICRON – OMIKRON) is really a compound of two separate words, namely עמי (OMI – AMI) and קרון(KRON – with Koph) or כרון (CRON, with Kaph). Since each word in the mnemonic verse designates a specific letter and we assert that the letter name Omicron is really a compound of two Hebrew words, it follows that the Greek alphabet will be lacking the Hebrew letter whose name is incorporated in Omicron. In other words, Omicron must be found to contain two letter–names from the original Hebrew alphabet. Since the letter Koph does not exist in Greek, one may assume that in the original mnemonic verse this letter was denoted by the word KRON קרון Accordingly one must start with this letter (Koph). On the other hand, the fragment (CRON – with Kaph) by itself is meaningless; its meaning in the alternative spelling (KRON – with Koph) will emerge after we shall have dealt with the next letter PI, which transcribes ... פִּי (Pi) it is immediately apparent that this is a grammatically modified form of the word פֶּה (PE = mouth). Yet as we saw earlier, the whole of our verse is in the second person masculine form, and hence this name will have to appear in the Hebrew restoration as פִּיך (PI– KHA = thy mouth.)

We are now in a position to elucidate the meaning of קרון(KRON), for by joining the two words togethe ,we get קרון פִּיך (KRON PI – KHA) which is very similar to the Hebrew expression קרוֹא ־ פּיך KRO PI–KHA) ="proclaim (call) it with thy mouth" . Accordingly it may be surmised that originally the word קרון (KRON) included the letter א (Aleph), which being vowelless, was however elided in speech, and in this form passed on to the Greeks. Yet there can be no doubt that the original form of the word was – קרואן (KRO–HON), which may be translated "Do thou proclaim–call".[37]

---

37 Cf."...and his mouth calleth for strokes", (Pr. 18: 6) "And they tell him...call thou with thy mouth" (Yoma, 1: 3). See also the book of Ruth, 1: 9; 12; 20; (in the hebrew text) Metzen; Lekhn; Kren Instead of Metzena; Lekhna; Krena.,

After Pi we come to the letter RO, which transcribes... רו (RO). Its corresponding letter in Hebrew and Aramaic is RESH, and in Ethiopian RES. As can be seen, in each of these languages a final S or SH sound is added. We shall therefore complete our word fragment RO in the same way; this gives us ROSH, i. e. – ראש = רוש (="head, summit").

Ro is succeeded by Sigma, of which the corresponding Hebrew letter is SHIN (שׁ), As we know the letters Shin (שׁ) and SIN (שׂ) were interchangeable in archaic Hebrew, and hence in its Hebrew restoration Sigma will have to start with the letter Shin. We thus obtain the phonetically equivalent שקמה (SHIKMA), which is a proper Hebrew word (=Sycamore). Here one may recall that in the preceding word ראש (ROSH) the final SH sound (or S – Sin) was assimilated by the Greeks to the initial sound of שקמה (SIGMA–SHIKMA), and accordingly these two words came to be pronounced as RO and SIGMA (SHIKMA) respectively.

The next letter–name in the Greek alphabet is Tau, which transcribed into Hebrew should start with the letter – ת (Tav). Its phonetics strongly suggest that the second letter of the original Hebrew word or word fragment must have been one of the vowels: א (Aleph), or ע (Ayin) or ה (Heh); and its third letter U – ו (waw); that is, the original word must have read ...תאו (TAU, with Aleph), or תעו (TAU, with Ayin), or תהו (TAHU, with Heh). the first two spellings are meaningless In the context of the mnemonic verse, but the third spelling – תהו (TAHU) appears to be a slight corruption of the word תהו ("TOHU=vain", "worthless"). Accordingly we shall transcribe this letter–name as תהו(TOHU)[38].

Upsilon, the letter following on Tau, was discussed already in connection with the letter Epsilon. It was found that this letter – name should appear in its Hebrew restoration as ופסילונים (U–PSILONIM). Continuing now the mnemonic verse from where we left off, one gets the following: NUN KSIL AMI KROHON PIKHA ROSH SHIKMA TOHU UPSILONIM...

The next letter–name is Phi, which transcribes... פי Though in itself meaningless, this word fragment may now be added to the preceding: (NUN KSIL AMI KROHON PIKHA ROSH SHIKMA TOHU U–PSILONIM PHI...). The fact that in this sequence the conjunction U– (waw) = "and" comes before פסילונים(PSILONIM) clearly indicates that this word is linked conceptually with the beginning of the passage: (ROSH SHIKMA TOHU U... PSILONIM PHI...) which implies that the completed and restored form of the word fragment (PHI) must be a synonym or an antonym of the word תהו(TOHU). To our mind, the only feasible word in the Hebrew language

---

38 Cf."They that make a graven image are all of them vanity" (Heb. Tohu). (Is. 44: 9); "Yet turn not aside from following the Lord...for then should ye go after vain things (Heb. Ha–TOHU), which cannot profit or deliver; for they are vain (Heb. Tohu)." (1Sam. 12: 20–21).

in this case is פיגול(PHIGUL=stench, filth), which also fits the context of the phrase: ROSH SHIKMA TOHU UPSILONIM PHIGUL.[39]

The remaining letters of the Greek alphabet are: Khi, Psi, and Omega . Khi is difficult to transcribe into Hebrew, but it is obvious that the Hebrew word represented in this letter– name must start with the letter כ (Kaph). Ḥeth ח will not do here, because being a guttural, it is pronounced in non–Semitic languages like the letter Heh ה as ,e. g ., in the case of the Greek letter Eta (=HETTAA).[40]

The letter Psi transcribes... פְּסִי (PSI.)

The final letter in the Greek alphabet is Omega, which transcribes אומג. (OMEGA – with Aleph) or... עומג (OMEGA with Ayin). However there is no word in the Hebrew language which begins with either of these two syllables. At first blush it might be thought that here also, as in the case of Omicron, we have a compound of two separate Hebrew words. Of course, the initial letters... או (O) make a proper Hebrew word (= or); and it is thus reasonable to assume that אומג ... really consists of the two words או (O = or) and מג ...(MEGA). Yet when these last three letter–names are written together they yield no meaning: KHI. . PSI...O MEGA . .As to the word fragment פסי ... (PSI) we recall that the word פסילונים (PSILONIM) already appeared in our verse, and accordingly we suggest that in this instance also Psilonim is the acceptable completion. We now read... כ... פסילונים או מג KHI...PSILONIM O MEGA... It should be noted that in the Hebrew Bible the verb לגדע – (Le–GADEA=hew down) is often met in conjunction with the word פסילים (PSILIM = idols), quite a few times in the imperative mood: e. g. ופסילי אלהיהם תגדעון (UPSILEI ELOHEHEM TEGADEUN) – "you shall hew down the graven images of their gods"[41]; and thus, just as before it was assumed that Psi completes PSILONIM, it is reasonable to assume that the fragment ... מג (MEGA...) should be completed מגדע (MEGADEA = hew down.)

The last three letter–names now transcribe as follows: פסילונים או מגדע . . כ (KHI. . PSILONIM O MEGADEA. .). The presence of the word או (O=or) in this passage clearly indicates that the completed Hebrew word represented in the word KHI must either be a synonym of MEGADEA or its complete antonym. A second requirement is, as we saw above, that the word must start with the letter Khaph כ. Since the only synonym of the verb – לגדע LeGADEA starting with this letter is כרות (KHROT= cut down)[42]. we may

---

39 Cf. Ez. 4: 14 "abominable flesh" (Heb. Basar phigul); Is. 65: 4" and broth of abominable (Heb. phigulim) things is in their vessels". Lev. 7: 18"it shall be an abomination" (Heb. Phigul yihye).

40 For the Greek pronunciation of the letter Ḥeth as Heh, see also Harris, A Grammar of The Phoenician Language, New Haven, 1936, p. 16.

41 For instance, Deut. 12: 3 ; Deut. 7: 5.

42 Cf. Mi. 5: 12; Deut. 12: 3 ; Ex. 34: 13.

assume that this is the looked – for word, and the passage (in emended form – to keep in line with the plural of Psilonim) now reads: כרות פסילונים או מגדעם (KHROT PSILONIM O MEGADEAM = cut idols or hew them down.) Our reconstruction completed, the original mnemonic Hebrew verse of the alphabet now reads from beginning to end:

אַלְפָּה בֵּיתָ(ךְ) גַּם־עַ(ל) דַלְתָ(ךְ) הַפְּסִילוֹנִ(ים) זֹאת־הַחְטָאָה טַטָ(הֵר).

יוֹדַ(עֵ) כַּפַּ(יִים) לַמְדָה מוּ(סָר) ;נ(וּן) כְּסִי(ל) עַמִי־קְרוֹאַנָ(ה) פִּי(ךְ) רֹא(ש)

שִׁקְמָה תֹהוּ וּפְסִילוֹנִ(ים) פִּי(גוּל) כ(רוֹת) פְּסִי(לוֹנִים) אוֹ מַגְ(דְעָם).

ALPHA BETA(kh) GAM A(l) DELTA(kh) EPSILON(im) ZOT–A HETTA(a) TETTA(her) IODA KAPPA (yim) LAMDA MU(sar) NU(n) KSI(l) AMI – KROHN(a) PI(kha) RO(sh) SHIKMA TOHU UPSILON(im) PHI(gul) KH(rot) PSI(lonim) O –MEGA(deam).

This restored mnemonic verse may be construed word for word: ALPHA BETAKH – "teach (thou) thy household"; GAM AL DELTAKH – "also upon thy door (write thou)"[43]; EPSILONIM ZOT A HETAA TETTAHER – "the idols, this sin purify (thou)" (this phrase you shall teach your household and– write upon your door – post); YODA KAPPAYIM – "those who know the hands" (i. e."young children still in their mothers' arms"); LAMDA MUSAR– "teach (thou) morals"; And what morals are you going to teach them? NUN KSIL AMI KROHN PIKHA–"grow up simpleton (witless) in my nation, to apprehend say with your mouth "ROSH SHIKMA TOHU UPSILONIM PHIGUL – "the tree– top of a Sycamore is vanity and idols (are) filth (abomination)" (i. e. the worship of the Ashera is vanity and the adoration of the idols is abomination); KHROT PSILONIM O MEGADEAM – "cut down the idols or hew them down" (i. e. smash them).

As can be seen, the initial assumption that the Greek letter–names are merely fragmentary words from an original mnemonic Hebrew verse has been confirmed. The danger that this might be a mere haphazrd stringing together of Hebrew words is reduced to almost a vanishing point by limitations imposed through our basic principles, one of which required that each word (letter–name) should begin with the corresponding Hebrew character; and the other that the phonetics of the Greek letter–names should be preserved in the Hebrew reconstruction. That the Greek alphabet HAS NOT BEEN TAMPERED WITH IN ANY WAY is confirmed by the reconstruction itself where the Greek letter–names appear unchanged. Yet, the Hebrew verse

---

43   Cf. The Jewish custom of affixing an inscribed scrollet (MEZUZAH) on the door–frame, and also the Biblical verses And thou shalt write them upon the door posts of thine house, and upon thy gates". (Deut. 11: 21); and "Behind the doors also and the posts hast thou set thy remembrance" (Is. 57: 7–8): See also the Lachish letters letter 4: "And I wrote upon the door all that your lordship sent to me". As these quotations show, It was customary in ancient times to write anything one wished to remember on one's door–frame.

that emerged in the reconstruction is entirely plausible and meaningful homogenously throughout.

The mnemonic verse established, we can now return to the discussion of the two letter–names Omicron and Omega, deferred at an earlier stage. As mentioned, some scholars think that these two names are Greek words meaning small –O and big –O, i. e. Omicron and Omega denote the short and long vowel O respectively. Yet if this is so, the question inevitably arises why we should have this form of letter–names only for the O; after all, there are other long and short vowels in the alphabet where this form could apply. Why are ETA and EPSILON, which also denote a long and short vowel, not called E– Mega and E–Micron analogously to O–Mega and O–Micron (granted we accept the reading MICRON and MEGA) and similarly to such designations in other languages, e. g. Hebrew: QAMATZ GADOL ("big Qamatz"), QAMATZ KATAN ("small Qamatz"); PATAKH GADOL ("big Patakh"), PATAKH KATAN ("small Patakh")? Why should different names be required to designate the same functions? After all, it would only be logical, once the principle of the long and short vowels was understood, that this would apply to all the vowels and not merely to the O.

Yet to us it seems that the contrary of what is asserted about Omicron and Omega is true. Reading the mnemonic Hebrew verse it is obvious that from the phonetic view point the o–sound in the two words עומי־קרואן (Omi– Krohn) and או–מגדעם (O–Megadeam) is short in the first case (Omi) and long in the second (O–Megadeam). In accordance with this perception, the first sound came to be regarded in the course of time as a short vowel and the second as a long vowel; furthermore, the following syllables of each word were construed, due to phonetic resemblance, as meaning "small" and "big" respectively, i. e. Mi–krohn – small and Mega – big[44]. the same long–short vowel distinction can be observed in the letter–words EPSILONIM (Epsilon) and HE– TTAA (Eta).

Confirmation of our argument may be seen in a passage from Higginus[45]: "Simonides, a native of Ceos, introduced into Athens...where he was domiciled, the double consonants Psi and Xi, the distinction between the vowels Omicron and Omega (short and long O) and distinction between the vowels Eta and Epsilon (long and short E). These changes were not, however, publicly adopted there until the Archonship of Euclides – (403 B. C.)"

With regard to the notion that the final "a" sound of the letter–names Alpha, Beta, Gamma, Delta, Lamda, Kappa, Iota, Teta, Eta, Zeta, Omega, was not originally part of these words but a later Greek addition, or a vestigial Aramaic root, it is now possible from the evidence of the reconstructed verse

---

44   In a similar way the letter Delta, whose derivation from the word Delet (door) is not in dispute, came to mean a "Delta" i. e. a river estuary.

45   The English translation is cited from Graves, op. cit. p. 226.

to perceive that this sound represented the most suitable breaking off place, from the phonetic viewpoint, within the words meant to be turned into letter–names. Confirmation of this is found in the later development of the Greek alphabet and in the way it was taken over by other languages. When we examine the letter–names in languages, where we know that they are derived from the Greek alphabet we discover that in these instances the names became A, Be, De etc. and did not become, for instance, Al, Del, Eps, Ep, Yo, Lam, Om, etc., but that they were derived (i. e. cut from the Greek alphabet) mainly at a vowel segment, in the way best suited to the character and phonetics of the particular language. The same principle that obtained when the Greek alphabet was taken over by other peoples must also have obtained when the original Hebrew verse was taken over by the Greeks.

From its context in the mnemonic verse it is apparent that the "Phoenicians" must be identified as the Israelites. For the "Phoenicians" are said to be the inventors of the alphabet whereas the verse reads: "Epsilonim Zot Ha–Hettaa Tettaher" (the idols this sin purify (thou) etc. – an idea exclusive to the Israelite nation and to the monotheistic belief it held. Moreover, from the words "Gam Al Deltakh" – "also upon thy door", it is also evident that the phrase: "Epsilonim Zot HaHettaa Tettaher" (the idols this sin purify) was written on the door posts, And here we encounter a surprising fact; to this day it is customary for the Jews to fix to their door–frames a small wooden or metal case (Mezuzah) containing a parchment scroll inscribed with two passages from Deuteronomy:

"Hear o Israel: The Lord our God is one Lord; and thou shalt love the Lord thy God with all thine heart, and with all thy soul, and with all thy might. And these words, which I command thee this day, shall be in thine heart: AND THOU SHALT TEACH THEM DILIGENTLY UNTO THY CHILDREN, and shalt talk of them when thou sittest in thine house, and when thou walkest by the way, and when thou liest down, and when thou risest up. And thou shalt bind them for a sign upon thine hand, and they shalt be as frontlets between thine eyes. AND THOU SHALT WRITE THEM UPON THE POSTS OF THY HOUSE, AND ON THY GATES."[46] (emphasis–N. G.).

"And it shall come to pass, if ye shall hearken diligently unto my commandments which I command you this day, to love the Lord your God, and to serve him with all your heart and with all your soul, that I will give you the rain of your land in his due season, the first rain and the latter rain, that thou mayest gather in thy corn, and thy wine and thine oil. And I will send grass in thy fields for thy cattle, that thou mayest eat and be full. Take heed to yourselves, that your heart be not deceived, and ye turn aside AND SERVE OTHER GODS, AND WORSHIP THEM; and then the Lord's

---

46 Deut. 6: 4–9.

wrath be kindled against you, and he shut up the heaven, that there be no rain, and that the land yield not her fruit; and lest ye perish quickly from off the good land which the Lord giveth you. Therefore shall ye lay up these my words in your heart and in your soul, and bind them for a sign upon your hand, that they may be as frontlets between your eyes. AND YE SHALL TEACH THEM YOUR CHILDREN, speaking of them when thou sittest in thine house, and when thou walkest by the way, when thou liest down, and when thou risest up. AND THOU SHALT WRITE THEM UPON THE DOOR POSTS OF THINE HOUSE, AND UPON THY GATES: that your days may be multiplied and the days of your children, in the land which the Lord sware unto your fathers to give them, as the days of heaven upon the earth."[47] (My emphasis–N. G.)

The content of these passages is almost identical with the reconstructed verse; both texts include several parallel commands, though they are phrased somewhat differently. the one states: "And thou shalt teach them diligently unto thy children...and thou shalt write them upon the posts of thy house and on thy gate", while the other reads: "ALPHA BETAKH GAM AL DELTAKH" ("teach thy household and also on thy door"– write it). or "YODA KAPAYIM LAMDA MUSAR" ("those still carried on the arms – i. e. the young children– teach them morals"). In one case we read: "EPSILONIM ZOT HaHETTAA TETTAHER" or "KHROT PSILONIM O MEGADEAM" ("the idols this sin purify, cut down the idols or hew them down."), while in the other: "Beware you shalt not forget the Lord...Ye shall not go after other gods".

It is easy to see that the Biblical passages on the Mezuzah scroll are concerned with the same ideas as the alphabetic verse; viz., do not worship idols and other gods, and teach this also to your household, and also write it on your door–posts.

In the light of the alphabetic verse it is worthwhile mentioning the following sentences in the book of Jeremiah (31: 31–34): "Behold the days come, saith the Lord, that I will make a new covenant with the house of Israel and with the house of Judah; not according to the covenant that I made with their fathers in the day that I took them by the hand to bring them out of the land of Egypt; which my covenant they brake, although I was an husband unto them, saith the Lord; But this shall be the covenant that I will make with the house of Israel; After those days, saith the Lord, I will put my law in their inward parts, and write it in their hearts; and will be their God, and they shall be my people. And they shall teach no more every man his neighbour, and every man his brother, saying know the Lord, for they shall know me from the least of them unto the greatest of them..."

It is deducible from the content of these sentences, that in the old

---

47 Deut. 11: 13–22.

covenant existed the command to teach one's neighbour and one's brother, to know the Lord, a command which is identical to that of the passsages in the Mezuzah.

The same command is also encountered in the book of Psalms: "For he established a testimony in Jacob and a law in Israel, which he commanded our fathers, that they should make them known to their children: That the generation to come might know them, even the children which should be born; who should arise and declare them to their children: That they might set their hope in God and not forget the works of God, but keep his commandments;" (Ps. 78: 5–8).

The similarity between these sentences, the reconstructed alphabetic verse and the passages in the Mezuzah, is quite evident. But what is this covenant that has been established between God and the nation of Israel? It is generally accepted that the covenant refers to the Decalogue (The tables of the covenant). But in Exodus (24: 7–8), we read: "And he took the BOOK of the covenant, and read in the audience of the people; and they said, all that the Lord hath said will we do, and be obedient." This is FOLLOWED by a description of Moses going up the mountain of Sinai (Horeb) and bringing the tables of the covenant (Ex. 24: 12). We learn therefore of two different episodes in the life of the nation of Israel; the first – a covenant between God and the nation. It is linked with the reading of the BOOK of the COVENANT; and the second which FOLLOWS, is the giving of the TABLES of the covenant.

The contents of the book of the covenant is presented to us in two passages in Deuteronomy: "Only take heed to thyself, and keep thy soul diligently, lest thou forget the things which thine eyes have seen, and lest they depart from thy heart all the days of thy life; AND TEACH THEM THY SONS AND THY SON'S SONS; specially the day that thou stoodest before the Lord thy God in HOREB, when the Lord said unto me, Gather me the people together, and I will make them hear my words, THAT THEY MAY LEARN TO FEAR ME all the days that they shall live upon the earth, AND THAT THEY MAY TEACH THEIR CHILDREN." (Deut. 4: 9–11). We learn therefore that what was said on the mount of Horeb is mainly: fear God and teach thy sons and thy son's sons to fear him. This same idea is expressed in the book of Jeremiah and in the Alphabetic verse.

Accordingly I am inclined to surmise that the book of the covenant which PRECEDED the Tables of the covenant refers to the receiving of the Alphabetic script, and thus it is quite simple to understand the passage: ". if you will obey my voice indeed, and keep my COVENANT, then ye shall be a peculiar treasure (Hebrew–Segula) unto me above all people". (Ex. 19: 5). The Israelites became the chosen (treasured) nation because with the acceptance of the book of the covenant, namely – the Alphabeth – they became the sole nation in the world to use a phonetic script.

It is worthwhile noting the verses in the Book of Isaiah: "Thus saith the Lord, the King of Israel, and his redeemer the Lord of Hosts; I am the first, and I am the last; and besides me there is no God, and who, as I, shall call and shall declare it, and set it in order for me, since I appointed the ancient people (Heb. Am Olam – = עם־עולם = eternal; everlasting people) and the things that are coming (Heb. Otiot אתיות) and shall come, let them shew unto them." (Is. 44: 6–7). In Hebrew:

כה־אמר יהוה מלך־ ישראל וגאלו יהוה צבאות אני ראשון ואני אחרון ומבלעדי אין אלהים: "ומי־כמוני יקרא ויגידה ויערכה לי משומי עם־עולם ואתיות ואשר תבאנה יגידו למו:"

"Thus said the Lord, the holy one of Israel and his maker (Heb. veyozro), Ask me of things to come (Heb. Ha–Otiot האתיות) concerning my sons, and concerning the work of my hands command ye me." (Is. 45: 11). In Hebrew:

"כה־אמר יהוה קדוש ישראל ויצרו האתיות שאלוני על־בני ועל־פעל ידי תצוני:"

In these verses the words אתיות(Otiot) were understood and translated as אתות(Otot) meaning signs – miracles – things to come. It must be borne in mind that in Hebrew the word אות (Ot) in singular has a double meaning; sign – (figuratively also miracle) and letter (alphabetic). But in the plural form the first one – sign– miracle, becomes Otot אתות– while the second – letter – becomes Otiot אתיות as in the above verses.

The reasons for the above translations and interpretations are various and we shall not discuss them here[48]. We would only like to suggest that if we examine these verses literally we can see and interpret them as relating to the creation of the Alphabetic letters. namely: "Since I appointed the eternal (everlasting)[49] people (Israel) and the letters (alphabetic)"etc. and "thus saith the Lord the Holy One of Israel and the creator (Heb. Veyozro) of the letters" The ending ...ו (o) in the word (Veyozro) is not to be regarded as third person genitive attached to the Preceding word Israel but must be regarded as a stylistic form and attached to the following word "Ha–Otiot".[50]

Let us not forget that in antiquity the formation of writing was attributed to God: "And the Tables were the work of God. and the writing was the writing of God." (Ex. 32: 16). The Egyptians attributed it to their god Thoth. The Babylonians attributed it to the godess Nisaba and the Greeks – to Mercury.

---

48 They are mainly based on: 1. The Septuagint translation. 2. The interpretation of the word Otiot in Is. 41: 23; 3. Yehuda ben Quraysh (c. 900 B. C.) ; The Risala, part 1; (22)

49 Erroneously translated "ancient people".

50 Like: Maayno Mayim – מעינו מים (Ps. 114: 8): Hayto Eret –חיתו ארץ – z(Gen. 1: 24): Yarho Asif ירחו אסיף – (calendar of Gezer): Bno Zipor –בנו ציפור – (Nu. 23: 18): Beno Beor –בנו בעור – (Nu. 24: 315 –): and others. See also Gesenius p. 254 § 90–o.

The Bible ascribes to Moses the writing of the Tables of the covenant. the writing of the journeys of the Israelites in the desert[51] and "all the words of the Lord".[52]

As pointed out in the preface. the phonetic alphabetic script was first thought to have originated around the year 1000 B. C. From here arose the inevitable tendency of Wellhausen, Alt and others to see biblical literature as the result of oral transmissions. But new epigraphical discoveries made investigators advance the origins of phonetic script to about 1500 B. C. Therefore, there is no reason whatsoever to deny the biblical text which ascribes to Moses the writing of events and the laws of the nation of Israel Nevertheless. with the change of attitude towards the script. there was no parallel change towards the biblical text. still considered to be a collection of orally transmitted sayings.

We must assume that Moses wrote in Hebrew (perhaps not in the language used in a later period. but still Hebrew). for the culture that follows is based on his teachings and is written in Hebrew. This assumption is supported by what is written in the Talmud[53]: "In the beginning the Torah (O. T.) was given to Israel in the Hebrew script and in the Holy language..." etc Namely the Talmud ascribes to Moses the writing in the Hebrew script. As already stated. Moses was brought up on Egyptian culture. therefore two possibilities arise:

1. Moses learned the Hebrew script from the Hebrews.

2. The Hebrews learned the Hebrew script from Moses

The first possibility seems implausible. as it is illogical that the Hebrews, who before leaving Egypt were on a very low cultural level, would have used an alphabetical script – an integral part of a higher culture. It is more logical to assume that the Hebrews learned the script from Moses, and again. two possibilities arise: either Moses borrowed the script from another nation and transferred it to the Hebrews. or, secondly, that he himself invented it.

The first possibility does not seem valid. for when a nation borrows a script from another. it adjusts it to its own needs and necessarily there are certain anachronisms. Letters or syllables appropriate to one language do not necessarily suit the other. An example of this is the borrowing of the Greek script from the "Phoenicians". The Greeks adapted the script to their needs but the letter order and names remained "Phoenician". We are not aware of such an anachronism in the Hebrew script. Though the belief exists that the Hebrews copied their alphabet from the "Phoenicians". In the light of this book, there is no basis for such a belief.

---

51   Nu. 33: 2.
52   Ex. 4: 4.
53   Talmud Bavli. Sanhedrin 21.

Berger[54] states that "the Phoenician language belongs to the Semitic family of languages and maintains its place between the Aramaic and Hebrew. It is closer to Hebrew than Aramaic. The points of agreement with Hebrew are more numerous and so much deeper that we must assume that one nation borrowed the dialect from the other. This does not mean that there are no evident differences between the two languages. but it seems that the Phoenician language stopped at an earlier stage of development.".

consequently there remains the other possibility that Moses invented the Hebrew script. and together with a new religion he gave the Israelites a new script. This supposition is supported by the Talmud:[55]

"Rabi Yosi says: It was fitting for Ezra to have given the Torah (Tables of the Covenant). if Moses had not anticipated him. It was said about Moses that he ascended (Mount Sinai): so it was said about Ezra that he ascended (to Israel). and despite the fact that he did not give the Torah. he did change the script. and also he received (gave) a script and language". Namely, ALSO HE Ezra, gave script and language. The emphasis of "also he" indicates that one must deduce that Moses also gave a script and a language. This Talmudic evidence strengthens our conclusion that the Israelites (Moses) invented the alphabetic script.

This supposition is not new. The jews Artapanos and Eupolemos (1st century B. C.). the Samaritan Margali (4th century A. C.). Isidore of Seville (6th century A. C.), and others have already maintained that Moses invented the phonetic alphabet. I would here like to mention an article[56] whose writer comes to the same conclusion on the supposition that as the consonants are not pronounced by themselves but are always linked with vowels. It is only the stutterer who pronounces them in their "chemical" elementary form: therefore. Moses, who according to the Bible was a stammerer. was naturally qualified to understand the development and the formation of phonetics and invent a phonetic script.

Renan[57], Sir Charles Marston,[58] and Tur–Sinai maintain also that the Israelites invented the phonetic script, but, to exclude Tur–Sinai whose theory we cited above, the beliefs of the other two are based solely on suppositon.

It is self–evident that Moses based the writing on his own culture which was the Egyptian Culture. This explains the Egyptian influence on the Alphabetic script.

To sum up: Moses invented the Hebrew phonetic script and the Israelites were the first to use it, therefore they were called by the Greeks "Phoenicians".

---

54   Berger. Phénicie, La Grande Encyclopedie: pp. 620–621.
55   Tosefta, Sanhedrin 4. 7: Jerushalmi. Megila. 8.
56   Kraus. La tribune de Geneve. 6. July. 1949.
57   Renan, Histoire Du Peuples D'isreal.
58   Marston, The Bible Comes Alive, 1938, ch. 8 (the story of the Alephbeth).

a name which may be explained "Phonicians"= Syllable Possessors, namely – possessors of a phonetic script, for it was an innovation and exception to the other nations of the world then. While in the region of Canaan (Israel) they were called the nation of Israel namely, the nation of "Asera El", for their worship of the Ashera.

Different names for one nation are not exception. The Greeks, for example, called themselves "Hellenes" and their country "Hellas". In Hebrew "Yevanim" and "Yavan". The Romans called them "Graeci"and their country – "Graecia".

The Germans were called "Germani" by the Romans. whereas the French call them "Allemands", the Italians –"Tedesci"; the Slavons –"Niemci", while the Germans call themselves"Deutsche".

The Romans referred to France and the French as "Gallia" and "Galli". In Hebrew the name of the country is "Zarfat" and the people "Zarfatim", and in English –"France" and "French".

The same is true with many other nations.

ARCHAEOLOGICAL FINDINGS AND MISCELLANUS ITEMS

When considering an archaeological finding, the arcaeologist does not regard it as an object by itself but classifies it according to concepts and suppositions formed and accepted in the course of time as proven basic evidence. Such a finding in its turn will become the ground for the explanation of new findings, and so on. Therefore an erroneous explanation of findings will inevitably lead to a chain–reaction of error. If the basic concepts and suppositions are changed then the explanation of the different findings must also inevitably undergo change. For example the finding of pottery vessels of identical style, in Israel and in Crete, may indicate interrelationship between the two countries, but when these pottery vessels are examined in the light of the concepts and suppositions that the Israelites entered Israel in the period of Mernephtah (c. 1200 B. C.), and that the Philistines are originally from Crete, then the conclusion will inevitably be that the Cretans were those whose culture influenced the Israelites and the findings will also be classified accordingly. But if the entry of the Israelites into Canaan occurred at a prior period (i. e. in the reign of Amenhotep III – c. 1406 B. C.), and if the Philistines did not come from Crete, then the conclusion would inevitably be completely opposite –The Israelites would be those who had influenced the Cretans.

If we assume that the Israelites entered Canaan in the period of Mernephtah (c. 1200 B. C.) then we will classify all findings from a prior period (c. 1400 –1200 B. C.) as being that of Canaanites, Hittites and others, but not that of the Israelites. who supposedly entered the region later. The same is true regarding geographical places which were not supposed to have been conquered by the Israelites, so that findings found in these sites will not be classified as Israelite objects. In a discussion about the date of the conquest of the land of Canaan by the Israelites, Albright remarks[1] that: "The excavation of Gezer, Ta'anach, Megiddo and Beth shan were not taken into account for the classifcation of this issue since all these cities remained in Canaanite hands during the period of the Judges, in accordance with Hebrew tradition".

It is generally agreed that the region of Sidon and the northern part of

---

1   Albright, Archaeology and The Date of The Hebrew Conquest of Palestine, BASOR, 1935, (58), p. 10

the country was not conquered by the tribe of Asher, In the light of such an assumption, it is natural that findings such as Ras Shamra (Ugarit) Tablets, and others (see below) were ascribed to the "Canaanites – Phoenicians". Therefore proximity of these tablets to the Hebrew language and the context of biblical poetry, led scholars inevitably to see in them "a proof" that the Israelites copied the Bible and their way of life from the "Canaanites – Phoenicians".

On the other hand if the invasion of the Israelites into Canaan occurred in the period of Amenhotep III and if as we have already seen they conquered the whole region including Sidon, then the picture is Reversed.

Many scholars[2] regard the verses in the Bible (Ex. 20: 4) "Thou shalt not make unto thee any graven image..."etc. as evidence and explanation for the paucity of such findings among Israelite findings, But at the same time it must be deduced from the Bible that idolatry worship was a widespread custom among all Israelite classes. Why therefore should idolatrous findings found in the country be referred to as non – Israelite objects (Canaanite and others)? Why should we not regard them as Israelite objects?

---

2   For example see: Wright, How Did Early Israel Differ From Her Neighbours, BA. (6), (I), 1943, p. 16.

RAS SHAMRA — UGARIT TABLETS

During the years 1929–1939 Schaeffer excavated at Ras Shamra on the Syrian coast about eleven kilometers north of Latakia. The site is identified with Ugarit mentioned in the el–Amarna Tablets. He unearthed clay tablets most of them written in a special alphabetic scripture. This writing called "Ugarit writing" was deciphered by the German scholar Bauer and the French scholars D'horme and Virrolleaud. These tablets were revealed to have contained fragments of religious and mythological epic poetry and literature, and their language is very similar to Hebrew.[1] According to Virrolleaud "The vocabulary of Ras Shamra is the same as that of the biblical books"[2]. and their geographical scenery is in the south of the land of Israel, in the Negev region. According to him the ancestors of the Phoenicians lived in the Negev early in the second millenium B. C. In these tablets he found mention of the tribe of Zeboulun, Terah (the patriarch Abraham's father). Dussaud also, believes that the background for the writing of these tablets is in the south of the country of Israel therefore he concludes that the Phoenicians came from the south of Israel. He finds in the tablets also references to names such as

---

1   Dussaud, Yahwe Fils De El, SY. 1957, p. 233
    Dahood, Ugaritic – Hebrew Philology.
    Albright, The North Canaanite Poems of Al'eyan Ba'al and The Gracious Gods, JPOS. 1934, pp. 114–115
    – A Hebrew Letter From The Twelfth Century, BASOR. (73), 1939, pp. 10, 12.
    – Specimens of Late Ugaritig Prose, BASOR. 1958, 150. pp. 36 – 38
    D'horme, Le Déchiffrement Des Tablettes de Ras Shamra, JPOS. XI, 1931, p. 5.
    Contenau, La Civilisation Phénicienne, p. 265
    Kaperlud, The Ras Shamra Discoveries and The Old Testament, p. 15.
    Driver, Ugaritic and Hebrew Words, Ugaritica, VI, pp. 181–186.
    Ginzberg, Kitvei Ugarit, p. 14. (Hebrew)
    Courtois. J. C. The Excavations At Ugarit, 1929–1966, Qadmoniot, Vol. II, 3 (7), 1969, (Hebrew)
    Sukenik. Devices For The Death Ritual In Canaanite Ugarit and In Shomron The Israelite, Kedem, 2, 1945, p. 42 (Hebrew) Let us note that the Germans Bauer, Friedriech and Goetz regard Ugarit language as an intermediate between Hebrew and Aramaic, Whereas Cantineau (La langue de Ras Shamra, Sy. 1932, 1940), believes it is not Canaanite neither Phoenician or Aramaic, but an unknown new language.
2   Virolleaud, Le Déchiffrement Des Tablettes Alphabetiques De Ras Shamra, Sy, 1931, (X), p. 20

Ashdod, Kadesh–barnea, and the Red Sea[3], and claims that "The language of the Ras Shamra tablets actually has a Phoenician – Hebrew vocabulary to the extent that it might well be asserted that Phoenician and Hebrew derive from this primitive Canaanite"[4]. Elsewhere when referring to the findings in Ras Shamra, he remarks: "The first levels of Ras Shamra (XVe, XIIs) revealed a civilisation that by the language, the phonetical construction of the alphabet more important even the very form of the letters, extending to ceramics and art products, show large analogies with those of Israel".[5]

According to Montgomery and Harris "The dialect of the semitic tablets of Ras Shamra belongs to the Hebraic stock (including Phoenician) it is an early Hebrew dialect"[6]. They call the tablets "cuneiform Hebraic Texts".[7] Gaster refers to this language as "proto Hebrew"[8]. Ginzberg remarks that; "The similarity of Ugarit language to the Biblical language is very great".[9] Schaeffer calls the Ugaritic language; "Language of the Canaanites that is to say archaic Hebrew or Proto Phoenician",[10] and points out: "The rules of composition for these tablets are exactly those of Hebrew poetry, and even the language in certain parts of the Ras Shamra tablets are definitely biblical"[11].

The deeper scholars delved into the material of the tablets, the more it was remarked that there are striking affinities between these fragments of literature and epic verse and between biblical passages and textual content. This similarity is not confined to context or vocabulary and grammar alone, but it was proved that there exists an exact parallelism in thought, imagery, stylistic terminology and idioms.[12] Such parallels even reach the point of

---

3   Dussaud, Ras Shamra, AAA. 1934.
     La Notion D'Âme Chez Les Israelites Et Les Phéniciens. SY. 1935, (XVI), pp. 267–277.
4   Dussaud, Les Découvertes de Ras Shamra et L'ancien Testament, Paris, 1937, p. 50. As cited by Schaeffer, The Cuneiform Texts of Ras Shamra, p. 57, n. 44. See also: Dussaud, Ras Shamra, AAA, p. 95.
5   Dussaud, Yahwe' Fils de El, SY., 1957, p. 233.
6   Montgomery – Harris, The Ras Shamra Mythological Texts, p. 16
7   Montgomery – Harris, ibid. p. 1.
8   Gaster, Ras Shamara, 1929–1939, Antiquity XIII, 1939, p. 309.
9   Ginzberg, Kitvei ugarit (Geb.) p. 14.
10   Schaeffer, The Cuneiform Texts of Ras Shamra – Ugarit, p. 57
11   Schaeffer, ibid. pp. 58–59.
12   Held, The Action Result Sequence of Identical Verbs, etc., JBL, 1965, p. 275.
     Albright, New Canaanite Historical And Mythological Date, BASOR, 1936, p. 32.
     The Bible And The Ancient Near East, p. 339.
     Gordon, Ugarit And The Minoan Crete.
     Gray, The Legacy of Canaan, VT., (V), 1957, pp. 4, 189, 208.
     Oberman, Ugaritic Mythology, Preface; XV – XVI
     Schaeffer, Ibid, pp. 76–77
     Barton, Archeology And The Bible, p. 19.
     Gaster, ibid. pp. 315– 316.

verbal identity with the same appropriate stereotyped formulas and correlated synonyms being used for the expression of certain ideas. Composite idioms characteristic of biblical literature are found word for word in the Ugarit Tablets, and as Ginzberg points out "The Canaanite and Hebrew poets have some fixed pairs of synonymous words or phrases for certain concepts which poets have frequent occasion to express. Many such fixed pairs are common to Ugaritic and Biblical poetry...Such a pair are with apparently no exceptions in Ugaritic poetry and with very few in Hebrew – always employed in the same order and that order is also nearly always the same in both literatures common to both is the rule that it is the more usual expression that comes first. Such agreement of synonyms goes beyond agreement of form and results in considerable similarity of diction".[13]

Scholars pointed out the similarity between biblical and Ugaritic literature and most of them concluded that the Hebrews (Israelites) borrowed from the "Phoenicians–Canaanites" their culture – language, religious rituals, poetry, Literature, Way of life and so on.[14] Cassuto who studied Ugaritic

---

Kaperlud, ibid.

Gazelles, Essai Sur Le Pouvoir De La Divinité A' Ugarit et en Israel, Ugaritica, VI, pp. 25–44

Rin, Alilot Haelim, p. 4 (Hebrew)

Loewenstamm, Kitvei Ugarit Vesafrut Hamikra, Kadmoniot, 1969, 3, (7). (Hebrew)

13 Ginzberg, Ugaritic Studies And The Bible, BA, 1945, p. 55 – Kitvei Ugarit, p. 15 (Hebrew)

14 Albright, Recent Progress In North Canaanite Research, BASOR, (70), 1938, p. 23.
– A Hebrew Letter From The Twelfth Century, BASOR, (73), 1939, pp. 9–13.
–The Bible And The Ancient Near East, p. 339
–The Archaeology of Palestine, pp. 230–237
Dussaud, Cultes Canaaneen Aux Source Du Jourdain, SY., XVII, 1936, pp. 283–295.
La Notion D'ame Chez Les Israelites Et Les Phéniciens, SY., (XVI), 1935, pp. 273–274.
Jahwe' Fils de El, SY. 1957, (XXXIV), p. 233
Wright, How Did Early Israel Differ From Her Neighbours, BA, (Vi), 1943, P. 4 and on.
Gray, The Legacy of Canaan, VT, 1957, pp. 4; 208.
Ginzberg, Ugaritic Studies And The Bible, BA, 1945, p. 55
Cullican, The First Merchant Venturers, 1966, pp. 121–122.
Oberman, Ugaritic Mythology, 1948, Preface XV.
Del Medico, La Bible Canaaneen, Payot, 1950, pp. 14–16.
Cross Jr., Notes On Canaanite Psalm In The Old Testament, BASOR, 117, 1950, pp. 19–21.
Kaperlud, The Ras Shamra Discoveries And The Old Testament, pp. 73; 76.
Scaeffer, The Cuneiform Texts of Ras Shamra Ugarit.
Contenau, La Civilisation Phénicienne, pp. 83; 84.
Hours – Miedan, Carthage, pp. 15– 16; 48– 49; 197.
Gaster, The Ras Shamra Texts and The Old Testament, PEQ, 1934, pp. 141–146.

Poetry, also remarked its similarity in context and language to the Bible, but concluded that there is no question of borrowing or adapting, but that there is a common origin for Ugaritic and Biblical Literatures."one of the characteristics common to Ugaritic and Hebrew Literatures was that of fixed pairs of parallel words in both hemistichs of the poetic verse. In the literary tradition a nearly constant association has been formed between a certain word and another synonymous word such as Eretz– Afar, The same words exactly appear in both languages the actual words Eretz and Afar in Ugaritic as in Hebrew".[15] According to Cassuto this parallelism does not exist in word–pairs only, but also in specific uses of verbal forms: locutions and composite expressions, metaphors, ornamental phrases and nomenclatures, imagery etc. Cassuto concludes: "...It is clear that not only in certain details but in the whole range of its literary language and in all the stylistic forms used, there exists a tradition common to Ugaritic and Biblical writings and there is no doubt that from the point of view of stylistic form both Literatures are merely two different branches of one tree". Therefore, according to Cassuto "We must explain the fact that the earliest biblical literary works are already composed in perfect style as though preceded by long development... The originality of Biblical Literature is in its context and spirit. Whereas stylistically it continues in the ancient Canaanite literary tradition".[16]

The Ugarit Tablets were discovered as we know in an archaeological stratum ascribed to the period from about the 14th to the 12th century B. C.[17] On the other hand, the el Amarna Tablets are ascribed to the period of Amenhotep III and IV, Hence the el Amarna and Ugarit Tablets refer to about the same period of time.[18] This fact raises two questions:

1) The el Amarna tablets which preceded the Ugarit tablets by several

---

Weil, Phoenicia And Western Asia etc., p. 30.

Held, The Action Result (Factitive–Passive) Sequence of Identical Verbs In Biblical Hebrew And Ugaritic, JBL. 1965, pp. 272–282

15 Cassuto, Parallel Words In Hebrew And Ugaritic, (Heb.), Leshonenu, 15, 1947, pp. 97–102.
    See also: Held, ibid. p. 275; Dahood, Ugaritic – Hebrew Philology, 1965, pp. 43–44.

16 . Cassuto, Tarbitz 13, 1942, pp. 197– 217; Tarbitz, 14. 1943, p. 10. ; Leshonenu, 15, 1947, p. 97. (Heb.)

17 Ginzberg, Ugaritic Studies And The Bible, BA. VIII, 1945. – Kitvei Ugarit, pp. 4–5; 14. (Heb.).
    Gaster, Ras Shamra, 1929–39; Antiquity, 13, 1939, p. 309.
    Dussaud, Ras Shamra, AAA. 1934, p. 94.
    Montegomery– Haris, The Ras Shamra Mythological Texts, 1935, p. 7
    d'Horme, Le Déchiffrement Des Tablettes De Ras Shamra, JPOS. 1931, p. 1
    Driver, Canaanite Myths And Legends, 1956, p. 1'
    Rin, Alilot Haelim, p. 5 (Hebrew)
    Yeivin, On The Origin of The Alphabetetc, Leshonenu, 17, 2–3 p. 68 (Hebrew).

18 See: Hours – Miedan, Carthage, p. 15.

years, are written in Akkaddian and not in Ugaritic script, whereas from the Ugaritic Tablets it is evident that the Ugaritic alphabet was then in quite an advanced and developed stage and not at its formation stage. In other words, if the el Amarna tablets were written to the Egyptian kings not in their proper language – in hieroglyphic but in Akkaddian, why were they not written in Ugaritic – which according to Ugarit findings was much more developed and more suitable for writting?

2) If the Ugaritic writing served the Canaanite population in the region, how was it that the writing style and modes of expression in the el Amarna Tablets are not identical to those of the Ugaritic tablets, While at the same time the identity and parallelism between the Ugaritic tablets and the Bible is so astonishing?

The solution to these questions must be in that the el Amarna tablets and the Ugaritic do not belong to the same population. Scholars believe that from a political point of view there was no real change in the region following the el Amarna wars. Such an assumption is founded mostly on another assumption which is that Aziru and Abd Ashera (Asirta) which are mentioned as having conquered the region in the el Amarna period, were also Amorites – Canaanites. Autran[19] relying on the verse "Neither did Asher drive out the inhabitants of Acco and the inhabitants of Sidon ..."(Ju. 1: 27 – 36), states: "The arrival of the Hebrews in Canaan did not therefore create any substantial change".

But we have seen that the Israelites invaded the country at the beginning of the 14th century, namely in the el Amarna Tablets period, and that they also conquered the region of Sidon and the northern part of the country. It is evident therefore, that with the wars of el Amarna one period comes to an end and a new period begins with a new population in the region. It must be concluded therefore that if in the period of the Ugarit tablets the region was inhabited by Israelites, why should we not see in these tablets an ancient Hebrew Literature antedating the Exile, in contrast to the Biblical literature which was crystalised after the changes brought about by Ezra? Here lies the answer to the amazing affinities and similarities between the Ugaritic tablets and the Bible, and an explanation for Cassuto's conclusion that "doubtless from the point of view of stylistic form both literatures are merely two different branches of one tree".

There remains the question as to why these tablets are written in a special cuneiform script and not in the ancient Hebrew alphabetic writing. The answer to this question may perhaps be sought in the geographical position of Ugarit: perhaps an attempt was made to form a new alphabetical notation on the basis of cuneiform writing on the one hand, and on the basis of

---

19   Autran, "Phéniciens", pp. 63 – 64.

"Phoenician" culture i. e. The Israelite culture on the other. Reyny[20] states that: "The most interesting indication of origins in ancient lands is that of the Canaanites (U. T. 311: 7) in a context which clearly shows the Canaanites considered as foreigners in Ugarit, just as with the Assyrians and Egyptians. Such an interpretation for the manner in which Canaanites are mentioned has recently been reconfirmed by Nogayroll who described an unpublished tablet concerning the payment made by the Ugarit people, of 3500 shekels to the chief of a Canaanite people...clearly a distinction is here being made between Ugarit and Canaanite citizens". Elsewhere[21] he sums up by saying: "Ugarit cannot be called a Canaanite city. For the Ugarit people the Canaanite was a foreigner as are the Egyptian and the Assyrian". Cullican[22] also concludes that "The Ugarit people did not see themselves as Canaanites", which is what can be implied from the above as well.

In 1933 Grant discovered a clay tablet at Beth Shemesh in Israel, which was written in a script recognised by Albright as Ugaritic script except that it was inversed.[23] Other tablets written in Ugarit script were found in Israel, at Taanach in 1963 and also at Nahal Habor (Wadi Bireh),[24] Yeivin points out to the discovery of a metal knife with an Ugarit inscription found near Kaukab el Hawa[25].

Let us add here that the prophet Isaiah prophesies on Tyre[26]: "...Whose merchants are princes whose traffickers are the honourable of the earth". The Hebrew verse reads Kinaaneaha ("כנעניה") translated – Traffickers. Some scholars read Knaaneaha instead of Kinaaneaha. In Hebrew Knaaneaha means "its Canaanites" and this was explained and regarded as proof that the population of Tyre was Canaanite.[27] Also if we accept "Kinaaneaha" to be read "Knaaneaha"(its Canaanites), then from the very emphasis that "its Canaanites" are the honourable of the earth, it must be deduced that all the rest of the population are not Canaanites. For the verse must be interpreted that in a population of non–Canaanites the Canaanites became conspicous as being the honorable of the earth and therefore such an interpretation does not necessarily indicate Tyre as a Canaanite city.

20   Rayni, A Social structure of Ugarit, pp. 7 – 8 (Hebrew)
21   ibid. p. 109.
22   Cullican, ibid. p. 52.
23   Albright, A Cuneiform Tablet From Beth Shemesh, BASOR, 53, 1934, pp. 18–19. See also Gaster, ibid. p. 310.
24   Rayni, A Clay Tablet From Taanach, (Heb.). Kadmoniot, 1965, (7) 3. pp. 89–90.
25   Yeivin, Ugaritic Inscription From Israel, (Heb.). Kedem, 1945, pp. 32; 41
26   Is. 23: 8
27   For example see: Aharoni ; Eretz Israel In Bible Period, p. 20 (Hebrew).
      Mazar, The Phoenicians on The Eastern Shore of The Mediterranean Sea, p. 8. in the book ;
      Western Galilee And The Coast of Galilee. (Heb.).
      Maisler, Canaan And Canaanites, BASOR, 102, 1946, pp. 9–10

In the light of the above the following verses on Tyre[28] Become clearer: "Thou shalt die the death of the UNCIRCUMCISED by the hand of strangers; . . Thou wast the ANOINTED CHERUB that covereth: and I set thee, so that THOU WAST UPON THE HOLY MOUNTAIN OF GOD; thou hast walked up and down in the midst of the stones of fire. THOU WAST PERFECT IN THY WAYS FROM THE DAY THAT THOU WAST CREATED, till unrighteousness was found in thee. By the abundance of thy traffic they filled the midst of thee with violence, AND THOU HAST SINNED: therefore have I CAST THEE as PROFANE OUT OF THE MOUNTAIN OF GOD; and I have destroyed thee, O covering cherub, from the midst of the stones of fire...By the multitude of thine iniquities, in the unrighteousness of thy traffic, thou HAST PROFANED THY SANCTUARIES; therefore have I brought forth a fire from the midst of thee; it hath devoured thee..." (emphasis – N. G.). If Tyre is a Canaanite city what does, uncircumcised, being perfect in the ways...; Sin, profaning of Sanctuaries and casting out of the Holy mountain of God, have to do with a profane Canaanite town?

---

28 Ezk. 28: 10 ; 28: 14 – 19.
    Let us note here that the Hebrew verses are throughout in the past tense. However, in some versions they are translated in the future tense (see: King James' A. V.), and so rendering a different meaning to the context. The English version cited above is from American Revised Standard Edition 1901. The French translation by Louis Segond reads also in the past tense.

SCRIPT AND LANGUAGE

It seems that scholars are unanimous in regarding the Phoenician script and language as nearly complete in identity with those of the ancient Hebrew. The same alphabetic letters are used in both languages, and most scholars tend to refer to the alphabetic script as "the Canaanite–Hebrew script". and to regard the language in both as different dialects of the same language.[1] The pronunciation of consonants and syllables, to our best knowledge, was identical.[2] Perrot who differentiates between Hebrews and Phoenicians remarks though, that "they spoke almost the same language",[3]

---

1   Rawlinson, Phoenicia, p. 327.
     Harden, The Phoenicians, p. 116
     Dahood, Ugaritic – Hebrew Philology, p. 2
     Albright, Recent Progress In North Canaanite Research, BASOR. 70, 1938, p. 13.
     A Hebrew Letter From The Twelfth Century, BASOR. 73. 1939, p. 10.
     The North Canaanite Poems of Al'eyan Ba'al, JPOS, 1934, p. 115.
     Harris, A Grammar of The Phoenician Language, pp. 6, 9, 68–69.
     Autran, Phéniciens, p. 4.
     Weill, Phéniciens, Égéens et Hellénes Dans La Mediterranée Primitive, SY., (II), 1921, p. 126.
     Berger, La Grande Encyclopédie, Paris, Tome 26, Phénicie, pp. 620 – 621.
     Smith Robertson, The Religion of The Semites, Meridian Library, 1956, p. 6.
     Moscati, The World of The Phoenicians, pp. 91 –93.
     Eisfeldt, The Beginnings of Phoenician Epigraphy etc. PEQ. 1947, p. 69 (notes).
     Renan, L'histoire Du Peuple D'israel, tome I. pp. 11, 101, 102.
     Barnette, Phoenician – Punic Art, EWA, p. 295.
     Perrot – Chipiez, History of Art In Phoenicia And Its Dependencies, 1885, pp. 12, 13 – 14, 63.
     Virolleaud, Les Inscriptions Cuneiformes de Ras Shamra, SY., 1929, p. 304.
     Le Déchiffrement Des Tablettes Alphabetiques De Ras Shamra, SY., (XII), 1931, p. 20.
     Gesenius, Hebrew Grammar, p. 10, § 2f; p. 6, § 1k ; p. 25, § 5a.
     Conder, Phoenician Inscription From Joppa PEF. 1892, p. 171.
     The Hebrew– Phoenician Inscription From Tel el Hesy, PEF, 1892, p. 126.
     Gordon, Before The Bible, p. 249 (Hebrew ed. 1966).
     Yeivin, On Problems of Alphabet Origin etc. Leshonenu, 17, 2– 3 p. 67. (Hebrew)
     Vance D. R.; Literary Sources for The History of Palestine and Syria: The Phoenician
     Inscriptions, B. A. 57: 1(1994). pp. 4, 5.
2   For example: Harris, ibid. p. 22
3   Perrot – Chipiez, ibid. p. 63.

and elsewhere; "...since the Phoenician inscriptions have been deciphered it has been recognized that the Phoenician and Hebrew languages resembled each other very narrowly – so narrowly that they might almost be called two dialects of one tongue".[4] He adds furthermore "On the other hand if you refuse to admit that the Phoenicians were of the same blood as the Jews how do you account for their speaking and writing not one of the idioms which we encounter at their best in Africa, but a language that differs little from pure Hebrew".[5] Renan remarks[6]: "They (the Phoenicians – N. G.) spoke a completely analogous language to what we call Hebrew". In his book "Otzar Haketovot Hafinikiot" Slouschz claims that "Between it (Phoenician – N. G.) and the Biblical Hebrew there are merely dialectical differences".[7] and on page 28 he remarks, " Everyone who reads Phoenician inscriptions remarks – not unsurprisingly – that the similarity between Phoenician and Hebrew is so great that it is even difficult to decide and say we have two dialects of the same language". He is more definite elsewhere[8]: "In my opinion – and let people say whatever they wish about the Phoenician language – There is no distinct difference between classical Hebrew and Phoenician, and the prophets rightly regarded the expression 'language of Canaan' as synonymous with Hebrew, the only differences to be found in Phoenician texts are located in the spelling and pronunciation, which are more primitive in Phoenicia and which tradition did not change and formulate according to our biblical Hebrew." In this context he remarks[9]: "The further we go back into the past of the Israelite nation the more do documents and spelling of the Israelite Texts show their fundamental affinities with those of the Phoenicians". Gesenius[10] remarks: "Phoenician is nearly identical with ancient Hebrew writing". Cassuto writes: "The language of the Canaanites and that of the Israelites was in fact one language"[11]. According to Tur–Sinai: "In the days of the Judges and first kings of Israel, the Canaanite– Hebrew language was principally one language"[12] Whereas Schaeffer remarks about the Ugaritic language as the "... language of the Canaanites that is to say archaic Hebrew or proto Phoenician".[13] Refering to the Siloam inscription (Jerusalem area) of king Hezekiah's time. Sayce[14] who bases, himself on the orthography of

4   ibid. p. 12

5   ibid. p. 13.

6   Renan, Ibid. p. 11

7   Slouschz, Otzar Haketovot Hafenikiot, Mosad Bialik, 1942, preface p. 26 (Hebrew).

8   Slouschz, La Civilisation Hebraique et Phénicienne A' Carthage, p. 16.

9   Ibid. Note 1. p. 16.

10   Gesenius, Hebrew Grammar, §a, p. 25.

11   Cassuto, The Godess Anat, p. 2o (Hebrew).

12   Tur Sinai. Halashon Vehasefer, 1959, Vol. I, p. 32. (Hebrew)

13   Schaeffer, The Cuneiform Texts of Ras Shamra, p. 57

14   Sayce, The Inscription At The Pool of Siloam, PEF. 1881, p. 72.

this inscription claims that it is principally a Phoenician inscription,

Hence, he believes, the writer of this inscription was a Phoenician. These words of Sayce point to the lack of any definable line separating the two languages. Rin[15] who refers to some of the above–mentioned ideas. remarks that "It is strange that even those who maintain as much...are still not prepared to accept the logical conclusion of their own deductions namely that Hebrew and Canaanite are one and the same". According to Rin "There is no doubt whatsoever that in the days of the Judges and first kings there was no difference between the 'Judean and Ugaritic' pronunciation system and all the arguments, based on phonological differences that 'Ugaritic' is 'a special language' are self refuting".[16]

Indeed the "Phoenician" language is identical with the Biblical language, both having the same vocabulary, verbs, and adverbs[17], the same inflections of verbs in plural. past perfect. and imperfect, the same prepositions as well as noun case endings for subject, object and possesive forms. In both the formation of plurals for the feminine and masculine gender is by adding the suffixes–Yim (ם'). T (ת) The names of numerals are identical, sentence structure is similar [18]Many words are identical including words of religious significance.[19] The consonantal pattern and pronunciation is identical, etc. and as Offord puts it[20]: "It is not merely in their vocabularies that the connection between the Hebrew and Phoenician peoples and languages is demonstrated, but also by the similarities of thought and the manner of expressing in writing their identical sentiments".

---

15   Rin, Acts of The Gods (Alilot Haelim), p. 9. (Hebrew).
16   Ibid. p. 12.
17   Albright, Specimens of Late Ugaritic Prose, BASOR, 1958, pp. 36–38.
     Conder, The Syrian Language, PEF. 1896, pp. 60–77
     D'horme, Le Déchiffrement DesTablettes De Ras Shamra, JPOS, XI, 1931, pp. 1 – 6.
     Gray, The Legacy Of Canaan, VT. 1957, p. 189.
     Torrey, A New Phoenician Grammar, JAOS, 1937, p. 398.
     Harris, ibid. pp. 57, 62.
     Virolleaud, Les Déchiffrements DesTablettes Alphabetiques De Ras Shamra, SY. XII, 193, pp. 5; 20.
18   Harris, ibid, p. 61.
     Rawlinson, p. 24.
     D'horme, ibid, p. 5.
     Dahood, Ugaritic – Hebrew Philology, pp. 14, 17.
     Torrey, ibid, p. 398.
     Gray, ibid. p. 4.
     Rin, Alilot Haelim, pp. 12–13. (Hebrew).
19   Albright, The North Canaanite Poems of Al'eyan Ba'al And The Gracious Gods, JPOS. 1934, p. III.
     Held, ibid. pp. 272–282
20   Offord, Archeological Notes, PEQ. 1917, p. 94.

RELIGION

Concerning the "Phoenician" religion most scholars are united in their belief that there exists nearly complete identity between "Phoenician" religious values, as reflected in different archaeological findings and the idolatrous worship that the Bible ascribes to the Israelites before they were taken into captivity.[1] Slouschz says that "The Hebrews held the same religion as the Phoenicians, and therefore it is impossible to differentiate between them".[2] The "Phoenician" hierarchy both in structure and in terminology resembles that of the Israelites. The servants in the Temples called Kohanim, and the higher in position among them is called Rav – Kohen.[3] The names of the sacrifices are the same (Zebah, Asham, Minha, Kalil, Shalem). The tariffs of sacrifices in the "Phoenician"Temples are identical barring a few slight differences, to those used by the Israelites as described in the Bible.[4]

---

1   Cook, Phoenicia, EB. edit. 1929.
    Contenau, La Civilisation Phénicienne, p. 82 ff.
    Berger, Phénicie, La grande Encyclopédie, Tome 26.
    Della Vida Giorgio Levi, Fenici, EI. 1932, p. 1000.
    Ribichini, Beliefs and Religious Life. p. 104 in The Phoenicians, Bompiani, 1988.
2   Slouschz, La Civilisation Hebraique Et Phénicienne a' Carthage, pp. 27 – 28.
3   Della Vida, ibid. p. 1000
    Contenau, ibid. pp. 105, 108.
    Hours–Miedan, Carthage, 1949, pp. 48– 49, 53.
    Lods, Les Prophèts d'israel etc. 1935, p. 294.
    Barrois, Manuel d'Archéologie Biblique, 1953, (II), pp. 340, 334
    Hooke, The Origins of Early Semitic Ritual, pp. 66–67.
    Gray, ibid. p. 143.
    Gaster, The Ras Shamra Texts And The Old Testament, PEQ. 1934, p. 141
    Slouschz, Hebraeo – Phéniciens Et Judeo – Berbéres, p. 126.
    Wright, How Did Early Israel Differ From Her Neighbours, BA, 1943, pp. 4–5.
    Warmington, Histoire Et Civilisation De Carthage, p. 193.
    Harden, The Phoenicians, 1962, p. 105.
    Moscati, The World Of The Phoenicians, p. 143.
    Kaperlud, The Ras Shamra Discoveries, 1965, pp. 17, 73.
4   Della Vida, ibid. p. 1000
    Contenau, ibid. pp. 105, 108.
    Hours–Miedan, Carthage, 1949, pp. 48– 49, 53.
    Lods, Les Prophèts d'israel etc. 1935, p. 294.
    Barrois, Manuel d'Archéologie Biblique, 1953, (II), pp. 340, 334
    Hooke, The Origins of Early Semitic Ritual, pp. 66–67.
    Gray, ibid. p. 143.

Robertson Smith remarks[5]: "It is clear from the Old Testament that the ritual observnces at a Hebrew and at a Canaanite sanctuary were so similar that to the mass of the people Jehovah worship and Baal worship were not separated by any well–marked line".[6]

A similar remark is made by Miedan[7]: "A striking analogy is immediately apparent between Phoenician religious ritual and that of the Hebrews". Slouschz writes: "It can be seen that the official literature of the ancient Carthaginians is largely permeated with religious concepts and are evident in those same literary aspects. in expression and culture, as those of the jews in ancient time. it reveals the same traditions and the same frame of mind mainly noticeable from a purely structural perspective. What we know of the social formation of Carthage leads us to that of Jerusalem and the scribes".[8]

In 1845 while excavating the foundations for a cathedral in Marseille, France, a stone was found on which a list of sacrificial tariffs was carved and its content closely resembles certain portions in the Book of Leviticus. This resemblance has already been referred to by Slouschz, Conder, Harden, Contenau and Others.[9] Such resemblance to portions of the Book of Leviticus can also be found in similar lists of tariffs discovered at Carthage[10] Just as in all other spheres, here too, because of the similarity between the Israelite religion and that of those called Phoenicians, most scholars came to the conclusion that the Israelite nation borrowed its culture and religious

Gaster, The Ras Shamra Texts And The Old Testament, PEQ. 1934, p. 141
Slouschz, Hebraeo – Phéniciens Et Judeo – Berbéres, p. 126.
Wright, How Did Early Israel Differ From Her Neighbours, BA, 1943, pp. 4–5.
Warmington, Histoire Et Civilisation De Carthage, p. 193.
Harden, The Phoenicians, 1962, p. 105.
Moscati, The World Of The Phoenicians, p. 143.
Kaperlud, The Ras Shamra Discoveries, 1965, pp. 17, 73.
5   Smith Robertson, The Religion of The Semites, p. 254
6   For Robertson Smith "Canaanite" equals to "Phoenician"
7   Hours – Miedan, Carthage, p. 55
8   Slouschz, La Civilisation Hébraique Et Phénicienne A' Carthage, p. 22.
9   CIS., I. 165.
     Slouschz, ibid, pp. 17, 23, 27, 28.
     –Otzar Haketovot Hafenikiot, 1942, Tab. 129 p. 141 (Hebrew)
     – Hebreo–Phéniciens Et Judeo–Berbeères, p. 126.
     Contenau, ibid, pp. 108 – 109.
     Harden, ibid. p. 105.
     Conder, Phoenician Notes, PEF. 1889, p. 144.
     Della Vida, ibid, p. 1000.
     Sayce, Early History of The Hebrews, pp. 204–207.
10   Perrot–Chipiez, History of Art In Phoenicia And Its Dependancies, 1885, p. 271.
     Smith Robertson, ibid. pp. 217 – 220, 237.
     Hours – Miedan, ibid. pp. 48 – 49.
     Dussaud, Les Origines Canaaneen de Sacrifice Israelite, p. 134

customs from the "Canaanites – Phoenicians".[11]

Conder who refers to the burial customs among the Phoenicians", remarks: "The Phoenicians and the Hebrews buried their dead in an identical fashion in niches"[12], and elsewhere:

"Similarities can be found in tomb construction between Jerusalem and Carthage".[13] Such similarity in burial customs is also pointed out by Slouschz, Barnette, and Perrot.[14] While Sukenik remarks that "In the excavations of the unified expedition to Samaria remnants from the Israelite period were found Showing a similar formation to that in Ugaritic tombs".[15] It must be noted that in texts related to burials found at Carthage, we find identical terms to those used in Jewish burial rituals e. g. Lezekher Olam – (for eternal memory), Beth Olam – (eternal House = tomb), Aron (=coffin) and the like.[16]

According to Dussaud[17] the tablets of Ras Shamra point to a complete identity between the Phoenicians and the Israelites in those concepts concerning spirit and soul from which, he believes the same burial rituals, the same lamentation ritual, and identity in sacrificial rituals derive.

11 Wright, ibid, pp. 4–5.
    Hooke, ibid, p. 67.
    Gray, ibid, pp. 4, 208.
12 Conder, Syrian Stone Lore, pp. 93 (notes), 94, 132.
13 Conder, ibid. p. 104.
    See Also Slouschz, Hebreo – Phéniciens et Judeo–Berbères, p. 345
14 Perrot – Chipiez, History of Art In Phoenicia etc. p. 149.
    Barnette, Phoenicia, EB. (1968), p. 892.
    Phoenician – Punic Art, EWA., p. 306.
    Slouschz, La Civilisation Hebraique Et Phénicienne A Carthage, pp. 18, 22.
15 Sukenik, Instalations For The Dead Ritual In Canaanite Ugarit And Israelite Samaria, Kedem 2, pp. 43, 45 (Hebrew)
16 Slouschz, La Civilisation Hebraique Et Phénicienne A Carthage, pp. 18, 22
17 Dussaud, La Notion D'ame Chez Les Israelites et les Phéniciens, SY. 1935, pp. 272–275.

THE GOD OF MEDICINE

Among the many deities the "Phoenicians" worshipped we encounter one called "Eshmun". The ancient Greek writers are unanimous in affirming that Eshmun and the Greek deity Asklepios are the same.[1] As we know Asklepios was the Greek god of Medicine and many Temples were erected to him. The ruins of many of those still exist in Thessaly, Epidaurus, Cos etc. This god is commonly represented with a club–like votive staff with a serpent coiled around it or in the form of a snake. In the Temples to this god snakes were cultivated for the ritual.[2] Why should a serpent symbolise this god of medicine? What connection is there between the snake and Medicine? In Greek mythology we do not find any explanation for this. But it is known that the Greeks adopted this god from the Phoenicians. In the light of what we have shown to prove that "Phoenicians" was the name given to the Israelites, let us therefore search for an explanation in the Israelite tradition.

The Bible tells us[3] that when the Israelites were in the desert a plague broke out of fiery serpents which bit the people many of whom died, "And Moses made a serpent of brass and set it upon the standard: and it came to pass, that if a serpent had bitten any man, when he looked unto the serpent of brass, he lived". In the book of Kings we read about King Hezekiah, one of the last Judean kings, as follows: "...and he brake in pieces the brazen serpent that Moses had made; for unto those days the children of Israel did burn incense to it; and he called it Nehushtan"[4] Therefore, over a very long period, from that of Moses till nearly that of the captivity, the Israelites burned incense to the serpent of brass, i. e. they worshipped it as a god. This brazen serpent, as we are told, was formed to heal those who were bitten by the snakes, therefore if the Israelites continue to worship it, it must be supposed that in their conciousness it was a healing deity – a deity of medicine, Similar to the snake on a club like staff which later on represented the god of Medicine – Asklepios. Here archaeology comes to our aid. In 1901 Macridy bey excavated in Sidon and unearthed a temple to the god Eshmun,[5] In this temple an inscription was discovered dedicating the construction to the god

---

1   Contenau, ibid. p. 92.
2   Untill today a serpent coiled around a votive staff symbolises medical associations and world wide medicine.
3   Nu. 21: 6–10.
4   2Kn., 18: 4
5   Contenau, ibid. p. 142.

Eshmun who was in this inscription named "God Eshmun sar Kadesh (ruler of Kadesh – N. G.).[6]

Reading about the wanderings of the Israelites in the desert, we find that they arrived "in the wilderness of Zin, which is Kadesh" [7]. From Kadesh they move to Mount Hor,[8] and on their leaving Mount Hor they come across the snakes, i. e. the brazen serpent is formed when they left the site of Kadesh but were still in the desert of Kadesh.

The Israelites worship the brazen – snake which represents a healing – god. The Greek god Asklepios is identical to the "Phoenician" god Eshmun called also "Eshmun Sar Kadesh" – Eshmun ruler of Kadesh. It was seen that the Israelites were called Phoenicians by the Greeks, therefore it might be assumed that "Eshmun Sar Kadesh" is the representation of the brazen–serpent that Moses created in the desert of Kadesh, and hence its appellation "Sar Kadesh". It is probable that the name Eshmun is a distortion of the Hebrew name "Yeshimon" (= wilderness) and we might see this as a reference to its creation in the wilderness. Virrolleaud remarks that the name Eshmun is met also in the form "Yashimunu" in the seventh century B. C. in a treaty between Esarhadon and the king of Tyre.[9]

According to Contenau,[10] Damascius (sixth century A. D.) identifies Adonis with the gods Asklepios and Eshmun and cites him saying that this god is "neither Egyptian nor Greek, but Phoenician".

Adonis is generally accepted as a Greek transcription for the Semitic name Adon. and according to Damascius, Adonis and Asklepios are the same, it might therefore be assumed that the brazen – serpent created by Moses was originally formed only to symbolise the god Adon, and that Moses did not intend giving the Israelites a new god which they created out of the brazen serpent.

---

6   Slouschz, Otzar Haketovot Hafenikiot, p. 23, 28, 30. (Hebrew) see also: Contenau, ibid. p. 143. Deuxième Mission Archéologique A' Sidon, SY. 1924, p. 16.

7   Nu. 33: 36 ; 20: 1 ; 27: 14.

8   Nu. 20: 22.

9   Virolleaud, Six Texts De Ras Shamra Provenant De La XIV Campagne (1950), SY., 28, 1951, p. 164. see also: Dussaud, Melqart, SY., 25; 1946, (48), p. 209.

10 Contenau, La Civilisation Phénicienne, p. 94–95.

ART AND ARCHITECTURE

In art and architecture we find a high degree of similarity between the Israelites and the "Phoenicians". Scholars point out that the Israelites as well as the Phoenicians, were influenced in their art by the Babylonians and the Egyptians.[1] Perrot and Chipiez say that "Cypriot art and Jewish art are no more than varieties or as a grammarian would say, dialects of the Art of Phoenicia".[2] They also point out the similarity in the style of construction between the walls of Arvad and Jerusalem,[3] from which they concluded that in the realm of art the Israelites borrowed from the "Phoenicians". Albright remarks that "at Ugarit and in Megiddo similar ground plans show corresponding thickness of walls", because of the same masonry characteristics he concludes that "Solomonic masonry shows clear indications of having been borrowed from the Phoenicians".[4] However he notes with astonishment that "at Megiddo were a number of proto – Ionic (better perhaps, proto Aeolic) pilaster capitals...similar ones have been found at a number of other sites in Palestine...Curiously enough, none has yet been reported from Phoenicia itself, ...But the Greeks of Cyprus and Ionia borrowed them from the Phoenicians..."[5] A similar remark is made by Harden.[6]

Avi–Yonah in a treatise which deals with the influence of "Phoenician" art on Jewish art says[7]: "If we compare the ornamentation in the Temple of Baal–Bek with those of the coffin found in the tomb of the Adiabene kings in Jerusalem we will discover an extraordinary similarity. In both we observe the same circles formed by the twisting of plants. In both they completely cover the whole decorated area, and in both the decoration is from the plant world in the form of a continuous band along the edges. Another analogy with Phoenician ornamentation are the wavy curliness in the plant The

---

1   Moscati, The World of The Phoenicians, pp. 45, 78 ;
    Albright, The Archaeology of Palestine, p. 253.
    Harden, The Phoenicians, p. 105
    Dunand, Byblia Grammata, p. 14
    Conder, Syrian Stone Lore, pp. 116, 123.
2   Perrot–Chipiez, History of Art In Phoenicia etc. p. 100.
3   Ibid, p. 278
4   Albright, ibid. pp. 104, 125.
5   Albright, ibid. p. 125 – 126.
6   Harden, ibid. p. 196.
7   Avi–Yonah, Phoenician Art And Jewish Art, article in book – Western Galilee
    and the coast of Galilee, Jerusalem, 1965, p. 23 (Heb.)

belief that king Solomon and the Jews borrowed their architecture from the Phoenicians is widely prevalent, and is based on the biblical narrative that Hiram from Tyre built the Temple in Jerusalem. Since Tyrians were regarded as non–Israelites, this caused the above mentioned belief. decoration found on coffins from Jewish tombs from the Second Temple period, discovered on the Mount of Olives. Similar curliness may be observed on the door post of the Temple of Kasr Naos". Elsewhere[8] he writes: "One of the most famous mosaics is the one found one hundred years ago in the tomb of Hiram near Tyre, and which today is in the Louvre. The vine coils and comes out of four amphora in the four corners of the floor. It forms circles in which there are a multitude of country life drawings and of flora and fauna. Another drawing of the same model, yet simpler, is found in the Lebanese church in Genah. Such mosaic ornamentation, WHICH IS NEARLY UNIQUE FOR THAT PERIOD TO PHOENICIAN AND THE LAND OF ISRAEL ALONE calls to mind the drawings in the floor of the synagoque in Maon (Nirim) based on the same ornamental principle". (emphasis–N. G.)

Though Avi–Yonah is trying to trace the influence of "Phoenician" art upon the Israelite, he points in fact to the "extraordinary similarity"between the two.

Chehab[9] also stresses the similarity in ornamentation of Sidonian sarcophages to those discovered along the coast of the land of Israel Herodotus (II, 44) tells us that in the temple of Baal Melkart in Tyre there were two pillars, one of pure gold, the other of emerald. Their like can be found in Malta and Carthage in the Temple of Tanit. Perrot[10], quoting Herodotus, notes that pillars similar to these stood in the Temple of Jerusalem, the pillars Yachin and Boaz[11]. Berard and Moscati also point to this similarity.[12]

In the Arch of Titus in Rome, there is a relief of the Temple's candelabrum, the base of which is square and with the form of a dragon designed on it. In the Talmud (Masekhet Avoda Zara, chap. III) we learn that "any one who finds objects with the form of the sun, the form of the moon, the form of a dragon shall take it (throw it into) to the Dead Sea." It is a strange thing to find the figure of a dragon on the Temple's candelabrum, for it contradicts one of the basic principles of Jewish religion. Scholars have already pointed out this matter. Reinach[13], tried to explain this by saying that the artist carved

---

8   ibid. pp. 28–29
9   Chehab, Sarcophages En Plomb, du Musée Nationale Libanais, SY. XV, 1934, p. 338, note 1.
10   Perrot – Chipiez, ibid. pp. 75, 84
11   ibid. p. 123. see: 2Chr. 3: 17
12   Berard, De L'origine De Cultes Arcadiens, 1894, pp. 74, 75.
     Moscati, ibid. p. 45.
13   Reinach, L'arc De Titus, REJ, XX, 1890, p. 83.
     Strauss, The Form And Fate of The Hasmonean Candlestick, article in Eretz Israel, pp. 122–129.

the candelabrum without having the original in front of him. He therefore assumed there was no identity between the carved candlestick and the authentic original. His assumption was accepted by most scholars. But this conjecture raises two questions 1) How is it that the artist was extraordinarily precise when carving the branches, as described in the Bible, "a knob and a flower" etc. Whereas when carving the base of the candlestick he did not do it accurately? 2) If the Roman artist carved the base according to his own conception and was not faithful to the original, we may expect a certain similarity between the figured candlestick and other Roman candelabra in general, but is that the case?

Kon[14] who analysed the ornamentation of the candelabrum figured on the Arch of Titus assumes that Josephus' words about the candelabrum having three feet were misunderstood. In fact, its base is made of one piece . In his view the dragon figured on the base of the candelabrum is of a kind whose figuration is permitted by Jewish law, this is taken from the Talmud (Tosephta, Avoda Zara, V, VI): "All kinds of visages could be found (pictured) in Jerusalem except that of man...What kind of dragon was prohibited? Rabbi Simon ben Elazar says: All those with spikes emerging from its neck. If it was smooth, it was permitted". And indeed this is the kind of dragon figured on the base of the candelabrum in the Arch of Titus. Kon rightly asks: "If this were true, why then, did he (the supposed Roman sculptor – N. G.) replace the human torso of the Didymian Temple by a smooth naked dragon – The only dragon permitted by Jewish law?". Moreover, he believes that a thorough analysis of the ornamentation of the candelabrum in Titus' Arch, shows all the signs of being closely related to Phoenician candelabra of the 9th century B. C.

This belief of Kon, that the base of the candelabrum in Titus' Arch is authentic, is in accord with the description of the candelabrum in the Bible, namely, that it was formed of one piece and had one leg (Ex. 25: 31–32). Indeed, Rashi explains"... its shaft is the lower leg made like a box and three legs come out of it downward". This explanation is not clear, for if it is the lower leg which is formed as a box, where do the legs come out from? In Yalkut Truma (in the Talmud) the description is simpler "How did Bezalel make the candelabrum? He fashioned it like a beam and made a square at the base." Josephus[15] also remarks that: "It (the candlestick) was made up of globules and lilies along with pomegrenates ...of these it was composed from its single base right up to the top". And elsewhere:[16] "A lampstand, likewise

---

14   Kon Maximillian, The Menorrah of The Arc of Titus, PEQ. 1950, pp. 25–30.
15   Josephus, ANT. Book III, 145. Translation by Thackeray & Marcus, Heinemann, 1950.
16   Josephus, Jewish wars, VII, 5: 5 Translation by Thackeray & Marcus, Heinemann, London, 1950.

made of gold, but constructed on a different pattern from those which we use in ordinary life. Affixed to a pedestal was a central shaft from which there extended slender branches". Whereas in book 7, chapter X section 3 he remarks: "Onias erected a fortress and built his temple (which was not like that in Jerusalem but resembled a tower) of huge stones... The altar, however, he designed on the model of that similar offerings, the fashion of the lampstand excepted; for, instead of making a stand, he had a lamp wrought of gold..."

We learn, therefore, that the Menorah (Candelabrum) in the Temple had a base. This candelabrum was similar in its form and ornamentation to "Phoenician" candelabra from the 9th century B. C.

Chester[17] reports about a gem found at Beyrouth that has for its design three stars the upper one being winged. Below these, and divided from them by two lines, is an early Phoenician inscription from right to left – ישעא – (Yesha'a) from the root Yesha. Prof. Sayce consider the characters to be of the 7th or 8th century B. C., and remarks that "The two lines which divide the name from the stars and the winged solar disk (for so he deciphers the winged star) explain the origin of the similar names which divide in half the inscriptions on early Hebrew seals". Chester believes that the seal is Hebrew and the name would be the short form of Yeshaya (Isaia), however he remarks that "The winged star seems however rather to point to a heathen owner". Conder[18] refers also to this gem as well as to two scarabs: one of the 7th century B. C. with a Phoenician legend of the "wife of Joshua" and the other shows a sphinx with the Egyptian pschent headdress and the title as "a memorial of Hoshea".

---

17   Chester, Notes On Some Phoenician Gems, PEF. 1885, p. 131.
18   Conder, Syrian Stone Lore, p. 75.
      See also Perrot–Chipiez, ibid, pp. 244, 246.

MISCELLANEOUS ITEMS

The calendar used by the "Phoenicians" was identical to that of the Israelites. The names of months were identical to those of the Israelites before the captivity period, and differed from the Babylonian.[1] The same is true with the monetary and weight systems. The names of the coins (currency) and weights were identical for both "Phoenicians" and Hebrews.[2] Conder remarks that the palm tree figure on Jewish coins figures on Carthaginian coins as well.[3]

Grace in an essay referring to jars found in two tombs at Mycenae and Tholos at Menidi, in a stratum ascribed to the 13th century B. C., concludes that these are Canaanite (Phoenician) jars. Accordingly, and on the basis of findings by Prof. Wace at Mycenee, she remarks: "The generally accepted view, that Phoenician influence on Greece was greatest in the 9th – 8th centuries B. C. when the alphabet was borrowed, may have to be revised in the light of this evidence from the 13th century".[4]

In the Book of Psalms we read the following psalm (Ps. 29)."Give unto the Lord, O ye Mighty, give unto the Lord glory and strength. Give unto the Lord the glory due unto his name; Worship the Lord in the beauty of holiness. The voice of the Lord is upon the waters; the God of glory thundereth; The Lord is upon the many waters. The voice of the Lord is powerful; the voice of the Lord is full of majesty. The voice of the Lord breaketh the cedars; yea, the Lord breaketh the cedars of Lebanon. He maketh them also to skip like a calf; Lebanon and Sirion like a young unicorn..."etc. How is it that in an Israelite hymn the subject is Lebanon and Sirion, considered to be a region outside of Israel? This does not only apply to this hymn, but the author of Song of Solomon for example, refers many times in his songs to that same

---

1   Langdon, Babylonian Menalogies And The Semitic Calendars, pp. 13, 23, 24–25.
     Conder, The Hebrew Months, PEF, 1889, p. 21.
     Offord, Palestinian and Phoenician Month Names, Archaeological Notes On Jewish
     Antiquities, PEQ, 1917, p. 100

2   Contenau, La Civilisation Phénicienne, p. 137.
     Ginzberg, Ugaritic Studies And The Bible, BA. 1945, p. 48.
     Pilcher, Weights of Ancient Palestine, etc. PEQ. 1912, pp. 136–144
     Conder, Phoenician Notes, PEF. 1889, p. 142.

3   Conder, Syrian Stone Lore, see notes, p. 192.

4   Grace, The Canaanite Jar p. 98 in The Aegean and the Near East Studies.

region."Come with me from Lebanon my spouse, with me from Lebanon: Look from the top of Amana, from the top of Shenir and Hermon"[5]; "and the smell of thy garments is like the smell of Lebanon"[6]. "A fountain of gardens, a well of living waters, and streams from Lebanon." (Sol. 4: 15); "Thy nose is as a tower of Lebanon which looketh towards Damascus"[7]; "The righteous shall flourish like the palm–tree: He shall grow like a cedar in Lebanon" (Ps. 92: 12).

The name Sirion occurs in the Book of Deuteronomy (3: 9) "which Hermon the Sidonians call Sirion; and the Amorites call Shenir". Hence we learn that the bible differentiates between Amorites and Sidonians and that it is the Sidonian name Sirion, which appears in the Israelite hymn in the Book of Psalms.

Ginsberg already noted the difficulty resulting from this mention of the name Sirion in the above–mentioned psalm, and from the verse in Deuteronomy. He explained it by saying that it refers to the region of Kedesh in the Syrian desert and that the Israelites borrowed this psalm from the "Phoenicians – Canaanites" just as they borrowed their culture.[8] He bases this view on the assumption that the Israelite entry into the land took place at a later period and that they did not conquer this region, so that Lebanon was not within their borders.[9] Nevertheless, he notes elsewhere[10]: "Perhaps the Ugarit letters will prove that prior to the Israelite period there were close cultic ties between Syria and the land of Israel". However Ginzberg does not explain the fact, that a nation employs in religious hymns and songs place names, which supposedly belong to another country, without changing them in the slightest and adapting them to its own nature and knowledge. Ginzberg's explanation is founded on basically erroneous assumptions. We have seen how the region of Lebanon and Hermon were conquered by the Israelites, and therefore they were within Israelite territory. As we read in the Bible: "and the children of the half tribe of Manasseh dwelt in the land: they increased from Bashan unto Baal–Hermon and Senir, and unto Mount Hermon".[11] The Hebrew text reads "and the children of the half tribe of Manasseh dwelt in the land FROM Bashan unto Baal–Hermon and Senir, and unto Mount Hermon they were outnumbered". Whereas about the Reubenites we read: "and Bela the son of Azaz, the son of Shema, the son of

---

5   Ps. 4: 8
6   Sol. 4: 11
7   Sol. 7: 4 (in the Hebrew text 7: 5)
8   Ginsberg, Kitvei Ugarit, pp. 129–131 (Heb.).
      Ugaritic Studies and The Bible, BA. 1945, pp. 53, 55
      See also: Cross Jr. Notes On Canaanite Psalm In The Old Testament, BASOR. 117, 1950, pp. 19–21
9   Ginsberg, ibid, pp. 53–54.
10   Ginsberg, ibid. p. 131.
11   1Chr. 5: 23

Joel, who dwelt in Aroer, even unto Nebo and Baal—meon: And eastward he inhabited unto the entering in of the wilderness from the river Euphrates: because their cattle were multiplied in the land of Gilead".[12] We also learn about the conquest of the region from the following verses in the book of 2Kn (14: 25; 28) concerning Jeroboam son of Joash: "He restored the coast of Israel from the entering of Hamath unto the sea of the plain", "and how he recovered Damascus, and Hamath which belonged to Judah, for Israel". The Hebrew verse reads: "and he recovered Damascus and Hamath to Judah and Israel". Namely Jeroboam RECONQUERED the region including Hamath and Damascus.

In the book of Joshua (11: 17) it is told that Joshua reached in his conquests as far as Baal—Gad in the valley of Lebanon under Mount Hermon. The site of Baal Gad is identified by Conder as Ein –Gedida, north of the Hermon[13], While according the Samaritan version of the book of Joshua, Joshua reached Armenia.[14]

12   1Chr. 5: 8.
13   Conder, Baal Gad, PEP, 1891, p. 251
14   Slouschz, Hebreo – Phéniciens et Judeo – Berbères, p. 150.

COLONIES AND PLACE NAMES

As we know the Phoenicians extended their trade routes to all countries in the Mediterranean basin, passing through the pillars of Hercules (today's Gibraltar) and reached the British Isles. For trading purposes they used to settle and remain in many places, which in the course of time developed into cities. Their most well known city is Carthage (Carta – Hadta) which was established as a colonial settlement on the North African coast (in the region of today's Tunis). It is generally accepted that the name Carthago = Carta Hadta means New town (Keret = town, Hadta = new),[1] But, as is known the word Keret means a metropolis, such an explanation of the name implies that the city from its inception was built to be a large city, a fact which does not fit in with the legend of the building of Carthage. Was the building of Carthage so different from that of other Phoenician colonies, which were built as trading posts[2], some of which became cities only in the course of time? On the other hand the term "Kiria" (town) or "Keret" for a metropolis occurs in the Bible[3] and in the Ugarit tablets but not "Karta", not even in apposition to Keret. Why therefore should the case be different with the name "Karta Hadta"? , And why "Hadta" and not "Karta" alone? .

The explanation "New Town" given to Cartago is not plausible even though we find in it the adjective New (= Hadta).

The adjective "New" can be found in many town names in our own era. Such as: New–England, New–Orleans, New Mexico, New–Bedford, New–York, New Brunswick, New Amsterdam, New Hampshire and many others. The common denomination for all of them is that the adjective "New" is intended to differentiate these cities from cities having the same name

---

1 Carpenter, Phoenicians In The West, AJA, 1958, (62), p. 42
   Neiman, Phoenician Place Names, JNES, 1965, p. 114, note 14.
   Carchedon –New City, JNES, 1966, pp. 42–47.
   Conder, Syrian Stone Lore, p. 66.
   Whitaker, Motya – A Phoenician Colony In Sicily, p. 29.
   Contenau, La Civilisation Phènicienne, p. 74.
   Moscati, The Carthaginian Empire, p. 54 in The Phoenicians, Bompiani, 1988.
   Moscati, The World of The Phoenicians, p. 116.
2 Moscati, ibid. p. 117.
   Moscati, Colonisation of The Mediterranean, p. 49 in The Phoenicians, Bompiani, 1988.
3 In Proverbs 8: 3 we read "Fi Karet"(in the Hebrew text) translated "at the entry of the city".

in the home country of the town builders e. g. – England, Mexico, York, Amsterdam, Hampshire etc. Such a practice is not unique for our era but can also be seen in antiquity. In the book of Joshua for example we come across the names Hazor, and Hazor Hadta (Jos. 15: 22–23) namely Hazor and New Hazor. Such must we also understand "Karta Hadta" namely "New Karta", and "Karta" is simply the name of the city from which the builders of the city of "Karta Hadta" came. A town called Karta is to be found in the inheritance of the tribe of Zebulun[4], who are considered to be seafarers. It is worth mentioning that another Phoenician colony with a similar name "Carteia" was known to have existed in the bay of Algeciras.[5]

By analogy with our own times we may also learn about other "Phoenician" colony names. As noted above many city names were formed by adding the adjective "new" to the name of a town in the country of origin, but we often see that the names of new towns correspond identically to the town names in the country of origin. For instance: Plymouth, Cambridge, Dartmouth, Bridgwater, Weymouth, Gloucester, Bristol etc. in England with exactly the same names to be found in America[6].

This phenomenon is not rare but occur in all periods, even in ancient times. We find for cities in different regions identical city names. e. g. Luz, Gilgal, Kedesh, Hazor, Arad, Carmel, Carthage, Melita (Malta), Thebes and others[7].

On the basis of what has been said above, let us examine the names of some Phoenician towns and colonies.

The founding of the city of Toledo in Spain is ascribed to the Phoenicians. Around this town we find today towns called Escalone, Avila, Joppa Maqueda. – names which phonetically recall the names Ashkelon, Avel (Abel), Jaffo (=Joppa=Jaffa), Makkeda. All these names appear in the days of king Solomon in the region of Judah,[8] and before that in the regions of the tribes of Judah and Dan. And there we find in the lot of the tribe of Judah, a town by the name of Eltolad (Jos. 15: 30) which is also mentioned as Tolad (1Chr. 4: 29) a name very similar to that of Toledo. As we know the present day Spanish city of Cadiz was built as a Phoenician colony named Agadir Strabo (3, 4,

---

4   Jos. 21: 34
5   Rawlinson, ibid. Phoenicia, p 68.
6   Plymouth, Cambridge, Dartmouth, Bridgwater, Wymouth etc. see also: "El Nombre de 'Sefarad' by A. I. Laredo and D. G. Maeso. in revista de La Escuela De Estudios Hebraicos año IV madrid 1944. Fasc. 2.
7   Bet–el was called Luz (Ju. 1: 23), and a man from this town built a city in the land of the Hittites, and called it Luz (Ju. 1: 26), Kedesh in Judah (Jos. 15: 23) and Kedesh in Naphtali
     (Jos. 19: 37). Hazor in Judah (Jos. 15: 23) and Hazor in Gallilee (Jos. 19: 36) ; Carthage on the African coast and Carthage on the Spanish coast.
8   Jos. 15: 41; Ju. 1: 18.

2), as mentioned by Slouschz[9] calls it Gadara. Whereas Pliny (3, 3) calls it Gades from which the name Cadiz derives.[10] No less than a city by the name Gederah is to be found in the region of the tribe of Judah (Jos. 15: 36). Near the city of Cadiz there are two cities called Jeres (חרס–Ḥeres)[11] and Sidonia, which are similar to the names Ḥeres in the tribe of Dan (Ju. 1: 35) and Sidon in the tribe of Asher. The city Constantin in Algeria was called Kirta while coins found there had the name Cartan (כרטן) impressed on them[12]. A name Kartan, which phoneticaly is identical to the name of the city Kartan occurs in the list of the cities of the tribe of Naphtali. (Jos. 21: 32). Near this city there is a town built by the Phoenicians called Igilgili[13] which is identical to the name Gilgal in Judah. (Jos. 15.)

Other names of known "Phoenician"colonies are Thebes (in Greece), Golos (near Malta), Kitera, Beerot (today's Syracuse), Motya, Araden, Lebena (in Rhodes), Idalium (in Cyprus). These names are to be found in Israelite cities. Thebez (Ju. 9: 50) Giloh–in Judah (Jos. 15: 51) ; Kitron in the lot of the tribe of Zebulun (Ju. 1; 30); Beeroth in Benjamin's lot (Jos. 9: 17); Moza (Jos. 18: 25) ; Arad in Judah (Ju. 1: 17); Idalah in Zebulun (Jos. 19: 15) ; Libnah in Judah (Jos. 15: 42). In Lixos on the coast of Morocco (today's Larach) a coin with a bilingual inscription was found with the name L. K. S. (ל.כ.ש.)[14] which might be read as Lachish (לכיש). in Judaea

According to Prof. Slouschz[15] the name of the city Tripoli in Lybia was Oea. Coins found in the place have the name Ha – Ayat (– ה-עית – The Ayat) in Punic letters –inscribed on them, and he ascribes this name to a Judean town Ayat – עית (Aya – עיה–) "He is come to Ayath he is passed to Migron" (Is. 10: 28), "The children also of Benjamin from Geba dwelt at Michmash, and Aija"– (עיה –Aya), (Ne. 11: 31) Conder[16] remarks that in Rhodes there is a holy place, probably Phoenician, named Zeus Atabyrius which Reland identifies with the name Tabor (in the lot belonging to the tribe of Zebulun). Berard[17] also points to this fact but adds that a similar name existed also in Sicily.

In the Bible we encounter genealogical tables of certain families[18] together

---

9   The name Agader אגדר הגדר is inscribed on coins found on the site: Slouschz Otzar Haketovot Hafenikiot p. 52 (Hebrew); See also: Rawlinson, Phoenicia, p. 290.: Neiman,
      Phoenician Place Names, JNES. 1965, p. 114, note 12.

10   Slouschz, Otzar Haketovot Hafenikiot, p. 152 (Hebrew)
      See also Moscati, ibid. p. 122

11   The Spanish j is pronounced as KH.

12   Slouschz, ibid. p. 219.

13   Barnette, Phoenician – Punic Art, EWA, p. 295. ; Moscati, ibid. p. 122.

14   Slouschz, Otzar Haketovot Hafenikiot, pp. 219, 227 (Hebrew)

15   Slouschz, Masai Beertz Luv, part II, pp. 13, 121. (Hebrew)

16   Conder, Syrian Stone Lore, note, p. 127.

17   Berard, Les Phéniciens Et L'odysée, p. 193.

18   See Genealogy of Judah: 1Chr. chaps. 2; 4; Gen. 10. See also

with their places of settlement, such that the place names are identical with the name of the head of the family.

Clermont Ganneau who refers to the town Arsuf (Reseph) in the territory of Ephraim remarks[19]: "In accordance with old Semitic fashion many of the names of towns are enumerated under the forms of eponymous personages: Reseph, רשף is one of these (1Chron. VII. 25.)"

As known Reshef was the name of the "Phoenician" Apollo, while a town by the name of Reshef (Arsuf – Apollonia) existed in the territory of the Ephraimite tribe. Ganneau points out this fact and says: "Therefore the ancient Ephraimite town of Arsuf would be one of the principal centers of the worship of the Phoenician Apollo"[20].

In the light of the above it may be presumed that the names of Sardinia and Sardes (in minor Asia) derive originally from the name "Sered" which was the head of a family in the tribe of Zebulun (Gen. 46: 14) which was known as a seafarer tribe.

Today's Spanish settlement of Ibica was formerly called Ibasim, and later Ebusus. On a coin the name of the place appears "יבשם" and "איבשם" (Ibsam)[21], and the very name יבשם (Ibsam) appears also as a name of the head of a clan in the tribe of Issachar. (1Chr. 7: 2)

The town of Monaco is known to be considered a "Phoenician" settlement by the name Manahat. This name is found in 1Chr. (2: 54) as that of the head of a clan (המנחתי) The Manahathite = that pertains to Manahat.

In this way we may also explain the name "Crete" perhaps based on the name of the Creti who dwelt in the south of Judah (1Sam. 30: 14). It is worth mentioning also a river with the name of Krit (transcribed in English Cherit) in Israel (1Kn. 17: 3)

In Crete there is a mountain called "Ida" which might be regarded as a distortion of Yehuda (Judah), and even Tacitus[22] tells about the origins of the Judeans as follows: "...it is said that the Jews were originaly exiles from the island of Crete who settled in the farthest parts of Libya at the time when Saturn had been deposed and expelled by Jove. As argument in favour of this is derived from the name: ...There is a famous mountain in Crete called Ida, and hence the inhabitants were called the Idaei..."

This story of Tacitus is interpreted in many ways, but it is agreed by all that Tacitus was mistaken and confused the name Ida with Yehuda (Judah), a confusion which results from the fact that he bases his story upon common

Aharoni, Eretz Israel In Biblical Time, Geographical History, 1962, pp. 78, 211

19   Ganneau, Notes, PEP. 1896, pp. 259–261
20   Ganneau, ibid. p. 260.
21   Slouschz, Otzar Haketovot Hafenikiot, p. 151
22   Tacitus, The Histories, translation Moore, Heineman, Harvard University Press, MCMLXII, p. 177.

hearsay. I will refrain from discussing these interpretations, and will refer only to Tacitus words alone. From his words (in the first half), it appears that the Judeans lived in Crete from where they were expelled and then settled in Libya. In other words the Judeans who settled in libya immigrated there from Crete. But the Judeans are known to have settled in Judah, and therefore Tacitus words were considered as erroneous.

From his words (in the second half) it may be understood that they emigrated from Egypt to the surrounding countries. Therefore we might see in Tacitus words a reference to two emigrations: the one from Egypt to Judah and the second from Crete to Libya . Such an account falls in well with the immigration of the "Phoenicians" (i. e the Israelites) from Israel to Crete and then onward to Libya and other places.

It is interesting that Homer[23] points out a river in the same region of Crete called Jordan, which indicates just as with the name Ida, a certain link with Judah.

A river by the same name of Jardanus also existed in Greece. Indeed Kohler[24] believed the name to be derived from the ancient Persian language (he explains: yar – year; Danus – river)namely Jordan is a river that flows the year long. All my efforts to find a basis for his belief were unsuccessful. Why should a river in Israel, in Greece and in Crete be called Jordan, presumably a Persian name, while there are no rivers in Persia itself called Jordan?

Victor Berard[25] lived for several years in the Greek islands studying the names of sites and his conclusion is that "most of the Greek islands bear names which have no meaning in Greek and do not seem to be Greek originally"[26]. According to him "each island has a few names one of which is authentically Greek, whereas the next is incomprehensible".[27] For the understanding of these names Berard drew upon the narratives and descriptions in the Iliad and the Odyssey as well as on descriptions and information from ancient historians. According to him the names of most Greek islands and many cities in the Mediteranean region, are of Semitic derivation, either from Hebrew or from what he calls Phoenician. Here are some examples:

The island "Siphnos"was also called "Merope" and "Akis". Pliny notes that "Siphnos ante Meropia et Acis apellata". Akis in Greek means healing and according to Berard Akis is the Greek transcription of the semitic word

---

23   Homer, Odyssey, III, 276 – 300. p. 38 in translation by Lang, Leaf and Myers, The Modern
    Library edit. N. Y. p. 35 in translation by Alexander Pope, The world's popular classics, Books, inc. N. Y.
    See also Berard, V. ibid. Vol. II, p. 280.
24   Kohler, Lexicologische Geographisches, ZDPV. (62), pp. 115, 120
25   Berard. V. Les Phéniciens Et L'odysèe
26   Berard, ibid. p. 117.
27   Berard, ibid. p. 123.

"marpe"(מרפא) meaning healing – medicine, which was corrupted into Meropia. (ibid. p. 157).

In Cyprus and Messina there exists the name Aipeia which in Greek means: hard–stiff. Aipeia is also called "Soloi" and according to Berard the name Soloi is given to regions in high places. A town by the name of Soloi is found in a rocky region on the Cilician coast. as well as the city Soloies in Sicily who later changed into Solontum. According to Berard Soloi is simply the Hebrew name Sela (סלע = rock), and Aipeia is its transcription into Greek (ibid. pp. 171–177). Not far from Soloi in Cilicia there is a river the Greeks call Koiranos or Saros. In the Homeric epics the name Koiranos is synonymous with king, chieftain, whereas Saros is its exact transcription into Hebrew – Sar (chieftain–שר) (ibid. p. 178).

In Messina there was a place called Aipeia which in the course of time came to be called Turia. This is seen by Berard to be the Hebrew–Aramaic name Tur = mountain and strangely enough in Beotia there is a mountain the Greeks call Orthophagus but which is called also Turion (ibid. p. 179) In the light of Homer's Odyssey, Berard explains the names Scyla and Charybdis as a corruption of the Hebrew words Skilla (stoning) and Khorban (destruction). The name Solyma which is a place name and is applied also to a ridge of mountains around a bay, is according to Berard of Hebrew derivation: Sulam = ladder, such as "Sulam of Tyre". He gets support for this in Strabo's words depicting the mountain ridge of Solyma, In the form of a ladder. (ibid. p. 190) In this ridge of Solyma not far from the sea there is a volcano crater called Chimaira where, according the Iliad (VI, 182), there lived a monster spouting fire. Berard regards the name chimaira derived from semitic etymology "Yehemar – = יחמר to seeth, boil." The same name Issa Chimaiara is also to be found in the island of Lesbos; in Sicily near the "Phoenician" city of Solontum – where there are hot water springs said to be generated by Hercules. The Greeks built thermal baths there named Chimaira (today called Termini) (Ibid. p. 190–192.)

The place name Aegilia is called Ogilus in Greek, and Berard regards it as an Hebrew name Agol, (=round),[28]

The name Amorgos–Amargo, he equates with the Hebrew word Margoa (=rest–repose). Strabo remarks[29] that "Neda is the name of a river that comes down from the Arcadian mountains and its well springs were opened by Rhea who came there to get purified after she had given birth to Zeus". While Pausanias[30] remarks that "the river of Neda receives near Phigali the stream of impurity Lumax which derives its name from the purification of Rhea".

---

28 Berard, ibid. p. 209.
29 VII. 3, 22
30 VIII. 41–1

Berard who cites those passages[31], remarks that "the Greek name for impurity–Lumax, is the exact translation of the Hebrew word 'Nida' which denotes in Hebrew every kind of impurity but especially the impurity of the woman during her menstruation period, or after giving birth, and in the scriptures we find 'Nida waters' to denote unpurified waters. Neda–Lumax is a couplet of Greek–Semitic names to denote this river of unpurification". This river of impurity flows, as mentioned, near the town of Phigali. According to Berard, also the name Phigali is the Hebrew word "Phigul" which is synonymous with impurity (defilement).

I have mentioned here only a few of Berard views and examples, and even if not all of Berard's statements are accepted by the reader nevertheless most of them are well founded and his line of inquiry leaves the reader full of admiration. Bochart (1599–1667) who regarded the Hebrew language as a base for the understanding of European languages and culture, tried before Berard to explain many names in Europe according to Semitic (Hebrew) etymology. But his theory collapsed, and as Berard (who was not Jewish) explains, The reason for this was that: "The xviii century by separating truth from religion, also separated 'sacred history' from history proper, and expelled Phoenicians and Jews from the ancient world of philosophy"[32].

In the Bible we are told that king Solomon traded with many countries, and greatly increased the wealth of the country till "silver was nothing accounted of in the days of Solomon. For the king had ships that went to Tarshish..." (2Chr. 9: 20–21). He sent ships to Tarshish, Ophir and the lands beyond the sea. Where is Tarshish?

The Septuagint sometimes translates Tarshish as Carthage (Is . 22: 1 ; 18, 27: 12; 38: 13) at other times it leaves the name as it is, Tarshish (Gen. 10: 4 ; Is. 60: 9 ; Jona. 1: 3 ; Ez. 1: 16 ; 1Chr. 1: 7), and occasionally translates it as sea. The Aramaic translation sometimes reads Tarshish – Carthago, though not always corresponding to the verses in the Septuagint. At other times the Aramaic translation reads –Tarsos for Tarshish. and occasionally translates sea as in the Septuagint. Eusebius believes that Tarshish is Carthage (Onomasticon v. Carchedon) It seems therefore that in these translations Tarshish is identified either as Carthage or as Tarsos in Cilicia. But it is generally accepted that Tarshish be equated with a city by the name of Tartesos, Why?

Herodotus (IV, 152) tells about Greek sailors who passed through the pillars of Hercules (today's Gibraltar), and arrived at a town by the name of Tartesos bringing gold from there to Greece. D'horme who refers to this story sees it as analogous to the biblical narrative on the bringing of gold from Tarshish. As in the ancient Hebrew the letters Shin and Sin are

---

31   Berard, v. ibid. p. 351.
32   Berard, ibid. p. 120

interchangeable, therefore he believes that the name Tarshish might be read Tarsis and according to him Tarsis is a distortion of the name Tartesos[33], which, as pointed out, is the generally accepted view on the issue today[34], and it finds support from Diodorus Siculus who remarks (V–35) that "this land (Iberia–N. G.) possesses, we may venture to say, the most abundant and most excellent known sources of silver...Now the natives were ignorant of the use of the silver, and the Phoenicians, as they pursued their commercial enterprises and learned of what had taken place, purchased the silver"[35] So Tartesos was identified with Tarshish. On the basis of Latin and Greek writers from ancient times Cintas[36] concludes that Tartesos is Cadiz.

In the biblical list of nations (Gen. 10: 4; 1Chr. 1: 7) it reads as follows: "And the sons of Javan; Elishah, and Tarshish, Kittim, and Dodanim", (Javan in Hebrew = Greece. – N. G.) It is obvious that the Bible links Tarshish with Yavan (Javan – Greece), and since in ancient Hebrew the letters Shin and Sin are interchangeable, therefore we are right in reading Tarsis, and it may be assumed that Tarshish – Tarsis is only a slight distortion of the Greek city of Tarsos in Asia minor. Josephus in Antiquities also identifies Tarshish with "The city Tarsos in Cilicia"[37], and some scholars agree with him[38]. As mentioned above, the Aramaic Translation to the Bible sometimes translates Tarshish – Tarsos. This city of Tarsos was known in antiquity as a very wealthy city, inhabited by many Phoenicians.

The trade expansion of the "Phoenicians" reached its peak between the years c. 900 –1000 B. C.[39] a period which parallels that of King Solomon's trading activity. Harden[40] asks why the Phoenicians did not set out on their travels across the sea before then? and he answers: "Some infusion of new ideas and of new blood must be postulated to account for their sudden maritime activity, and these probably came from the Mycenaeans.", But in

---

33   D'horme, Les Peuples Issue De Japhet, SY. XIII, 1932, p. 45
34   For example: Slouschz, Sefer Hayam, p. 143 (Hebrew)
      Cullican, The First Venturers, 1966, p. 114.
      Maspero, The struggle of the nations, Egypt, Syria, And Assyria, 1910, p. 740.
      Moscati, The World Of The Phoenicians, 1968, pp. 96, 100, 231–232,
      Carpenter. R. Tartesos, p. 123. EB, 1929 edit. (part archaeology –article Spain).
35   Diodorus Siculus, transalation Oldfather. C. H. London, Heinemann
36   Cintas, Tarsis – Tartesos – Gadess, Semitica, XVI, 1966, pp. 5–37.
37   Josephus, Ant. IX, 209 ; I, 127.
38   Conder, Notes, PEF, 1892, pp. 44–45.
      Notes, PEF. 1896, p. 168.
      The Onomasticon, PEP, 1896, p. 239.
      Mieses, Les Juifs et Les Etablisments Puniques en Afrique Du Nord, p. 116.
39   For example see: Harden, The Phoenicians, pp. 22, 52.
      Contenau, La Civilisation Phénicienne, p. 56
      Albright, The Archaeology of Palestine, 1949, p. 122
40   Harden, ibid. p. 51.

the light of what has been said before the answer must lie in the coming of the Israelites (The Phoenicians) who replaced the Canaanites. In this same sense we must also understand Hecateus when he says that Phoenicia was formerly called Chna, (Canaan), and Philo of Byblus words: "Chna who was afterwards called Phoinix".[41] namely that a change of cultural values took place in the region.

---

41   Fr. Hist. Grec. I, 17 ; III, 569. see also Phoenicia, EB. 1929 edit. p. 766a

SPARTA

In the first Book of Maccabees[1] we read about a correspondence between Jonathan the high priest in Israel and the people of Sparta, and the context is as follows: "Jonathan, the High Priest, the council of the nation, the priests and the rest of the Jewish people to their Spartan BROTHERS, greetings! Even before this, a letter was sent to Onias the High Priest from Areius who was then king among you, to the effect that you are OUR KINSMEN,[2] as the copy herewith submitted sets forth. Onias received the man who was sent honorably, and accepted the letter in which declaration was made about alliance and friendship. Although we are not in need of these pledges, since we find encouragement in the holy books which we possess, we have undertaken to send to you to renew the pact of brotherhood and friendship, that we may not BECOME ESTRANGED from you; for much time has gone by since you sent word to us, So we remember you at every opportunity incessantly ON THE FESTIVALS and at other appropriate days, IN THE SACRIFICES which we offer and IN OUR PRAYERS, as it is right and fitting to recall OUR KINSMEN" (my emphasis–N. G.)

In this letter the Spartans are named kinsmen (brothers in the Hebrew translation). Perhaps this is only a manner of speech, but the astonishing facts in this letter are that Areius king of Sparta initially sent a letter to Onias the priest, and "although we are not in need of these pledges... we have undertaken to send to you...that we may not become estranged from you..." and "we remember you at every opportunity incessantly on the festivals and other appropriate days, in the sacrifices which we offer and in our prayers, as it is right and fitting to recall our kinsmen". What have festivals, sacrifices, and prayers to do with all this and what does estrangement mean in this context, if all that is at issue here is a pact? It is even more strange when reference is made to letters sent in bygone days, in the period of Areius and Onias and "Much time has gone by since you sent word to us..." etc. The significance of the text most probably implies much stronger ties than a simple pact.

The Book of Maccabees includes the letter that Areius King of Sparta sent

---

1   The First Book of Maccabees, 12: 5–12, English translation by Tedesche, Harper & Brothers, New York, 1950.
2   In note no. 7 to this verse the translator writes: "Apparently there was a legend in the Orient that the Spartans and the Jews were of the same ancestry ".

to Onias the priest, and which Jonathan the priest refers to in his letter to the Spartans.

"This is the copy of the letter which they sent to Onias, Areius King of Spartans to Onias the High priest greetings! IT HAS BEEN FOUND IN A DOCUMENT ABOUT THE SPARTANS AND JEWS THAT THEY ARE RELATED, AND THAT THEY ARE OF THE FAMILY OF ABRAHAM[3]. SINCE WE HAVE LEARNED THIS will you please write us about your welfare. We are writing in turn to you that your cattle and property are ours, and ours are yours. We charge then, therefore, to report this to you."[4] (my emphasis–N. G.).

In this letter it is explicitly noted that they are brothers jointly descended from Abraham, and when this fact was discovered, after it was found in a document, they wrote this letter. Hence the reason for their writing was not to suggest the formation of a pact, but to impart the knowledge that they are brothers (kinsmen) and common descendants of Abraham. The Spartans' dwelling on the fact they are related to Abraham is thus not just fanciful phraseology and rhetoric. After all the reference is not to the sons (descendants) of Adam or Noah – names inclusive of the entire human race, but to the sons of Abraham, that is to a specific ethnic group. Today even the Jews are called the sons of Abraham, Isaac and Jacob. Therefore the term "kinsmen" (brothers) in this letter is to be understood as indicating a blood relationship between the Jews (Judeans) and Spartans. The indicated kinship may be inferred from what is written about Jason the High priest who went "to the Lacedaemonians, with the hope of obtaining shelter there by reason of their common origin"[5]. As noted by Herodotus (V, 57 ; I, 56: IV, 147), the Spartans – the Lacedemons – were related to the Phoenicians. We may now also understand the kinship between the Spartans and the Jews as indicated in the book of Maccabees, since "Phoenicians" is the name given to the entire nation of Israel

It may be noted here that Neiman[6] derives the name Sepharad (the Hebrew name for Spain) from the name Sparta or Sparda which according to Strabo was the name of a place near Taraco. In course of time this name came to embrace the entire peninsula. According to Neiman Sparta –Lacedemonia was also called Sepharad[7]. Perhaps this will serve to explain the verse in the book of Obadia: "and the captivity of Jerusalem, which is in Sepharad shall possess the cities of the south"[8]. So it is the dispersion of Jerusalem which

---

3   The translator here refers the reader to note no. 7 above.
4   The First Book of Maccabees, 12: 19–23,
5   The Book of Maccabees, II 5: 9. The translator notes here: "Apparently there was a legend that the Lacedaemonians and the Jews were of the same ancestry".
6   Neiman, Sefarad The Name Of Spain, JNES. 1963, pp. 128–132.
7   Neiman, ibid. p. 132
8   Obadiah, 1: 20

is in Sparta which "We remember at every opportunity incessantly on the festivals and at other appropriate days, in the sacrifices which we offer and in the prayers, as it is right and fitting to recall our kinsmen" (Hebrew reads "brothers").

Prof. Slouschz pointed to the many similarities in different spheres between those called Phoenicians and the Israelites. According to him the language is the same language.[9] the culture is the same culture. In his own words: "From the way in which this (culture)emerges before the Hebrew scholar out of numerous texts found at Carthage which were interpreted through Phoenician inscriptions and Israelite literature, Carthaginian civilisation appears to be purely and simply Hebraic."[10] He suggests that the figures of Samson and Joshua have their origine in the same mythical conceptions as does the figure of Melkart in Tyre. The Bull is the Emblem of the Israelite Sun God just as it is of Melkart,[11] The social structure was the same. In Carthage as in Jerusalem there existed a Sanhedrin (a council of 71 elders)[12], In Carthage as in Israel there were Judges (Shofetim) at the head of the nation. The religious structure was also identical. Moreover even linguistic changes and periods of linguistic shifts developed at Carthage parallel to those in Israel[13] Any place originally inhabited by Phoenicians later became inhabited by Jews.

Prof. Slouschz was led to conclude that because of their identical characteristics the so–called Phoenicians and the Hebrews in the days of the Judges formed a single ethnic group.[14] On the other hand he also interpreted the biblical verse "Asher lo horish' the inhabitants of Sidon" etc. as meaning Asher did not conquer these cities. However since the town of Tyre is not mentioned in the list of towns that Asher did not "lehorish" Prof. Slouschz concluded[15] that Tyre was indeed conquered by the Israelites while Sidon was not conquered. This inevitably led him to assume that the Israelites and "Phoenicians" were two different nations and that the many similarities between them resulted because the two nations belonged to a single ethnic group, which group was part of the Benei Kedem (children of the East). He thinks that some of the Hebrews joined with the Phoenicians to form a new race which he labels "Phoenician–Hebrews", with an identical language, script, religion and a homogeneous culture, this new race of "Hebrew–Phoenicians" set out on its travels throughout the Mediterranean and practised commerce

9   Slouschz, La Civilisation Hebraique et Phénicienne A' Carthage
10   Slouschz, ibid. p. 6.
11   Slouschz, Hebreo – Phéniciens et Judeo–Berbères, p. 59.
12   Slouschz, ibid, p. 183. cites Justin. I. 18, 7.
13   Slouschz, La Civilisation Hebraique et Phénicienne A' Carthage, p. 16.
     –Hebreo–Phéniciens et Judeo–Berbères, p. 180.
14   Slouschz, ibid. p. 60.
15   Slouschz, La Civilisation Hebraique et Phénicienne A' Carthage, p. 8.

and established colonies. The religion of these Hebrew–Phoenicians was primitively Jewish notably different from the Jewish religion after the Exile (The Ezra period).[16]

I consider Prof. Slouschz to have been mistaken in his interpretation of the particular biblical verse by his assuming that the Israelites did not conquer Sidon; and this led him to the conclusion that the "Phoenicians" and the "Israelites" were two different nations.

Slouschz is by no means not the only scholar to point to the similarities between the so–called Phoenicians and the Israelites. Most scholars in fact do so, as discussed in previous chapters.

---

16   Slouschz, Hebreo–Phénicens et Judeo–Berbères, pp. 136–137, 448

CONCLUSION

There can be observed a close identity between the so–called "Phoenicians"and the Israelites in all spheres of life and culture, such as language with all its ramifications, religious and social structures, a Sanhedrin (i. e. supreme religious council), the rule of Judges; also in psalmody, mythology, cosmogony, burial rites, tomb forms, tariffs and names of sacrifices, art, monetary system, names of the months, system of weight etc. Along with all this, there existed a parallel identity in historical events: The Israelites conquer the land about the 14th century B. C. (the Amarna Period). There occurred at that time a period of political and cultural changes among the Canaanite population and there were also changes in writing; the rule of Judges is substituted for the rule of kings; moreover names like Rib–Adi (Hadad) change to Rib–Baal indicating substitution of deities (Hadad to Baal) etc.[1], and also we note the first appearance of the name "Phoenicians".

The pinnacle of expansion for the "Phoenician" empire overlaps in time with the Israelite expansion of king Solomon's period.

Those–called "Phoenicians" are supposed to be the inventors of the Alphabetic writing, whereas according to the Talmud Moses was its inventor. Moreover we have already shown in this book that from the Greek alphabeth a rhymed verse having a definite unified meaning in Hebrew, has been derived.

The period of the appearance of the Alphabetic writing among the Israelites is identical with the period when this writing is considered to appear among those–called Phoenicians.

The names of "Phoenician" settlements are identical to those of Israelite cities.

Scholars have treated each sphere and subject separately and explained the identities and similarities by claiming that the Israelite people imitated and borrowed from the "Phoenicians–Canaanites". But is there another instance in history where one nation borrowed from and imitated another nation so completely in all phases of its life and culture? This is not just an imitation

---

1   Warmington, Histoire et Civilisation De Carthage, p. 173.
     Perrot – Chipiez, History of Art In Phoenicia And Its Dependancies, pp. 26–27.

of external forms, but is an "imitation" in every tiny detail and minutae including of historical events and their dates!

We have seen that the Exodus occurred in c. 1446 B. C. and the Israelites in the Amarna period conquered the whole land of Canaan including the region of Sidon and Tyre, which afterwards became known as Phoenicia. This conquest must have brought about political and social changes in the region which are reflected in the changes cited above (writing, names, Judges etc.), and also the appearance of "Phoenician" culture. It thus becomes necessary to draw a demarcation line separating the Canaanite period from the "Phoenician". Clearly Canaanites–Amorites are not Phoenicians . It should be borne in mind that the name "Phoenicians" appears for the first time in history after the Amarna period and there is no basis whatever to link "Canaanites" with "Phoenicians", Hecateus' statement that "Phoenicia was formerly called Chna", along with Philo Byblius' statement that "Chna who was afterwards called Phoinix" brings out this change.

Assembling all the data and treating it as a whole and not as separate items leads one to the inevitable conclusion that Phoenicians was the name given to the Israelites by the Greeks, and moreover there is reason to believe that Herodotus includes the Israelites under the name "Phoenicians". Diodorus Siculus is refering to the origins of the Jewish nation regards them as part of those Phoenicians who did not sail with Cadmos to Greece. The Book of Maccabees refers to the Spartans – Lacedemonians, (who are known to be related to the Phoenicians), as the sons of Abraham and brothers to the Jews. We have seen and discussed the political and religious development within the Israelite nation, a development which led to a political rift and the formation of the Judean nation from within the Israelite one, while the name Phoenicia, which at first was given by the Greeks to the whole Israelite nation, remained attached only to the rejected part (i. e. ten tribes). In the course of time the Judean nation expanded and its borders extended as far as Carmel, Acre etc. The name Phoenicia then was applied only to the coastal strip between Carmel and Aradus. Here most likely is the answer and explanation for Raymond Weill's astonished question: "How is it that the term Phoenicia gradually narrowed down geographically".[2]

---

2   Weill, Phoenicia And Western Asia To The Macedonian Conquest, pp. 15–17.

BIBLIOGRAPHY

Abel, F. M., Les confins de la Palestine et de l'Égypte sous les Ptolémées, RB. 1939, pp. 207–236.

Abramski. S. The Kenites. article in Eretz–Israel edit. Israel Exploration Society, vol. III, 1954. pp. 116–124 (Hebrew)

Aharoni, Y. Eretz Israel in late Canaanite period and the period of the Israelite conquest, 1959, Matkal edit. (Hebrew).

The settlement of Israelite tribes in upper Galilee, Magnes, Jerusalem, 1957. (Hebrew).

Eretz Israel in biblical period–Historical geography. Mosad Bialik, Jerusalem, 1962. (Hebrew)

The conquest of the land, article in: "Iyunim besefer Yehoshua", Kiriat–Sefer, Jerusalem 1960. pp. 8–9. (Hebrew).

Carta's Atlas to Biblical period. Carta, Jerusalem, 1964. (Hebrew).

Albright, W. F., The Archeology of Palestine, Pelican edit. 1951.

The Bible and the Ancient near east, Doublday, 1961.

New Canaanite Historical and Mythological date, BASOR. 63, 1936, pp. 23–32

The town of Selle (Zaru) in the Amarna Tablets, JEA. 1924, pp. 6–8.

The Israelite conquest of Canaan in the light of Archeology, BASOR. 74, 1939, pp. 11–23.

The kyle memorial excavation at Bethel, BASOR. 56, pp. 2–15.

Specimen of late Ugaritic prose, BASOR. 150, 1958, pp. 36–38.

Was the patriarch Terach a canaanite moon god, BASOR. 71, 1938, pp. 35–40.

– Exploring in Sinai with the university of California African Expedition, BASOR, 109, 1948, pp. 5–20.

An early Alphabetic Inscriptions from Sinai and their decipherment, BASOR. 110, 1948, pp. 6–22.

Some important recent discoveries, Alphabetic origins and Idrimi statue, BASOR, 118, 1950, pp. 11–20.

A revision of early Hebrew chronology, JPOS. 1920 – 21, pp. 49–79.

The Amarna letters from Palestine; Syria, the Philistines and Phoenicia, CAH. vol. 2. chap. 20, 33, 1966.

A colony of Cretan mercenaries on the coast of the Negeb, JPOS. 1921, pp. 187–194.

Palestine in the earliest historical period, JPOS, 1922, pp. 110–138.

New light on early Canaanite language and literature, BASOR., 46, 1932, pp. 15–20.

The Egyptian correspondence of Abimilki prince of Tyre, JEA., 1937, pp. 190–203.

Archeology and the date of the Hebrew conquest of Palestine, BASOR, 1935, 58, pp. 10–18.

Recent progress in North canaanite research, BASOR., 70, 1938, pp. 18–24.

The origin of the Alphabeth and ugaritic A. B. C. again, BASOR., 119, 1950, pp. 23–24.

A Hebrew letter from the twelfth century, BASOR., 73, 1939, pp. 9–13.

The north canaanite poems of Al'Eyan Ba'al and the gracious gods, JPOS., 14, 1934, pp. 101–140.

New light on Early History of Phoenician Colonisation, BASOR. 83. 1864. pp. 14–22.

The smaller Beth Shan stele of Sethos I., BASOR. no. 125. Feb. 1952. pp. 24–32.

Astour, M. C., Greek names in the semitic world and semitic names in the Greek world, JNES., 1964, pp. 193 –201.

The origin of the terms Canaan, Phoenician and Purple, JNES. 24, 1965, pp. 346–350.

Atkinson, Alphabeth, EB., 1929 edit.

Atkinson and Whatmough, J., Alphabeth, EB., 1968 edit.

Autran, G., "Phéniciens, Essai de contribution a' l'histoire Antique de la Mediterranée, Geuthner, Paris, 1920.

Avishur Yitschak. Phoenician inscriptions and the Bible. edit. Rubenstein, Jerusalem 1979. (Heb.)

Avi–Yona, M., Phoenician and Jewish Art, article in: Western Galilee and the coast of Galilee, pp. 20–29, IES. Jerusalem, 1965. (Hebrew)

Baedeker's Egypt and the Sudan. Handbook for travelers, Leipzig, 1908, 6th edition.

Bar–Deroma, H., Wezeh Gevul Haares, The true boundaries of the Land according to the sources, Beer, Jerusalem, 1958. (Heb.)

The Negev ; Jerusalem, 1934. (Heb.).

Barnette, R. D., Phoenician – Punic art, pp. 294 – 312. EWA, vol. XI. McGraw – Hill book co., N. Y. 1966, pp. 294–312.

Phoenician and Syrian ivory carving, PEQ., 1939, pp. 4–19.

Phoenicia and the ivory trade, Ar., 1956, Vol. 9; 2, pp. 87–97.

The sea peoples. CAH, vol. 2, chap. 28, 1969.

Phoenicia, EB., 1968 edit.

Barns, H., La révélation du nom divin "Tetragammaton", RB., 1893, pp. 329–350.

Barrois, A. G., Manuel d'archeologie biblique, edit. Picard, 1953.

Barton, G. A., Archeology and the Bible, 7th edit. American Sunday School Union, 1952.

The Habiri of the el Amarna Tablets and the Hebrew conquest of Palestine, JBL., Vol. 48, 1929, pp. 144–148.

Baumgarten, A. I., The Phoenician History of Philo of Byblos, a commentary. Brill – Leiden, 1981.

Baurain, c., Portées chronologique et geographique du terme "Phénicien". Studia Phoenicia

IV. p. 7–28. Namur, 1986.

Benson, J. L., A Problem in orientalizing cretan birds; Mycenean or Philistine prototypes, JNES.

Vol. XX, 2, 1961, pp. 73–84.

Berard, V., De l'origine des cultes arcadiens, Librairie des ecoles francaises d'Athenés et de Rome. edit. Thorin. Paris, 1894.

Les Phéniciens et l'odyssée Tomes I – II, Collin, Paris, 1927.

Le nom des Phéniciens, RHR., 1926, p. 87.

ItaAQUE et la grèce Des Achéen, collin, 1927.

Berard, J. Philistines et Préhellenes, RAr., 37, 1951, pp. 129–142.

Les Hyksos et la légende d'Io, SY., 29, 1952, pp. 1–43.

Berger, P., "Phénicie", article in: "La grande encyclopedie", Tome 26 ième., Paris, pp. 617–623.

Bliss, F. J., A mound of many cities, PEF 2nd. edit., 1898.

Bondi, S. F., The Origins in the East, pp. 28–37 in book: "The Phoenicians". edit. Bompiani, 1988.

– The Course of History, in ibid . pp. 38–45.

Bonfante, G. Who were the Philistines, AJA., 50, 1946, pp. 251–262.

The name of the Phoenicians, classical philology, 36, 1941, pp. 1–20.

Bottero, J. Le problem des Habiru a' la 4e. rencontre assyriologique internationale, Cahiers de la Societé Asiatique, Paris, 1954.

Bourdon, C., La Route de l'Exode de la terre de GESSÉ A Mara, RB., 1932, I– pp. 370– 392, I– 538–549.

Braver, Haharetz, Dvir, 1929. (Hebrew).

Breasted, J. H., Ancient Records of Egypt, Historical documents, University of Chicago press, 1906.

A history of Egypt, N. Y., 1951, 2nd edit.

Bright, J., A history of Israel, London, SC. M. 1960.

Brugsch – Bey H., Egypt under the Pharaohs, Murray, London, 1891.

L'Exode et les monuments Égyptiens, discours prononcé a l'ocassion du Congrès

Internationale d'Orientalistes a' Londres, Leipzig, 1875.

Burney, C. F., Israel settlement in Canaan, the Biblical tradition and its historical background,

Schweich lectures, 1917, Published for British Academy Press by Oxford university, 1921.

Campbell, E. F., The Amarna letters and the Amarna period, BA. Vol. XXIII, (1), 1960, pp. 2–22.

Cantineau, J., La langue de Ras Shamra, SY., XIII, 1932, p. 164.

La langue de Ras Shamra, SY., XXI, 1940, pp. 38–61

Carpenter, R., Phoenicians in the West, AJA, Vol. 62, 1958, pp. 35–53

Cassuto, M. D., Parallel words in Hebrew and Ugaritic, Leshonenu, vol. 15, 1947, pp. 97–102. (Hebrew).

Biblical literature and Ugaritic literature, Tarbitz, 13, 1942, pp. 197–217; Tarbitz, 14, 1943,

pp. 1–10 . (Hebrew).

Biblical Encyclopedia, entry: Baal. (Hebrew).

A commentary on the Book of Exodus, Magnes press, Jeruslem, 1965, 4th edit. (Hebrew)

Cazelles, H., Essai sur le pouvoir de la Divinité á Ugarit et en Israel, Ugaritica, VI, paris. 1969.

Les localisations de l'Exode et la critique literaire, RB. Tome LXII, 1955, pp. 321–364.

Hebrew, Ubru et Ḥapiru, SY., XXXV, 1958, pp. 198–217.

Chadwick, J., The prehistory of the Greek language, CAH., vol. II. 1963.

Champollion, le jeune, Dictionnaire Egyptien, Paris, Didot freres, MDCCCXLI.

Chehab, M. E., Sarcophages en plomb, Musée National Libanais, SY., XV, 1934, pp. 337–350.

Chester, Gr. J., Notes on some Phoenician gems, PEQ. 1885, pp. 129–132.

More notes on Phoenician gems and Amulets, PEQ., 1886, pp. 43–50.

A journey to the Biblical sites in Lower Egypt, etc., PEP. 1880, pp. 133–158.

Notes on the topography of the Exodus, PEP. 1881, pp. 104–110

Chiera, E., Ḥabiru and Hebrews, AJSLL., 1932–33, pp. 115–124.

Chomsky, W. Hebrew the eternal language edit. Rubin Mass, Jerusalem, 1972. (Hebrew)

Cintas, P., Tarsis–Tartessos–Gades, Semitica, XVI, 1966, pp. 5–37.

Clarke, C. P., The Exodus, PEP., 1883, pp. 90–96.

The route of the Exodus, PEP., 1883, pp. 225–236.

C. M. W., The Exodus, PEP., 1883, pp. 98–100.

Cohen, M. La grande invention de l'ecriture et son evolution, Paris, Klincksieck, 1958.

Colb, N. Topography of the Jews of medieval Egypt, JNES., XXIV, 1965, pp. 251–270.

Conder, R. C., The Date of the Exodus, PEQ. 1896, pp. 255–258.

Topography of the Exodus, PEP., 1880, pp. 231–234.

The Onomasticon, PEQ., 1896, pp. 229–245.

Notes (on Philistines), PEQ., 1896, p. 341.

The Hebrew Months, PEQ., 1889, pp. 21–24.

Note on the supposed date of the Exodus, in book TEAT Published by P. E. F. 1893.,

Appendix pp. 191–193.

The Exodus, PEF., 1883, pp. 79–90.

The Canaanites, PEP., 1887, pp. 227–231.

The Syrian Language, PEF. 1896, pp. 60–77.

Phoenician Notes, PEF. 1889, pp. 142–145.

The Alphabeth, PEF. Vol. XI, 1889, pp. 17–20.

Kadesh Barnea, PEQ., 1885, pp. 21–25.

Notes (on Phoenician Antiquities), PEP., 1886, pp. 15–19.

Syrian Stone Lore, or the monumental history of Palestine, edit. PEF, 1896.

The Hebrew of the Tell Amarna Letters, PEP, 1891–2, p. 251.

The ten tribes, PEP., 1888, pp. 144–150.

Lieutenant Conder Reports, PEP., 1881, pp. 158–208.

Notes, PEF., 1891, p. 72.

Baal Gad, PEP., Vol. xii. 1891, p. 251.

Monumental notice of Hebrew victories, PEP., 1890, pp. 326–329.

Notes (Alosha, Tarsis), PEP., 1892, pp. 44–45.

Phoenician Inscription from Joppa PEP., 1892, p. 171.

The Tell Amarna Tablets (TEAT), PEF. edit. 1893.

Notes, PEF., 1896, pp. 168–171.

Contenau, G. La civilisation Phénicienne, Paris, Payot, 1949.

–Deuxième mission archeologique à Sidon, SY., IV, 1924, p. 16.

Manuel d'Archeologie Orientale, Edit. A. Picard, 1927.

Coode, J., The passage of the Israelites across the Red Sea, PEP., 1885, pp. 97–99.

Cook, S. A., Notes on Excavation (Jericho), PEQ., 1926, pp. 206–214.

Phoenicia, EB. edit. 1929.

Carthage and Gezer, PEP., 1906, pp. 159–160.

Courtois. J. C., The Excavations at Ugarit 1929–1966, Qadmoniot Vol. II, 1969, 3 (7). pp. 74–83. (Hebrew).

Cowley, A. E., The origin of the Semitic Alphabeth, JEA. 1916, pp. 17–21.

The Sinaitic inscriptions, JEA., Vol. XV, 1929, pp. 200–218.

Crace, J. D., The route of the Exodus, PEQ., 1915. pp. 64–66.

Cross, F. M. Jr. Notes on a canaanite psalm in the Old Testament, BASOR., 117, 1950, pp. 19–21.

The evolution of the proto– canaanite alphabeth, BASOR., 134; 1954, p. 15–24.

The Origin and Early Evolution of the Alphabet, pp. 17–18, in Western Galilee and the Coast

of Galilee, 19th Archeological convention 1963, Jerusalem, 1965, (Hebrew).

Crowfoot, J. W., On the Ivories from Samaria, JPOS., 1933, pp. 121–127.

Culican. W., Carthage, EB., edit. 1968.

The first merchant venturers, Thames and Hudson, 1966, London

Cesnola Bowl 4555 and Other Phoenician Bowls, Opera Selecta from Tyre to Tartessos.

Goteborg, 1986.

Dahood, M., Ugaritic – Hebrew philology, Pontifical Biblical Inst. Rome, 1965.

Danby, H., Translation –The Mishna, Oxford University Press, London, Geoffrey Cumberlege. 1954.

Del–Medico, H. E., La Bible Canaaneèn, Paris, Payot, 1950.

De la Jonquière, C., L'Expedition d'Egypte 1798–1801, edit. Lavauzelle, Paris.

Della Vida G. Levi, "Fenici", Enciclopedia Italiana, Di scienze, Lettere Ed Arti. publicata sotto L'alto

Patronato di S. M. il Re d'Italia, edizioni instituto. CMXXXII ., Treves–Trecani, 1932.

De Rougé, E., Memoire sur l'origine Egptiènne de l'alphabeth Phénicien, 1874.

De Tillesse, G. M., Section "Tu" et "Vous" dans le Deuteronome, VT., XII, 1962, pp. 29–87.

De Vaux, R., Le problem des Ḥapiru après quinze anneèes, JNES., 1968, pp. 221–228.

El et Baal, le Dieu des Pères et YaHweh, Ugaritica, VI, pp. 501–517.

Les Patriarches Hébreux et les Decouvertes modernes, RB., 1948, pp. 321– 347.

Dhorme, E., Les peuples issus de Japhet d'après le chapitre X de la Genèse, SY., XIII, 1932, p. 46.

La question des Ḥabiri, RHR., 1938, (118), pp. 170–187.

Les Nouvelles Tablettes d'El Amarna, RB., 1924, pp. 5–32.

Les Ḥabiru et les Hebreux, JPOS. IV, 1924, pp. 162–168.

Le Dechiffrement des tablettes de Ras Shamra, JPOS., XI, 1931, pp. 1–6.

Le pays Biblique au Temp d'El Amarna. RB., 1909, pp. 50–73.

La langue de Canaan, RB., X, 1913, pp. 369– 393 ; RB., XI, 1914, pp. 344–372.

Première traduction des textes phéniciens de Ras Shamra, RB. 1931, pp. 32–56.

Un Nouvel Alphabet semitique, RB., 1930, pp. 571–577.

Diodorus Siculus, translation Oldfather, C. H., Harvard University Press, Heinemann, London.

Translated by Walton. Edit Heinemann, London, MCMLXVII.

Diringer, D., The origins of the Alphabet, Antiquity, 1943, pp. 77–90.

The Early Greek Alphabets, Antiquity, 1963, pp. 270–273.

The story of the Aleph Beth, Thomas Yoseloff, 1960.

The Palestinian Inscription and the origin of the Alphabeth, JAOS., (63), 1943, pp. 24–30.

Writing, Thames and Hudson, 1962.

The Early Hebrew Book Hand, PEQ., 1935, p. 16.

The Alphabeth a key to history of Mankind, 2nd edit., Philosophical library, N. Y. 1953.

Biblical study and the archaeological research, Eretz Israel, vol. III, 1954, p. 42. (Hebrew).

Dothan T., The Philistines and their material culture, Bialik Inst. and the I. E. S. Jerusalem, 1967. (Hebrew).

Driver, G. R., Semitic writing from pictograph to Alphabeth, Schweich Lectures, 1944, London, edit. 1948.

Jehovah, EB., 1929 edit.

Ugaritic and Hebrew words, Ugaritica. (VI), (tome XVII), Mission de Ras Shamra, Institut

Francais d'Archeologie de Beyrouth, Paris, 1969.

Canaanite myths and legends, Old Testament Studies, (3), 1956

Dunand, M. Byblia Grammata, Tome II, Beyrouth, 1945,

Dussaud, R., Breves remarques sur les Tablettes de Ras Shamra, SY., XII, 1931, pp. 67–77.

Ras Shamra, AAA. 1934,, pp. 93–98.

Melquart, SY., XXV, 1946 – 48, pp. 205–230.

YaHwe Fils de El, Sy., XXXIV, 1957, pp. 232–242.

Notes, PEQ., 1936, p. 54.

Les Inscriptions Phéniciennes du Tombeau d'Ahiram, SY., V, 1924. p. 152.

Bibliographie, SY., 1925, p. 195.

L'origin de l'Alphabeth et son evolution première d'après les decouvertes de Byblos, Sy,

XXV, 1946– 48, pp. 36–52.

La Notion d'âme chez les Israelites et les Phéniciens, SY. XVI, 1935, pp.

267–277.

Les origines Cananèen du sacrifice Israelite, Paris. 1921.

Observation sur la céramique du 2e millenaire avant notre ère, SY., IX, 1928, pp. 131–150.

Note Additionelle, SY., XVI, 1935, pp. 346–352.

Cultes Cananeen aux sources du Jourdain, SY., XVII, 1936, pp. 283–295.

Ebers, G., Egypt– Descriptive, Historical, and Picturesque. Translated from the original german by Clara Bell with an introduction and note by S. Birch; Cassel, Petter Galpin & Co. London, Paris and New York, 1887.

Eissfeldt, O., The beginnings of Phoenician epigraphy according to a letter written by Wilhelm Gesenius in 1835, PEQ. 1947, p. 69.

The Exodus and Wanderings, CAH. 1975, ch. xxvi. P. 321 ff Engelbach, R., The Egyptian name of Joseph, JEA., (X), 1924, pp. 204–206.

Eusebii Pamphilli, Episcopi Caesariensis – Onomasticon, edit. Larsow & Parthey; Williams & Nortgate, London, 1862.

Evans, Sir Arthur, The Palace of Minos at Knossos, MacMillan, London, 1921.

Faulkner, R. O., Egypt from the inception of the nineteenth Dynasty to the death of Ramesses III, CAH., (52), Vol. II. Chap. XXIII, 1966.

Flavius Josephus, Jewish Antiquities, English translation by Thackeray and R. Marcus. The Loeb Classical Library, Harvard University Press, London, W. Heinemann, MCML.

Jewish Antiquities, Hebrew translation by A. Shalit, Bialik Inst. – Masada. 1944.

Contra Apionem, Hebrew translation by Simhoni, Masada, 1959.

Against Apion, Harvard University press, London, Heinemann, MCMLVI

The Jewish wars (against the Romans) Hebrew translation by Simhoni, Y. N. Masada, 1961.

The Jewish wars, English Tran. London, Heinemann, MCMLVI.

Freedman, D. N., The name of the god of Moses, JBL., vol. 79. 1960, pp. 151–156.

Freud, S., Moise et le Monotheism, nrf., Gallimard, 1958.

Furumark, A., The settlement at Ialysos and Aegean History, c. 1550–1400 B. C., OA. vol. VI, 1950, pp. 150–2

Ganneau, C. Notes, PEQ., 1896, pp. 259–261.

Hiram king of Tyre, PEQ. 1880, pp. 174–181.

Ganor, N. R. The Lachish Letters, PEQ., 1967.

Who invented the Alphabet, Bulletin 12, 1970, Museum Haaretz Tel–Aviv, Israel

Who were the Phoenicians, "Ot". Geneva, 1952. (Hebrew).

Who were the Phoenicians, authors' edit. Israel, 1962. (Heb.)

Who were the Phoenicians, Reshafim edit. Israe, 1974. (Heb.)

Garbini, G. The question of the Alphabet, pp. 86–103 in book, "The Phoenicians", edit. bompiani, 1988.

Gardiner, A. A., Tanis and Pi Ra'messe, a Retractation, JEA, XIX. 1933, pp. 122–128.

The geography of the Exodus, an answer to Prof. Naville and others, JEA. vol. X, 1924,

pp. 87–96.

The geography of the Exodus etc., pp. 203–215 in Recueil d'etudes Egyptologique dedié a la memoire de J. F. Champollion, Bibliotheque de l'école Des hautes etudes . Paris, 1922.

The Sinai Script and the origin of the Alphabeth, PEQ. 1929, pp. 48–55.

The Egyptian origin of the Semitic Alphabeth, JEA, 1916, pp. 1–16.

Garstang, J., A third season at Jericho; city and Necropolis, PEQ., 1932, pp. 149–153.

The Archeology of Palestine and the Bible, PEQ. 1932, pp. 221–230.

The story of Jericho, PEQ. 1941, pp. 168–171.

Joshua–Judges, London, Constable & co., 1931.

The fall of Bronze Age Jericho, PEQ., 1935, pp. 61–68.

The walls of Jericho, PEQ, 1931, pp. 186–196.

Sir Charles Marston's Expedition of 1930, PEQ, 1930, pp. 123–133.

The date of destruction of Jericho, PEQ., 1927, pp. 96–100.

Garstang – Rowe, The ruins of Jericho (a letter to the editor), PEQ., 1936, p. 170.

Gaster, Th., The Chronology of Palestinian Epigraphy, 1) PEQ., 1935, pp. 128–140, 2) PEQ., 1937, pp. 43–58.

Ras Shamra 1929 – 39, Antiquity, XIII. 1939, pp. 304–319.

Ugaritic Philology, JAOS., Vol. 70, 1950, pp. 8–18.

The Ras Shamra Texts and the Old Testament, PEQ. 1934, pp. 141–146.

Geheman, H. S. Manuscripts of the Old Testament in Hebrew, BA., Vol. viii. 1945, pp. 100–103.

Gelb. I. J. A study of Writing. Phoenix Books, university of Chicago press 2nd. edit. 1962.

Gell, F., The Exodus, PEP, 1883, pp. 96–98.

Gerleman, G., The song of Deborah in the light of stylistics, VT. Vol. I. 1951, pp. 168–180.

Gesenius. Gesenius' Hebrew Grammar, edit., by Kautsch, 2nd. English edit., revised by Cowley, Oxford – clarendon press, 1960.

Hebrew and English Lexicon of the Old Testament, Oxford, 1968.

Hebräisches und Aramäisches Handwörterbuch uber Das Alte Testament, 13e Auflage, Leipzig, 1899.

Hebräisches und Chaldäisch Handwörterbuch uber das Alte Testament, 7e Auflage, Leipzig 1868.

Hebrew–Chaldee Lexicon to the Old Testament, translated by Samuel Prideaux Tregelles. Baker Book House. Michigan. 1982.

Gibson, D., Correspondence, PEQ., 1936, p. 102.

Gibson, J. C. L., Textbook of Syrian Semitic Inscriptions, Vol. I, Clarendon, Oxford, 1971.

Ginsberg, H. L. Ugaritic Studies and the Bible, BA., VIII, (2) 1945, pp. 1–58.

Interpreting Ugaritic Texts, JAOS, (70) 1950, pp. 156–160.

The Ugarit Texts, Bialik Foundation, Jerusalem, 1936. (Heb.).

Ugaritic Studies and the Bible in The Biblical Archaeologist Reader vol. II Anchor books 1964. edited by E. F. Campbell & D. N. Freedman.

Goetze, A., The city Khalbi and the Khapiru people, BASOR., 1940, (79), pp. 32–34.

Goitein, S. D., YHWH the passionate, the monotheistic meaning and origin of the name YHWH., VT., VI, 1956, pp. 1–9.

Gordon, C. H., The Role of the Philistines, Antiquity, (vol. XXX), 1956, pp. 22–26.

Ugarit and the Minoan Crete, the bearing of their Texts on the origin of western culture, Norton, 1966.

Before The Bible, Am Oved – Dvir, Israel, 1966. (Heb. Trans.).

Grace, V. R., The Canaanite Jar, pp. 80 – 109, in: The Aegean and the Near East studies presented to Hetty Goldman on the ocassion of her 75th birthday, Weinberg, Augustin. N. Y. 1956.

Graves, R., The White Goddess, Faber & Faber, London, 1960.

Gray, J., The God YW in the religion of Canaan, JNES., 1953, pp. 278–283.

The Legacy of Canaan, supplement to VT. (V), 1957.

Greenberg, M. The Hab/piru, American Oriental Series Vol. 39. American Oriental Society 1955.

Greene, J. Baker, The Route of the Exodus, PEP., 1885, pp. 67–73.

The Route of the Exodus, PEP., 1884, pp. 230–237.

Greenfield, J. C., entry "Philistines", in the Interpreters' dictionary of the Bible, Abingdon press, N. Y., 1962.

Griffith, G., The Egyptian derivation of the name Moses, JNES. 1953, (vol. XII), pp. 225 – 231.

Grinz, I. M. in "Iyunim Besefer Yehoshua", Israel Society for Biblical Research, 1960. (Hebrew)

Guillaume, A., The Habiru, Hebrews and the Arabs, PEQ., 1946, pp. 64–85.

Halevi, J., Nouvelles considerations sur l'origin de l'Alphabeth, RS., 1901, (IX), pp. 356 – 370.

Hall, H. R., Annual Meeting (Philistines), PEQ, 1923, pp. 124–133.

The Keftiu Fresco in the tomb of Senmut, BSA . (X), 1903 – 4, pp. 154–157.

The peoples of the sea a chapter of the History of Egyptoplogy, pp. 297–329 in Recueil d'Etudes Égyptologique Dedieés a' la memoire de J. F. Champollion, Paris, 1922.

Keftiu and the peoples of the sea, BSA, VIII, 1901– 2, pp. 157–189.

Hallock. F. H., The Habiru and the Sa. gaz in the Tell El Amarna Tablets, in Mercer, TEAT, 1939, Excursus VII, pp. 838–845.

Haran, M. The Routes of the Exodus, article in Tarbitz, 1971, pp. 113–143. (Hebrew).

Harden, D. The Phoenicians, Thames and Hudson, 1962.

The Phoenicians on the west coast of Africa, Antiquity, vol. XXII. 1948, (87), pp. 141–150.

Harris, Z. S., A grammar of the Phoenician Language, American Oriental Series, 1936.

Hayes, W. C., Most Ancient Egypt, JNES, 1964.

Haynes, A. E., The Route of the Exodus, PEP., 1896, pp. 175–185.

The Date of the Exodus PEP, 1896, pp. 245–255.

Headlam, A. C., Sixty sixth Annual Meeting–The Bible as an Historical source, PEQ., 1931, pp. 121–138.

Held, M., The Active Result (Factitive–Passive) sequence of identical verbs in biblical Hebrew and Ugaritic, JBL. 1965, vol. LXXXIV. pp. 272–282.

Herm Gerhard, The Phoenicians, English trans. William Morrow & co. New York 1975.

Herodotus, The Histories., New edition. Penguin Classics. translated by Aubry de Selincourt, revised, by John Marincolor. 1996.

Herodotus, The History of, Translated by G. Rawlinson, edit. Komroff. Tudor Pub. N. Y. 1947.

Herodotus, Translation by Godley, A. D., Loeb Classical Library. Harvard University Press, London, Heinemann, MCMXLVI.

Herodotus, Hebrew translation by Shorr, A. Jerusalem, Mass, 1934.

Heurtley, W. A., The relationship between "Philistine"and Mycenaean Pottery, QDAP., 1936, pp. 90–110.

Hooke, S. H., The origins of early Semitic Ritual, Schweich Lectures, 1935, edit. 1938.

Hours – Miëdan, M. Carthage, Presse Universitaire de France, 1949.

Hull, E., On the relations of land and sea in the Isthmus of Suez at the time of the Exodus, PEP, 1884, pp. 137–141.

–The Route of the Exodus, PEP, 1885, pp. 65–67.

–Narrative of an expedition through Arabia Petrae, PEP., 1884, pp. 114–136.

Hutchinson, R. F., The Exode, PEP., 1887, pp. 239–250.

Hyatt, Ph. J., Yahweh as "The God of my Father", VT. (V), 1955, pp. 130–136.

Hygini Fabulae, H. I. Rose, Lvgdvni Batavorum 1933, Sythoff, Leyden

Isserlin, B. S. J., The Israelite Conquest of Canaan: A Comparative Review of the Arguments Applicable. PEQ. 1983. pp. 85–94.

Jack, J. W. The Date of the Exodus in the light of external evidence, edit. Clark, 1925.

New light on the Habiru – Hebrew question, PEQ. 1940. pp. 95–113.

Jannāh Rabbi Yonah Ibn., (Abu- l Walid Marwan; died 11th century), Sefer Hashorashim, (Kitab al Usul), Berlin 1896. Co. Mekizei Nirdamim, Photocopy Jerusalem 1966. (Hebrew).

Sefer Harikma (Kitab al–ulama), Vilenski, Hebrew language Academy, Jerusalem 1964.

• (Hebrew).

Perush lekitvei Hakodesh, (Exegesis to the O. T). Heb. assembled by A. Z. Rabinovitch, Tel–Aviv. 1926.

Javis, C. S., The Forty Years' Wanderings of the Israelites, PEQ. 1938, pp. 25–41.

Jean, Ch., F. Les Hyksos sont ils les inventeurs de l'Alphabeth. SY . (IX), 1928, pp. 278–299.

Josephus Flavius, See Flavius Josephus.

Kahana, A. The Apocrypha, Masada, Tel–Aviv 1959. (Hebrew).

Kaufman Y., The biblical account of the conquest of Palestine, Magness, Jerusalem, 1953.

Kapelrud, A. S., Phoenicia, The Interpreters' Dictionary of The Bible, N. Y. Abingdon, 1962.

The Ras Shamra Discoveries and the Old Testament, Basil – Blackwel, Oxford, 1965.

Katzenstein, H. Y., Hiram I and The Israelite Kingdom, Beth Mikra quarterly, Vol. 28 (4), 1966, pp. 28 –61, (Hebrew).

Kent, Ch. F., Biblical geography and History, Edit. Elder, London, 1911.

Kenyon, K. M., Excavations at Jericho, 1952, PEQ. 1952, pp. 62–82.

Kittel, R., The Religion of The People of Israel Translated – Caryl Micklem. London, Allen & Unwin ltd. 1925.

Klausner. J. Kitvei Kodshenu, pp. 180–220; New investigation and old sources, edit. Massada 1957. (Heb.)

Knudtzon, J. A., Die El Amarna Tafeln, Hinrichs, Leipzig, 1915.

Kohler, L., Lexikologisch geographisches, ZDPV, (62), 1939, pp. 115–120.

Kon, M. The Menorrah of the Arch of Titus, PEQ. 1950, pp. 25–30.

Kraeling, E. G., The origin of the name "Hebrews", AJSL. 1941, pp. 237–253.

Light from Ugarit on the Khabiru, BASOR. (77), 1940, pp. 32–33.

Aram and Israel, Columbia University Oriental Studies, Vol. XIII, AMS. press. 1966.

Lagrange, R. P., L'Itineraire des Israelites du pays de Gessen aux bords du Jourdain, RB. (1) 1900, pp. 63–86.

Introduction Au livre des Juges, RB. 1902, pp. 5–30.

Lambdin, T. O., Alphabet, article in The Interpreters' Dictionary of the Bible. N. Y. Abingdon, Nashville, 1962.

Langdon, S., Babylonian Menalogies and the Semitic Calendars, Schweich Lectures, 1933, The British Academy, London 1935.

Laredo A. I. y Maeso David Gonzalo – El Nombre de "Sefarad" ; Revista de la Escuela De Estudios Hebraicos año iv, Madrid 1944, Fasc. 2. ; laredo – pp. 349– 358; Maseo – Pp. 359–363.

Leibovitz, J. Sinai and Midian, Journal of the Jewish Palestine Exploration Society, Jerusalem 1934, pp. 117–144. (Hebrew).

Lemaire, A. ; Divinités Égyptienne Dans L'onomastique Phénicienne – Studia Phoenicia. IV. pp. 87–98. société des Études classiques, Namur, 1986.

Lenormant, F., entry – Alphabetum, pp. 188–218, Dictionnaire des Antiquités Grecques et Romaines, sous la direction de Ch. Darenberg et E. Saglio, Paris, Hachette, 1877.

Lepsius, R., Letters from Egypt, Ethiopia and the peninsula of Sinai with extracts from his chronology of the Egyptians, with reference to the Exodus of the Israelites, Translated By Leonora and Johanna Horner . MDCCLIII. Henry. Bohn. London. .

Lidzbarski, M.; Handbuch der Nordsemitischen Epigraphik (I–text), G. Olms, Hildesheim, 1962.

Alphabet, article in The Jewish Encyclopedia, 1916, p. 439.

Livor, J. The character of the sources in the Book of Joshua, related to their historical aspects, Iyunim Besefer Yehoshua, pp. 42–70, Kiryat – Sefer, 1959, Israel (Hebrew).

Lods, A. Israël, des origines au milieu du VIII siècle, Edit. Albin Michel ; Paris 1949.

Les Prophètes D'Israël et les débuts du Judaism, Edit. La renaissance du livre, Paris, 1935.

Loewenstamm, S. E., The tradition of the Exodus in its Development, Magnes, Jerusalem, 1965; 2nd edit. 1972. (Hebrew).

Ugaritic Literature and the Bible, Qadmoniot, Vol. II, 3 (7), 1969, pp.

83–88. (Hebrew).

New light on the History of the Alphabeth, Israel Exploration Society, 1951, Vol. XVI, 3, 4, pp. 32–36.

Lucas, A. The route of the Exodus of the Israelites from Egypt. Edward Arnold, London, 1938.

The number of Israelites at the Exodus, PEQ., 1944, pp. 164–168.

The Date of the Exodus, PEQ., 1941, pp. 110=112.

Macalister. R. A. S., The Philistines, their History and Civilisation, The Schweich Lectures 1911, Argonaut Inc. 1965.

Maccabees, The first Book of Maccabees, an English Translation, by S. Tedesche, Introduction and commentary by S. Zeitlin, Harper & Brothers, N. Y. 1950.

Maclaurin, E. C. B., YHWH, the origin of the Tetragammaton, VT. (vol. VII), 1962, pp. 439–463.

Maisler, B., Canaan and Canaanites, BASOR., 102, 1946, pp. 7–12.

Mallon, A., Les Hebreux en Egypte, Orientalia, (3), 1921.

Les Hyksos et les Hebreux, JPOS (V), 1925, pp. 85–91.

Marston Sir Ch., The Bible comes alive, Spottiswoode, London, 1937.

The Bible is true, Eyre and Spotiswoode, London, 1934.

Masar . B. The sancturay of Arad and the family of Hobab the Kenite. JNES. XXIV, 1965, pp. 297–303.

The Philistines and the foundation of the kingdoms of Israel and Tyre, pp. 1–17 in Vol. I, Proceeding of the Israel Academy of Sciences and Humanities, 1966. (Hebrew).

The Phoenicians on the Eastern Shore of the Mediterranean Sea, pp. 1–16 in: Western Galilee and the coast of Galilee, The 19th Archaeological convention, 1963, Israel Exploration Society, Jerusalem 1965. (Hebrew).

Masar – Shapira, Atlas for biblical period, 1957. (Hebrew).

Maspero, G., Egypt, Syria, and Assyria, The struggle of the Nations, Society for promoting Christian Knowledge, 2nd. edit., Sayce, London, 1910.

Histoire Ancienne des peuples de l'Orient, 7e. edit. Hachette, Paris 1905.

May, H. G., Moses and the Sinai Inscriptions, BA. 1945, (VIII) p. 93.

The ten lost tribes, BA . (VI), 1943, pp. 55–60.

Mazza. F., The Phoenicians as Seen by The Ancient World, pp. 548–567 in book, "The Phoenicians", edit. Bompiani, 1988.

McCown, Ch. Ch., The Ladder of Progress in Palestine, Harper, 1943

Meek, Th. J., Hebrew Origins, Harper Torchbooks, N. Y. 1960.

The Israelite Conquest of Ephraim, BASOR. (61), 1936, p. 17–19.

Mendels. D., Hellenistic Writers of the Second Century B. C. on the Hiram–Solomon Relatiomship. pp. 429–441 in Studia Phoenicia, Leuven,

1983.

Mendenhall. G. E. The Hebrew Conquest of Palestine. BA. (XXV), 3, 1962, pp. 66–87.

Mercer, S. A. B. The Tell El Amarna Tablets, Macmillan, Toronto, 1939.

Miller, J. M., Archaeology and the Israelite Conquest of Canaan: Some Methodological Observations. pp. 87– 93, PEQ. 1977.

Mishna, The Mishna translation, Danby, H. Oxford University Press, London, Geoffrey Cumberlege, 1954.

Montet, P. L'origine Egyptiénne de l'Alphabeth Phénicien, in Byblos et l'Egypte, Quatre campagnes de fouilles a Gebeil, 1921–2–3–4. Bibliothéque archeologique et Historique, tome XI, Geuthner, Paris 1928.

Montgomery, J. A. and Harris, Z. S., The Ras Shamra Mythological Texts, The American Philosophical Society, 1935.

Moscati Sabatino, The world of the Phoenicians, English trans., Weidenfeld–Nicolson, London, 1968. — The Canaanites and the Aramaeans. pp. 194–223 in book The face of the ancient orient, Routledge & kegan 1960.

A Civilisation Rediscovered, pp. 16–23 in Book "The Phoenicians" edit. Bompiani, 1988.

Who were the Phoenicians, pp. 24–25 in ibid.

The carthaginian empire, pp. 54–61 in ibid.

Colonisation of the Mediterranean, pp. 46–53. in ibid

Moyal, D., Or Mimizrah, Commentary on the Book of Genesis, Tel–Aviv, 1941. (Hebrew).

Muhly, D. J., Homer and the Phoenicians, Berytus – Archeological studies, Vol. XIX, 1970, pp. 19–64.

Murray, Egypt, Murray's Handbook for Travellers, 8th edit. 1891.

Naish, J. P., The Ras Shamra Tablets, PEQ., 1932, pp. 154–163.

Naville, E. The Geography of the Exodus, JEA. (X), 1924, pp. 18–39.

The Egyptian name of Joseph, JEA. (XII), 1926, pp. 16–18.

The Exodus, and the crossing of the Red Sea, article in Illustrated Bible Treasury, p. 165, Edit. W. Wright, London, Nelson and Sons, 1896.

Neiman, D., Carchêdôn – New City, JNES, 1966, pp. 42–47.

Phoenician Place Names, JNES., vol. XXIV. 1965, pp. 113–115.

Sefarad, The name of Spain, JNES., vol. XXII. 1963, pp. 128–132.

Nelson, H. H., et al. Medinet Habu, Vol. I. University of Chicago, 1930.

Noth, M. Exodus, S. C. M. press 1962

Oberman, J., Ugaritic Mythology, Yale University Press, 1948

Oesterley, W. O. E and Robinson, Th. H., A History of Israel, Oxford, Clarendon press, 1955.

Hebrew Religion, its origin and development, London, Society for

Promoting Christian Knowledge, 1940.

Offord, J., Archaeological Notes on Jewish Antiquities, the semitic name of Pithom, PEQ., 1919, p. 182—184.

Archaeological Notes, PEQ. 1920, pp. 77–78.

On Anu, Heliopolis in a semitic inscription and the Gilgals and Massebatu of Palestine, PEQ., 1919, pp. 123–133.

The Red Sea, PEQ., 1920, pp. 176–181.

Babylonian and Hebrew Theophoric names, PEQ., 1916, pp. 85–94

The localities of the Exodus and a new Egyptian Papyrus, PEQ., 1912, pp. 202–205.

Archaeological Notes on Jewish Antiquities, PEQ. 1917, pp. 94–103.

The mountain throne of Jahve, PEQ, 1919.

Palmer, E. H. The desert of the Exodus, parts I+II, Cambridge, Deighton Bell, London, Bell & Daldy 1871.

Parzen, H., The problem of the Ibrim (Hebrews) in the Bible, AJSL. 1932–33, pp. 254–261.

Patai, R., The Goddess Ashera, JNES, XXIV, 1965, pp. 1—2.

Paton. L. B."Phoenicians" article in Encyclopaedia of Religion and Ethics. edit. by James Hastings New York, c. Scribners, sons.

Peet, T. E., Egypt and the Old Testament, The University Press of Liverpool, London, Hodder and Stoughton, MCMXXII.

Perrot G. –Chipiez Ch., History of Art in Phoenicia and its dependencies, Vol. II, Chapman and Hall, 1885.

Petrie, F., Egypt and Israel, London, Society for Promoting Christian Knowledge, 3rd reprint 1912.

Researches in Sinai London, John Murray, 1906.

The Date of the Exodus, PEF., 1896, pp. 335–337.

Hyksos and Israelite Cities, British School of Archaeology in Egypt, London, 1906.

Revision of History, Ancient Egypt, Mars 1936.

Palestine and Israel, Historical Notes, London, Society for Promoting Christian Knowledge, 1934.

A History of Egypt, Methuen, London 1895.

The formation of the Alphabet, BSAE (Vol. III), Macmillan, London, 1912.

Phytian–Adams, W. J. Aiguptos: A Derivation and some suggestions, JPOS., Vol. II, 1922, pp. 94–100.

Mirage in the Wilderness, PEQ. 1935, pp. 69–78; 114–127.

Jericho, Ai and the occupation of Mount Ephraim, PEQ. 1936, pp. 141–149.

Israelite Tradition and the date of Joshua, PEQ., 1927, pp. 34–47.

Pilcher, E., Weight of Ancient Palestine, Coinage and Weights, PEQ., 1912, pp. 136–144.

Pliny, Pliny Natural History, English translation, Eicholz D. E. The Loeb Classical Library, London, Heinemann, 1961.

Prignaud, J. Caftorim et Kerétim, RB. (71), 1964, pp. 215–229.

Pritchard, J. B., Ancient Near Eastern Texts relating to the Old Testament, Princeton, 1950 (ANET).

Ancient Near East, 2 Vol. An Anthology of Texts and Pictures, Princeton Paperback print 1973, (ANE).

Archaeology and the Old Testament, Princeton University Press, 1958.

Pyres, Philistine Graves in Gezer, PEQ, 1907, pp. 240–243.

Rawlinson, "Phoenicia", The story of the Nations, London – N . Y. 1889, 2nd. edit.

Raymond, A., The divine name Yahweh, JBL, LXXX, 1961, pp. 320–328.

rayney, A. F. A social structure of Ugarit, Hebrew translation, Bialik inst. Jerusalem, 1967.

Redford, D. B., Exodus I 11, VT. (XIII), 1963, pp. 401–418.

Some observations on Amarna chronology, JEA (45), 1959. pp. 34–37.

Reinach, M. S., L'Arc de Titus, conference faite a' la société des études juives, le 3 Mai 1890, REJ. 1890, pp. LXV–XCI.

Renan, E., Histoire du Peuple d'Israel, 2e. edit., Calman – Levy, Paris, 1891.

Reuveni, A. Kadmut Haivrim, Mass. edit. Jerusalem, 1962 (Hebrew).

Ribichini. S., Beliefs and Religious life, pp. 104–125 In "The Phoenicians", edit. Bompiani, 1988.

Questions De Mythlogie Phénicienne D'après Philon de Byblos. Studia Phoenicia IV. Pp. 41–52. Société des Études Classique. Namur 1986.

Rin. Z. Acts of the gods (Alilot Haelim), The Ugaritic epic Poetry, Israel Society for biblical research, (Heb.) 1968.

The Third Column of Acts of the Gods. Inbal. Philadelphia 1992.

Robert, Ch., La Révélation du nom divin JEHOVAH, RB., 1894, pp. 161–181.

Robinson, E., Biblical Research in Palestine, Murray, MDCCCXLI, Vol. I.

Rose, H. I. Hygini Fabulae, see: Hygini Fabulae.

Rosenbaum. M Rev. and Silberman A. M. – pentateuch, translated with Targum Onkelus, Haphtaroth and Rashi's commentary, Jerusalem 1930.

Rothenberg, B., An Archaeological Survey of South Sinai 1st. season, 1967/ 68, PEQ., 1970, pp. 4–29.

Rowley, H. H., From Joseph to Joshua, Biblical tradition in the light of Archaeology, Schweich Lectures, 1948.

Israel's Sojourn in Egypt, Reprint from the Bulletin of the John Rylamds

Library, Vol. 22, (1), 1938, Manchester University press.

The date of the Exodus, PEQ, 1941, pp. 152–157.

The Exodus and the Settlement in Canaan, BASOR, 85, 1942, pp. 27–31.

Habiru and Hebrews, PEQ., 1942, (74), pp. 41–53.

Ras Shamra and the Habiru question, PEQ, 1940, pp. 90–94.

Rowton, M. B., The Problem of the Exodus, PEQ., 1953, pp. 46–60.

Salama, R. N., What has become of the Philistines, PEQ., 1925, pp. 37–45; 68–79.

Saussey, E. La céramique Philistine, Syria, V, 1924, pp. 169–185.

Sayce, A. H. The inscription of the Pool of Siloam, PEP., 1881, pp. 69–73.

The Early History of The Hebrews, 2nd edit. Rivingtons, London 1899.

The "Higher Criticism" and the verdict of the monuments, London 1894.

Fresh Light From The Ancient Monuments, 5th. Edit. The religious tract society. 1890.

Scarth, J., A few thoughts upon the Route of the Exodus, PEP. 1882, pp. 235–246.

Schaeffer, C. The Cuneiformes Texts of Ras Shamra Ugarit, Schweich Lectures, 1936, Oxford university press. 1939.

Schild, E., On Exodus III 14. I am that I am, VT. vol. 4. 1954, pp. 296–302

Servin, A., La tradition Judeo–Chrétienne de l'Exode, BIE., 1949. Tome XXXI. pp. 315–355.

Shiloh Y., The Proto – Aeolic Capital–the Israelite Timorah Capital. pp. 39–52, PEQ. 1977

New Proto – Aeolic Capitals found in Israel BASOR. 222. 1976.

Slouschz, N., Hébraeo–Phéniciens et Judéo–Berbères, Paris, Leroux, 1908 (Paru dans Archives Marocaines, vol. XIV).

La civilisation Hebraique et Phénicienne a' Carthage, Extrait de la Revue Tunisienne, Tunis 1911.

Otzar Haketovot Hafenikiot, Bialik Inst., 1942. (Hebrew).

My travel in Lybia, vol II, Tel–Aviv 1943, (Hebrew)

Sefer Hayam (The book of the sea), Palestine Maritime league, Tel–Aviv, 1948. (Hebrew).

Motzaei Haivrim, edit. Sifriat Hashaot, (Hebrew).

Smith, A. C., The Route of the Exodus, PEP., 1883, pp. 223–224.

Smith, G. A. The Historical Geography of the Holy Land. Fontana Library Edit., London, 1968.

Smith Robertson, W., The Religion of the Semites, Meridian Library, N. Y. 1956.

Snaith, N. H., "Yam Suf" The Sea of reeds, the Red Sea, VT. Vol. XV, 1965, pp. 395–398.

Speiser, E. A., The name Phoinikes, pp. 324–331 in: Oriental and Biblical Studies. Collected Writings of E. A. Speiser, . edit. university of Pennsylvania press, Philadelphia 1967.

Ethnic movements in the Near East in the second Millenium B. C., The Hurrians and their connection with the Habiru and the Hyksos, AASOR (XIII), 1931–1932, pp. 13–54.

A Note on Alphabetic Origins, BASOR. 1951. no 121.

Spinoza B.; Tractatus Theologico Politicus (Heb Trans. Ch. Wirszubski). Magnes Press. Jerusalem 1983. The Philosophy of Spinoza. edited by J. Ratner. The world's popular classics books. Inc. N. Y

Stanley, A. P., Sinai and Palestine, Murray, London, 1881.

Steindorff, G. Outline of the History of Egypt, pp. lxxvi ff. in Baedeker's handbook – Egypt. 1908.

Stern E.; When Canaanites Became Phoenician sailors. BAR. vol 19, No. 1 Jan / Feb 1993. pp 24–31; 76–78.

Stolper. M. W., A note on Yahwistic Personal names In The Murasu Texts . BASOR. Apr. 1976. no. 222 . pp. 25–28.

Straus, H. The Hasmonaite Candelabre, its fate and form. Eretz Israel– Archaeological, Historical and Geographical studies, Publication of the I. E. S. Jerusalem, vol. vi, 1960. pp. 122–129. (Hebrew).

Stutchkoff, N. Thesaurus of the Hebrew Language, Shulsinger, 1968

Sukenik, A. L., Installations in Connection with the cult of the Dead in Canaanite Ugarit and in Israelite Samaria. Kedem II studies in Jewish Archaeology. Jerusalem 1945. pp. 42–47.

Swiggers P., Byblos dans les Lettres d'El Amarna: Lumières sur des relations obscures. pp. 53–55

in Studia Phoenicia tome. III. Leuven, 1983.

Tacitus, History, Hebrew Translation, Dvoretzki, S., Bialik Inst. Jerusalem, 1965.

Annals, Hebrew Transalation Dvoretzki, S., Bialik Inst. 1962.

The Histories, English trans. C. H. Moore, London, Heinemann, Harvard University Press, McMlxii.

Thorley – Kelso, Palestinian Pottery in Bible times, BA., VIII, No. 4. 1945, pp. 82–93.

Tomkins, H. G., Egyptology and the Bible, PEQ., 1884, pp. 54–57.

Exploration of the Delta of Egypt, PEQ. 1885. pp. 114–116.

Tor–Sinai N. H. Who created the Alphabeth, 2 articles in daily paper; Palestine Post, Oct. 14 & 21, 1949.

"Ketav Hatorah", Halashon Vehasefer, Bialik Inst. 1959, Vol. Halashon, pp. 123–164. (Hebrew)

"Mereshit Torat Israel Bemasoret Haaleph Beth", Halashon Vehasefer, Bialik inst. 1959, Vol. Hasefer, pp. 150–194. (Hebrew)

Alephbeth, entry in Biblical Encyclopedia, Bialik Inst. 1950. (Heb.)

Torrey, C. Ch., Commentary on the book "A new Phoenician Grammar", JAOS, (57), 4. 1937, pp. 397–410.

Trager, G. L., Language – essay in E. B. edit. 1961.

Trumbull, H. C., Kadesh–Barnea, its importance and probable site, Hodder & Sloughton, London, 1884.

Trumper, V. L. The Route of the Exodus from Pithom to Marah, PEQ., 1915, pp. 22–29.

Tunyogi, A. C., The Book of the Conquest, JBL., LXXXIV, 1965, pp. 374–380.

Uphil, E. P., Pithom and Raamses, their location and significance JNES, 1969, (28), 1, pp. 15–39.

Vance Donald, R. ; Literary Sources for the History of Palestine and Syria: The Phoenician

Inscriptions. BA. 57: 1 (1994), pp. 2–19.

Vandersleyen C. L' Étymologie de Phoïnix, "Phénicien" pp. 19–22 in Studia Phoenicia, V. Leuven, 1983.

Vaughan Stooke, G., Remarks on the 'Jam –Suph', PEP, 1881, pp. 322–323.

Vendryes, J. Le Langage, Introduction linguistique a' L'histoire, edit. Albin Michel 1968.

Vincent, L. H. Chronique, (Les fouilles Anglaises d'Ascalon), RB. 1922, pp. 99–111.

L'Aube de l'Histoire a' Jericho, RB., 1938, pp. 561– 589. ; RB. 1939, pp. 91–107.

Ceramique et Chronologie, RB., 1932, pp. 264–284.

La chronologie de Ruines de Jericho, RB., 1930, pp. 403–433.

The chronologie of Jericho, PEQ., 1931, pp. 104–105.

Virey, Ph., Note sur le Pharaon Ménephtah et les temps de l'Exode, RB., 1900. pp. 578–586.

Virolleaud, Ch. Kaftor dans les poémes de Ras Shamra, RES., 1937, (3), pp. 137–141.

Les Inscriptions Cuneiformes de Ras Shamra, SY., X, 1929, p. 304–310.

Six Textes de Ras Shamra provenant de la XIV campagne 1950, SY. (XXVIII), 1951, pp. 163–179.

Le dechiffrement des Tablettes Alphabetique de Ras Shamra, SY. (XII), 1931, pp. 15–23.

Wainwright, G. A., Caphtor, Keftiu and Cappadocia, PEQ. 1931, pp. 203–216.

Some sea people and others in the Hittite Archives, JEA. 1939, vol. 25, pp. 148–153.

Caphtor Cappadocia, VT., VI, 1956, pp. 199–210

Some early Philistine History, VT., (IX), 1959, pp. 73–84.

Keftiu and Karamania (Asia Minor), AS., IV, 1954, pp. 33–48.

Some sea Peoples, JEA, 1961, Vol. 47, pp. 71–90.

Warmington, B. H. Histoire et civilisation de Carthage, Payot, Paris, 1961.

Wathlet p., Les Phéniciens et la Tradition Homerique, pp. 235–243 in Studia Phoenicia, tome. I – II. Leuven 1983.

Watson, Sir Ch. M., Egypt and Palestine, PEQ. 1915, pp. 132–143.

The Desert of the Wanderings, PEQ. 1914, pp. 18–23.

Weill, Raymond, Phoenicia and Western Asia to the Macedonian Conquest, Harrap & Colt, 1940.

Phéniciens, Ēgéens et Hellénes dans la Mediterranée primitive, SY. II, 1921, pp. 120–144.

Welch, F. B., The Influence of the Aegean Civilisation on South Palestine, PEP. 1900, pp. 342–350; –BSA, VI, 1899–1900, pp. 117–124.

Weld, A. G., The Route of the Exodus, PEP. 1883, pp. 139–142.

Wellhausen, J., Prolegomena to the History of Israel with a Reprint of the article Israel from the Encyclopaedia Britanica. Translated from the German under the author's Supervision by J. Sutherland Black and Alan Menzies. MDCCCLXXXV. Edinburgh: Adam & Charles Black.

Whitaker, J. I., Motya, a Phoenician colony in Sicily, London, Bell 1921

Wiener, H. M., The Conquest narratives, JPOS. IX, 1929, pp. 1–26.

Wilson, J. A. The 'Eperu' of the Egyptian Inscriptions, AJSLL, 1932 – 1933, pp. 275–280.

Wright G. E., Biblical Archaeology, Westminster Press, London 1957.

The literary and Historical problem of Joshua 10 and Judges I. JNES, vol. V, no. 2. 1946, pp. 105–114.

Epic of Conquest, BA., Vol. III, 1940 (3), pp. 25–40.

How did early Israel differ from her neighbours, BA. Vol. VI no. 1. 1943, pp. 1–20.

Philistine Coffins and Mercenaries, BA., 1959 (3), Vol. XXII, pp. 54–66.

Biblical Archaeology today, BA., Vol. X, 1947, (1), pp. 7–24.

Two misunderstood items in the Exodus – Conquest cycle, BASOR., 86, 1942, pp. 32–35.

Wright William, The Illustrated Bible Treasury, London, Nelson 1896.

Wunderlich, H. G., The Secrets of Crete, Fontana / Collins, Macmillan Pub. 1978.

Yadin, Y. Military and Archaeological aspects in the Conquest description, in the Book of Joshua, article in: "Iyunim Besefer Yehoshua", pp. 71–

100, Israel Biblical research Society, Kiriat Sefer, (9), 1960. Jerusalem. (Hebrew).

Yahuda, A. S. The Accuracy of the Bible, 1935, Dutton, U. S. A.

Yeivin, S. On problems nowadays of the origin of the Alphabeth, Leshonenu, vol. 17, (2–3), pp. 67–71, Jerusalem, 1951. (Hebrew).

Mekhkarim Betoldot Israel Veartzo (studies in the History of Israel and his country), Newmann, 1960. (Hebrew).

The conquest of the land, Maarkhot, 1945, Feb. pp. 61–74. ; Mai, pp. 59–70. (Hebrew).

The History of the Hebrew Script, Library of Palestinology of the Jewish Palestine Exploration Society, Jerusalem 1939. (Hebrew).

Notes on Archaeology and the Israelite invasion. PEQ. 1930. pp. 226–227.

The History of Jewish Script, JPOS, 1938.

Zimerman, F., El and Adonai, VT., 1962, pp. 190–195.

Drawing no. 1

A Relief, Temple Medient Habu – A battle between Ramses 3rd and those named "Sea People"

Drawing no. 2

A Relief, Temple Medient Habu – Battle between Ramses 3rd and those named "Sea People"

Drawing no. 3

Philistine prisoners; from a relief, Temple Medinet Habu

Drawing no. 4

Relief; Temple Medinet Habu – Prisoners from Amuru; Conventionally identified as (From Left): A Libyan, A Syrian Semite, Hittite, From the Sea people, Syrian. Please note that the Syrian-Semite Apron is identical to the Sea People prisoner Apron.

Drawing no. 5

INDEX

Y